Computer Application in Management

Nirupma Pathak

First Edition: 2010

Himalaya Publishing House

MUMBAI • NEW DELHI • NAGPUR • BENGALURU • HYDERABAD • CHENNAI • PUNE • LUCKNOW • AHMEDABAD • ERNAKULAM • BHUBANESWAR • INDORE • KOLKATA

First Edition : 2010
Reprint . 2016

Published by : Mrs. Meena Pandey for **Himalaya Publishing House Pvt. Ltd.,**
"Ramdoot", Dr. Bhalerao Marg, Girgaon, **Mumbai - 400 004.**
Phone: 2386 01 70/2386 38 63, Fax: 022-2387 71 78
Email: himpub@vsnl.com Website: www.himpub.com

Branch Offices

New Delhi : "Pooja Apartments", 4-B, Murari Lal Street, Ansari Road, Darya Ganj, New Delhi - 110 002. Phone:23270392, 23278631 Fax: 011-23256286

Nagpur : Kundanlal Chandak Industrial Estate, Ghat Road, Nagpur - 440 018. Phone: 2738731, 3296733 Telefax: 0712-2721215

Bengaluru : No. 16/1 (Old 12/1), 1st Floor, Next to Hotel Highlands, Madhava Nagar, Race Course Road, Bengaluru - 560 001. Phone: 22281541, 22385461, Telefax: 080-22286611

Hyderabad : No. 3-4-184, Lingampally, Besides Raghavendra Swamy Matham, Kachiguda, Hyderabad - 500 027. Phone: 040-27560041, 27550139, Mobile: 09848130433

Chennai : No. 85/50, Bazullah Road, T. Nagar, Chennai - 600 017. Phone: 044-28144004/28144005

Pune : First Floor, "Laksha" Apartment, No. 527, Mehunpura, Shaniwarpeth (Near Prabhat Theatre), Pune - 411 030. Phone: 020-24496323/24496333

Lucknow : Jai Baba Bhavan, Church Road, Near Manas Complex and Dr. Awasthi Clinic, Aliganj, Lucknow - 226 024. Phone: 0522-2339329, 4068914, Mobile: 9305302158, 9415349385, 9389593752

Ahmedabad : 114, "SHAIL", 1st Floor, Opp. Madhu Sudan House, C.G.Road, Navrang Pura, Ahmedabad– 380 009. Phone: 079-26560126, Mobile: 09327324149,09314679413

Ernakulam : 39/104 A, Lakshmi Apartment, Karikkamuri Cross Rd., Ernakulam, Cochin – 622011, Kerala. Phone: 0484-2378012, 2378016, Mobile: 09344199799

Bhubaneswar : 5 Station Square, Bhubaneswar (Orissa) - 751 001. Mobile: 9861046007

Indore : Kesardeep Avenue Extension, 73, Narayan Bagh, Flat No. 302, IIIrd Floor, Near Humpty Dumpty School, Narayan Bagh, Indore 452 007(M.P.) Mobile: 09301386468

Kolkata : 108/4, Beliaghata Main Road, Near ID Hospital, Opp. SBI Bank, Kolkata - 700 010, Mobile: 09910440956

Typeset by : HPH Editorial Office, Bhandup (Rajani Tambe).

Printed by : A to Z Printer, Delhi.

PREFACE

The primary objective of " **Computer Application in Management**" is to provide materials that not only introduce the student to the field of computer science, but also acquaint the student with specific issues related with information technology industry. I wrote this book in recognition of the ever growing importance of information and the unique challenges faced information technology industry. In order to remain ahead of other competitors, industries are taking the advantage of information. Information is playing a major role in all the spheres. Whether it is information technology industry, banking sector, pharma industry, education sector, automobile industry etc. This is an era of information, the entire world is globalised and it has become global village and singe society just after revolution of IT that lead to easy access of information.

The book exhaustively explains the basic concepts of some computer applications like computer network as well as MS Office, Computer Hardwares, E-Commerce as well as applications of IT. We hope that this book will serve as a sufficient study material to first year students of MBA of UP Technical University as well as to the beginners in the field.

Nirupma Pathak

CONTENTS

Unit I

Unit II

Unit III

Unit IV

Unit I

CHAPTER 1

Components of Computer

COMPUTER COMPONENTS

Hardware

The **hardware** are the parts of computer itself including the **Central Processing Unit (CPU)** and related **microchips** and **micro-circuitry, keyboards, monitors, case** and **drives** (hard, CD, DVD, floppy, optical, tape, etc...). Other extra parts called **peripheral components** or **devices** include **mouse, printers, modems, scanners, digital cameras** and **cards (sound, colour, video)** etc... Together they are often referred to as a **personal computer**.

Central Processing Unit – Though the term relates to a specific chip or the **processor** a CPU's performance is determined by the the rest of the computer's **circuitry** and **chips**.

Currently the Pentium chip or processor, made by Intel, is the most common CPU though there are many other companies that produce processors for personal computers. Examples are the CPU made by Motorola and AMD.

With faster processors the **clock speed** becomes more important. Compared to some of the first computers which operated at below 30 **megahertz** (MHz) the Pentium chips began at 75 MHz in the late 1990's. Speeds now exceed 3000+ MHz or 3 **gigahertz** (GHz) and different chip manufacturers use different measuring standards (check your local computer store for the latest speed). It depends on the **circuit board** that the chip is housed in, or the **motherboard**, as to whether you are able to upgrade to a faster chip. The motherboard contains the circuitry and connections that allow the various component to communicate with each other.

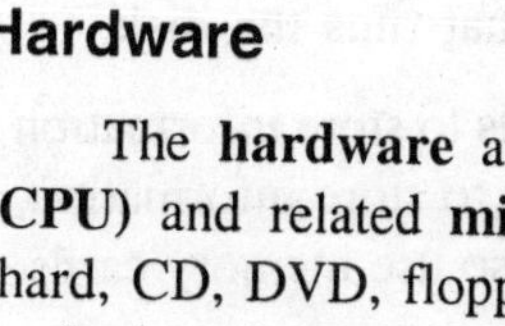

Though there were many computers using many different processors previous to this I call the 80286 processor the advent of home computers as these were the processors that made computers available for the average person. Using a processor before the 286 involved learning a proprietary system and software. Most new software are being developed for the newest and fastest processors so it can be difficult to use an older computer system.

Keyboard – The keyboard is used to type information into the computer or **input** information. There are many different keyboard layouts and sizes with the most common for Latin based languages being the QWERTY layout (named for the first 6 keys). The standard keyboard has 101 keys. Notebooks have embedded keys accessible by **special** keys or by pressing key combinations (CTRL or Command and P for example). **Ergonomically** designed keyboards are designed to make typing easier. Hand held devices have various and different keyboard configurations and **touch screens.**

Some of the keys have a special use. There are referred to as **command keys**. The 3 most common are the Control or CTRL, Alternate or Alt and the Shift keys though there can be more (the Windows key for example or the Command key). Each key on a standard keyboard has one or two **characters**. Press the key to get the lower character and hold Shift to get the upper.

Removable Storage and/or Disk Drives – All **disks** need a **drive** to get information off - or **read** - and put information on the disk - or **write**. Each drive is designed for a specific type of disk whether it is a CD, DVD, hard disk or floppy. Often the term 'disk' and 'drive' are used to describe the same thing but it helps to understand that the disk is the **storage device** which contains computer files - or **software** - and the drive is the mechanism that runs the disk.

Digital flash drives work slightly differently as they use **memory cards** to store information so there are no moving parts. Digital cameras also use Flash memory cards to store information, in this case photographs. **Hand held devices** use digital drives and many also use memory cards.

Mouse – Most modern computers today are run using a mouse controlled pointer. Generally if the mouse has two buttons the left one is used to **select** objects and text and the right one is used to **access menus**. If the mouse has one button (Mac for instance) it controls all the activity and a mouse with a third button can be used by specific software programs.

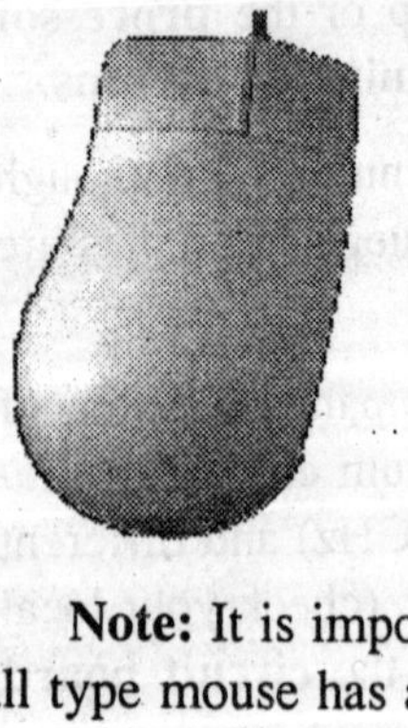

One type of mouse has a round ball under the bottom of the mouse that rolls and turns two wheels which control the direction of the pointer on the screen. Another type of mouse uses an optical system to track the movement of the mouse. **Laptop** computers use touch pads, buttons and other devices to control the pointer. Hand helds use a combination of devices to control the pointer, including touch screens.

Note: It is important to clean the mouse periodically, particularly if it becomes sluggish. A ball type mouse has a small circular panel that can be opened, allowing you to remove the ball. Lint can be removed carefully with a tooth pick or tweezers and the ball can be washed with mild detergent. A build up will accumulate on the small wheels in the mouse. Use a small instrument or finger nail to scrape it off taking care not to scratch the wheels. Track balls can be cleaned much like a mouse and touch-pad can be wiped with a clean, damp cloth. An optical mouse can accumulate material from the surface that it is in contact with which can be removed with a finger nail or small instrument.

Monitors – The monitor shows information on the screen when you type. This is called **outputting** information. When the computer needs more information it will display a message on the screen, usually through a **dialog box**. Monitors come in many types and sizes. The resolution of the monitor determines the sharpness of the screen. The resolution can be adjusted to control the screen's display.

Most desktop computers use a monitor with a **cathode tube** or **liquid crystal display**. Most notebooks use a liquid crystal display monitor.

To get the full benefit of today's software with full colour graphics and animation, computers need a color monitor with a display or **graphics card**.

Printers - The printer takes the information on your screen and transfers it to paper or a **hard copy**. There are many different types of printers with various levels of quality. The three basic types of printer are: **dot matrix**, **inkjet**, and **laser**.

Dot matrix printers work like a typewriter transferring ink from a ribbon to paper with a series or 'matrix' of tiny pins.

Ink jet printers work like dot matrix printers but fires a stream of ink from a cartridge directly onto the paper.

Laser printers use the same technology as a photocopier using heat to transfer toner onto paper.

Modem - A modem is used to translate information transferred through telephone lines, cable or line-of-site wireless.

The term stands for **modulate and demodulate** which changes the signal from **digital**, which computers use, to **analog**, which telephones use and then back again. **Digital modems** transfer digital information directly without changing to analog.

Modems are measured by the speed that the information is transferred. The measuring tool is called the **baud rate**. Originally modems worked at speeds below 2400 baud but today analog speeds of 56,000 are standard. Cable, wireless or digital subscriber lines can transfer information much faster with rates of 3,00,000 baud and up.

Modems also use **Error Correction** which corrects for transmission errors by constantly checking whether the information was received properly or not and **Compression** which allows for faster data transfer rates. Information is transferred in **packets**. Each packet is checked for errors and is re-sent if there is an error.

Anyone who has used the Internet has noticed that at times the information travels at different speeds. Depending on the amount of information that is being transferred, the information will arrive at its destination at different times. The amount of information that can travel through a line is limited. This limit is called **bandwidth**.

There are many more variables involved in communication technology using computers, much of which is covered in the section on the **Internet**.

Scanners – Scanners allow you to transfer pictures and photographs to your computer. A scanner 'scans' the image from the top to the bottom, one line at a time and transfers it to the computer as a series of **bits** or a **bitmap**. You can then take that image and use it in a paint program, send it out as a fax or print it. With optional **Optical Character Recognition** (OCR) software you can convert printed documents such as newspaper articles to text that can be used in your word processor. Most scanners use **TWAIN** software that makes the scanner accessible by other software applications.

Digital cameras allow you to take digital photographs. The images are stored on a memory chip or disk that can be transferred to your computer. Some cameras can also capture sound and video.

Case – The case houses the microchips and circuitry that run the computer. Desktop models usually sit under the monitor and tower models beside. They come in many sizes, including desktop, mini, midi, and full tower. There is usually room inside to expand or add components at a later time. By removing the cover off the case you may find plate covered empty slots that allow you to add cards. There are various types of slots including IDE, ASI, USB, PCI and Firewire slots.

Depending on the type notebook computers may have room to expand. Most Notebooks also have connections or ports that allows expansion or connection to exterior, peripheral devices such as monitor, portable hard-drives or other devices.

Cards – Cards are components added to computers to increase their capability. When adding a peripheral device make sure that your computer has a slot of the type needed by the device.

Sound cards allow computers to produce sound like music and voice. The older sound cards were 8 bit then 16 bit then 32 bit. Though the human ear can't distinguish the fine difference between sounds produced by the more powerful sound card they allow for more complex music and music production.

Colour cards allow computers to produce colour (with a colour monitor of course). The first colour cards were 2 bit which produced 4 colours [CGA]. It was amazing what could be done with those 4 colours. Next came 4 bit allowing for 16 [EGA and VGA] colours. Then came 16 bit allowing for 1064 colours and then 24 bit which allows for almost 17 million colours and now 32 bit and higher allow monitors to display almost a billion separate colours.

Video cards allow computers to display video and animation. Some video cards allow computers to display television as well as *capture* frames from video. A video card with a digital video camera allows computer users to produce live video. A high speed connection is required for effective video transmission.

Network cards allow computers to connect together to communicate with each other. Network cards have connections for cable, thin wire or wireless networks. For more information see the section on Networks.

Cables connect internal components to the **Motherboard**, which is a board with series of electronic path ways and connections allowing the CPU to communicate with the other components of the computer.

Memory – Memory can be very confusing but is usually one of the easiest pieces of hardware to add to your computer. It is common to confuse **chip memory** with **disk storage**. An example of the difference between memory and storage would be the difference between a table where the actual work is done (memory) and a filing cabinet where the finished product is stored (disk). To add a bit more confusion, the computer's hard disk can be used as **temporary memory** when the program needs more than the chips can provide.

Random Access Memory or **RAM** is the memory that the computer uses to temporarily store the information as it is being processed. The more information being processed the more RAM the computer needs.

One of the first home computers used 64 **kilobytes** of RAM memory (Commodore 64). Today's modern computers need a minimum of 64 Mb (recommended 128 Mb or more) to run Windows or OS 10 with modern software.

RAM memory chips come in many different sizes and speeds and can usually be **expanded**. Older computers came with 512 Kb of memory which could be expanded to a maximum of 640 Kb. In most modern computers the memory can be expanded by adding or replacing the memory chips depending on the processor you have and the type of memory your computer uses. Memory chips range in size from 1 Mb to 4 Gb. As computer technology changes the type of memory changes as well making old memory chips obsolete. Check your computer manual to find out what kind of memory your computer uses before purchasing new memory chips.

Software

The software is the information that the computer uses to get the job done. Software needs to be accessed before it can be used. There are many terms used for process of accessing software including running, executing, starting up, opening and others.

Computer programs allow users to complete tasks. A program can also be referred to as an application and the two words are used interchangeably.

Examples of software programs or applications would be the Operating System (DOS, Windows 9x/Millenium/XP/Vista, O/S2, UNIX, MacOS 9.x/10.x and various others), Wordprocessor (typing letters), Spreadsheet (financial info), Database (inventory control and address book), Graphics program, Internet Browser, Email and many others.

Any document that you create, graphic you design, sound you compose, file you make, letter you write, email you send or anything that you create on your computer is referred to as software. All software is stored in files.

Software is stored on a **disk**, card, tape or one of the dozens of other **storage devices** available.

There are millions of different pieces of software available for almost every conceivable need. Software is available commercially through stores and mail order and also available on the **Internet**. Software is also available through an Open Source license which allows anyone to use the Open Source software free of charge as long as the license is maintained. If you can't find the application that you need **software development** companies can custom design software for you.

The largest software companies offer packages of software or **suites** that include many of the programs that the average person or business needs. Software packages or suites contain programs that work together and share information, making it easier to combine that information in versatile ways. For example when writing a letter you can get the mailing address from an address book, include a letterhead from a graphics program and include a financial chart from a spreadsheet and combine this collection of information in the body of the letter.

The three basic types of software are: **commercial**, **shareware** and **open source** software. Some software is also released into the public domain without a license.

Commercial software comes prepackaged and is available from software stores and through the Internet.

Shareware is software developed by individual and small companies that cannot afford to market their software world wide or by a company that wants to release a demonstration version of their commercial product. You will have an evaluation period in which you can decide whether to purchase the product or not. Shareware software often is disabled in some way and has a notice attached to explain the legal requirements for using the product.

Open Source software is created by generous programmers and released into the public domain for public use. There is usually a copyright notice that must remain with the software product. Open Source software is not public domain. In that the company or individual that develops the software retains ownership of the program but the software can be used freely. Many popular Open Source applications are being developed and upgraded regularly by individuals and companies that believe in the Open Source concept.

Operating Systems

All computers need some sort of Operating System (OS). The majority of modern home computers use some form of Microsoft's operating systems. The original Microsoft operating system was called DOS (Disk Operating System) though most computers use Windows. Windows comes in various versions beginning with version 3.x then 95, 98, ME and currently XP. A few computers use IBM's O/S2. Apple's Mac use their own operating system beginning with OS 1 though most modern Macs use version 8.x or 9.x. Apple's latest version is OS 10.1.x. In the past large companies and institutions would have an operating system design exclusively for them but as the commercial operating systems become more sophisticated the benefits of this practice is becoming less apparent. Some computer professionals, Internet Service Providers (ISP) and mainframe computer users use an operating system such as UNIX (or a variant such as Linux), Windows NT or 2000 (Win2k) or one of the other network or server based operating systems.

There are many smaller operating systems out there. The problem is that software is currently being developed only for the main operating systems and only the newest versions of these OS. Many older computers with unique operating systems have lots of software already developed for them but there is very little new software being developed for the older computers. The older proprietary operating systems are less likely to offer **technical support** than the more modern operating systems.

The operating system controls the **input and output** or directs the flow of information to and from the **CPU**. Much of this is done automatically by the system but it is possible to modify and control your system if you need to.

When you turn your computer on, it first needs to load the operating system sometimes referred to a **booting up**. Basically the computer starts from scratch every time you turn the power on.

It checks all its components and will usually display a message if there is a problem. Loading the system is usually automatic.

Once the system is loaded the user can start the application or program that they are going to use.

Most computer users will run Microsoft Windows, Mac OS or Linux as their operating system. These OS are **Graphic User Interface (GUI)** which allows the user to control or run the computer using a **Mouse** and **Icons**. The user simply moves the mouse on a flat surface, rolls the trackball or moves their hand over the touchpad to control a pointer. They then choose the option they want by pressing a button or touching the pad.

Without a GUI the user controls the computer using the keys on the keyboard. This is referred to as a **Command Line Interface (CLI)**

Disk and Storage

Disks and cards are used to store information. All information on computers are stored in **files**. The size of a **file** is measured in bytes.

A byte **is** approximately **one character (letter 'a', number '1', symbol '?' etc....).**

A byte is made up of **8 bits**. A bit is simply an **on** or an **off** signal which passes through the computers circuitry. Every piece of software can be broken down into a series of **on** or **off** signals or it's **Binary Code**.

About a thousand bytes is a kilobyte **(Kb).**

About a million bytes is a **megabyte** (Mb).

About a billion bytes is a **gigabyte** (Gb).

About a trillion bytes is a **terabyte** (Tb)

Editor's Note: I say 'about' because everything in computers must be divisible by 8 so a kilobyte is actually 1,024 bytes. The reason for this goes beyond the scope of an introductory level document but as it can cause some confusion I thought it should be mentioned.

Disk is a common way of transporting information such as bringing files home from work or sharing files. **Floppy disks** have become less useful as file sizes increase and **Compact disks** (CDs), Flash drives and Digital Video Devices (DVDs) are becoming more popular. Most software is sold on a CD. Internal **Hard disks** are the most common storage device.

Compact disks or CDs can store large amounts of information. One disk will store 650 Mb. One type is a CD-ROM which stands for **Compact Disk Read Only Memory**. Another type is a CD-RW which stands for **Compact Disk - Read/Write**. CD drives can copy information or **burn** information on to a blank CD. Common **Read Only CD** blanks can only be written to once though more expensive **Read/Write CD's** can be used over and over again.

DVD disks can store 4.5 Gb on standard disk, 8 Gb on a dual layer disk and 16 Gb on a blue-ray disk.

Digital recorders allow you to store large files, such as movies, on a single disk.

Hard disks store the majority of information on today's modern computer. Some of the first hard disk stored 10 to 40 Mb. Today the standard hard disk stores 150 Gb or more (this number is constantly increasing). Information can be stored and deleted as necessary. As files get larger the speed that hard disks can read and write become more important.

Flash drive or thumb drives range in size.

Floppy disk or diskette comes in two basic sizes: 5.25 inch and 3.5 inch. Both have a low and high density versions though 3.5 inch high density disks are the most common though many modern computers are being sold without floppy disk drives.

Disk size	Amount of storage	Approximate printed 8.5 x 11 inch pages
3.5 high density	1.44 Mb	720 pages
CD	650 Mb	a small library
DVD	4.5 Gb	a feature length movie
DVD dual layer	8 Gb	a long feature length movie with extras

There are many other storage devices including **tapes**, **Panasonic's LS120 3.5 inch diskettes**, **Iomega's Zip & Jazz disks**, **VCR tape** and many others. Innovation in storage technology is advancing rapidly and some technologies become obsolete.

Information is stored in an **electromagnetic** form much like a cassette or video tape.

Note: Keep disks away from strong electric or magnetic fields including x-rays. Be aware of high electromagnetic areas in the room such as televisions, speakers, high tension wires, etc... Use disks only at room temperature and keep them out of direct sunlight. If possible avoid passing electromagnetic storage devices through airport x-rays. In theory, information stored on a disk will last indefinitely but the physical storage device will wear out with usage and time so be sure to **back up** (copy) your important files to a second storage device.

BASIC COMPUTER OPERATIONS

How Computers Work

Input: Information and programs are entered into the computer through Input devices such as the keyboard, disks or through other computers via network connections or modems connected to the Internet. The input device also retrieves information off disks.

Output: Output Device display information on the screen (monitor) or the printer and sends information to other computers. They also display messages about what errors may have occurred and brings up message or dialog box asking for more information to be input. The output device also saves information on the disk for future use.

Processing: The CPU or central processing unit is sometimes called the Control Unit and directs the operation of the input and output devices. The **Co-processor** or the **Arithmetic-Logic Unit** does arithmetic and comparisons. The memory or RAM temporarily stores information (files and programs) while you are using or working on them. The BIOS or basic input/output system controls the dialogue between the various devices.

Keyboard Layout and Data Entry

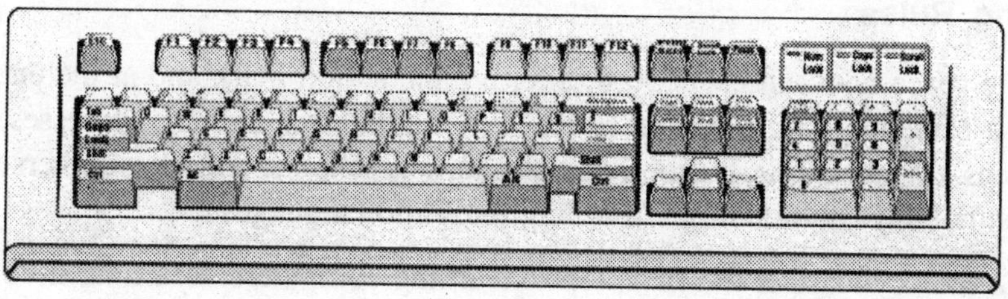

ENTER or RETURN – Moves the cursor down one line and to the left margin. Enter also process commands such as choosing an option in a dialog (message) box and submitting a form.

DEL or DELETE – Deletes the character at cursor to the right of the cursor and all highlighted (or selected) text.

BKSP or BACKSPACE – Deletes the character to the left of cursor and all hightlighted (or selected) text.

SPACE BAR – Moves the cursor one space at a time to the right.

SHIFT KEY – Use the shift keys to type capital letters and to type the upper character on keys with two characters on them.

CAPS LOCK – Locks the keyboard so it types capital letters (a light goes on when caps lock is on)

TAB – Moves the cursor five spaces to the right (number of spaces are usually adjustable). Tab moves to the next field in a form or table (Shift-Tab for previous field).

ESC or **ESCAPE** – Cancels a menu or dialog box.

ARROW KEYS – Moves the cursor around document without changing text.

FUNCTION KEYS or **F KEYS** – Access commands by themselves or in combination with the three **command** keys: CTRL, SHIFT and ALT

Command or Special Keys

Command keys normally do nothing on their own but work in combination with other keys. Each piece of software uses the command keys differently though there is a move to standardize some functions. The Control key or Ctrl is often used to access commands. The Alternative key or Alt is often used to access menus. The Shift key is used to type CAPITAL LETTERS. As well the command keys are all used to move through documents and edit text faster and easier. As well many computers have Special keys design specifically for the particular computer. Apple computers have the Apple keys and Macs have Command keys. Many keyboards now have a Windows key specifically for Windows 9x and newer systems. Many older computers also have special keys used for a variety of different functions.

Some Notebook or Laptop keys are left out because of space limitations and they usually have a Special function key which allows other keys to double for the missing ones.

Basic Typing Rules

Place one space between each word, after a punctuation mark and at the end of a sentence. Always start a sentence with a capital letter. Use capitals for names, addresses, provinces and countries, places, organizations, businesses, associations, schools, colleges, universities, days of the week, months, holidays, nationalities, ethnic groups and languages.

Learning the keyboard is the first step to learning computers. Learning involves practice. It really is as simple as that. There are two kinds of typing:

The first is called **Touch Typing**. The Touch Typist uses the **Home Keys** (*asdf* for the left hand and ***jkl;*** for the right) and all the fingers on both hands as well as the thumbs for the Space Bar while typing. There are many commercial and public domain programs that are designed to teach this method.

The other method is some times called 'Hunt and Peck' or depending on finger strength 'Search and Destroy'. This involves using one or more fingers on one or two hands to type. It is a perfectly acceptable way of using a computer and many people get along fine with this technique.

Keyboard Symbols

The following chart displays the character symbols, name and Latin-1 number on a standard keyboard in their approximate position on the keyboard. Most characters from any Roman based language can be created on any computer using the **American Standard Code for Information Interchange** or **ASCII**. Most computers and software also recognize **American National Standards Institute (ANSI)** formatting standards as well. View the entire ISO Latin-1 Character Set.

Computer Viruses

A virus is a **program** designed by a computer programmer (**malicious hacker**) to do a certain unwanted function. The virus program can be simply annoying like displaying a happy face on the user's screen at a certain time and date. It can also be very destructive and damage your computer's programs and files causing the computer to stop working.

The reason why hackers create viruses are open for speculation. The most quoted reason is simply to see if it can be done. Other reasons are Ludite based "smash the machine" motivations, anti-establishment/anti-corporate actions, criminal intent, and various others that range into the "conspiracy theory" realm.

Viruses take two basic forms

One is **boot sector** viruse which infects the section of a disk that is first read by the computer. This type of virus **infects** the boot or master section of any disks that it comes in contact with. The second is a **program virus** that infects other programs when the infected program is run or executed. Some viruses infect both and others change themselves (polymorphic) depending on the programs they encounter.

Though viruses do not damage computer **hardware** there have been attempts to create programs that will do things like run the hard drive until it fails or lodge itself in the computer's clock (which has a rechargeable battery) allowing it to remain active even months after the computer has been unplugged. Other viruses affect certain microchips (BIOS chip for instance). These microchips need to be modified under normal computer use but the virus program can produce changes which cause them to fail. Other viruses will affect the characters or images displayed on the screen which may give the impression of monitor failure.

Viruses can cause a great deal of damage to the computers it infects and can cost a lot of time and money to correct it.

Computer viruses have been around for a long time, even before computers became widely used and they will likely remain with us forever. For that reason computer users will always need ways to protect themselves from virus programs. The main, common feature of a virus is that it is **contagious**! Their sole purpose is to spread and infect other computers.

A computer gets a virus from an infected **file**.

The virus might attach themselves to a **game**, a **program** (both shareware and commercial) or a **file** downloaded from a bulletin board or the Internet.

You cannot get a virus from a plain **email** message or from a simple **text** file! That is because the virus needs to be **'run'** or **executed** before it can take effect. This usually happens when the user tries to open an infected program, accesses an infected disk or opens a file with an infected macro or script attached to it. A plain email message is made up of text which does not execute or run when opened.

Modern email programs provide the ability to allow users to format email messages with HTML and attach scripts to them for various purposes and it is possible for a malicious hacker to attempt to spread a virus by building a virus script into an HTML type of email message.

When you are accepting software or scripts on Internet sites or reading mail from unknown senders it is best not to run a program from that site or sender without checking it with an **anti-virus program** first.

Protect yourself

You can take safeguards against virus infection. The first thing is to get an anti-virus program. Most reputable companies that create virus protection programs release an **evaluation copy** that a Internet user can download for free and use for a certain amount of time. This anti-virus program will be able to **check your computer** for viruses and **repair damage** or **delete files** that are infected with viruses. You may have to replace infected files that cannot be repaired.

The second thing you can do is **purchase a copy** of the program. The reason for this is that viruses are constantly being created. When you purchase an anti-virus program you are also purchasing **periodical updates** which keep your anti-virus program up-to-date and are able to deal with new viruses as they are encountered. Commercial virus programs also allow the user to customize when and how the program will check the computer for viruses. You will need to renew this updating service periodically.

If you find that your computer has been infected with a virus use an anti-virus, program to clean your computer and make sure to **check all the disks** that you use. This includes all the hard drives on your computer(s) and all your floppy disks and CDs as well as any media that you save information on. Remember that the virus can easily re-infect your computer from one infected file!

If you have to reload your computer programs, use the original program disks. You may want to check your original disks before reinstalling the software. If your original disks are infected contact the distributor to get replacements.

Always take the time to ensure that your computer is properly protected. Spending money on a good virus checking program could save you hundreds of dollars and lots of time later.

A discussion of viruses would not be complete without mentioning **hoaxes.** Malicious people without programming skills will send out fake virus warnings causing people to take unnecessary measures which often cause harm to your computer. One example is that it tries to get the unsuspecting computer user to delete an important system file by warning them that it is a virus. A legitimate virus warning will provide a link to a website operated by an anti-virus company with more information about that virus. Don't forward a virus warning until you have check out whether it is legitimate.

Computer Security

There is a lot of discussion these days about computer security as more people use email and more services such as banking, mail orders and subscriptions become available through the Internet. But how secure is the Internet and what is computer security?

Updating Software

It is very important to update your software periodically. When a program is released, particular internet browsers may contain flaws usually referred to as bugs. These bugs may not appear to be a problem but criminals will attempt to use these flaws for their own use. Keeping your software up to date will help keep your computer secure.

Computers & Security

Before the Internet, computer security was limited to 'closed systems' or network computers such as offices or banks where only people physically in the office could use the computer system. It was quite easy for the network supervisor to set up user names and passwords and since that time people have become used to logging on before they can use these types of computers or resources.

With the advent of the Internet, computer users can now work in an 'open system' and security has become much more complicated. Even though you can now connect your home or office computer to the Internet and perform remote transactions without leaving the building you still want to be sure that the transaction is secure. The transaction takes place through the Internet by bouncing the information through various computers before it reaches, for example, the bank's computer. You want to be sure that no one observes the transaction along the way and collects or modifies your transaction information.

This is where computer security comes in. There are many different types of security systems though most use a process called **encryption**. When you connect to your bank or other service to make a transaction you are often required to send your account number or user name as well as a Personal Identification Number (PIN) or password for verification. This information should only be sent after establishing a **secure connection**. If you are using an Internet browser you will see a small closed lock appear in the window of the browser. Once you are connected to a **secure server** any information you send or receive is scrambled or **encrypted** using a mathematical formula and then reassembled or **decrypted** at the other end. The computer user u.ually will not notice this happening as they perform their **secure transaction**. Anyone with criminal intent who intercepts your transaction will be treated to a stream of garbled nonsense - (e.g., qANQR1DBwU4D560EJv6XqrMQB)!

If this is the first time you use a new service you most often will need to **setup an account** and possibly **download** a small piece of software called a **plug in** which allows your computer to create the secure connection or link.

The transaction often involves the exchange of a small file that keeps track of the transaction and can act as a flag or bookmark when you next visit that website. These small files are called **cookies** and are set by the website you are visiting. They can contain information such as the type of server you are connecting from, the type of browser you are using, the last site you visited and any information you volunteer. You can view the information stored in the cookie. Try a search for 'cookie' to find the cookies folder. Windows users can view any cookies they are storing in the folder C:\Windows\Cookies.

Setting up security

As most people won't be setting up their own secure server, the scope of this section is limited to the topics of protecting email and small business or organizational transactions.

Email can be protected using a service or an application (program). There are others but the two that stand out currently are S/MIME and PGP. S/MIME requires the user to register with a 3 party service which issues a digital id that you attach to your message. Though this is usually a commercial service there is often a free introductory period. PGP is free for personal use or a commercial application for business use and is run from your own computer.

Both methods allow users to sign or attach a digital identification to the email message which verifies, to the recipient, that the message is from the original person or organization and that the information wasn't tampered with in transit. These methods also allow the user to encrypt their message so that anyone intercepting the message wouldn't be able to read it. You can also decide the level of encryption from low; in which a nerd with some good software and enough time on their hands could possibly decrypt to high (128 bit) which would take a whole mountain of an expert's week to decrypt if even then. Most of us will choose somewhere in between as this process involves increased time and file size.

Both methods use key pairs of public and private keys. Your public key is sent to everyone that you communicate through email. Your public key can be sent through various methods including posting it to an internet service or sending it as a part of an email message. Public keys can also be posted on your website in a file. Your friends and associates can add your public key to a file called a key ring. When someone wants to send you a secure email the sender encrypts their messages with your public key. When you receive the email you must decrypt it using your private key. Many email programs will automatically verify that the message is authentic. You will need to type in your password to view the message.

Encryption also involves using the key pair but in reverse. Once your message is completed you encrypt the file using the recipient's public key ensuring that only the recipient can access that message with their private key. (Editor's note: Don't lose your private key!).

Small businesses and organizations that wish to offer transactions over the Internet or Ecommerce can take their chances and set up an unsecured system, set up their own secure server or purchase a service from a third party. There are various types including service that take a percentage of the transaction and/or charge a service fee and/or charge for each transaction. Some organizations are more reliable and you should always shop around before committing to a service. Because this type of service is so new the length of time a company has been operating is not always a way to decide. Things to watch for is downtime. If your company's website is operating properly yet the customer or user can't access the transaction server because it is down, too busy or misconfigured, they will easily be put off perhaps entirely. Watch for contracts that lock you in as the market is still developing and prices tend to fluctuate. It is easy to switch services by simply changing the address on your website's order forms.

Questions

(1) What is a computer? Explain its functional units?

(2) What is CPU? Explain the role of arithmetic and logical unit (ALU) and control unit (CU)?

(3) What is the difference between a microcomputer and a microprocessor?

(4) Why computers are said to be more versatile machines man has ever made?

(5) What are the functional units of a computer? Whether these units could be located in different places and can be accessed? If so, explain how?

❑ ❑ ❑

CHAPTER 2

Computer-Introduction to Memory

The Role of Memory

The term "**memory**" applies to any electronic component capable of temporarily storing data. There are two main categories of memories:

- **Internal memory** that temporarily memorises data while programs are running. Internal memory uses microconductors, i.e. fast specialised electronic circuits. Internal memory corresponds to what we call random access memory (RAM).
- **Auxiliary memory** (also called *physical memory* or *external memory*) that stores information over the long term, including after the computer is turned off. Auxiliary memory corresponds to magnetic storage devices such as the hard drive, optical storage devices such as CD-ROMs and DVD-ROMs, as well as read-only memories.

Technical Characteristics

The main characteristics of a memory are:

- **Capacity**, representing the global volume of information (in bits) that the memory can store
- **Access time**, corresponding to the time interval between the read/write request and the availability of the data
- **Cycle time**, representing the minimum time interval between two successive accesses
- **Throughput**, which defines the volume of information exchanged per unit of time, expressed in bits per second
- **Non-volatility**, which characterises the ability of a memory to store data when it is not being supplied with electricity

The ideal memory has a large capacity with restricted access time and cycle time, a high throughput and is non-volatile.

However, fast memories are also the most expensive. This is why memories that use different technologies are used in a computer, interfaced with each other and organised hierarchically.

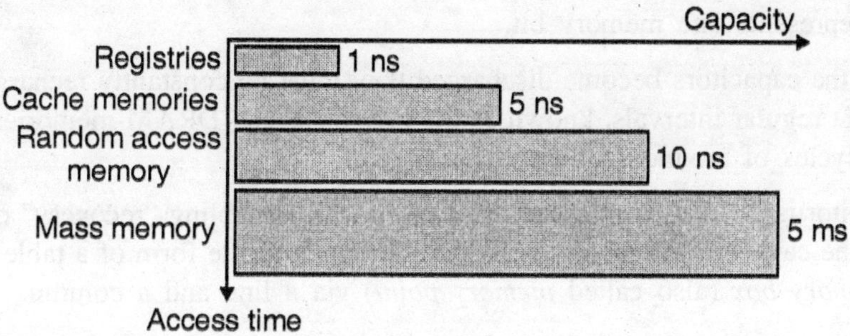

The fastest memories are located in small numbers close to the processor. Auxiliary memories, which are not as fast, are used to store information permanently.

Types of Memories

Random Access Memory

Random access memory, generally called **RAM** is the system's main memory, i.e. it is a space that allows you to temporarily store data when a program is running.

Unlike data storage on an auxiliary memory such as a hard drive, RAM is volatile, meaning that it only stores data as long as it supplied with electricity. Thus, each time the computer is turned off, all the data in the memory are irremediably erased.

Read-Only Memory

Read-only memory, called **ROM**, is a type of memory that allows you to keep the information contained on it even when the memory is no longer receiving electricity. Basically, this type of memory only has read-only access. However, it is possible to save information in some types of *ROM* memory.

Flash Memory

Flash memory is a compromise between RAM-type memories and ROM memories. Flash memory possesses the non-volatility of ROM memories while providing both read and write access However, the access times of flash memories are longer than the access times of RAM.

Types of random access memory

There are generally two broad categories of random access memory:

- **DRAM** memories (*Dynamic Random Access Module*), which are inexpensive. They are used essentially for the computer's main memory.

- **SRAM** memories (*Static Random Access Module*), which are fast and costly. SRAM memories are used in particular for the processor's cache memory.

OPERATION OF THE RANDOM ACCESS MEMORY

The random access memory comprises hundreds of thousands of small capacitors that store loads. When loaded, the logical state of the capacitor is equal to 1, otherwise it is 0, meaning that each capacitor represents one memory bit.

Given that the capacitors become discharged they must be constantly recharged (the exact term is *refresh*) at regular intervals, known as the **refresh cycle**. DRAM memories for example require refresh cycles of around 15 nanoseconds (ns).

Each capacitor is coupled with a transistor (*MOS-type*) enabling "recovery" or amendment of the status of the capacitor. These transistors are arranged in the form of a table (matrix) thus we access a *memory box* (also called *memory point*) via a line and a column.

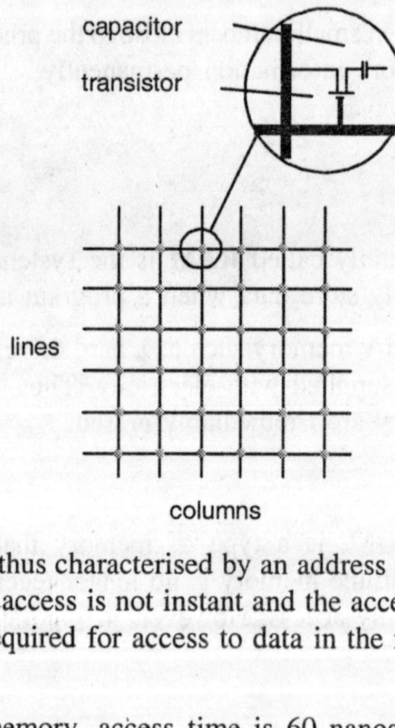

Each memory point is thus characterised by an address which corresponds to a row number and a column number. This access is not instant and the access time period is known as **latency time**. Consequently, time required for access to data in the memory is equal to cycle time plus latency time.

Thus, for a DRAM memory, access time is 60 nanoseconds (35ns cycle time and 25ns latency time). On a computer, the cycle time corresponds to the opposite of the clock frequency; for example, for a computer with frequency of 200 MHz, cycle time is 5 ns ($1/200*10^6$)).

Consequently a computer with high frequency using memories with access time much longer than the processor cycle time must perform **wait states** to access the memory. For a computer with frequency of 200 MHz using DRAM memories (and access time of 60ns), there are 11 wait states for a transfer cycle. The computer's performance decreases as the number of wait states increases, therefore we recommend the use of faster memories.

RAM module formats

There are many type of random access memory. They exist in the form of memory modules that can be plugged into the mother board.

Early memories existed in the form of chips called *DIP* (*Dual Inline Package*). Nowadays, memories generally exist in the form of modules, which are cards that can be plugged into connectors for this purpose. There are generally three types of RAM module:

- modules in ***SIMM*** format (*Single Inline Memory Module*): these are printed circuit boards with one side equipped with memory chips. There are two types of SIMM modules, according to the number of connectors:

  ⇨ SIMM modules with 30 connectors (dimensions are 89x13mm) are 8-bit memories with which first-generation PCs were equipped (286, 386).

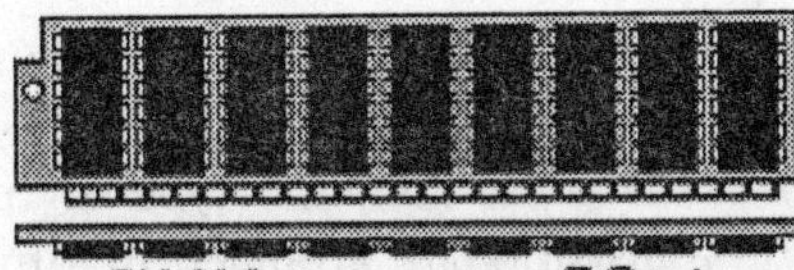

SIMM memory - 30 pin

  ⇨ SIMM modules with 72 connectors (dimensions are 108x25mm) are memories able to store 32 bits of data simultaneously. These memories are found on PCs from the 386DX to the first Pentiums. On the latter, the processor works with a 64-bit data bus; this is why these computers must be equipped with two SIMM modules. 30-pin modules cannot be installed on 72-connector positions because a notch (at the centre of the connectors) would prevent it from being plugged in.

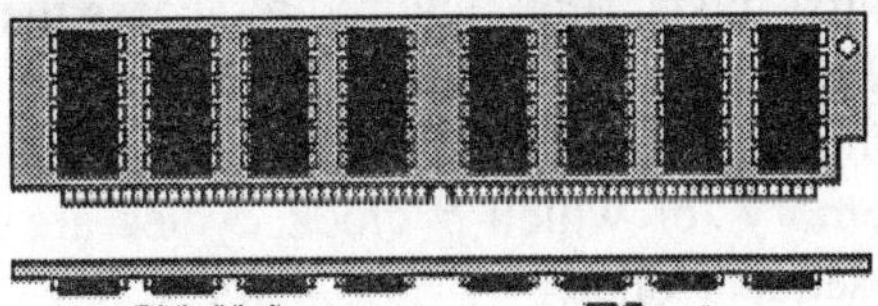

SIMM memory - 72 pin

- modules in **DIMM** format (*Dual Inline Memory Module*) are 64-bit memories, which explains why they do not need pairing. DIMM modules have memory chips on both sides of the printed circuit board and also have 84 connectors on each side, giving them a total of 168 pins. In addition to having larger dimensions than SIMM modules (130x25mm), these modules have a second notch to avoid confusion.

DIMM memory

It may be interesting to note that the DIMM connectors have been enhanced to make insertion easier, thanks to levers located on either side of the connector.

Smaller modules also exist; they are known as **SO DIMM** (*Small Outline DIMM*), designed for portable computers. *SO DIMM* modules have only 144 pins for 64-bit memories and 77 pins for 32-bit memories.

- modules in **RIMM** format (*Rambus Inline Memory Module*, also called *RD-RAM* or *DRD-RAM*) are 64-bit memories developed by Rambus. They have 184 pins. These modules have two locating notches to avoid risk of confusion with the previous modules.

- Given their high transfer speed, RIMM modules have a thermal film which is supposed to improve heat transfer.

As for DIMMs, smaller modules also exist; they are known as **SO RIMM** (*Small Outline RIMM*), designed for portable computers. *SO RIMM* modules have only 160 pins.

DRAM PM

The **DRAM** (*Dynamic RAM*) is the most common type of memory at the start of this millennium. This is a memory whose transistors are arranged in a matrix in rows and columns. A transistor, coupled with a capacitor, gives information on a bit. Since 1 octet contains 8 bits, a DRAM memory module of 256 Mo will thus contain 256 * 2^10 * 2^10 = 256 * 1024 * 1024 = 268,435,456 octets = 268,435,456 * 8 = 2,147,483,648 bits = 2,147,483,648 transistors. A module of 256 Mo thus has a capacity of 268,435,456 octets, or 268 Mo! These memories have access times of 60 ns.

Furthermore, access to memory generally concerns data stored consecutively in the memory. Thus **burst mode** allows access to the three pieces of data following the first piece with no additional latency time. In this burst mode, time required to access the first piece of data is equal to cycle time plus latency time, and the time required to access the other three pieces of data is equal to just the cycle time; the four access times are thus written in the form X-Y-Y-Y, for example *5-3-3-3* indicates a memory for which 5 clock cycles are needed to access the first piece of data and 3 for the subsequent ones.

DRAM FPM

To speed up access to the DRAM, there is a technique, known as **paging**, which involves accessing data located in the same column by changing only the address of the row, thus avoiding repetition of the column number between reading of each row. This is known as **DRAM FPM** (*Fast Page Mode*). FPM achieves access times of around 70 to 80 nanoseconds for operating frequency between 25 and 33 Mhz.

DRAM EDO

DRAM EDO (*Extended Data Out*, sometimes also called *hyper-page*") was introduced in 1995. The technique used with this type of memory involves addressing the next column while reading the data in a column. This creates an overlap of access thus saving time on each cycle.

EDO memory access time is thus around 50 to 60 nanoseconds for operating frequency between 33 and 66 Mhz.

Thus the RAM EDO, when used in burst mode, achieves 5-2-2-2 cycles, representing a gain of 4 cycles on access to 4 pieces of data. Since the EDO memory did not work with frequencies higher than 66 Mhz, it was abandoned in favour of the SDRAM.

SDRAM

The **SDRAM** (*Synchronous DRAM*), introduced in 1997, allows synchronised reading of data with the mother-board bus, unlike the EDO and FPM memories (known as *asynchronous*) which have their own clock. The SDRAM thus eliminates waiting times due to synchronisation with the mother-board. This achieves a 5-1-1-1 burst mode cycle, with a gain of 3 cycles in comparison with the RAM EDO. The SDRAM is thus able to operate with frequency up to 150 Mhz, allowing it to achieve access times of around 10 ns.

DR-SDRAM (Rambus DRAM)

The **DR-SDRAM** (*Direct Rambus DRAM*) is a type of memory that lets you transfer data to a 16-bit bus at frequency of 800Mhz, giving it a bandwidth of 1.6 Go/s. As with the SDRAM, this type of memory is synchronised with the bus clock to enhance data exchange. However, the RAMBUS memory is a proprietary technology, meaning that any company wishing to produce RAM modules using this technology must pay royalties to both RAMBUS and Intel.

DDR-SDRAM

The **DDR-SDRAM** (*Double Data Rate SDRAM*) is a memory, based on the SDRAM technology, which doubles the transfer rate of the SDRAM using the same frequency.

Data are read or written into memory based on a clock. Standard DRAM memories use a method known as **SDR** (*Single Data Rate*) involving reading or writing a piece of data at each leading edge.

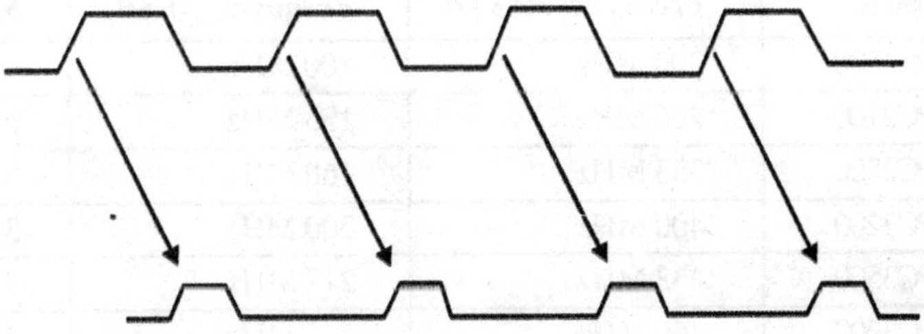

The DDR doubles the frequency of reading/writing, with a clock at the same frequency, by sending data to each leading edge and to each trailing edge.

DDR memories generally have a product name such as PC*XXXX* where "*XXXX*" represents the speed in Mo/s.

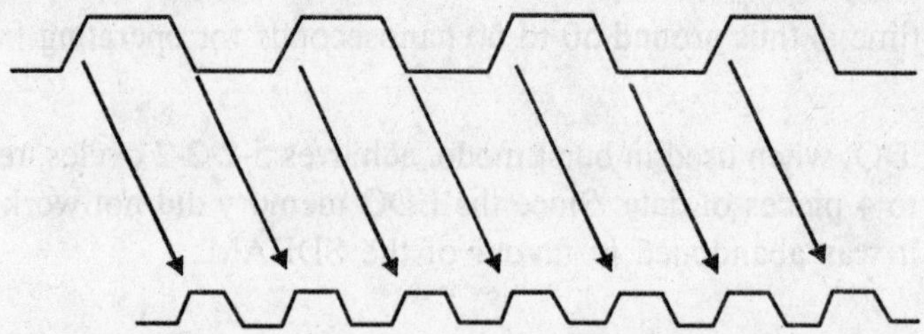

DDR2-SDRAM

DDR2 (or DDR-II) memory achieves speeds that are twice as high as those of the DDR with the same external frequency.

QDR (*Quadruple Data Rate* or *quad-pumped*) designates the reading and writing method used. DDR2 memory in fact uses two separate channels for reading and writing, so that it is able to send or receive twice as much data as the DDR.

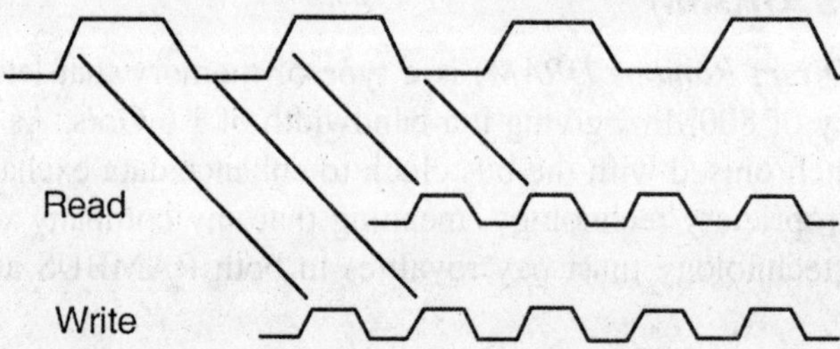

DDR2 also has more connectors than the classic DDR (240 for DDR2 compared with 184 for DDR).

Summary table

The table below gives the equivalence between the mother-board frequency (FSB), the memory (RAM) frequency and its speed:

Memory	Name	Frequency (RAM)	Frequency (FSB)	Speed
DDR200	PC1600	200 MHz	100 MHz	1.6 Go/s
DDR266	PC2100	266 MHz	133 MHz	2.1 Go/s
DDR333	PC2700	333 MHz	166 MHz	2.7 Go/s
DDR400	PC3200	400 MHz	200 MHz	3.2 Go/s
DDR433	PC3500	433 MHz	217 MHz	3.5 Go/s
DDR466	PC3700	466 MHz	233 MHz	3.7 Go/s
DDR500	PC4000	500 MHz	250 MHz	4 Go/s
DDR533	PC4200	533 MHz	266 MHz	4.2 Go/s
DDR538	PC4300	538 MHz	269 MHz	4.3 Go/s
DDR550	PC4400	550 MHz	275 MHz	4.4 Go/s
DDR2-400	PC2-3200	400 MHz	100 MHz	3.2 Go/s

DDR2-533	PC2-4300	533 MHz	133 MHz	4.3 Go/s
DDR2-667	PC2-5300	667 MHz	167 MHz	5.3 Go/s
DDR2-675	PC2-5400	675 MHz	172.5 MHz	5.4 Go/s
DDR2-800	PC2-6400	800 MHz	200 MHz	6.4 Go/s

Synchronisation (timings)

It is not unusual to see scores such as 3-2-2-2 or 2-3-3-2 to describe the parameterisation of the random access memory. This succession of four figures describes the synchronisation of the memory (*timing*), i.e. the succession of clock cycles needed to access a piece of data stored in the RAM. These four figures generally correspond, in order, to the following values:

- **CAS delay** or **CAS latency** (CAS meaning *Column Address Strobe*): This is the number of clock cycles that elapse between the reading command being sent and the piece of data actually arriving. In other words, it is the time needed to access a column.
- **RAS Precharge Time** (known as *tRP*, RAS meaning *Row Address Strobe*): This is the number of clock cycles between two RAS instructions, i.e. between two accesses to a row operation.
- **RAS to CAS delay** (sometimes called *tRCD*): this is the number of clock cycles corresponding to access time from a row to a column.
- **RAS active time** (sometimes called *tRAS*): this is the number of clock cycles corresponding to the time needed to access a row.

The memory cards are equipped with a device called **SPD** (*Serial Presence Detect*), allowing the BIOS to find out the nominal setting values defined by the manufacturer. It is an EEPROM whose data will be loaded by the BIOS if the user chooses "auto" setting.

Error correction

Some memories have mechanisms for correcting errors to ensure the integrity of the data they contain. This type of memory is generally used on systems working on critical data, which is why this type of memory is found in servers.

Parity bit

Modules with parity bit ensure that the data contained in the memory are the ones required. To achieve this, one of the bits from each octet stored in the memory is used to store the sum of the data bits. The parity bit is 1 when the sum of the data bits is an odd number and 0 in the opposite case.

Thus the modules with parity bit allow the integrity of data to be checked but do not provide for error correction. Moreover, for 9 Mo of memory, only 8 will be used to store data since the last mega octet is used to store the parity bits.

ECC modules

ECC (*Error Correction Coding*) memory modules are memories with several bits dedicated to error correction (they are known as *control bits*). These modules, used mainly in servers, allow detection and correction of errors.

Dual Channel

Some memory controllers offer a dual channel for the memory. The memory modules are used in pairs to achieve higher bandwidth and thus make the best use of the system's capacity. When using the Dual Channel, it is vital to use identical modules in a pair (same frequency and capacity and preferably the same brand).

Read-only memory (ROM)

There is a type of memory that stores data without electrical current; it is the ***ROM*** (*Read Only Memory*) or is sometimes called *non-volatile memory* as it is not erased when the system is switched off.

This type of memory lets you store the data needed to start up the computer. Indeed, this information cannot be stored on the hard disk since the disk parameters (vital for its initialisation) are part of these data which are essential for booting.

Different *ROM*-type memories contain these essential start-up data, i.e.:

- The BIOS is a programme for controlling the system's main input-output interfaces, hence the name *BIOS ROM* which is sometimes given to the read-only memory chip of the mother board which hosts it.
- The **bootstrap loader** a programme for loading (random access) memory into the operating system and launching it. This generally seeks the operating system on the floppy drive then on the hard disk, which allows the operating system to be launched from a system floppy disk in the event of malfunction of the system installed on the hard disk.
- The **CMOS Setup** is the screen displayed when the computer starts up and which is used to amend the system parameters (often wrongly referred to as *BIOS*).
- The **Power-On Self Test** (*POST*), a programme that runs automatically when the system is booted, thus allowing the system to be tested (this is why the system "counts" the RAM at start-up).

Given that ROM are much slower than RAM memories (access time for a ROM is around 150 ns whereas for SDRAM it is around 10 ns), the instructions given in the ROM are sometimes copied to the RAM at start-up; this is known as *shadowing*, though it is usually referred to as *shadow memory*).

Types of ROM

ROM memories have gradually evolved from *fixed read-only memories* to memories than can be programmed and then re-programmed.

ROM: The first ROMs were made using a procedure that directly writes the binary data in a silicon plate using a mask. This procedure is now obsolete.

PROM: PROM (*Programmable Read Only Memory*) memories were developed at the end of the 70s by a company called *Texas Instruments*. These memories are chips comprising thousands of fuses (or diodes) that can be "burnt" using a device called a " *ROM programmer*", applying high voltage (12V) to the memory boxes to be marked. The fuses thus burnt correspond to 0 and the others to 1.

EPROM: EPROM (*Erasable Programmable Read Only Memory*) memories are PROMs that can be deleted. These chips have a glass panel that lets ultra-violet rays through. When the chip is subjected to ultra-violet rays with a certain wavelength, the fuses are reconstituted, meaning that all the memory bits return to 1. This is why this type of PROM is called *erasable.*

EEPROM: EEPROM (*Electrically Erasable Read Only Memory* memories are also erasable PROMs, but unlike EPROMs, they can be erased by a simple electric current, meaning that they can be erased even when they are in position in the computer.

There is a variant of these memories known as **flash memories** (also *Flash ROM* or *Flash EPROM*). Unlike the classic EEPROMs that use 2 to 3 transistors for each bit to be memorised, the EPROM Flash uses only one transistor. Moreover, the EEPROM may be written and read word by word, while the Flash can be erased only in pages (the size of the pages decreases constantly).

Lastly, the Flash memory is denser, meaning that chips containing several hundred mega octets can be produced. EEPROMs are thus used preferably to memorise configuration data and the Flash memory is used for programmable code (IT programmes).

The action involving reprogramming of an EEPROM is known as flashing.

Introduction to Flash memory

Flash memory is a kind of semiconductor-based, non-volatile, rewritable computer memory; that is, it has many of the same characteristics as RAM, except that the data is not wiped out when the machine is turned off. Flash memory stores bits of data in memory cells, but the data remains saved even when electrical power is cut.

Due to its higher speed, durability, and low energy consumption, flash memory is ideal for many applications, such as digital cameras, mobile phones, printers, PDAs, laptop computers, and device that can record and play back sound, such as mp3 players. What's more, this kind of memory has no moving parts, which makes it very shock-resistant.

Types of memory cards

There are many competing, incompatible memory card formats, almost one for every manufacturer. Among these formats of memory cards, the most common are:

- Compact Flash
- Secure Digital cards (called SD Card)
- Memory Stick
- SmartMedia
- MMC (*MultimediaCard*)
- xD picture card

Comparison

	Dimensions (mm)	Volume (mm3)	Weight (g)	#of Transfer of connectors		Theoretical capacity	Theoretical size
Compact Flash type I	43 × 36 × 3,3	5 108	3,3	50	20 Mo/s	137 Go	128 Go
Compact Flash type II	43 × 36 × 5	7 740	4	50	20 Mo/s	137 Go	12 Go
SmartMedia	37 × 45 × 0,8	1 265	2	22	2 Mo/s	128 Mo	128 Mo
MMC	24 × 32 × 1,4	1 075	1,3	7	20 Mo/s	128 Go	8 Go
MMC Plus	24 × 32 × 1,4	1 075	1,3	7	52 Mo/s	128 Go	4 Go
RS-MMC MMC Mobile	24 × 16 × 1,4	538	1,3	13	8 Mo/s	128 Go	2 Go
MMC Micro	14 × 12 × 1,1	185	< 1	13		128 Go	2 Go
Memory Stick Standard, Pro	21,5 × 50 × 2,8	3 010	4	10	2 Mo/s	128 Mo	128 Mo
Memory Stick Duo, Pro Duo	20 × 31 × 1,6	992	2	10	20 Mo/s	32 Go	16 Go
Memory Stick Pro-HG	20 × 31 × 1,6	992	2	10	60 Mo/s	32 Go	32 Go
Memory Stick Micro M2	12,5 × 15 × 1,2	225	2	10	20 Mo/s	32 Go	8 Go
SD	24 × 32 × 2,1	1 613	2	9	20 Mo/s	32 Go	32 Go
mini SD	20 × 21,5 × 1,4	602	1	11	12 Mo/s	32 Go	4 Go
micro SD	15 × 11 × 1	165	0,3	8	10 Mo/s	32 Go	12 Go
xD	25 × 20 × 1,8	890	2,8	18	9 Mo/s	8 Go	2 Go

Memory card readers

It should be noted that there are multi-format memory card readers, most of which can be plugged into a USB port.

Compact Flash

Compact Flash memory (sometimes called *CF*) is a kind of memory card created in 1994 by the company *SanDisk*. Compact Flash is made up of a memory controller and a flash memory chip contained within a miniature casing (42.8mm wide and 36.4mm high), which is smaller than a matchbox and weighs only 11.4 grams.

There are two types of Compact Flash cards, with different dimensions:

- Type I Compact Flash cards, which are 3.3mm thick;

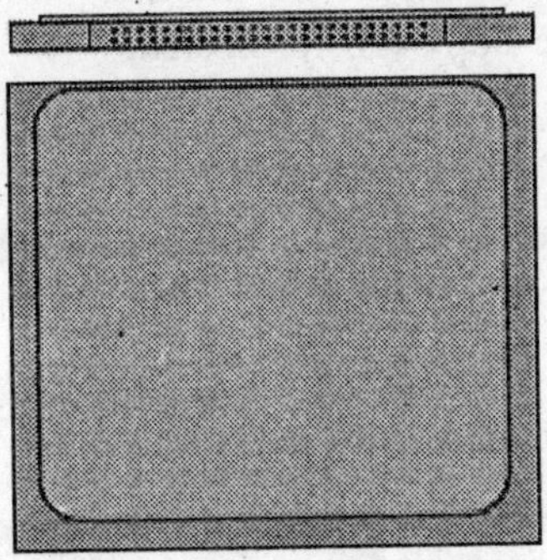

- Type II Compact Flash cards, which are 5mm thick.

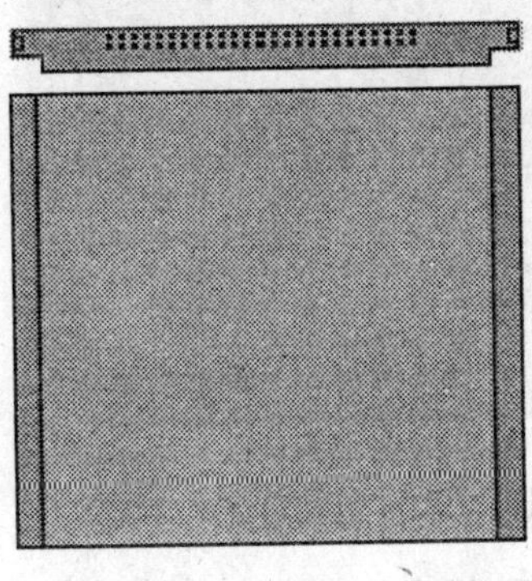

CompactFlash cards comply with the PCMCIA/ATA standard, although the connector has 50 pins instead of 68, as PCMCIA do. For this reason, a CompactFlash card can be inserted into a passive Type II PCMCIA slot

Memory Stick

The **Memory Stick** (written as *MS* or *MS Card*) is a type of memory card created jointly by Sony and SanDisk in January 2000.

The architecture of Memory Stick cards is based on NAND flash memory circuits (EEPROM).

Memory stick memories are very small (21.5 mm × 50.0 mm × 2.8 mm), which is equivalent to the size of a small box of matches, and weigh only 4 grams.

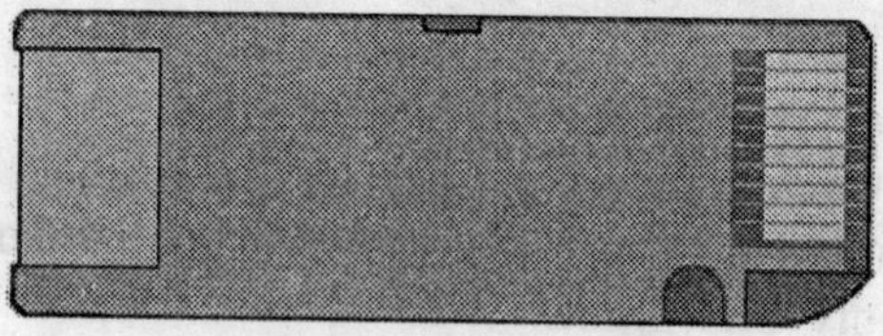

Data can be accessed by way of an edge connector with 10 pins, for a throughput of up to 14.4 Mb/s (up to a maximum of 19.6 Mb/s).

There are two types of Memory Sticks: the "normal" *Memory Stick* and the "Magic Gate", which protects documents that are copyright protected.

MMC - Multimedia Cards

Multimedia card memory (abbreviated as *MMC*) is a type of memory card created jointly by *SanDisk* and *Siemens* in November 1997.

Its architecture is based on a combination of read-only memory (ROM) for read-only applications and flash memory for read/write purposes.

Multimedia cards are very small (24.0 mm × 32.0 mm × 1.4 mm), which is equivalent to the size of a postage stamp, and weigh only 2.2 grams.

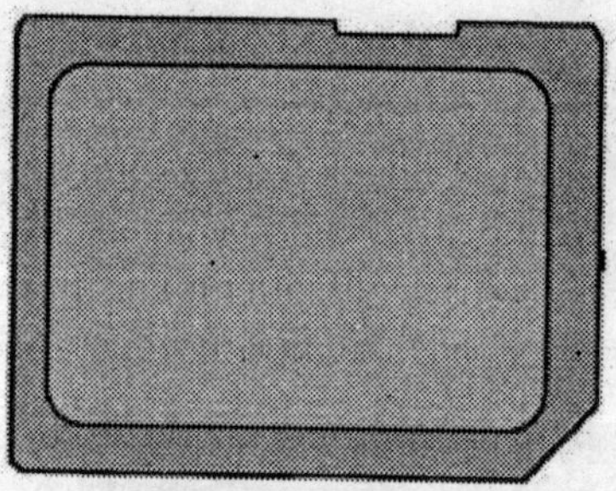

There are two types of MMC cards that have different voltages:

- MMC 3.3V, with a notch on the upper left-hand corner
- MMC 5V, with a notch on the upper right-hand corner

Data can be accessed by way of an edge connector with 7 pins, for a throughput of up to 2 Mb/s (perhaps even 2.5 Mb/s).

Secure Digital

Secure Digital memory (known as *SD* or *SD Card*) is a type of memory card created by Matsushita Electronic, SanDisk and Toshiba in January 2000. Secure Digital memory is a memory specifically developed to meet new safety requirements in the field of electronic audio and video devices. It therefore includes a copyright protection system that satisfies the **SDMI** (Secure Digital Music Initiative) standard.

The architecture of the SD cards is based on NAND-type flash memory circuits (EEPROM).

The Secure Digital memory has small dimensions (24.0mm × 32.0mm × 2.1mm), equivalent to those of a postage stamp, and weighs barely 2 grammes.

Data are accessed using a 9-pin lateral connector achieving a transfer speed of 2 Mb/s with the potential to go up to 10 MB/s.

SD memory access time is around 25μs for first access and cycles of *50 ns* for subsequent cycles.

Smart Media

SmartMedia memory is a type of memory card created by Toshiba and Samsung.

Its architecture is based on NAND type flash memory circuits (EEPROM)

SmartMedia memory is equivalent in size to a postal stamp (45.0mm x 37.0mm x 0.76mm) and weighs barely 2 grams.

There are two types of SmartMedia card with different voltages:

- 3.3V SmartMedia cards have a notch on the right

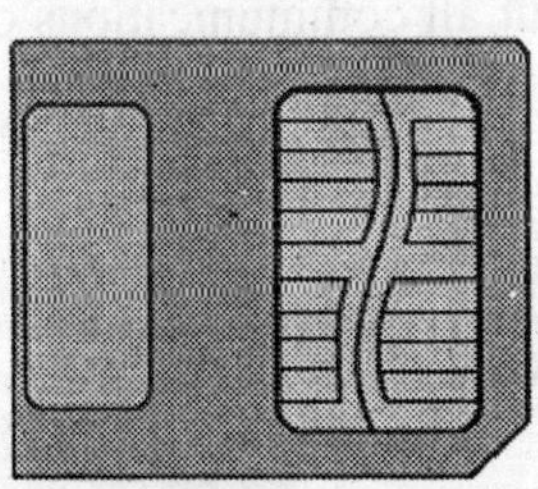

- 5V SmartMedia cards have a notch on the left

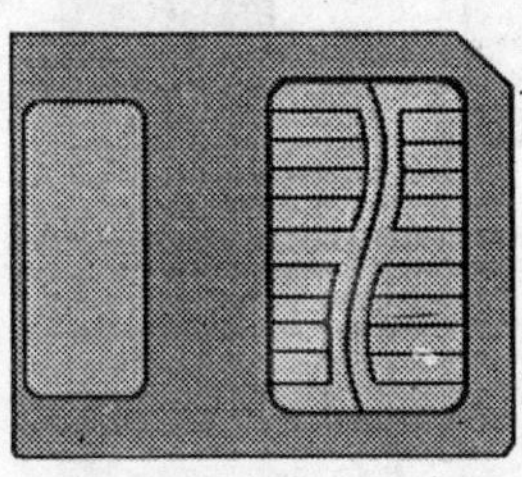

Access to the data is carried out via a chip with 22 pins. Whatever the capacity of the SmartMedia card, the dimensions and location of the chip are the same.

Access time for the memory is approximately 25μs for the first access and cycles of *50 ns* for the following ones.

Compatibility

There are two adapters making it possible to insert a SmartMedia card in a PCMCIA location, so as to enable the transfer of data directly from a SmartMedia card to a laptop.

xD Picture card

xD Picture memory (for *eXtreme Digital*) is a type of memory card created by Fuji and Olympus in August 2002.

The architecture of xD cards is based on NAND type flash memory circuits (EEPROM)

xD picture card memory is smaller in size than a postal stamp (20.0mm × 25.0mm × 1.7mm) and weighs barely 2 grams.

Access to the data is carried out via a lateral connector with 18 pins, allowing a transfer rate of 1.3 Mb/s to be reached and potentially up to 3Mb/s for writing and around 5 Mb/s for reading.

In time it is expected that xD picture cards will reach a capacity of 8Gb.

Introduction to the concept of a bus

A **bus**, in computing, is a set of physical connections (cables, printed circuits, etc.) which can be shared by multiple hardware components in order to communicate with one another.

The purpose of buses is to reduce the number of "pathways" needed for communication between the components, by carrying out all communications over a single data channel. This is why the metaphor of a "data highway" is sometimes used.

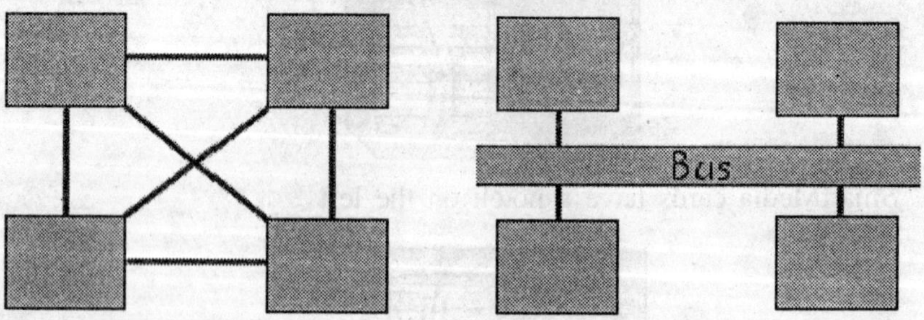

If only two hardware components communicate over the line, it is called a **hardware port** (such as a serial port or parallel port).

Characteristics of a bus

A bus is characterised by the amount of information that can be transmitted at once. This amount, expressed in bits, corresponds to the number of physical lines over which data is sent simultaneously. A 32-wire ribbon cable can transmit 32 bits in parallel. The term "**width**" is used to refer to the number of bits that a bus can transmit at once.

Additionally, the bus speed is also defined by its **frequency** (expressed in Hertz), the number of data packets sent or received per second. Each time that data is sent or received is called a **cycle**.

This way, it is possible to find the maximum **transfer speed** of the bus, the amount of data which it can transport per unit of time, by multiplying its width by its frequency. A bus with a width of 16 bits and a frequency of 133 MHz, therefore, has a transfer speed equal to:

$16 * 133.10^6 = 2128*10^6$ bit/s,

or $2128*10^6/8 = 266*10^6$ bytes/s

or $266*10^6 /1000 = 266*10^3$ KB/s

or $259.7*10^3 /1000 = 266$ MB/s

Bus subassembly

In reality, each bus is generally constituted of 50 to 100 distinct physical lines, divided into three subassemblies:

- The **address bus** (sometimes called the *memory bus*) transports memory addresses which the processor wants to access in order to read or write data. It is a unidirectional bus.
- The **data bus** transfers instructions coming from or going to the processor. It is a bidirectional bus.
- The **control bus** (or *command bus*) transports orders and synchronisation signals coming from the control unit and travelling to all other hardware components. It is a bidirectional bus, as it also transmits response signals from the hardware.

The primary buses

There are generally two buses within a computer:

- **the internal bus** (sometimes called the *front-side bus*, or *FSB* for short). The internal bus allows the processor to communicate with the system's central memory (the RAM).
- **the expansion bus** (sometimes called the *input/output bus*) allows various motherboard components (USB, serial, and parallel ports, cards inserted in PCI connectors, hard drives, CD-ROM and CD-RW drives, etc.) to communicate with one another. However, it is mainly used to add new devices using what are called **expansion slots** connected to the input/outpur bus.

Cathode ray tube monitor

Most monitors (computer screens) use **cathode ray tubes** (or **CRT** for short), which are glass vacuum tubes into which an electron gun emits a flow of electrons guided by an electrical field towards a screen covered in small phosphorescent elements.

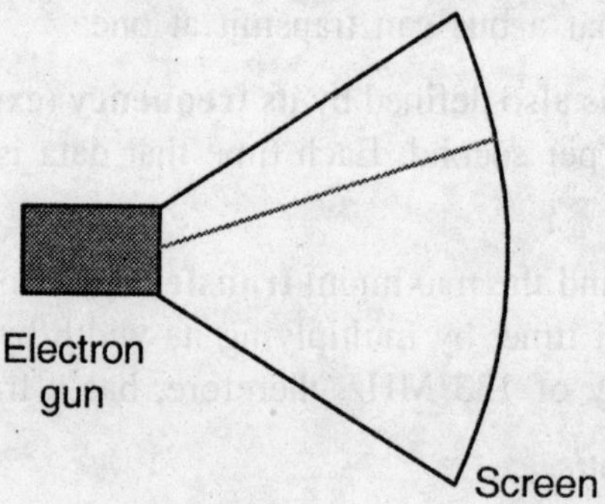

The electron gun is made up of a **cathode**, a negatively charged metallic electrode, and one or more **anodes** (positively charged electrodes). The cathode emits the electrons attracted by the anode. The anode acts as an accelerator and concentrator for the electrons, forming a flow of electrons aimed at the screen. A magnetic field guides the electrons from left to right and from top to bottom. It is created with two electrified X and Y plates (called *deflectors*) which send the flow horizontally and vertically, respectively.

The screen is covered with a fine layer of phosphorescent elements, called phosphors, which emit light by excitation when electrons strike them, creating a lit-up dot called a **pixel**.

Activating the magnetic field causes the electrons to follow a **scan pattern**, going from left to right and then down to the next row once they reach the end.

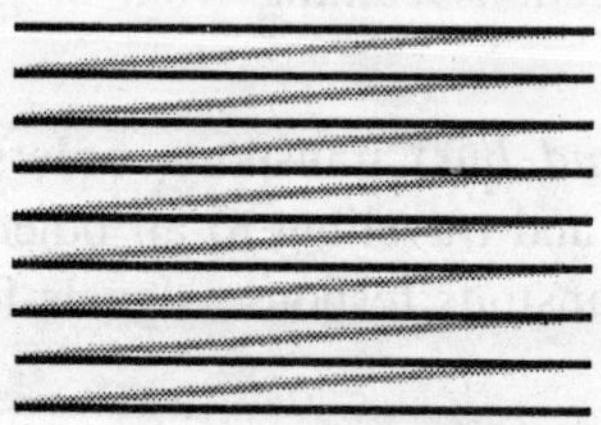

The human eye cannot see this scanning due to persistence of vision. Try waving your hand in front of your screen to view the phenomenon: You'll see several hands at once!

Combined with the firing and non-firing of the electron gun, scanning tricks your eyes into believing that only some pixels on the screen are lit up.

The colour monitor

A black and white monitor can display different tones (shades of gray) by varying the intensity of the flow.

For colour monitors, three electron beams (coming from three different cathodes) each strike a point with a specific colour: red, green, and blue (RGB).

Three points of colour are called a **triad** (or *dot trio*).

Blue phosphors use zinc sulfide, while green ones use zinc sulfide and cadmium sulfide. The red ones are hard to create, and are made from a mixture of yttrium and europium, or gadolinium oxide.

However, these phosphors are so close together than the eye cannot separate them enough to tell them apart; it sees a single colour made up of these three colours. Try flicking a tiny drop of water onto the glass of your monitor: It will magnify the phosphors so that you can see them.

What's more, to avoid smearing (such as an electron meant to strike a green phosphor colliding with blue instead), a metallic grid called the **shadow mask** is placed in front of the phosphoric layer to guide the electron flow.

There are several different categories of CRT monitors, which are set apart by the mask used:

- **FST-Invar** (*Flat Square Tube*), whose phosphors are round. These monitors use a grid called a *shadow mask*. They give the right colours overall, but have the disadvantage of distorting and darkening the image at the corners.

- Mitsubishi's **Diamondtron** tubes and Sony's **Trinitron**, whose masks are made up of vertical slots (called an *aperture grille* or *tension mask*), which lets through more electrons and therefore gives a brighter image.

- Nec's **Cromaclear** tubes, whose mask uses a hybrid system with dimpled slots, is the best technology of the three.

Technical specifications

The specifications for CRT monitors include:

- The **definition**: The number of pixels that the screen can display. This number is generally between 640 × 480 (640 pixels long, 480 pixels wide) and 1600 × 1200, but higher resolutions are technically possible.
- The **size**: This is calculated by measuring the diagonal of the screen, and is expressed in inches (an inch is about 2.54 cm). Be carcful not to confuse a screen's *definition* with its *size*. After all, a screen of a given size can display different definitions, although in general screens which are larger in size have a higher definition.
- The **dot pitch**: This represents the distance which separates two phosphors of the same colour. The lower the dot pitch, the better the image quality. A dot pitch equal to or less than 0.25 mm will be comfortable to use, while monitors with a dot pitch equal to or greater than 0.28 mm should be avoided.

- The **resolution**: This determines the number of pixels per surface unit (given in linear inches). This is abbreviated **DPI**, for *Dots Per Inch*. A resolution of 300 dpi means 300 columns and 300 rows of pixels per square inch, which means that there are 90,000 pixels per square inch. By comparison, a resolution of 72 dpi means that one pixel is 1"/72 (one inch divided by 72) or 0.353 mm, which corresponds to one *pica* (a typographical unit). The terms "resolution" and "definition" are often confused in the media.
- The **refresh rate**: This represents the number of images which are displayed per second, or more precisely the number of times the image is refreshed each second. Also called the **vertical scan rate**, it is expressed in Hertz. The higher this value is, the better the visual comfort (the image does not appear to flicker), so it must be much higher than 67 Hz (any lower than that, and the image appears to "blink"). Most people do not notice the flicker effect at 70 Hz or higher, so a value equal to or greater than 75 Hz is generally suitable.

Flat-screen monitors

Flat-screen monitors (also called *FPDs* for *Flat panel displays*) are becoming more and more widespread, as they take up less space and are less heavy than traditional CRT monitors.

What's more, the technology used by flat-screen monitors uses less energy (lower than 10W, as opposed to 100W for CRT monitors) and emits less electromagnetic radiation.

Liquid crystal displays

LCD (*Liquid Crystal Display*) is based on a screen made up of two grooved transparent parallel plates, oriented at 90° to one another; the space between them holds a thin layer of liquid containing certain molecules (liquid crystals) which change direction when they are exposed to electrical current.

Combined with a source of light, the first plate acts as a polarizing filter, letting through only those light components whose oscillation is parallel to the grooves.

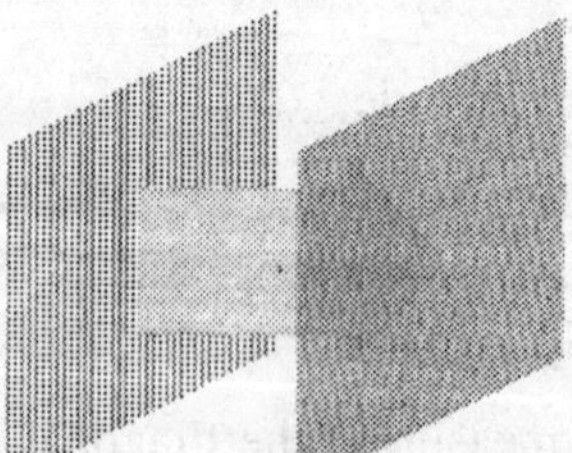

In the absence of electrical current, the light is blocked by the second plate, which acts as a perpendicular polarising filter.

When powered, the crystals align one by one in the direction of the electric field, and can cross the second plate.

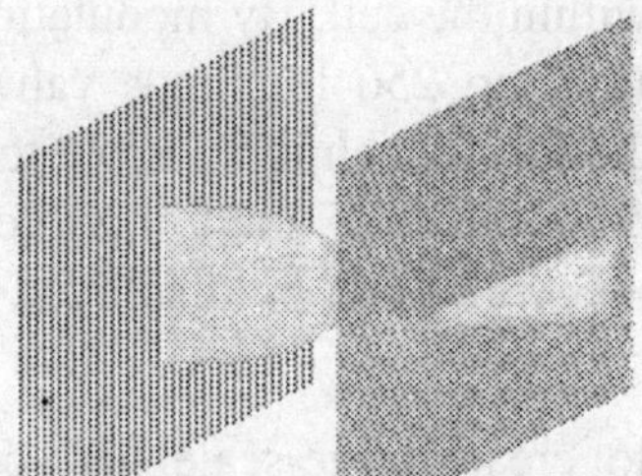

By locally controlling the orientation of the crystals, it is possible to make pixels. There are normally said to be two types of flat screens, depending on which control system is used to polarise the crystals:

- "**Passive matrix**" displays, whose pixels are controlled by row and column. Pixels are given a row/column address using transparent conductors located in the monitor's frame. The pixel lights up when it is addressed, and turns off in when refreshed.

Passive matrix monitors usually use **TN** technology (*Twisted Nematics*). Passive matrix monitors often suffer from a lack of brightness and contrast.

- "**Active matrix**" displays, in which each pixel is controlled individually.

The most common technology for this kind of display is **TFT** (*Thin Film Transistor*), which can control every pixel using three transistors (which correspond to the 3 RGB colours). Under this system, the transistor coupled with each pixel can memorise its state, and keep it lit between refreshes. Active matrix monitors are brighter and display a sharper image.

Whether the monitors are active or passive, they need a light source to function. The following terms define how the screen is lit:

- **Reflection** screens are light from the front, using artificial light or simply ambient light (as with most digital watches).

- **Transmission** screens use rear lighting to display information. This type of screen is especially well-suited for indoor use, or in dim light conditions, and normally provides a high-contrast, bright image. On the other hand, they become hard to read when used outdoors (in full sunlight)

- **Transflective** screens use rear lighting as well as a polariser made of a translucent material, which can transmit background light while reflecting some ambient light. This type of screen is especially suitable for devices that are meant to be used both indoors and outdoors (such as digital cameras and PDAs).

Plasma screens

Plasma technology (*PDP*, *Plasma Display Panel*) is based on emitting light by exciting gases. The gas used in plasma screens is a mixture of argon (90%) and xenon (10%). Gas is contained within cells, each one corresponding to a pixel that corresponds to a row electrode and column electrode, which excite the gas within the cell. By modulating the voltage applied by the electrodes and the frequency of excitation, up 256 luminous values can be defined. The gas excited this way produces ultraviolet radiation (which is invisible to the human eye). With blue, green, and red phosphors distributed among the cells, the ultraviolet radiation is converted into visible light, so that pixels (made up of 3 cells) can be displayed in up to 16 million colours (256 × 256 × 256).

Plasma technology can be used to create large-scale high-contrast screens, but plasma screens are still expensive. What's more, power consumption is more than 30 times higher than for an LCD screen

Specifications

The most common specifications for monitors are:

- The **definition**: The number of pixels that the screen can display. This number is generally between 640x480 (640 pixels long, 480 pixels wide) and 1600x1200, but higher resolutions are technically possible.
- The **size**: This is calculated by measuring the diagonal of the screen, and is expressed in inches (an inch is about 2.54 cm). Be careful not to confuse a screen's *definition* with its *size*. After all, a screen of a given size can display different definitions, although in general screens which are larger in size have a higher definition.
- The **resolution**: This determines the number of pixels per surface unit (given in linear inches). This is abbreviated **DPI**, for *Dots Per Inch*. A resolution of 300 dpi means 300 columns and 300 rows of pixels per square inch, which means that there are 90,000 pixels per square inch. By comparison, a resolution of 72 dpi means that one pixel is 1"/72 (one inch divided by 72) or 0.353 mm, which corresponds to one *pica* (a typographical unit).
- **Response time**: Defined by international standard ISO 13406-2, this corresponds to the amount of time needed to switch a pixel from white to black and back again. Response time (expressed in milliseconds) should be as low as possible (pragmatically, lower than 25 ms).
- **Luminance**: Expressed in candelas per square metre (Cd/m^2), this is used to define the screen's "brightness" The order of magnitude for luminance is about 250 cd/m^2.
- The **horizontal and vertical viewing angle**: Expressed in degrees, this is used to define the angle from which viewing the screen becomes difficult when the user is not looking at it straight-on.

The role of the hard drive

The **hard drive** is the component which is used to permanently store data, as opposed to RAM, which is erased whenever the computer is restarted, which is why the term *mass storage device* is sometimes used to refer to hard drives.

The hard drive is connected to the motherboard using a **hard drive controller** which acts as an interface between the processor and the hard drive. The hard drive controller manages the drives linked to it, interprets commands sent by the processor and routes them to the drive in question. Hard drives are generally grouped by interface as follows:

- IDE
- SCSI
- Serial ATA

When the USB standard appeared, external cases which could connect a hard drive using a USB port were released, making hard drives easy to install and increasing storage capacity for macking backups. These are called **external hard drives**, as opposed to internal hard drives which are plugged directly into the motherboard; still, they are the same disks, even though they are connected to the computer using a case plugged into a USB port.

Structure

A **hard drive** is made up of not just one, but several rigid metal, glass, or ceramic disks, stacked very close to one another and called **platters**.

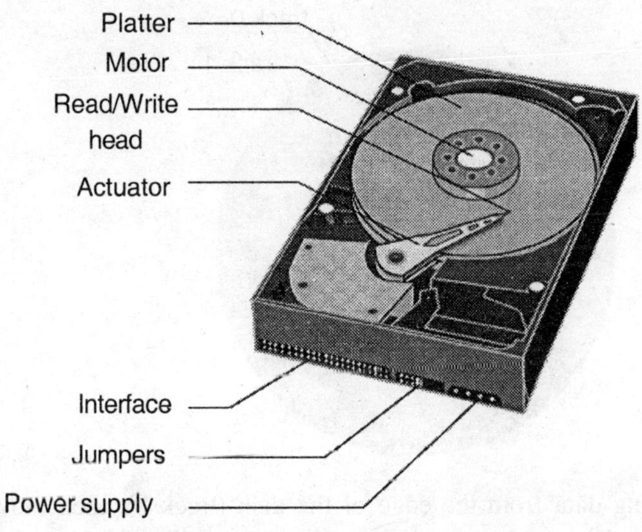

The disks turn very quickly around an axle (currently several thousand revolutions per minute) in a counter-clockwise direction. A computer works in binart mode, meaning that the data is stored in the form of 0s and 1s (called bits). Hard drives hold millions of these bits, stored very close to one another on a fine magntic layer a few microns thick, which is covered by a protective film.

They are read and written using **read heads** located on both sides of the **platters**. These heads are electromagnets which raise and lower themselves in order to read or write data. The read heads are only a few microns from the surface, separated by a layer of air created by the rotation of the disks, which generates a wind of about 250km/h (150 mph)! What's more, these disks are laterally mobile, so that the heads can sweep across their entire surface.

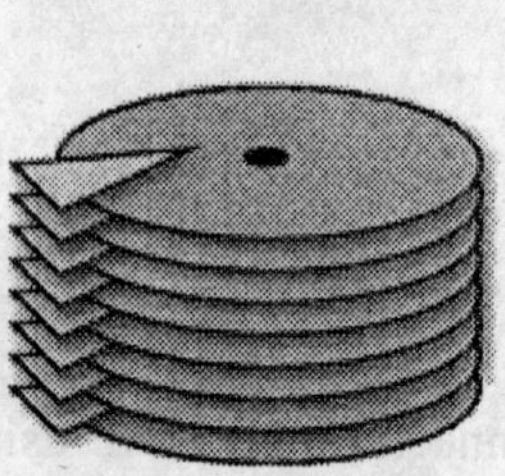

However, the heads are linked to one another and only one of them can read or write at a given moment. The term **cylinder** is used to refer to all the data stored vertically on each of the disks.

This entire precision mechanism is contained within a fully airtight case, as the smallest particle can degrade the disk's surface. This is why hard drives are closed shut with seals, and the warning "*Warranty void if removed*", as only hard drive manufacturers can open them (in particle-free "cleanrooms").

How it works

The read/write heads are said to be "inductive", meaning that they can generate a magnetic field. This is especially important in writing: The heads, by creating positive or negative fields, polarise the disk surface in a very tiny area, so that when they are read afterwards, the polarity reversal completes a circuit with the read head, which is then transformed by an analog-digital converter (ADC) into a 0 or 1 which can be understood by the computer.

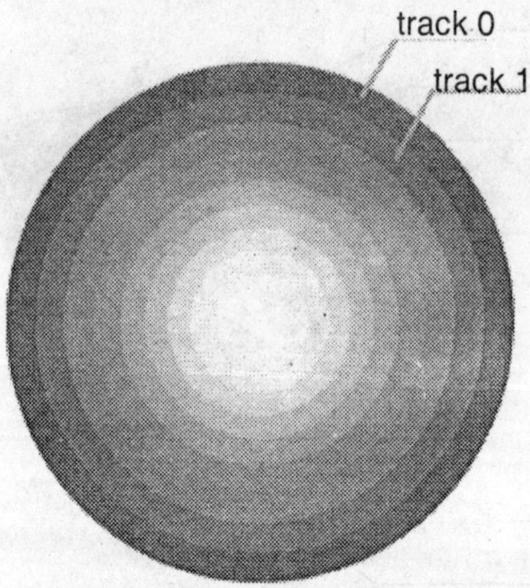

The heads start writing data from the edge of the disk (track 0), then move towards the centre. The data is organised in concentric circles called "**tracks**", which are created by low-level formatting.

The tracks are separated into areas (between two radii) called **sectors**, containing data (generally at least 512 octets per sector).

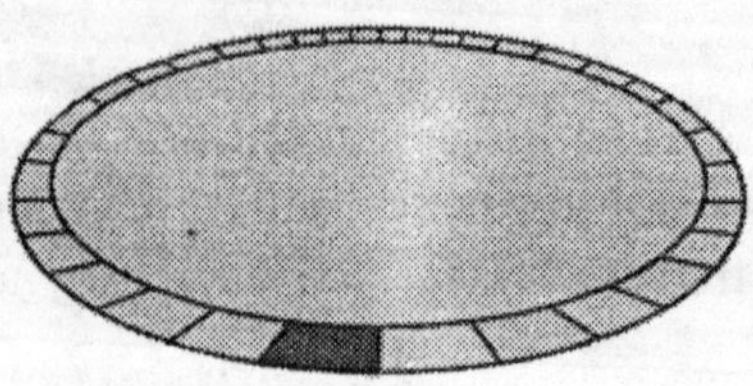

The term **cylinder** refers to all data found on the same track of different platters (i.e. above and below one another), as this forms a "cylinder" of data.

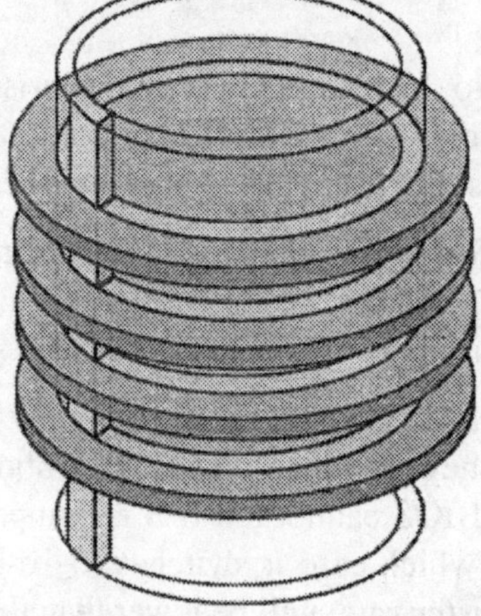

Finally, the term **clusters** (also called **allocation units**) refers to minimum area that a file can take up on the hard drive. An operating system uses ***blocks***, which are in fact groups of ***sectors*** (between 1 and 16 sectors). A small file may occupy multiple sectors (a cluster).

On old hard drives, addressing was done physically, by defining the position of the date from the coordinates *Cylinder/Head/Sector* (**CHS**).

Block mode

Block mode and **32-bit transfer** are used to get the best performance out of your hard drive. Block mode involves transferring data in blocks, usually in 512-byte packets, which keeps the processor from having to process a large number of tiny one-bit packets. This way, the processor has the "time" to perform other operations.

Unfortunately, this data transfer mode is only useful for older operating systems (such as MS-DOS), as recent operating systems use their own hard drive manager, which makes this management system obsolete.

There is a BIOS option (*IDE HDD block mode* or *Multi Sector Transfer*) which can sometimes determine how many blocks can be managed at once. It is a number between 2 and 32. If you don't know it, there are several solutions available:

- Check your hard drive's documentation
- Search for the drive's specifications on the Internet
- Carry out tests to determine it.

Still, block mode may generate errors in certain systems, due to redundancies in the hard drive manager. The system involves disabling one of the two managers:

- the 32-bit software manager in the operating system;
- block mode in the BIOS.

32-bit mode

32-bit mode (as opposed to 16-bit mode) is characterised by 32-bit data transfers. 32-bit transfer is comparable to 32 doors opening and closing all at once. In 32-bit mode, two 16-bit words (groups of bits) are transmitted one after another, then assembled.

The improvements in performance when switching from 16-bit mode to 32-bit mode are generally insignificant. In any event, it is no longer normally possible to select the mode, as the motherboard automatically determines which mode to use depending on the type of hard drive.

However, automatically selecting 32-bit mode may slow down IDE CD-ROM drives whose speed is higher than 24x when they are alone on an IDE ribbon cable. Indeed, when a CD-ROM drive is alone on the cable, the BIOS cannot tell if it is compatible with 32-bit mode (because it is looking for a hard drive), in which case it switches to 16-bit mode. In this case, the transfer speed (incorrectly called the *transfer rate*) will be lower than the one claimed by the manufacturer.

The solution is to plug the CD-ROM drive and a 32-bit-compatible hard drive into the same ribbon cable.

Technical specifications

- **Capacity:** Amount of data which can be stored on a hard drive.
- **Transfer rate:** Quantity of data which can be read or written from the disk per unit of time. It is expressed in bits per second.
- **Rotational speed:** The speed at which the platters turn, expressed in rotations per minute (*rpm* for short). Hard drive speeds are on the order of 7200 to 15000 rpm. The faster a drive rotates, the higher its transfer rate. On the other hand, a hard drive which rotates quickly tends to be louder and heats up more easily.
- **Latency (also called rotational delay):** The length of time that passes between the moment when the disk finds the track and the moment it finds the data.
- **Average access time:** Average amount of time it takes the read head to find the right track and access the data. In other words, it represents the average length of time it takes the disk to provide data after having received the order to do so. It must be as short as possible.
- **Radial density:** number of tracks per inch ***(tpi)*.**
- **Linear density:** number of bits per inch ***(bpi)* on a given track.**
- **Surface density:** ratio between the linear density and radial density (expressed in bits per square inch).

- **Cache memory (or buffer memory):** Amount of memory located on the hard drive. Cache memory is used to store the drive's most frequently-accessed data, in order to improve overall performance;
- **Interface:** This refers to the connections used by the hard drive. The main hard drive interfaces are:
  - ⇨ IDE/ATA
  - ⇨ Serial ATA
  - ⇨ SCSI
  - ⇨ However, there are external cases used for connecting hard drives with USB or FireWire ports.

The **Compact Disc** was invented by *Sony* and *Philips* in 1981 in order to serve as a high-quality compact audio storage device which allowed for direct access to digital sound tracks. It was officially launched in October 1982. In 1984, the Compact Disc's specifications were extended (with the publication of the *Yellow Book*) so that it could store digital data.

CD geometry

A **CD (Compact Disc)** is an optical disc 12cm in diameter and 1.2mm thick (its thickness may vary from 1.1 to 1.5 mm) for storing digital information: up to 650 MB of computer data (equivalent to 300,000 typed pages) or 74 minutes of audio data. A circular hole 15mm in diameter is used to centre it on the CD player's surface.

The makeup of a CD

A CD is built from a plastic (polycarbonate) substrate and a fine, reflective metallic film (24-carat gold or a silver alloy). The reflective layer is then covered with an anti-UV acrylic finish, creating a protective surface for data. Finally, an additional layer may be added so that data can be written on the other side of the CD as well.

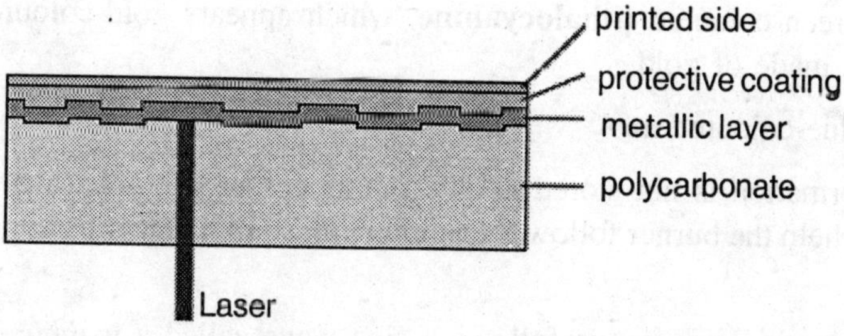

The reflective layer contains tiny bumps. When the laser passes over the polycarbonate substrate, light is reflected off the reflective surface, but when the laser reaches a bump, that's what allows it to encode information.

This information is stored in 22188 tracks engraved in grooves (though it's actually just one track spiralling inward).

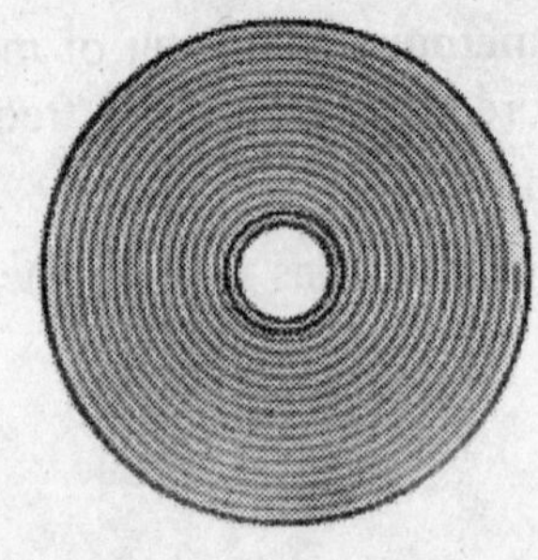

Commercially purchased CDs have already been pressed, meaning that the bumps have been created using plastic injected into a mold which contains the desired pattern in reverse. A metallic layer is then affixed onto the polycarbonate substrate, and this layer is itself covered with a protective coating.

Blank CDs (CD-R), by contrast, have an additional layer (located between the substrate and metallic layer) made of a dye which can be marked (or "burned") by a high-powered laser (10 times as powerful as the one used for reading them). It is the dye layer which either absorbs or reflects the beam of light emitted by the laser.

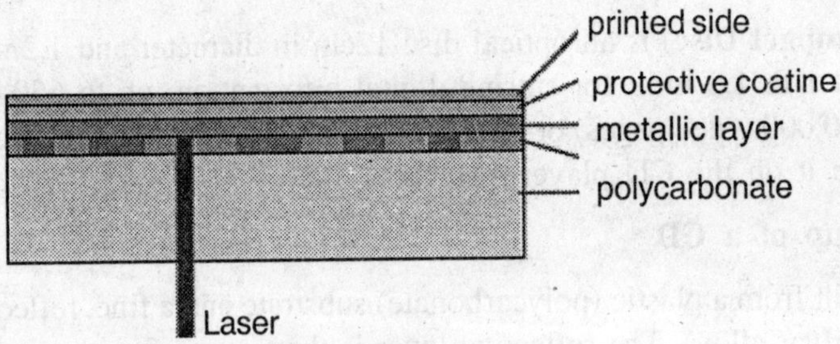

The most commonly used dyes are:

- Blue-coloured **cyanine**, which appears green when the metallic layer is made of gold
- Light-green-coloured **pthalocyanine**, which appears gold-coloured when the metallic layer is made of gold
- Dark-blue-coloured **azo**

As the information is not stored as pits but as coloured marks, a *pre-groove* is placed in the blank disc to help the burner follow the spiral path, so that precision engineering is not needed on CD burners.

What's more, this pre-groove follows a sine wave called a *wobble*, with an amplitude of +/-0.03μm (30nm) and a frequency of 22.05kHz. The wobble lets the burner know what speed it needs to record at. This information is called *ATIP* (*Absolute Time in Pre-Groove*).

Operation

The read head is made of a laser (*Light Amplification by Stimulated Emission of Radiation*) which emits a beam of light, and a photoelectric cell which captures the reflected beam. CD players use an infrared laser (with a wavelength of 780 nm), as it is compact and inexpensive. A lens located near the CD focuses the laser beam onto the pits.

A semi-reflective mirror allows the reflected light to strike the photoelectric cell, as shown in the following diagram:

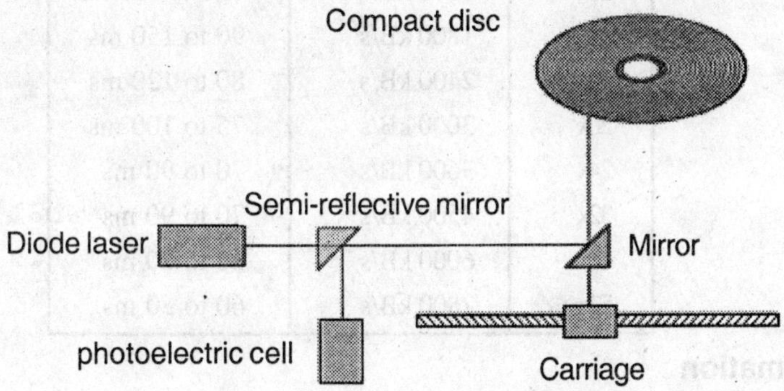

A "pickup" moves the mirror so that the read head can access the entire CD-ROM.

A CD has two basic operating modes:

- Reading at a **constant linear velocity** (or **CLV** for short). This was the operating mode of the earliest CD-ROM drives, based on how CD audio players and even old turntables work. When a disc turns, the grooves closer to the centre run more slowly than the grooves on the outer edge, so the read speed (and therefore the speed at which the disc rotates) has to adjust based on the radial position of the read head. With this process, the information density is the same throughout the disc, so there is an increase in capacity. CD audio players have a linear velocity between 1.2 and 1.4 m/s.
- **Reading at a constant angular velocity** (**CAV**) involves adjusting the information density depending on where the data is located, so that the rotation speed is the same at every point on the disc. This means that data density will be lower on the edge of the disc and higher near the centre.

A CD-ROM drive's reading velocity originally corresponded to the speed of an audio CD player, a rate of 150 kB/s. This speed was then adopted as a reference point and termed **1x**. Later generations of CD-ROM drives have been described using multiples of this value. The following table shows the read speed for each multiple of 1x:

	Read speed	Response time
lx	150 kB/s	400 to 600 ms
2x	300 kB/s	200 to 400 ms
3x	450 kB/s	180 to 240 ms
4x	600 kB/s	150 to 220 ms
6x	900 kB/s	140 to 200 ms
8x	1200 kB/s	120 to 180 ms
10x	1500 kB/s	100 to 160 ms
12x	1800 kB/s	90 to 150 ms
16x	2400 kB/s	80 to 120 ms
20x	3000 kB/s	75 to 100 ms
24x	3600 kB/s	70 to 90 ms
32x	4500 kB/s	70 to 90 ms
40x	6000 kB/s	60 to 80 ms
52x	7800 kB/s	60 to 80 ms

Encoding information

The physical track is made up of bumps 0.168μm deep and 0.67μm wide, with variable length. The "rings" in the spiral are spread about 1.6μm apart from one another. *Pits* are the term for the depressions in the groove, and *lands* are the spaces between them.

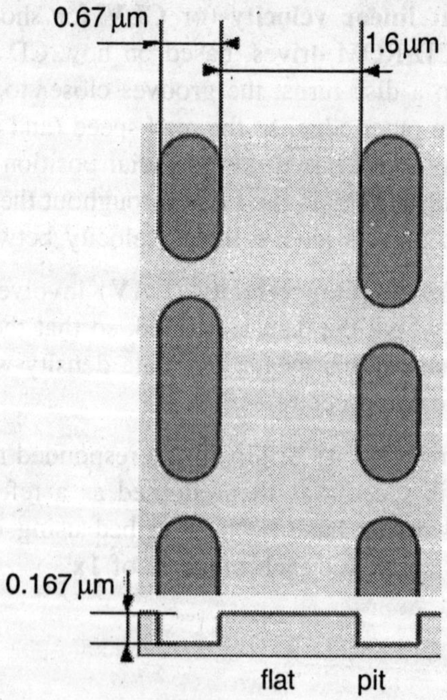

The laser used for reading CDs has a wavelength of 780 nm when travelling through air. As the polycarbonate's refractive index is 1.55, the laser's wavelength in the polycarbonate is equal to 780/1.55 = 503nm = 0.5μm.

Since the depth of the groove is one quarter the wavelength of the laser beam, a light wave reflected by a *pit* travels half again as long (125% as long to hit the disk and the same to return) as a wave reflects by a *land*.

This way, whenever the laser strikes a pitted groove, the wave and its reflection are dephased by a half wavelength and cancel one another out (destructive interference), so it's as if no light was reflected at all. Moving from a pit to a land causes a drop in the signal, which represents **one bit**.

The length of the groove is what stores the information. The size of a bit on a CD ("S") is standardised and corresponds to the distance travelled by the light beam in 231.4 nanoseconds, or *0.278µm* and the standard minimum velocity of 1.2 m/s.

In the *EFM* standard (*Eight-to-Fourteen Modulation*), used for storing information on a CD, there must always be at least two bits set to 0 between two consecutive 1 bite, and there cannot be more than 10 consecutive zero bits between two 1 bits, in order to avoid errors. This is why the length of a groove (or a land) is greater than or equal to the length needed to store the value *001* (*3S*, or *0.833µm*) and less than or equal to the length of the value *00000000001* (*11S*, or *3.054µm*).

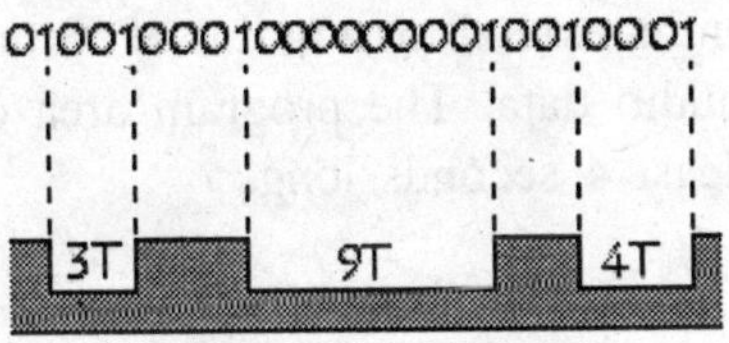

Standards

There are numerous standards describing the ways in which information must be stored on a compact disc, depending on how it is to be used. These standards are set out in documents called *books*, each of which has a colour assigned to it:

- **Red book** (also called *RedBook audio*): Developed in 1980 by Sony and Philips, it describes the physical format of a CD and the encoding method for an audio CD (sometimes called *CD-DA* for *Compact Disc - Digital Audio*). It defines a sample rate of 44.1 kHz and 16-bit resolution (in stereo) for recording audio data.
- **Yellow book:** Developed in 1984 in order to describe the physical format for data CDs (*CD-ROM* for *Compact Disc - Read Only Memory*). It includes two modes:
    - ⇨ **CD-ROM Mode 1**, used for storing data with error-correction (called *ECC*, for *Error Correction Code*) in order to avoid losing data due to degradation of the disc.
    - ⇨ **CD-ROM Mode 2**, used for storing compressed graphical, video, and audio data. To be able to read this type of CD-ROM, a drive must be *Mode 2 compatible*.

- **Green book**: Physical specifications for a CD-I (*CD Interactive*, by Philips)
- **Orange book**: Physical format for writable CDs. It is divided into three sections:
  - ⇨ *Part I*: The CD-MO format (magneto-optical disks)
  - ⇨ *Part II*: The CD-WO format (*Write Once*, now called *CD-R*)
  - ⇨ *Part III*: The CD-RW format (*CD Rewritable*)
- **White book**: Physical format for video CDS (*VCD*)
- **Blue book**: Physical format for "Extra" CDs (*CD-XA*)

Logical structure

The Orange Book dictates that a CD-R, whether it is an audio CD or a CD-ROM, is made up of three areas which form the *information area*:

- The **Lead-in Area** (sometimes called the *LIA*) only contains information which describes the contents of the disc (in the **TOC**, *Table of Contents*). The Lead-in Area extends from a radius of 23 mm from the edge to a radius of 25 mm. This size is required by the need to be able to store information about a maximum of 99 tracks. The Lead-in Area lets the CD player/drive follow the spiralling pits in order to synchronise itself with the data found in the *program area.*
- The **Program Area** is the section of the disc which contains the data. It starts 25 mm out from the centre, extends to a radius of 58mm, and can contain the equivalent of 76 minutes of audio data. The program area can contain up to 99 tracks (or sessions), each at least 4 seconds long.

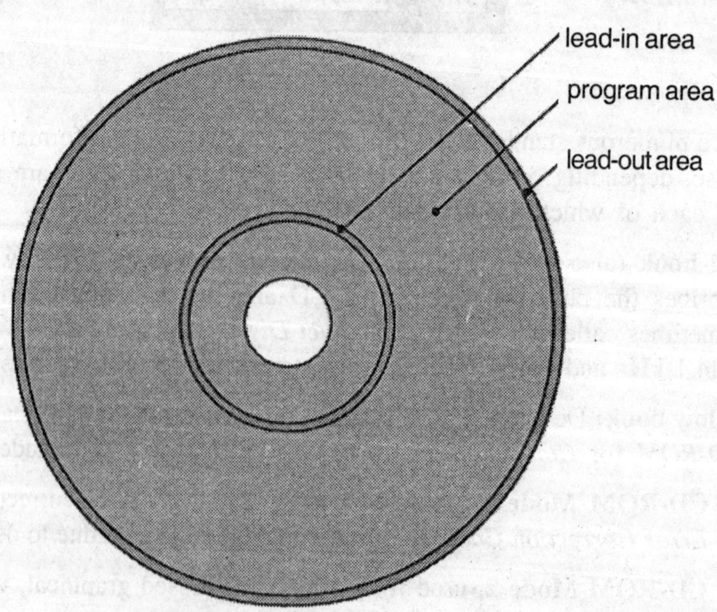

- The **Lead-Out Area** (or *LOA*), containing null data (silence on an audio CD) marks the end of the CD. It starts at a radius of 58 mm and must be at least 0.5 mm in width (radially). The Lead-Out Area must contain at least 6750 sectors, or 90 seconds of silence at minimum speed (1X).

Besides the three areas described above, a CD-R contains a *PCA* (*Power Calibration Area*) and a *PMA* (*Program Memory Area*), which together form the *SUA* (*System User Area).*

The *PCA* can be seen as a testing area for the laser, so that it can calibrate its power depending on the kind of disk being read. This area is what makes it possible to sell blank CDs that use different dyes and reflective layers. Each time it is readjusted, the burner notes that it has carried out a test. Up to 99 tests are allowed per disc.

File systems

The format of the CD (or more precisely, the *file system*) describes how the data is stored in the *program area.*

The earliest file system for CDs was the *High Sierra Standard.*

The **ISO 9660** format, standardised in 1984 by the ISO (International Standards Organization) revisited the *High Sierra Standard* in order to define the structure of files and folders on CD-ROMs. It is divided into three levels:

- **Level 1:** An ISO 9660 Level 1-formated CD-ROM may only contain files with names made up entirely of capital letters (*A-Z*), digits (*0-9*) and the character "_". Together, these are called *d-characters*. Folder names are limited to 8 d-characters and can be no more than 8 subfolders deep. Additionally, the *ISO 9660* standard requires each file to be stored continuously on a CD-ROM, without fragmentation. It is the most restrictive level. Compliance with Level 1 ensures that the disc will be readable on large number of platforms.
- **Level 2:** The format ISO 9660 Level 2 requires that each file be stored as a continuous flow of bytes, but is more flexible with file names, allowing the characters @ - ^ ! $ % & ( ) # ~ and up to 32 subfolders deep.
- **Level 3:** The format *ISO 9660 Level 3* does not restrict file names or folders.

Microsoft has also defined the *Joliet* format, an expansion of *ISO 9660* which allows long file names (*LFNs*) of up to 64 characters, including spaces and accented characters (based on Unicode).

The *ISO 9660 Romeo* format is a naming option offered by Adaptec, independent of *Joliet,* for storing files whose names can be as long as 128 characters, but which does not support Unicode encoding.

The *ISO 9660 RockRidge* format is a naming extension to *ISO 9660* which makes it compatible with UNIX file systems.

In order to make up for the limitations of *ISO 9660* (which make it unsuitable for DVD-ROM discs), the OSTA (*Optical Storage Technology Association*) has developed the *ISO 13346* format, known under the name *UDF* (*Universal Disk Format*).

Writing methods

- **Monosession:** This method creates a single session on the disc and does not allow new data to be added later.
- **Multisession:** Unlike the previous method, this one lets a CD be written to several times, by creating a 14MB-long table of contents (*TOC*) de 14Mo for each session.
- **Multivolume:** This is multisession recording which considers each session as a separate volume.
- **Track At Once:** This method is used for disabling the laser between two tracks, in order to create a two-second pause between each track on an audio CD.
- **Disc At Once:** Unlike the previous method, Disc At Once writes a whole CD all at once (without pausing).
- **Packet Writing:** This methods lets data be recorded in packets.

Technical specifications

A CD-ROM drive is defined by the following:

- **Speed:** The speed is calculated relative to the speed of an audio CD player (150 KB/s). A drive which can reach speeds of 3000KB/s would be called 20X (20 times faster than a 1X drive).
- **Access time:** This represents the average time it takes to go from one part of the CD to another.
- **Interface:** ATAPI (IDE) or SCSI;

Introduction to the DVD format

The **DVD** (*Digital Versatile Disc*, or less commonly *Digital Video Disc*) is an "alternative" to the compact disc (CD) with six times as much storage space (for the lowest-capacity kind of DVD — single-layer, single-sided). The DVD format was designed to provide a universal storage medium, while the CD was originally designed as an audio medium only.

The DVD is designed to make data addressable and accessible at random (non-sequentially). It has a complex structure which provides greater interactivity, but requires more advanced microprocessors

The DVD format was originally supported (starting 15 September 1995) by a consortium of ten multimedia companies (Hitachi, JVC, Matsushita, Mitsubishi, Philips, Pioneer, Sony, Thomson, Time Warner and Toshiba). Starting in 1997, a new consortium called "DVD Forum", succeeded the initial one.

A DVD can easily be confused with a CD, as both are plastic discs 12 cm in diameter and 1.2 mm thick, which are read using a laser beam. However, CDs use an infrared laser with a wavelength of 780 nanometres (nm), while DVD burners use a red laser with a wavelength of 635 nm or 650 nm. What's more, CD players generally use a lens with a focus of 0.5, while the lenses of DVD players have a focus of 0.6. For this reason, DVDs have grooves whose minimum height is 0.4μ with a pitch of 0.74μ, as opposed to 0.834μ and 1.6μ for a CD.

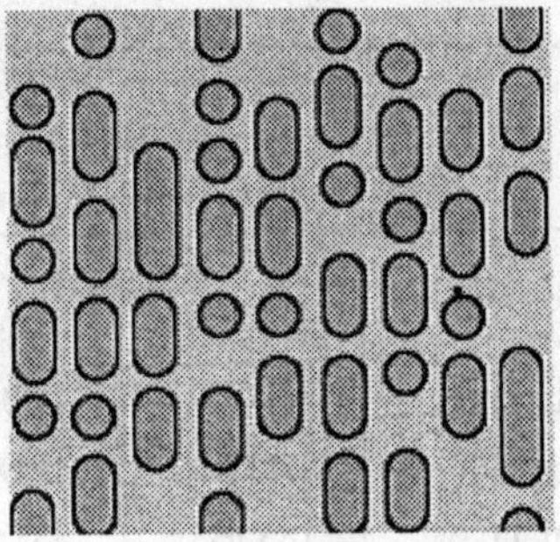

The main reason to use DVDs is their storage capacity, which makes them an excellent medium for video. A 4.7GB DVD can store more than two hours of compressed video in MPEG-2 (*Motion Picture Experts Group*), a format used for compressing images while still keeping them high-quality.

Physical structure

DVDs exist in both "single layer" and "dual layer" (DL) versions. Dual layer discs are made up of a translucent, gold-based semi-reflective layer and an opaque, silver-based reflective layer, separated by a bonding layer. In order to read both these layers, the drive has a layer which can change its intensity by modifying its frequency and focus:

- with low intensity the beam is reflected off the outer gold surface;
- with higher intensity, the beam passes through the first layer is reflected off the inner silver surface.

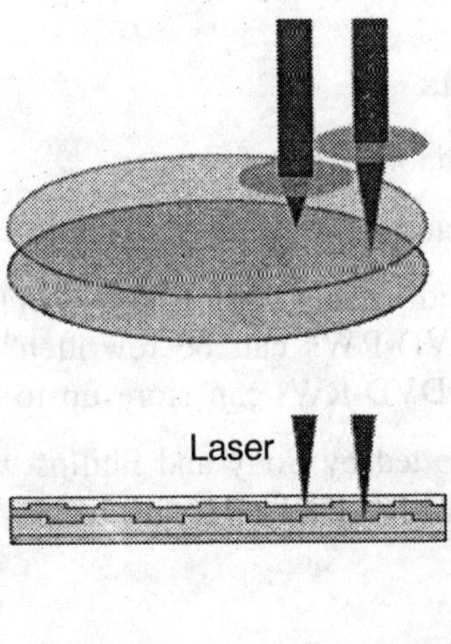

The inner layer, however, has a lower density. Additionally, it stores the information "upside down" on an inverted spiral, in order to limit latency when moving from one layer to the other.

What's more, DVDs exist both in single-sided and double-sided versions, like vinyl records. In the latter case, the information is stored on both sides of the disc.

DvD are generally divided into four families, each with different storage capacities depending on their physical characteristics:

Type of disc	Characteristics	Storage capacity	Equivalent in music (hours:minutes)	Equivalent in number of CDs
CD		650MB	1:14	1
DVD-5	single-sided, single layer	4.7 GB	9:30	7
DVD-9	single-sided, dual layer	8.5 GB	17:30	13
DVD-10	double-sided, single layer	9.4 GB	19:00	14
DVD-17	double-sided, dual layer	18 GB	35:00	26

Standard DVD formats

The official specifications for DVD are divided into five books:

- Book A for DVD-ROM;
- Book B for DVD Video;
- Book C for DVD Audio;
- Book D for writeable (DVD-R) and rewritable (DVD-RW) DVDs. The DVD-R format is Write-Once, while DVD-RW is a rewritable format, which lets data be rewritten using a phase-change metallic alloy;
- Book E for rewritable DVDs (also called DVD-RAM, for *DVD Random Access Memory*). DVD-RAM is a rewritable medium which uses phase-change technology to record data. DVD-RAMs are actually cartridges which are composed of a case and a DVD. Some cartridges are removable, so that a DVD-RAM can be played in a DVD player.

Standard DVD recording formats

There are currently three recordable DVD formats:

- **DVD-RAM** by Toshiba © and Matsushita ©. This format is mainly used in Japan.
- **DVD-R/DVD-RW**, supported by the DVD Forum. DVDs in DVD-R format can only be recorded once, while DVD-RWs can be rewritten up to about 1000 times. The DVD-R format, as well as DVD-RW, can store up to 4.7 GB on a disc.
- **DVD+R / DVD+RW**, supported by Sony and Philips within the DVD+RW Alliance, which also includes Dell, Hewlett-Packard, Mitsubishi/Verbatim, Ricoh, Thomson and Yamaha.

These three formats are incompatible with one another, despite their similar performance. The DVD-RAM format will not be discussed at length here, as it is mainly used in Japan. The DVD-R(W) and DVD+R(W) formats, on the other hand, are widely used in Europe and North America.

DVD-R/RW

The DVD-R/DVD-RW format is based on what is known as "**pre-pit**" technology. As with CD-Rs, writeable and rewriteable DVDs use a "pre-groove" (a spiral groove already engraved on the disc), which follows a sine wave called a *wobble*. The pre-groove defines the position for the record head to be placed on the disc (called *tracking*) while the oscillating frequency lets the burner adjust its speed. Address information (i.e. where the data is located), by contrast, is defined using recesses pre-engraved onto the disc in the pits between the disc's groove, called "land pre-pits" (or LPP for short).

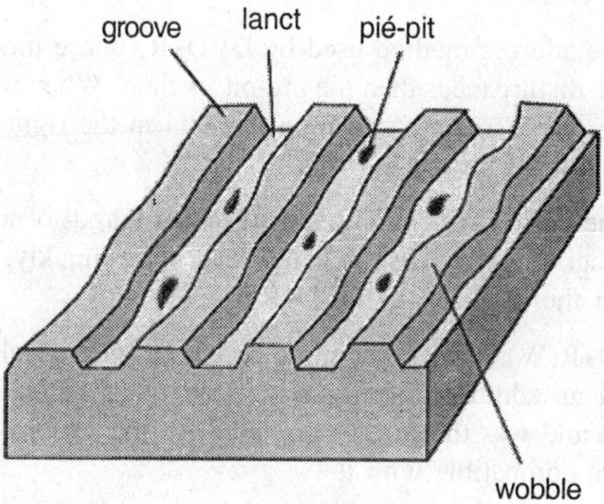

Pre-pits form a second signal, which used for positioning data. When the laser reaches a pre-pit, an amplitude peak appears in the oscillation, which lets the burner know that data must be recorded. The DVD-R specifications make it clear that a pre-pit must be at least one period long (1T).

The DVD-R/DVD-RW format offers error handling features, which are mainly software-based (called *Persistent-DM* and *DRT-DM*).

DVD+R/RW

The DVD+R/DVD+RW format uses a groove whose oscillation (wobble) has a much higher frequency than DVD-Rs (817.4 kHz for DVD+R versus 140.6 for DVD-R) and handles addresses by phase-modulating the wobble, a kind of phase-inversion encoding called **ADIP** (*ADdress In Pre-groove*). This phase inversion takes place every 32 periods (32T).

The DVD+RW format has an error-correction feature called DVD+MRW (*Mount Rainier for DVD+RW*) used to mark defective blocks. What's more, if readable data is found on that

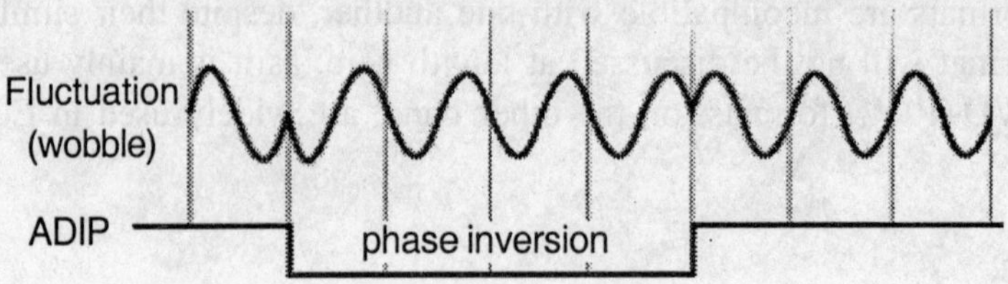

block, there is a mechanism for moving them to a healthy block and updating the file allocation table (this process is called *Logical to Physical Address Translation*).

What's more, the specifications provide for a check to run in the background, in order to check errors found on the disc while the reader is inactive. The user can still read the disc or eject it at any time; if this happens, the error check will continue where it left off as soon as the player is idle again.

Difference between DVD+ and DVD-

Generally speaking, the address method used by DVD+R (phase modulation) has a higher resistance to electromagnetic disturbances than the pre-pit method. When writing a disc, the write head must also read the pre-pits in order to position the data in the right place. Thus, the light emitted by the laser may cause disturbances.

What's more, given the period which corresponds to the length of a pre-pit (T1), the pre-pits are much harder to detect when the disc is being read more quickly. So it's not surprising that the first 16x burner on the market was DVD+RW.

This is why the DVD+R(W) format, for more recent technological specifications, offers better performance as well as additional features. On the other hand, DVD-R(W) has been ratified by the DVD Forum and was the first format used, so the majority of DVD drives (and especially DVD players) are compatible with it.

Most DVD burners support both formats. In conclusion, given that it is more compatible with standalone DVD players, DVD-R(W) is preferred for creating Video DVDs, while DVD+R(W) is superior for creating data discs.

DVD DL

The term "**DVD DL**" (*DVD Dual Layer*) refers to DVDs which can be recorded on two separate layers. These discs, which have more storage space than single-layer DVDs, use a technology similar to that of DVD-9 (dual-layer discs).

Logical structure

A DVD is essentially made up of three zones, which represent the *information area*:

- The **Lead-in Area** (or *LIA* for short) only contains data which describes the disc's contents (this information is stored in the *Table of Contents*, or **TOC**). The Lead-in Area lets the DVD player/drive follow the spiralling pits in order to synchronise itself with the data found in the *program area*.

- The **Program Area** is the area which contains the data.
- The **Lead-Out Area** (or *LOA* for short), containing null data (silence on an audio DVD) marks the end of the DVD.

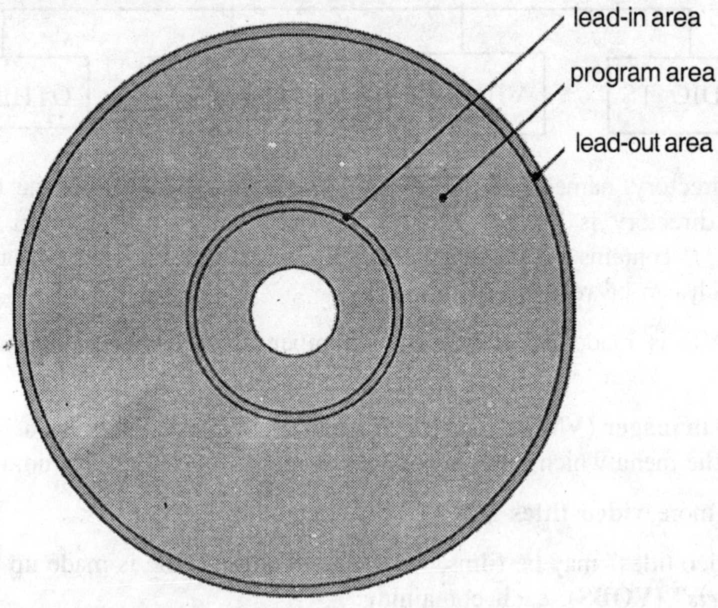

Besides the three areas described above, a recordable DVD contains a *PCA* (*Power Calibration Area*) and an *RMA* (*Recording Management Area*) located before the Lead-In Area.

The PCA can be seen as a testing area for the laser, so that it can calibrate its power depending on the kind of disc being read. This area is what makes it possible to sell blank CDs that use different dyes and reflective layers. Each time it is readjusted, the burner notes that it has carried out a test. Up to 99 tests are allowed per disc.

File and folder system

DVDs use the file system **UDF** (*Universal Disk Format*). In order to remain somewhat compatible with older operating systems, a hybrid file system called "UDF Bridge", which supports both UDF and the ISO 9660 file system used by CD-ROMs, has been created. Nonetheless, it is important to note that DVD video and audio players do not support UDF.

Structure of a video DVD

A video DVD may contain data for standalone DVD players, as well as additional data that can be read by a computer.

A video DVD has a hierarchical folder organisation for storing video and audio data. It normally relies on the following structure:

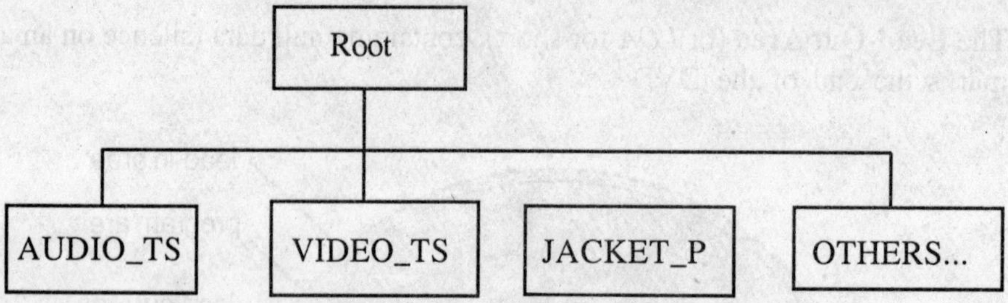

The main directory, named *VIDEO_TS* (for *Video Title Sets*), holds the DVD video files. The *AUDIO_TS* directory is for DVD audio, but it is sometimes required by certain DVD players. *JACKET_P* contains images of the DVD's cover art. Lastly, you can also add other folders to it, which can be read by a computer.

A video DVD is made up of a certain number of elements found in the *VIDEO_TS* directory:

- A **video manager** (**VMG**). The VMG generally includes the introductory video clip, as well as the menu which gives access to the other video titles (including the submenus).
- One or more **video titles sets** (**VTS**), containing video titles.

  The "video titles" may be films, videos or albums. A title is made up of "*Video Object Block Sets*" (**VOBS**), each containing:

  - a "control file" (called **VTSI**, for *Video Title Set Information*), and containing navigation data.
  - one or several video objects (*VOB*, *Video Object Block*). The video object (VOB) is the basic element of the DVD. It contains video and audio data and multiplexed images, all in MPEG2 format. A *.VOB* file may be read by a software video player by changing its extension to "*.MPG*". The DVD format's specifications require all VOB files to be no larger than one gigabyte. Each VOB is made up of "*cells*", which represent the various video or audio clips that make up the VOB, such as video chapters or the songs on an album.
  - a copy of the *VTSI* (**VTSI Backup**).

A DVD can contain up to 99 titles (*VTS*), each divided into 10 chapters.

The VIDEO_TS directory usually contains three types of files with the following extensions:

- **IFO**, containing navigation data (it corresponds to the Video Manager).
- **VOB** (Video Object Block), containing video streams, the audio channels and the subtitles for a video title.
- **BUP** (*BUP* stands for *Backup*), which contains a backup of the IFO files, in case they become unreadable.

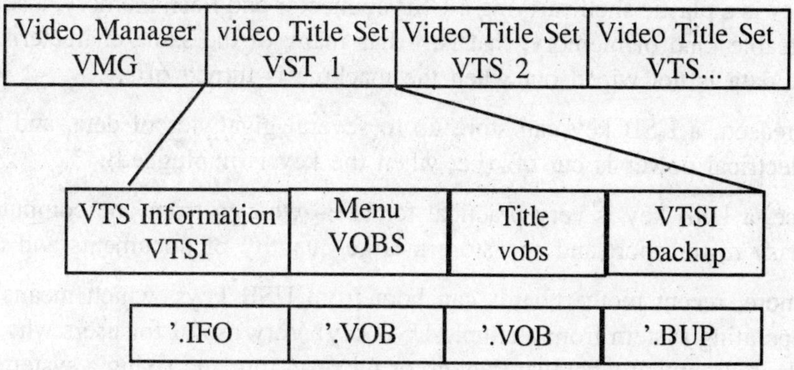

The special file named *VIDEO_TS.IFO* (*IFO* stands for *information*) contains the information needed for the DVD player to display the main menu. It is accompanied by the file*VIDEO_TS.VOB*, which contains the opening animation, as well as a backup file (named *VIDEO_TS.BUP*).

Regions

Video DVDs are designed to be readable in certain parts of the world only, which has been divided into regions (originally meant to limit the distribution of bootlegs). Theoretically, it is impossible to play a DVD from one region on a player from a different one. However, nearly all computer DVD drives and many standalone players can be made "region-free" using special tools.

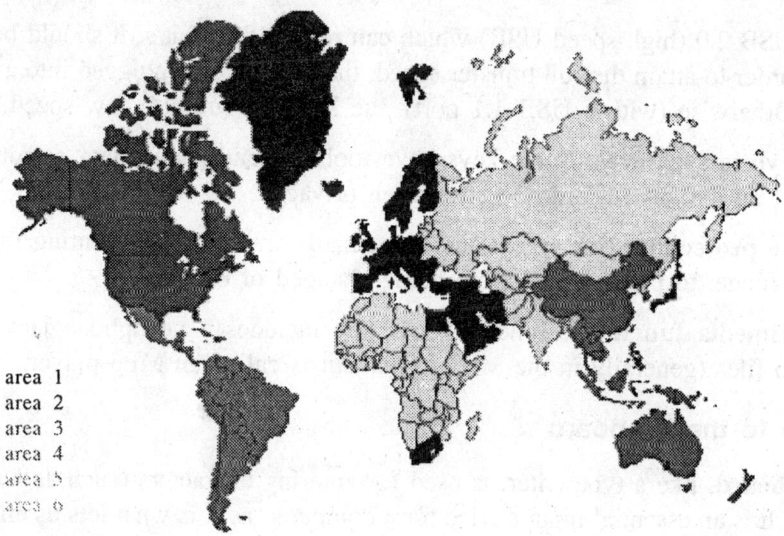

Introduction to USB keys

A **USB key** is a compact-format removable storage device which can be plugged into a computer's USB port.

A USB key is a plastic shell carrying a USB connector and flash memory, a solid-state, non-volatile, rewriteable kind of memory; that is, it has many of the same characteristics as RAM, except that the data is not wiped out when the machine is turned off.

For this reason, a USB key can store up to several gigabytes of data, and keep the data saved when electrical power is cut off (i.e. when the key is unplugged).

In practice, a USB key is very practical for users who go from one computer to another, as it is very easy to transport and can store a large quantity of documents and data.

What's more, recent motherboards can boot from USB keys, which means that you can now start an operating system from a simple USB key! Very useful for users who want to carry their own work environment wherever they go or for restarting and fixing a system after a crash.

Characteristics

The features to take into account when choosing a USB key are:

- **Storage capacity**
- **Transfer rate:** This is the speed at which data is transfered. It should be noted that the transfer rate when reading is different from the transfer rate when writing, as the process of writing to flash memory is slower. The transfer rate depends on the read speed and write speed of the Flash memory component, as well as the USB standard supported:
  - ⇨ USB 1.1 (low-speed USB), which can reach 12 Mbit/s,
  - ⇨ USB 2.0 (high-speed USB) which can reach 480 Mbit/s. It should be noted that in order to attain the full transfer speed, the key must be plugged into a USB 2.0 port. Otherwise (with a USB 1.1 port), the key will run at a low speed.
- **Encryption features:** Some keys have tools for encrypting data or some of the data found on the key, in order to strengthen privacy.
- **Write protection:** Some keys include a hardware switch for putting the key in read-only mode, to prevent data from being changed or erased.
- **Multimedia functions:** When a USB key includes a headphone jack and can play audio files (generally in the MP3 format), it is called an MP3 player.

Introduction to the keyboard

The **keyboard**, like a typewriter, is used for entering characters (such as letters, numbers, and symbols). It is an essential input device for a computer, as it is what lets us enter commands.

The term **"QWERTY"** (after the first six letter keys on the keyboard) refers to the type of keyboard which is used with nearly all computers in the English-speaking world. In other countries, keyboard layouts are different.

The **Qwerty** keyboard was designed in 1868 in Milwaukee by **Christopher Latham Sholes**, who placed the keys corresponding to the most commonly used letter pairs at opposite ends of the keyboard, in order to prevent the typewriter hammers of the time from becoming jammed with one another. This keyboard was first sold by the company Remington in 1873. Therefore, the Qwerty keyboard was designed from a purely technical perspective, hindering usability and efficiency. Legend has it that the placement of keys along the first row of the Qwerty keyboard was motivated by typewriter dealers of the time, who wanted all the keys needed to type the word "*typewriter*" to be conveniently located when demonstrating the product.

In 1936, August Dvorak (a professor at the University of Washington) created a keyboard whose keys were arranged solely with efficiency in mind. The **Dvorak keyboard** placed all the vowels of the alphabet and the five most common consonants on the central row so they could be easily accessed, while also evenly dividing the work between the left and right hands. What's more, the most frequent letters of the alphabet were placed at the centre of the keyboard.

Various studies showed that the increased efficiency of the Dvorak keyboard was small in practice and that the amount of effort required to switch from the *Qwerty* keyboard to Dvorak's was too much to be worth the trouble, which explains why all computers today still have Qwerty keyboards.

Keyboard connector

Keyboards are generally plugged into the rear of the CPU, on the motherboard, using a purple PS/2 connector:

How it works

Whenever a key is pressed, a specific signal is transmitted to the computer. The keyboard uses a crossbar network to identify every key based on its row and column

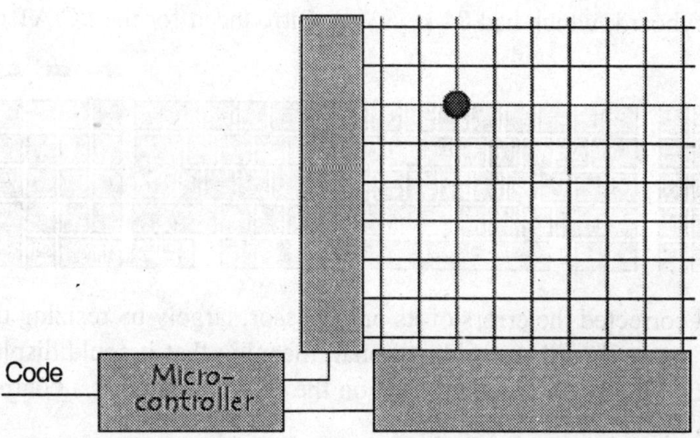

When a key is pressed, an electrical contact is formed between the row and column. The electric signals are transmitted to a microcontroller, which sends a code (BCD, ASCII or Unicode) to the computer describing the character which corresponds to that key.

Types of keyboards

There are four types of keyboards for PCs. The first three were invented by IBM, while the latter is the result of changes made when Microsoft Windows 95 was released. These are the four kinds of keyboards:

- The 83-key keyboard (PC/XT)
- The 84-key keyboard (PC/AT)
- The 102-key keyboard, called the *extended keyboard*
- The 105-key Microsoft Windows 95-compatible keyboard.

PC/XT keyboards

This was the first keyboard for the PC, and was unusual in that it was separate from the computer, unlike the other computers of the time (such as the Apple II and the Amiga), whose keyboards were integrated within them.

This keyboard included 83 keys, but was criticised for the arrangement of the keys and their disproportionate size (especially the *Shift* and *Enter* keys, which were too small and poorly placed). What's more, communication between the keyboard and the CPU was one-way, meaning that the keyboard couldn't include an LED indicator.

PC/AT keyboards

The PC/AT keyboard, which had 84 keys, was introduced for the PC/AT computer in 1984.

This keyboard corrected the errors of its predecessor, largely by resizing the *Shift* and *Enter* keys. Additionally, the keyboard was bidirectional, meaning that it could display its status using LED indicator lights. Finally, the motherboard on the PC/AT included a controller for adjusting the settings:

- The repetition frequency (the number of characters sent per second when a key was depressed)
- The repetition delay: The length of time before a computer would consider a key to be depressed, in order to distinguish typing a single character from holding down a key

Extended keyboards

The new IBM-compatible computers launched in 1986 came with 102-key keyboards.

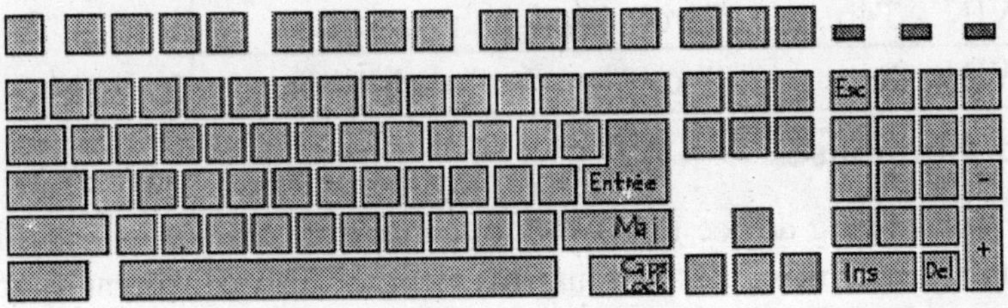

This new keyboard included different blocks of keys: Starting with this model, the function keys were moved to the top of the keyboard, while cursor control keys, represented by arrows, were added.

Microsoft Windows-compatible keyboards

Microsoft has defined three new keys, which are used for shortcuts to certain Windows features.

These three new keys are, from left to right:

- The *left Windows* key
- The *right Windows* key
- The *Application* key

Here are a few shortcuts using these new keys:

Combination	Description
WIN - E	Display the browser
WIN - F	Find a file
WIN - F1	Show help
WIN - M	Minimise all desktop windows
WIN - Pause	Show system properties
WIN - Tab	Scroll through the taskbar
WIN - R	Show the "Run" dialog box

Introduction to the mouse

The **mouse** is a pointing device used to move a cursor on the screen and allowing objects to be selected, moved and manipulated using the buttons. The consistent action of pressing (*clicking*) on a button in order to carry out an action is called a "**click**".

The first mouse was invented and developed by *Douglas Carle Engelbart* of the *Stanford Research Institute* (*SRI*): it was a wooden mouse containing two perpendicular discs and connected to the computer by a pair of twisted wires.

Mouse connector

The mouse is generally plugged in to the back of the central processing unit, into the motherboard, with a green PS/2 connector:

Some mouse, with advanced functionalities sometimes have a USB connector.

Types of mouse

There are several types of mouse, classified according to the positioning technology on the one hand and the data transmission to the central processing unit on the other.

We can therefore distinguish several large categories of mice:

- **Mechanical mouse**, where the operation is based on a ball (in plastic or rubber) encased in a frame (in plastic) transmitting the movement to two rollers;
- **Optical-mechanical mouse**, where the operation is similar to that of mechanical mouse, except the movement of the ball is detected by optic sensors.
- **Optical mouse**, capable of determining movement through visual analysis of the surface upon which they slide.

Mechanical mouse

The mechanical mouse comprises of a ball upon which two rollers turn. These rollers each comprise of a notched disc which turns between a photodiode and LED (Light Emitting Diode) allowing the light to pass through in sequence. When the light passes through, the photodiode sends a bit (1), when it meets an obstacle, the photodiode sends a zero bit (0). Using this information, the computer knows the position of the cursor and even its speed.

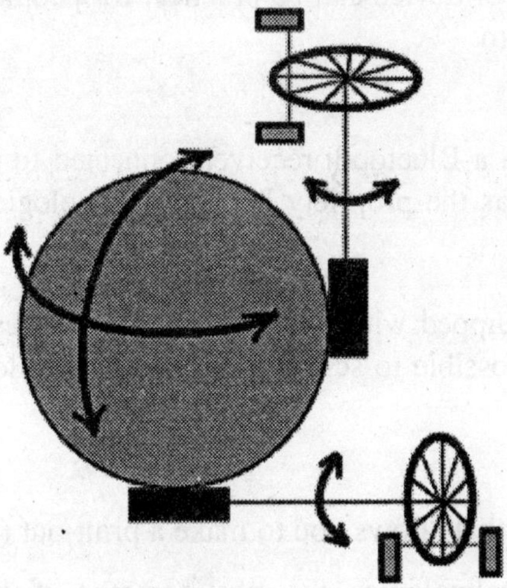

Tip: As you use it, dust settles on the mouse rollers preventing them from turning correctly and causing strange reactions in the cursor. To remedy this, simply open the cage containing the ball and clean the rollers (with a toothbrush for example).

Optical mouse

The optical mouse operates by analysing the surface on which it moves. So, an optical mouse is comprised of an LED, an image acquisition system (IAS) and a digital signal processor (DSP).

The LED is responsible for shining on the surface so as to enable the IAS to get an image of the surface. The DSP, through analysing the microscopic characteristics of the surface determines the horizontal and vertical movement.

Optical mouse operate on any slightly uneven or even coloured surface. The main advantages of this type of pointing device in comparison to the mechanical mouse are greater precision along with less dirtiness.

Cordless mouse

Cordless mouse are more and more popular because they can be used without physically being connected to the computer, which gives a sensation of freedom.

There are also several categories of cordless mouse, depending on the technology used:

Infrared mouse

(*IR*) There mouse are used with an infrared receiver connected to the computer. The range of this type of device is a few metres at most with direct line of sight in the same way as a television remote.

Hertzian mouse

These mouse are used with a hertzian receiver, generally proprietary to the manufacturer. The range of this type of device is around ten metres at most, not necessarily with direct line of sight to the computer. This type of device can be practical for people connecting their computer to their television in another room.

Bluetooth mouse

These mouse are used with a Bluetooth receiver connected to the computer. The range of this type of device is the same as the propriety hertzian technologies.

Mouse wheel

Mouse are increasingly equipped with a wheel. The wheel, generally located between the right and left buttons makes it possible to scroll through pages while enabling the user to move the cursor on the screen.

Printers

The **printer** is a peripheral that allows you to make a print-out (on paper) of computer data.

There are several printer technologies, the most common of which are:

- the daisy wheel printer
- the dot-matrix printer (also called *impact matrix printer*)
- the inkjet printer and the bubble jet printer
- the laser printer

Today, daisy wheel printers and matrix printers are hardly ever used.

Characteristics

The printer is generally characterised by the following elements:

- **Print speed:** expressed in *pages per minute* (*ppm*), print speed represents the printer's ability to print a large number of pages per minute. For colour printers, a distinction is generally made between monochrome and colour print speed.
- **Resolution:** expressed in *dots per inch* (abbreviated as *dpi*), resolution means the sharpness of printed text. Sometimes the resolution is different for a monochrome, colour or photo print-out.
- **Warm-up time:** the waiting time necessary before the first print-out. A printer cannot print when it is "cold". A certain temperature must be reached for the printer to run optimally.
- **Onboard memory:** the quantity of memory that allows the printer to store print jobs. The higher the amount of memory, the longer the printer queue can be.

- **Paper format:** depending on their size, printers are able to accept different sized documents, generally in A4 format (21 x 29.7 cm) or less frequently A3 (29.7 x 42 cm). Some printers allow you to print on other types of media, such as CDs or DVDs.
- **Paper feed:** the method of loading paper into the printer, characterising the way in which blank paper is stored. The paper feed can change depending on where the printer will be placed (rear loading is advised for printers that will be up against a wall).* The main paper feed modes are:
  - ⇨ The **feed tray**, which uses an internal paper feed source. Its capacity is equal to the maximum number of sheets of paper that the tray can fit.
  - ⇨ The **sheet feeder** is a manual feed method that allows you to insert sheets of paper in small quantities (of about 100). The sheet feeder in the back of the printer is either horizontal or vertical.
- **Cartridges:** Cartridges are rarely standard and depend highly on the printer brand and model. Some manufacturers favour multicoloured cartridges whereas others offer separate ink cartridges. Separate ink cartridges are on the whole cheaper because often one colour is used more than others.

  It is interesting to examine the printing cost per sheet. The size of the ink drop is especially important. The smaller the drop of ink, the lower the printing cost will be and the better the image quality will be. Some printers produce drops that are 1 or 2 picolitres.
- **Interface:** How the printer is connected to the computer. The main interfaces are:
  - ⇨ USB
  - ⇨ Parallel
  - ⇨ Network: This type of interface allows several computers to share one printer. There are also WiFi printers that are available through a wireless network

Daisy Wheel Printer

Daisy wheel printers are based on typewriters. A matrix in the shape of a daisy contains "petals" that each have one raised character. To print the text, a ribbon of ink is placed between the daisy and the sheet of paper. When the matrix hits the ribbon it leaves ink on paper in the shape of the character on the petal.

These printers are obsolete because they are extremely noisy and very slow.

Dot-Matrix Printer

The **dot-matrix printer** (sometimes called a *matrix printer* or an *impact printer*) allows you to print documents on paper thanks to the "back and forth" motion of a carriage housing a print head.

The head is made up of tiny metal pins, driven by electromagnets, which strike a carbon ribbon called an "**inked ribbon**", located between the head and the paper.

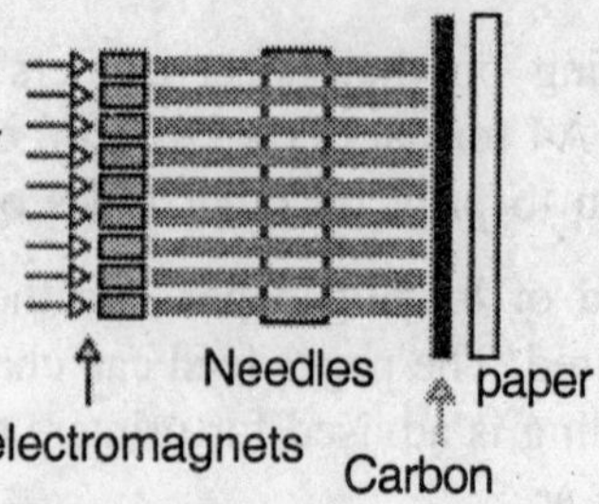

The carbon ribbon scrolls by so that there is always ink on it. At the end of each line, a roller makes the sheet advance.

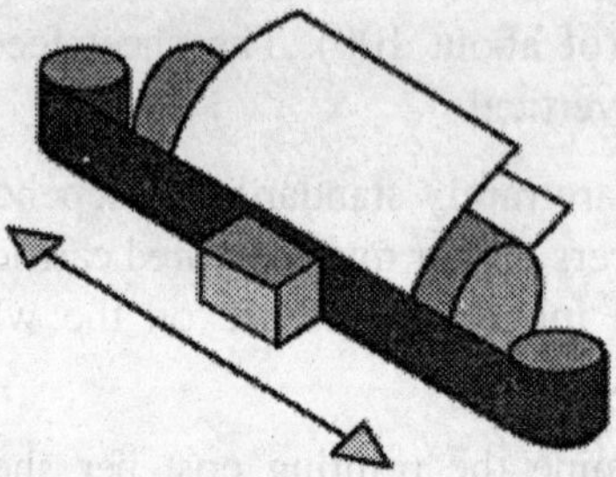

The most recent dot-matrix printers are equipped with 24-needle printer heads, which allows them to print with a resolution of 216 dpi (*dots per inch*).

Inkjet Printer and Bubble Jet Printer

The **inkjet** printer technology was originally invented by Canon. It is based on the principle that a heated fluid produces bubbles.

The researcher who discovered this had accidentally brought a syringe filled with ink into contact with a soldering iron. This created a bubble in the syringe that made the ink in the syringe shoot out.

Today's printer heads are made up of several nozzles (up to 256), equivalent to several syringes, which are heated up to between 300 and 400°C several times per second.

Each nozzle produces a tiny bubble that ejects an extremely fine droplet. The vacuum caused by the decrease in pressure creates a new bubble.

Generally, we make a distinction between the two different technologies:

- **Inkjet printers** use nozzles that have their own built-in heating element. Thermal technology is used here.
- **Bubble jet printers** use nozzles that have piezoelectric technology. Each nozzle works with a piezoelectric crystal that changes shape when excited by its resonance frequency and ejects an ink bubble.

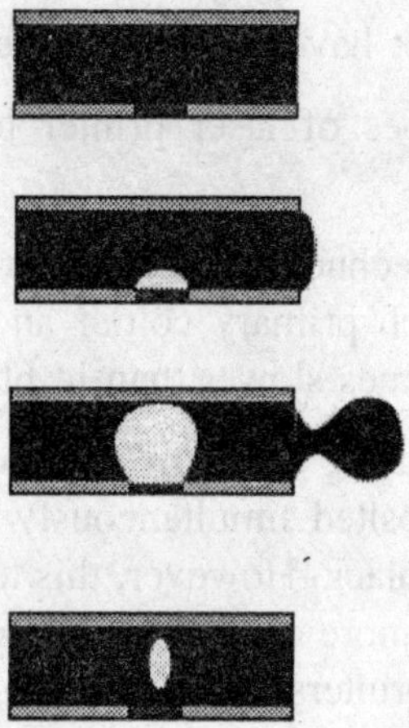

Laser Printer

The **laser printer** produce quality print-outs inexpensively at a high print speed. However, these printers are mostly used in professional and semi-professional settings because of their high cost.

Laser printers use a technology that is close to that used by photocopiers. A laser printer is mainly made up of an elecrostatically charge photosensitive drum that attracts the ink in order to make a shape that will be deposited on the sheet of paper.

How it works: a primary charge roller gives the sheets of paper a positive charge. The laser gives a positive charge to certain spots on the drum with a pivoting mirror. Then, negatively charged ink in powder form (**toner**) is deposited on the parts of the drum that were previously charged by the laser.

By turning, the drum deposits the ink on the paper. A heating wire (called a *corona wire*) finally attaches the ink to the paper.

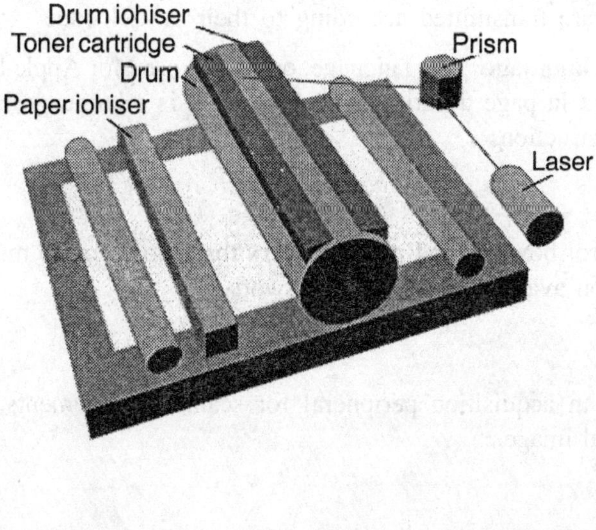

Because laser printers do not have mechanical heads, they are quick and quiet.

There are two different types of laser printer technology: "carousel" (four passes) or "tandem" (single-pass).

- **carousel**: with carousel technology, the printer passes over the paper four times to print a document (one for each primary colour and one for black, which in theory makes printing in colour four times slower than in black).
- **tandem**: a laser printer using "tandem" technology deposits each colour in one single pass. The toners are deposited simultaneously Output is as fast when printing in colour as it is when printing in black. However, this technology is more expensive because the mechanics behind it are more complicated. Therefore it is used only by middle to top-of-the-line colour laser printers.

LED Printer

Another printer technology competes with laser printers: **LED** (*Light Emitting Diode*) technology. With this technology, an electroluminescent diode printhead polarises the drum with a very fine light ray, making very small dots. This technology is particularly well adapted for obtaining high resolutions (600, 1,200 or 2,400 dpi).

Given that each diode is makes one point, print speed hardly affects resolution. Moreover, this technology lacks moving parts, which translates into less-expensive and more solid and reliable printers.

Printer Command Language

Page description language is the standard language that computers use to communicate with printers. Indeed, a printer must be able to interpret the information that a computer is sending to it.

The two main page description languages are:

- **Printer command language** (PCL): A language made up of binary sequences. The characters are transmitted according to their ASCII code
- **PostScript language**: This language, originally used for Apple LaserWriters, has become the standard in page description languages. It is a language in its own right based on a set of instructions

Print Servers

There are control boxes called **print servers** that allow you to make a printer with a USB or parallel connection available to a whole network.

The Scanner

A **scanner** is an acquisition peripheral for scanning documents, i.e. converting a paper document to a digital image.

There are generally three types of scanner:

- **Flat scanners** let you scan a document by placing it flat against a glass panel. This is the most common type of scanner.
- **Hand scanners** are smaller in size. These scanners must be moved manually (or semi-manually) in successive sections over the document in order to scan the whole document.
- **Sheet-fed scanners** feed the document through a lighted slot in order to scan them, similar to fax machines. This type of scanner is increasingly built into machines such as multi-function printers.

There are also scanners that are able to scan specific items such as slides.

Characteristics of a scanner

A scanner is generally characterised by the following elements:

- **Resolution:** Expressed in *dots per inch* (referred to as *dpi*), the resolution defines the fineness of the scan. The order of magnitude of the resolution is around 1200 per 2400 dpi. The horizontal resolution is very much dependent on the quality and number of captors, whereas vertical resolution is closely linked to the accuracy of the drive motor. However it is important to distinguish the optical resolution, which is the actual resolution of the scanner, from the **interpolated resolution**. Interpolation is a technique involving defining intermediate pixels from among actual pixels, by calculating the mean of the colours of neighbouring pixels. This technology helps achieve good results but the *interpolated resolution* thus defined is in no way a criterion that can be used to compare scanners.
- **The format of the document:** Depending on their size, scanners are able to accommodate documents of different sizes, generally A4 (21 × 29.7 cm), or more rarely A3 (29.7 × 42 cm).
- **Acquisition speed:** Expressed in *pages per minute* (*ppm*), the acquisition speed represents the scanner's ability to pick up a large number of pages per minute. The acquisition speed depends on the document format and the resolution chosen for the scan.
- **Interface:** This is the scanner connector. The main interfaces are as follows:
  - ⇨ FireWire. This is the preferred interface since its speed is particularly suited to this type of peripheral
  - ⇨ USB 2.0. This is offered on all recent computers. It is a standard interface which is recommended if the computer has no FireWire connection
  - ⇨ SCSI. Preferred interface for the scanner at the end of the 90s, the SCSI standard has now been abandoned in favour of the FireWire and the USB 2.0
  - ⇨ Parallel port. This type of connector is naturally slow and is used less frequently; it should be avoided if the computer has one of the preceding connectors

- **Physical characteristics:** other elements may be taken into account when choosing a scanner:
  - ⇨ Size, in terms of the physical dimensions of the scanner.
  - ⇨ Weight.
  - ⇨ Electricity consumption, expressed in Watts (W).
  - ⇨ Operating and storage temperatures.
  - ⇨ Noise level. Scanners can be very noisy and this may cause considerable disturbance.
  - ⇨ Accessories: The drivers and user manual are usually provided, but you must check that connection cables are also provided; if not they must be purchased separately.

How a scanner works

The operating principle for a scanner is as follows:

- The scanner moves over the document line by line
- Each line is broken down into "basic dots" which correspond to pixels.
- A captor analyses the colour of each pixel
- The colour of each pixel is broken down into 3 components (red, green, blue)
- Each colour component is measured and represented by a value. For 8-bit quantification, each component will have a value between 0 and 225 inclusive.

The rest of this article will specifically describe the operation of a flat scanner, although the operating mode for a hand scanner or sheet-fed scanner is exactly the same. The only difference is in the feeding of the document.

A flat scanner has a motor-driven lighted slot which scans the document line by line under a transparent glass panel on which the document is placed, with the scanning side face down.

The high-intensity light emitted is reflected by the document and converges towards a series of captors via a system of lenses and mirrors. The captors convert the light intensities received into electrical signals, which are in turn converted into digital data by an *analogue-digital converter*.

There are two categories of captors:

- **CMOS** captors (*Complementary Metal Oxide Semi-conductor)*, or *Complementary MOS*). This is known as the **CIS** technology (*Contact Image Sensor*). This type of device uses an LED ramp (*Light Emitting Diode*) for lighting the document and requires a very close distance between the captors and the document. The *CIS* technology, however, uses a lot less energy.
- **CCD captors** (*Charge-coupled devices*). Scanners using *CCD* technology are often thicker as they use a cold neon lamp. The quality of the scanned image is on the whole better however, since the signal/noise ratio is lower.

What is a Modem used for?

A **modem** is the peripheral used to transfer information between several computers over a wire transmission medium (e.g. telephone lines). Computers operate digitally using binary language (a series of zeros and ones), but modems are analogue. The digital signals pass from one value to another. There is no middle or half-way point. It is "*All or Nothing*" (one or zero). On the other hand, analogue signals do not move "in steps", but rather continuously.

For example, a piano works more or less digitally because there are no "steps" between notes. Conversely, a violin can modulate its notes to pass through all possible frequencies.

A computer operates like a piano and a modem like a violin. The modem converts binary information from the computer into analogue information in order to modulate it over the telephone line. You can hear bizarre noises if you turn up the sound from the modem.

Thus, a modem modulates digital information on analogue waves. In the opposite direction, it demodulates analogue data in order to convert them into digital data. The word "modem" is an acronym for "*MOdulate/DEModulate*".

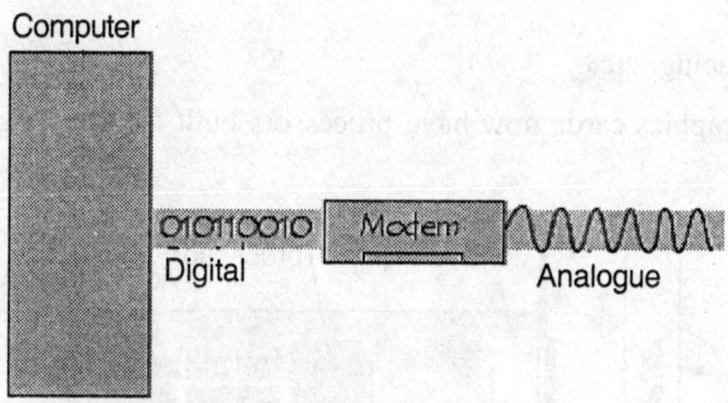

A modem's transmission speed is generally expressed in **bauds**, in tribute to Emile Baudot (11 September 1845 - 28 March 1903), a famous French engineer who worked in the area of telecommunications. This unit of transmission speed characterises the frequency of (de)modulation, i.e. the number of times the modem makes the signal change status per second. Thus, the bandwidth in bauds is not quite equal to the bandwidth in bits per second because a signal status change may be necessary to encode a bit.

Communication Standards

As modems proliferated, the need increased for standardised protocols for communication by modem, so that all the protocols would use a common language. This is why two organisations developed communication standards:

- The **BELL** laboratories, precursors in the area of telecommunications
- The *International Telephone and Telegraph Consultative Committee* (**CCITT**), known since 1990 as the *International Telecommunication Union* (**ITU**).

The goal of the ITU is to define international communications standards. Modem standards can be divided into 3 categories:

- Modulation standards (e.g. *CCITT V.21*)
- Error correction standards (e.g. *CCITT V.42*)
- Data compression standards (e.g. *CCITT V.42bis*)

2D Accelerator Cards

A **graphics card,** sometimes called a **graphics adapter, video card** or **graphics accelerator**, is a computer component which converts digital data into a graphical form which can be displayed on a monitor.

The initial role of a graphics card was to send pixels to a screen, as well as a variety of simple graphical manipulations:

- Moving blocks (such as the mouse cursor);
- ray tracing;
- polygon tracing; etc.

More recent graphics cards now have processors built for handling complex 3D graphical scenes.

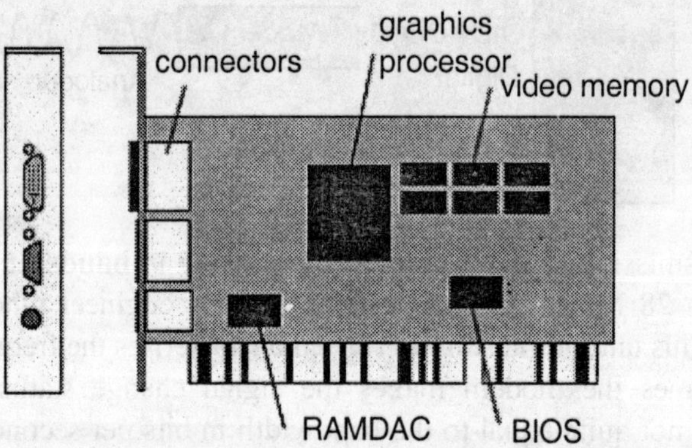

A video card's main components are:

- A **Graphical Processing Unit** (or **GPU** for short), the heart of a graphics card, which processes images based on the encoding being used. The **GPU** is a specialised processor with advanced image processing capabilities, especially for 3D graphics. Because of the high temperatures that the graphics processor can reach, a radiator and fan are often mounted on it.
- The job of the **video memory** is to store images processed by the GPU before they are displayed by the monitor. The larger the video memory, the better the graphics card can handle textures when displaying 3D scenes. The term *frame buffer* is generally used to refer to the part of the video memory which stores images before they are

shown onscreen. Graphics cards rely heavily on the type of memory that the card uses, as their response time is crucial for displaying images quickly, as is the amount of memory, which affects the number and resolution of the images that may be stored in the frame buffer.

- The **RAMDAC** (*random access memory digital-analog converter*) is used for converting digital images stored in the *frame buffer* as analog signals to send to the monitor. The **RAMDAC**'s frequency determines the refresh rate (number of images per second, expressed in Hertz - Hz) that the graphics card can support.
- The **video BIOS** contains the graphics card's settings, in particular the graphics modes that the adapter supports.
- The **interface**: This is a kind of bus used to connect the graphics card to the motherboard. The AGP bus is specifically designed to handle high dataflow, which is necessary when displaying video or 3D sequences. The PCI Express bus performs better than the AGP bus that it has ended up replacing.
- The **connections**:
  - ⇨ Standard VGA interface: Most graphics cards are built with a 15-pin VGA (Mini Sub-D, with 3 rows of 5 pins each), usually coloured blue, which is mainly used to connect the adapter to a CRT monitor. This type of interface is used to send 3 analog signals to the screen, corresponding to the red, blue, and green components of the image.

  - ⇨ The DVI (*Digital Video Interface*), found in some graphics cards, is used to send digital data to monitors which can support the interface. This bypasses the need to convert digital data into analog and then back again.

  - ⇨ S-Video interface: More and more graphics cards these days have an S-Video socket built in, so that the computer's output can be viewed on a television screen. This is why it is often called a **"TV-out"** plug.

3D Accelerator Cards

The field of 3D is much more recent, and is becoming more important. Some PCs can now compute faster than certain workstations.

Computing a 3D scene is a process which is roughly divided into four steps:

- **script:** laying out elements
- **geometry:** creating simple objects
- **setup:** cutting the objects into 2D triangles
- **rendering:** applying textures to the triangles.

The better the 3D accelerator card can compute these steps by itself, the faster it can be displayed. The first chips could only render, letting the processor take care of the rest.

Since then, graphics cards have included a "setup engine", which handles both of the last two steps.

For example, a 266 Mhz Pentium II which computes the first three steps can process 350,000 polygons per second; when it only computes two, it can reach 750,000 polygons per second.

This demonstrates how much of a load these cards remove from the processor.

The type of bus is also an important factor. While an AGP bus doesn't improve 2D images, cards that use that bus instead of the PCI bus are higher-performance. This is due to the fact that an AGP bus is directly linked to the RAM, which gives it much higher bandwidth than a PCI bus.

These high-technology products now require the same manufacturing quality as processors do, as well as etching between 0.25 μm and 0.35 μm in width.

Questions

(1) Explain the various peripheral devices?

(2) What is memory? What is the difference between register memory and main memory? Which is faster and why?

(3) Differentiate between static and dynamic RAM? Which one is faster and compact?

(4) Differentiate between the primary & secondary memory?

(5) What do you mean by physical storage media? Explain the memory hierarchy in brief?

❒ ❒ ❒

Unit II

CHAPTER
3

MS-Office and DBMS

INTRODUCTION TO MICROSOFT WORD FOR WINDOWS

Word Processors

Word processors are application programs used for *creating*, *editing*, *printing* and *saving* documents. By using a word processor it is possible to prepare reports, announcements, journals, books, etc. This week, you will learn about Microsoft Word, the most popular word processor of nowadays computer world. This product has so many features that it is not possible to learn all in one experiment, nevertheless after completing this experiment you will not only be able to do a lot of these things, but also learn how to learn the other features by yourself, using Help Menu.

Typing Text

When you start Word, a new, empty document file is automatically created, so you face an empty page. You can start typing anything you like. They will be seen on the screen. Use the Enter key **only** at the end of Paragraphs! (Not at the end of each sentence or line).

Using the Menus

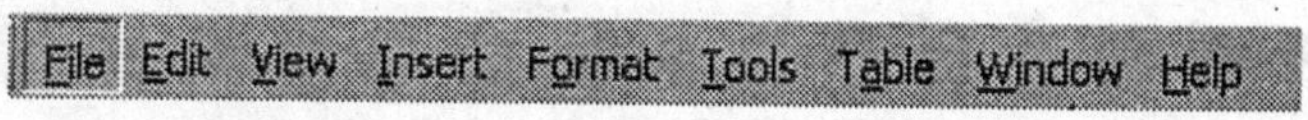

On the top of the screen there is a bar that contains many drop-down menus (File, Edit, View, etc). If you want to reach the menu bar with your keyboard, you can use the **Alt** key. A lot of operations are offered in these menus, and you can select any of them to do the corresponding operation, without having to write any commands. It is not possible to explore all the menu items in one experiment, however you can learn them in time, easily, by yourself. For this purpose, you may find the **Help** menu very helpful. Just use it. It is for you!

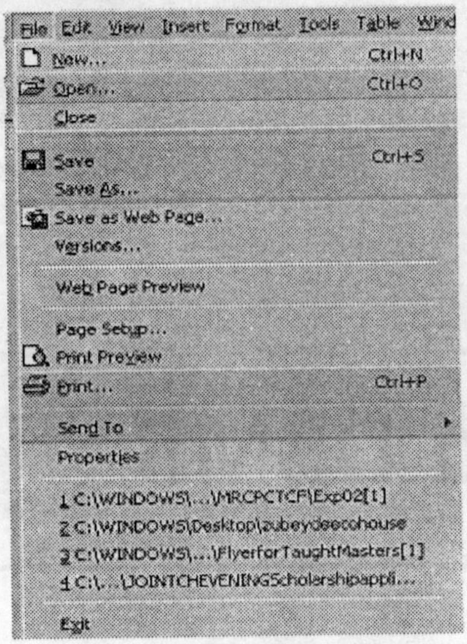

File Menu: The items on this menu are related with file operations. The default file type created with Word is document type (*.doc). **New** creates a new, empty document, **Open** opens a document which was created and saved before, **Save** saves the document to a disk (permanent storage device), **Save as** is used to save another (one more) copy of a file, with a different name, **Print** is used to take a print-out of the document, **Close** closes the currently open, active document, **Exit** is used to quit from Word.

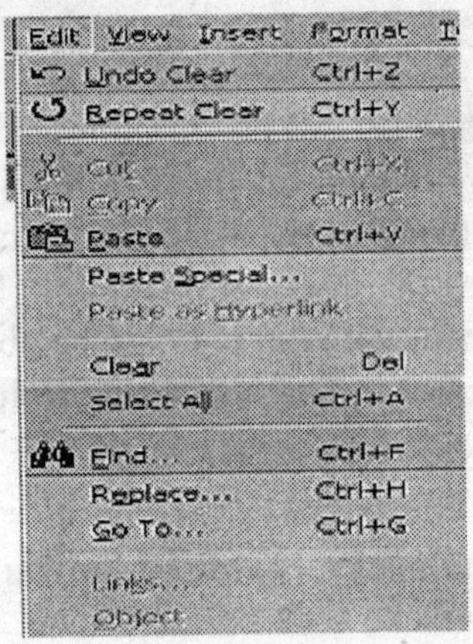

Edit Menu: **Undo** is used to cancel the last action (operation) you have made, **Repeat** is used to do a cancelled action once again, **Find** is used to search for some word or sentence in your document. **Cut** and **Copy** should be used together with **Paste**. Cut ~ Paste combination is used to change the place of a selected text by moving it into another part of your document. Copy ~ Paste is used to put an extra copy of a selected text into another part of the document. Please refer to "Selecting Text" part.

Using The Formatting Toolbar

Changing Font Size & Font Type

By default, the font size is usually 12. You can select any other value from the corresponding combo box. Larger the value, larger the size of the font.

Ex: This sentence is written with size 8. This sentence is written with size 20.

By default, the font type is usually Times New Roman. You can select any other type.

Ex: This sentence is written using "Times New Roman" type.

`This sentence is written using "Courier New" type.`

This sentence is written using "Arial" type.

Bold, Italic and Underlined Texts 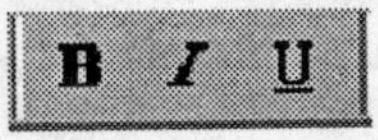

You can find the buttons for these three styles (**B** *I* <u>U</u>) on top of your screen. You can use any combination of them to write **Bold**, *Italic* and Underlined texts.

Ex: *This is an italic sentence.* **This is a bold sentence.** <u>This is an underlined sentence.</u> <u>*This is both italic and underlined.*</u> <u>**This is underlined and bold.**</u> <u>***This is italic & underlined & bold.***</u>

Paragraph Alignment 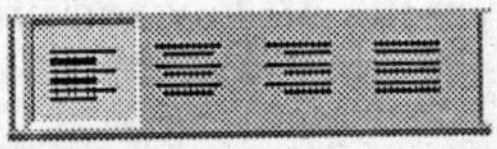

You can arrange the paragraphs as **left aligned**, **right aligned**, **centered** and **justified** (i.e. aligned from both left and right margins) by clicking one of the corresponding buttons shown above.

Ex: The first paragraph in the "Preliminary Explanations" part is left aligned. The second one is right aligned, and the third is centered. All the other paragraphs in the rest of the lab sheet are justified.

Selecting Text:

- *With mouse*
  1. Move your mouse pointer to the beginning of the text you want to select
  2. Click and hold the left mouse button
  3. Move the mouse to the end of the text you want to select.
  4. Release the mouse button.
- *With keyboard*
  1. Move the blinking cursor, by using the arrow keys, to the beginning of the text you want to select
  2. Press and hold the shift button
  3. Move the cursor to the end of the text that you want to select
  4. Release the shift button

When a text is selected, you see it highlighted. Now, you can do many operations on the selected text. (ex: move (cut~paste), copy (copy~paste), underline, change size, type, color, etc.)

Copying or Moving a selected text

To copy or move a text the first thing you have to do is to select it. Then click the **Copy** or **Cut** item from the **Edit** menu depending on what you want to do. (Cut is used to move). Move the cursor to the position that you want to insert the selected text. Click **Paste** in the Edit menu.

Using Shortcuts and Access Keys

- Many items in the menus have shortcuts that can be accessed by keyboard. Instead of clicking these items with your mouse, sometimes you may prefer to use the shortcuts. For example the shortcut for Save is Ctrl + S. Instead of clicking File and then Save, you can hold down *Ctrl* key and press S. This will do the same thing.
- Each menu item has one letter underlined. This is the access key of the item. If you get bored of using mouse, just hold down the *Alt* key and press the corresponding letters to travel in the menus.

Dividing a paragraph into columns

This paragraph is divided into three (equal width) columns. To divide a paragraph into columns, first select all the paragraph, then click **Columns** item in the **Format** menu, choose the "Number of columns" that you want to divide the selected text into, click the "Line between" check box to put a tick and make it checked if you want to have lines between these columns. It is also possible to have columns with different widths and arrange the space between the columns as you like.

Inserting Table into your document

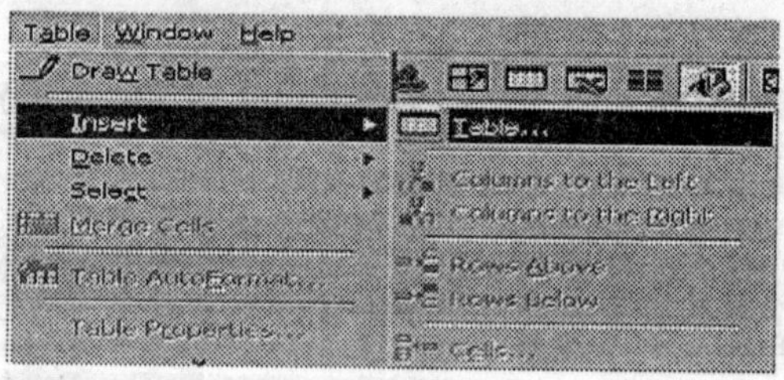

To insert a table into your document, click the **Insert table** item in the **Table** menu, enter the number of rows and columns and click OK. Here is a table with 6 rows and 5 columns:

ID	*Name*	*Surname*	*City*	*Country*
860815	Katarína	Kovalèíková	Dolný Kubín	Slovakia
882345	Gino Yman	Aguilar	Cercado de Lima	Peru
898123	Blanca Faci	Jiménez	Zaragoza	Spain
901573	Tapac	TopieMKO	Kiev	Ukraine
910723	Betty	Clichet	Buzy	France

Designing borders and shading of the table: Select the part of the table on which you want to do modifications, click **Borders and Shading** item in the **Format** menu, click the Borders tab or the shading tab and choose the line style and shading color that you like.

Inserting Equations into your documents

To insert an equation into a document, click the **Object** menu item in the **Insert** menu. Select "Microsoft Equation 3.0" from the list of object types available. You can now write any kind of formulae or equations by using the equation tool window.

Ex: $v_c = \sqrt{\dfrac{2gh}{1+\dfrac{I_{cm}}{mR^2}}}$ $\begin{bmatrix} 2 & -3 & 4 \\ 9 & 7 & 1 \\ 5 & 0 & -8 \end{bmatrix}\begin{bmatrix} x_1 \\ x_2 \\ X_3 \end{bmatrix} = \begin{bmatrix} 2 \\ 3 \\ -5 \end{bmatrix}$ $\sum_i \vec{F}_i = m\vec{a}$ $\vec{a} = \lim_{f \to 0} \dfrac{\vec{r}}{t} = \dfrac{\overrightarrow{dr}}{dt}$

- By using *Line spacing* commands, the distance between sentences can be arranged.(Single space, Double Space…etc.) For this command, from **Format** drop-down menu, **Paragraph** menu should be selected and from there "line spacing" can be arranged.
- By using *Effect* commands, Superscripts and Subscripts can be written. For this command, from **Format** drop-down menu, **Font** menu should be selected and from there "Effects" can be arranged.
- By using *Footnote* command, some necessary footnotes can be written. For this command, from **Insert** drop-down menu, **Footnote** menu should be selected.
- By using *Header and Footer* commands, some texts can be written to the top or bottom of your sheet (such as date, name…etc.). For this command, from **View** drop-down menu, **Header and Footer** menu should be selected.

INTRODUCTION TO MICROSOFT EXCEL

When you start Excel, you will see a **worksheet** (tables) in which you can write **text**, **numbers** or **formulae**. Texts can be used to create titles or labels, numbers are the data that we obtain from somewhere and formulae are used to do some operations or calculations on these numbers.

Tables are formed of **columns** and **rows**. Each box in a table (the intersection of a row and a column) is called a **cell**. Columns are named as A, B, C, D, etc, and rows are named as 1, 2, 3, 4, etc. Cells are named as A1, A2,…, B1, B2,…,…, Z1, Z2,… depending on the location they are found.

Ranges:

In an Excel Worksheet there are 16384 rows and 256 columns. **Range** is a group (rectangular block) of cells. A column or a row, for example, is a range, part of a column or a row is also a range. Ranges are represented with two cells: The first and the last.

Ex: A1:A5 is a range of 5 cells in the A column. More strictly, A1, A2, A3, A4, A5

B2:E4 is a range of 12 cells. The cells are B2, B3, B4, C2, C3, C4, D2, D3, D4, E2, E3, E4.

Formulae

In Excel, you can write formulae to do some calculations on cells or ranges of cells. For example, you can add the values in Fl and F2, and write the result into F3, by writing =F1+F2 into F3.

Functions

In these formulae you can also use some functions like SUM(), AVERAGE(), SIN(), etc. For example, instead of = F1+F2, you may use = SUM(F1:F2). Of course for adding only two numbers it may not be a very bright idea to use the function SUM(), but if you have many numbers to add, it will certainly be very useful.

If you want to see the complete list of these functions, just click the **Function** item in the **Insert** menu.

Writing Formulae

To write a formula into a cell, you should first put an equal sign (=) and then write the corresponding formula.

Ex: Write 1, 2, 3, 4, 5 into A1, A2, A3, A4 and A5 respectively. Then write = SUM(A1:A5) into the cell A6.

Do you see the result 15 in A6? Now change the number in any of the cells in range A1:A5 and see that the value of A6 is **automatically recalculated.**

Copying a formula to other cells:

Suppose you want to add the numbers in B1:B5, also. Instead of writing = SUM(B1:B5) into B6, you can just copy A6 to B6. You know that the formula in A6 was = SUM(A1:A5) but it will be automatically turned to = SUM(B1:B5) during the copy operation.

Constant Addressing vs Relative Addressing:

As you see in the section above, when you copy some formula to another cell, the range in it automatically changes. This is because there is relative addressing. To prevent this, you can use the $ sign in front of the cell addresses. Suppose that you write = SUM($A$1:$A$5) in A6. When you copy it to B6, the formula will remain exactly the same, and you will see 15 in both A6 and B6.

Using the Help Menu:

Sometimes, you may forget how to do something, or you may want to learn something new which would be very useful for what you are intending to do. In these cases, you can just refer to the **Help** menu. Try it! It is like a teacher who is always ready to answer your questions and solve your problems.

Sorting a column

You can sort some rows (or some range of cells) in the table, by any column, in ascending or descending order. To do this, just select a range of cells, click the **Sort** item in the **Data** menu, and select the columns by which you want to do the sort. It is so simple!

Inserting Charts into your worksheet

Charts (graphs) are visual representations of numbers. Instead of seeing many numbers all together, we usually prefer to see a chart that represents everything visually. Whenever there is an election, for example, all the TV channels show the results by using some kind of graphs. It is more easily understandable to human beings. To insert a chart, just select the corresponding columns (or ranges), and click **Chart...** item in the **Insert** menu. Then select the chart type that you want to use and click **Next** two times. Now enter the **Chart title**, and select a **data label** style, if you want, and click **Next** again. Be sure that "As object in: Sheet 1" is selected and click **Finish**. Now the chart is inserted into your worksheet. Change the values in some of the cells of the range that was used to prepare the chart. Realize that the **chart is automatically updated** to reflect these changes.

INTRODUCTION TO MICROSOFT POWERPOINT

Presenting ideas in a clear and concise manner is important when sharing information with others. For this reason Microsoft® PowerPoint® has become an indispensable tool for instruction. Originally, PowerPoint was used primarily for giving live slide presentations in front of groups of people; now it enables you to give Internet-based presentations that can transcend barriers of time and space. PowerPoint 2002 has several features that enable you to post presentations online for your students, parents or colleagues to view, and you don't need to know HTML or other programming.

In this workbook, you will learn:

- Creating a simple presentation and enhancing it by adding graphics, spreadsheet data, and voice narration.
- Saving your presentation as a Web document so that anyone with a capable browser can view your work.
- Setting up and delivering an online broadcast of your presentation over your network or the Internet. In addition, your online broadcast will be automatically archived so that others can view your slides, and can also see and hear your presentation. This will enable students to easily review a lecture when studying for an exam, clarifying notes, or catching up on a missed class.

Before you start using PowerPoint 2002, you should become familiar with its features. The following illustration shows a slide in the TriPane view with the task pane showing.

> **Words to know:**
>
> **HTML-HyperText Markup Language**—Programming language used to format Web pages.
>
> **Browser**—A program that allows viewing of HTML formatted documents (Web pages).
>
> **Online Broadcast**—A feature in PowerPoint 2002 that allows delivery of a presentation to an unlimited group of attendees over a network or the Internet.
>
> **Streaming (content)**—The act of delivering a constant flow of data to a receiving client. A live audio or video feed, for instance.
>
> **Microsoft Internet Explorer**—Microsoft's Web browser, which allows the displaying and editing of Web pages.
>
> **Windows Media Technologies**—A service that optimizes streaming media for unicast and multicast transmission.

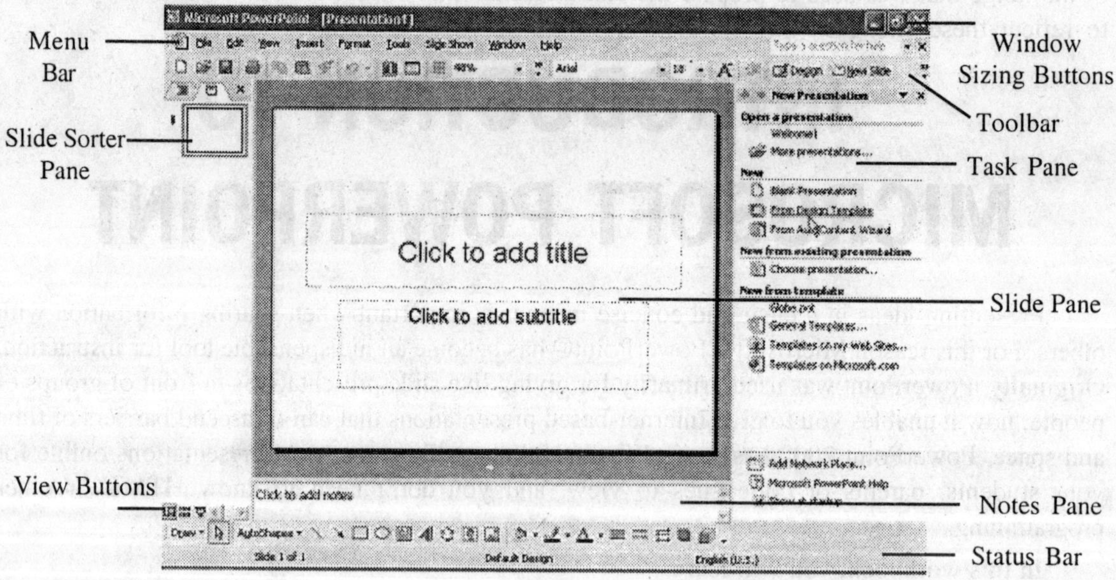

To create a presentation

1. Open PowerPoint. In the task pane under New select From Design Template and then click OK.
2. In the Slide Design task pane, click the design template you want to use by selecting the appropriate thumbnail (Global for this workshop). To see the name of the template, hover your cursor over the thumbnail and a Tool Tip will reveal the name of the template.

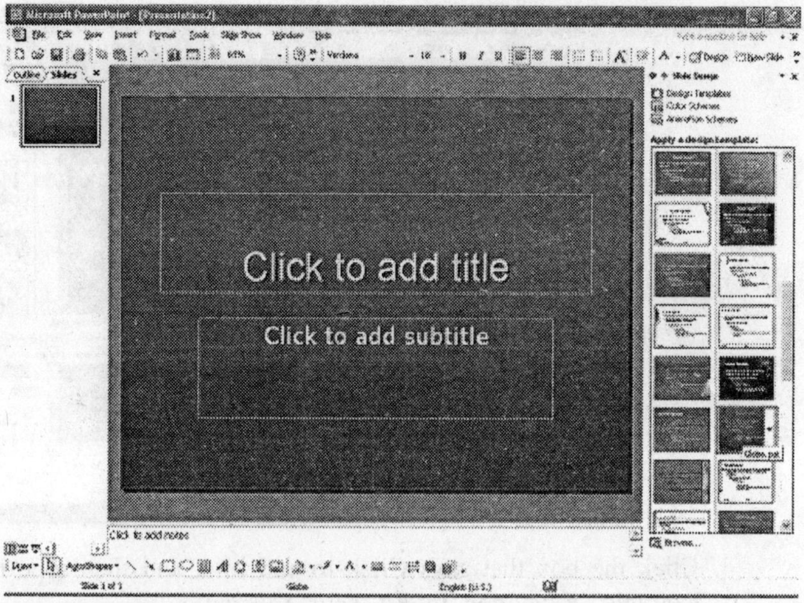

> WORK better
>
> PowerPoint has a TriPane view that allows simultaneous viewing of slides, notes and the slide sorter. The outline and the slide sorter may be switched by clicking on the appropriate tab above the slide sorter.

3. Click in the box that says Click to add title and then type the title for your presentation (for example, *Welcome to Your Online College*).
4. You can create a new design template by saving a customized template. From the **Save As** list, select Design Template.

   Click the box that says Click to add subtitle, and then type the subtitle of your presentation (for example, *A Global Educational Experience for Students in Your Career Area*).
5. From the File menu, click **Save**, and then enter a file name for your presentation (for example, *welcome1*). Click **Save** again to save your file.

> WORK better
>
> You can create a new design template by saving a customized template. From the **Save As** list, select Design Template.

To add graphics to your presentation

1. Click New Slide from the Insert menu.

   -or-

   Click the New Slide button on the Formatting toolbar to add a new slide to your presentation.
2. In the Slide Layout pane, click Title and Text (formerly Bulleted List) on the New Slide dialog box if it isn't already selected. Remember that a tool tip will divulge the auto layout name if hover on the object for a second.

> WORK better
>
> You can import an outline for your presentation from an external file by selecting **Slides from Outline** from the Insert menu.

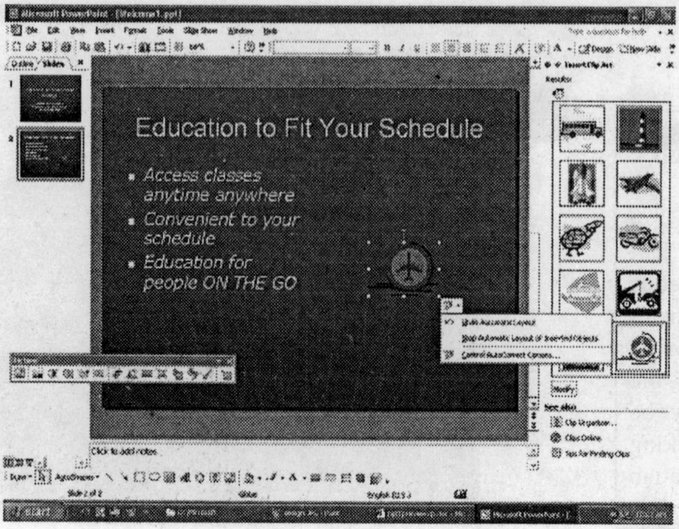

3. Click the box that says Click to add title, and then type the title for that page (for example, *Education to Fit Your Schedule*).

4. Click the box that says Click to add text, and then type two or three bullets (for example, *Access classes anytime anywhere, Convenient to your schedule, Education for people ON THE GO*).

5. From the Insert menu, point to Picture and then click Clip Art to open the Insert Clip Art task pane.

6. Type the name of the type of clip art you want, for example, type *Transporation* in the box under **Search For**, and then click **Search.** (Note: All clip art may not appear unless you have access to the Office CD in your CD-ROM drive or internal network and you have cataloged the images on your local hard disks. This is a simple one time process that is initiated the first time you insert clip art.)

2. From the search results, click the thumbnail for the image you want to insert. The clip art will be inserted on the slide. To change the format of the graphic, double-click the image. From the **Format Picture** dialog box, you can adjust the size and position of the graphic. To undo automatic formatting, click the SmartTag in the lower right corner of the image, and select **Undo Automatic Layout**.

3. From the File menu, click **Save** to save your work.

To add Excel data to your presentation

1. From the Insert menu click New Slide to add a new slide to your presentation.

2. From the Slide Layout task pane, under **Text Layouts**, click Title Only to change the format of the new slide. To see the name of the slide layout, hover your mouse over the slide for a tool tip.

3. Click the box that says Click to add title, and then type the title for that page (for example, *Annual Income in $K*).
4. From the Insert menu, click **Object,** and then click Create from file. Browse to a pre-existing Excel file, like *Annual_Income.xls* and then click OK.

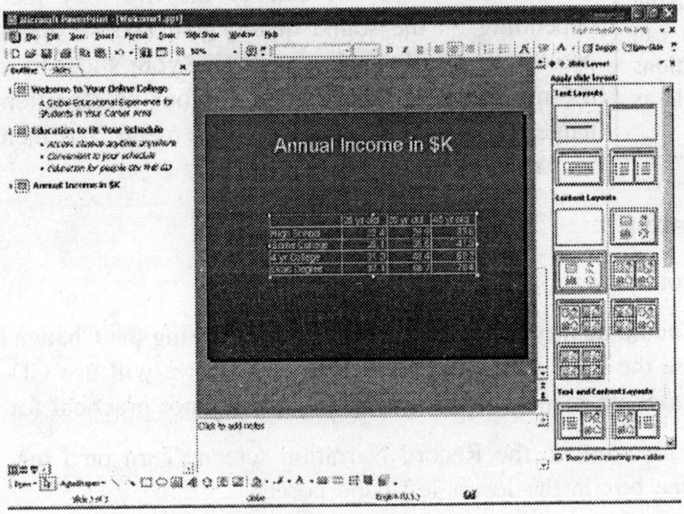

5. Position and resize the Excel worksheet as necessary, and then click Save to save your changes.
6. Click New Slide from the Insert menu to add a new page to your presentation.
7. From the Slide Layout task pane under **Other Layouts**, click Title and Chart.
8. Click the box that says Click to add title, and then type the title for the page (for example, *Education Pays Off Over Time*).
9. Double-click the box that says Double-click to add chart, and then click Import File from the Edit menu.
10. Browse to the same Excel worksheet that you used in step 4, and then click Open.
11. In the Import Data Options dialog box, select a sheet from the workbook, and then click OK.
12. Position and resize the chart as necessary, add any other pages that you want, and then select Save from the File menu to save your presentation.

Add another dimension of meaning to your presentation by using narration. Students can hear your descriptions and ideas, as well as your inflections.

PowerPoint enables you to record yourself while giving a presentation. This allows others to both view and listen to your lecture at any time. It also enhances a presentation that has been saved in a Web format. If you want, you can have someone else provide the voice that will be recorded as the narration. Special hardware is not required for this, just a sound card and microphone. (Most computers now come with sound cards and microphones.)

WORK better

Add another dimension of meaning to your presentation by using narration. Students can hear your descriptions and ideas, as well as your inflections.

It is best to start out with a script for a short presentation. This ensures that your finished product sounds professional without any stammering or fumbling for words.

You may also want to keep a copy of your presentation without narration, because the size of the file may increase dramatically depending on the sound quality you choose. Saving a copy of your presentation will enable you to give your slides to someone else to use the material. To save a copy of your presentation under a different name, click **Save As** from the File menu, and then type a new name for the file.

To Record Narration

1. Click Record Narration from the Slide Show menu.
2. Select the audio quality for your presentation by clicking the Change Quality button and then choose the level you want. For this workshop we will use CD Quality; however, this level uses up memory quickly and is probably not practical for most projects.
3. Click OK to return to the Record Narration screen. Turn on **Link Narrations in** by selecting the box in the lower left-hand corner
4. Click OK in the Record Narration dialog box and the first slide will appear. Begin recording the narration. Speak normally and as clearly as possible.
5. Click OK to advance to the next slide when you are finished with each recording. When you have finished, click the last slide to terminate the recording process.
6. Click Save to save the slide timings and review the slide timings.
7. Return to the first slide by clicking it in the slide sorter view, and then select View Show, or click the View Show button at the lower left corner of the presentation window. This will play your presentation.
8. If you do not like your narration and want to re-record it, select Undo Record Narration from the Edit menu and record the narration again. (Note: If you record the narration without clicking **Undo Record Narration**, you will record a second narration on top of the original one.)
9. Click Save from the File menu to save your presentation and narration.

WORK better

You can use features of Windows Media Technologies and the Windows operating platform to restrict access to presentations.

You can deliver your presentation over a network with the following features:

- *Save as Web Page*— converts your entire presentation into HTML based pages, which look exactly like your original slides, complete with narration.
- *Pack and Go* Wizard— leads you through the necessary steps that will compress your presentation exactly as is for distribution over a network or CD-ROM. The main benefit of this method is that it allows the receiver to view the complete presentation. (You are required to have PowerPoint or the PowerPoint Animation Player to view Pack and Go presentations.)
- *Online Broadcast*— allows real time delivery of your presentation over a network as it is being given. The presentation is broadcast much like a television news program; if you have audio or video hardware, you can include your speech and camera footage in your slide show. Your broadcast can be archived for playback on demand; however, if you are planning to broadcast to more than 10 people, you will need to increase the power of your broadcast by using a Windows Media Server. Windows Media Technology is a streaming technology that allows information to be viewed as it is received, instead of through the download and play method.

No matter which method you choose, there are great benefits to delivering your presentation over a local area network (LAN) or the Internet.

To save your presentation as a Web page

1. With the presentation open in PowerPoint, click Save As Web Page from the File menu.
2. Browse to the location where you want to store your presentation, and then enter a file name and title.
3. Click Save to save your presentation.
4. If you want to make the presentation available on a Web server, click Publish in the Save As dialog box.
5. Choose what you would like to publish (for example, number of slides, speaker note, custom shows).

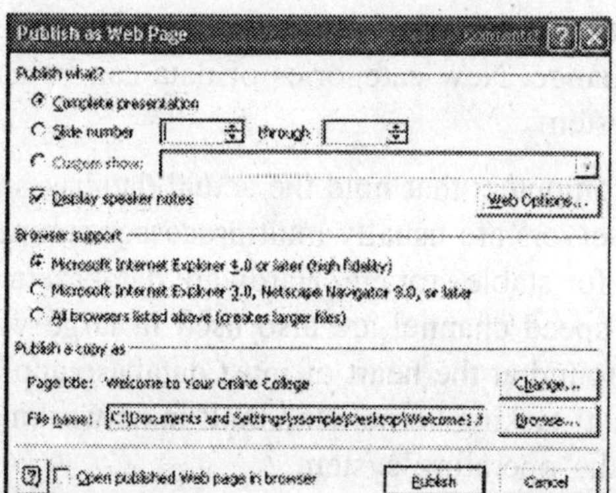

6. Click Web Options, and then select the check box for Show slide animation while browsing. This will display most of the animations and slide transitions you chose in your original presentation.
7. Click OK, and then select the browser you want to support. For best results, choose Microsoft Internet Explorer 4.0 or later (high fidelity).
8. Choose the location (Web server and full URL) where you want to publish your work, and then click Publish.

DATABASE MANAGEMENT SYSTEM

A **Database Management System (DBMS)** is a set of computer programs that controls the creation, maintenance, and the use of the database with computer as a platform or of an organization and its end users. It allows organizations to place control of organization-wide database development in the hands of database administrators (DBAs) and other specialists. A DBMS is a system software package that helps the use of integrated collection of data records and files known as databases. It allows different user application programs to easily access the same database. DBMSs may use any of a variety of database models, such as the network model or relational model. In large systems, a DBMS allows users and other software to store and retrieve data in a structured way. Instead of having to write computer programs to extract information, user can ask simple questions in a query language. Thus, many DBMS packages provide Fourth-generation programming language (4GLs) and other application development features. It helps to specify the logical organization for a database and access and use the information within a database. It provides facilities for controlling data access, enforcing data integrity, managing concurrency controlled, restoring database.

Overview

A DBMS is a set of software programs that controls the organization, storage, management, and retrieval of data in a database. DBMSs are categorized according to their data structures or types. The DBMS accepts requests for data from an application program and instructs the operating system to transfer the appropriate data. The queries and responses must be submitted and received according to a format that conforms to one or more applicable protocols. When a DBMS is used, information systems can be changed much more easily as the organization's information requirements change. New categories of data can be added to the database without disruption to the existing system.

Database servers are computers that hold the actual databases and run only the DBMS and related software. Database servers are usually multiprocessor computers, with generous memory and RAID disk arrays used for stable storage. Hardware database accelerators, connected to one or more servers via a high-speed channel are also used in large volume transaction processing environments. DBMSs are found at the heart of most database applications. Sometimes DBMSs are built around a private multi-tasking kernel with built-in networking support although nowadays these functions are left to the operating system.

History

Databases have been in use since the earliest days of electronic computing. Unlike modern systems which can be applied to widely different databases and needs, the vast majority of older systems were tightly linked to the custom databases in order to gain speed at the expense of flexibility. Originally DBMSs were found only in large organizations with the computer hardware needed to support large data sets.

1960s Navigational DBMS

As computers grew in speed and capability, a number of general-purpose database systems emerged; by the mid-1960s there were a number of such systems in commercial use. Interest in a standard began to grow, and Charles Bachman, author of one such product, Integrated Data Store (IDS), founded the "Database Task Group" within CODASYL, the group responsible for the creation and standardization of COBOL. In 1971 they delivered their standard, which generally became known as the "Codasyl approach", and soon there were a number of commercial products based on it available.

The Codasyl approach was based on the "manual" navigation of a linked data set which was formed into a large network. When the database was first opened, the program was handed back a link to the first record in the database, which also contained pointers to other pieces of data. To find any particular record the programmer had to step through these pointers one at a time until the required record was returned. Simple queries like "find all the people in India" required the program to walk the entire data set and collect the matching results. There was, essentially, no concept of "find" or "search". This might sound like a serious limitation today, but in an era when the data was most often stored on magnetic tape such operations were too expensive to contemplate anyway.

IBM also had their own DBMS system in 1968, known as *IMS*. IMS was a development of software written for the Apollo program on the System/360. IMS was generally similar in concept to Codasyl, but used a strict hierarchy for its model of data navigation instead of Codasyl's network model. Both concepts later came to be known as navigational databases due to the way data was accessed, and Bachman's 1973 Turing Award presentation was *The Programmer as Navigator*. IMS is classified as a hierarchial database. IMS and IDMS, both CODASYL databases, as well as CINCOMs TOTAL database are classified as network databases.

1970s Relational DBMS

Edgar Codd worked at IBM in San Jose, California, in one of their offshoot offices that was primarily involved in the development of hard disk systems. He was unhappy with the navigational model of the Codasyl approach, notably the lack of a "search" facility which was becoming increasingly useful. In 1970, he wrote a number of papers that outlined a new approach to database construction that eventually culminated in the groundbreaking *A Relational Model of Data for Large Shared Data Banks*.

In this paper, he described a new system for storing and working with large databases. Instead of records being stored in some sort of linked list of free-form records as in Codasyl, Codd's idea was to use a "table" of fixed-length records. A linked-list system would be very inefficient when storing "sparse" databases where some of the data for any one record could be left empty. The relational model solved this by splitting the data into a series of normalized tables, with optional elements being moved out of the main table to where they would take up room only if needed.

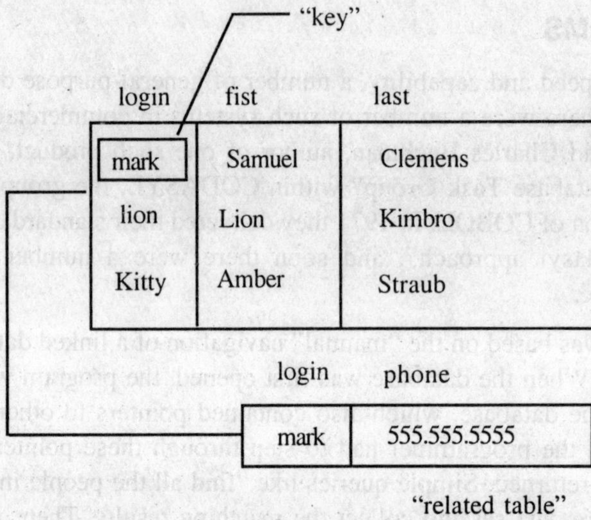

In the relational model, related records are linked together with a "key".

For instance, a common use of a database system is to track information about users, their name, login information, various addresses and phone numbers. In the navigational approach all of these data would be placed in a single record, and unused items would simply not be placed in the database. In the relational approach, the data would be *normalized* into a user table, an address table and a phone number table (for instance). Records would be created in these optional tables only if the address or phone numbers were actually provided.

Linking the information back together is the key to this system. In the relational model, some bit of information was used as a "key", uniquely defining a particular record. When information was being collected about a user, information stored in the optional (or *related*) tables would be found by searching for this key. For instance, if the login name of a user is unique, addresses and phone numbers for that user would be recorded with the login name as its key. This "re-linking" of related data back into a single collection is something that traditional computer languages are not designed for.

Just as the navigational approach would require programs to loop in order to collect records, the relational approach would require loops to collect information about any one record. Codd's solution to the necessary looping was a set-oriented language, a suggestion that would later spawn the ubiquitous SQL. Using a branch of mathematics known as *tuple calculus*, he demonstrated that such a system could support all the operations of normal databases (inserting, updating etc.) as well as providing a simple system for finding and returning *sets* of data in a single operation.

Codd's paper was picked up by two people at the Berkeley, Eugene Wong and Michael Stonebraker. They started a project known as INGRES using funding that had already been allocated for a geographical database project, using student programmers to produce code. Beginning in 1973, INGRES delivered its first test products which were generally ready for widespread use in 1979. During this time, a number of people had moved "through" the group — perhaps as many as 30 people worked on the project, about five at a time. INGRES was similar to System R in a number of ways, including the use of a "language" for data access, known as QUEL — QUEL was in fact relational, having been based on Codd's own Alpha language, but has since been corrupted to follow SQL, thus violating much the same concepts of the relational model as SQL itself.

IBM itself did one test implementation of the relational model, PRTV, and a production one, Business System 12, both now discontinued. Honeywell did MRDS for Multics, and now there are two new implementations: Alphora Dataphor and Rel. All other DBMS implementations usually called *relational* are actually SQL DBMSs. In 1968, the University of Michigan began development of the Micro DBMS relational database management system. It was used to manage very large data sets by the US Department of Labor, the Environmental Protection Agency and researchers from University of Alberta, the University of Michigan and Wayne State University. It ran on mainframe computers using Michigan Terminal System. The system remained in production until 1996.

End 1970s SQL DBMS

IBM started working on a prototype system loosely based on Codd's concepts as **System R** in the early 1970s. The first version was ready in 1974/5, and work then started on multi-table systems in which the data could be split so that all of the data for a record (much of which is often optional) did not have to be stored in a single large "chunk". Subsequent multi-user versions were tested by customers in 1978 and 1979, by which time a standardized query language, SQL, had been added. Codd's ideas were establishing themselves as both workable and superior to Codasyl, pushing IBM to develop a true production version of System R, known as *SQL/DS*, and, later, *Database 2* (DB2).

Many of the people involved with INGRES became convinced of the future commercial success of such systems, and formed their own companies to commercialize the work but with an SQL interface. Sybase, Informix, NonStop SQL and eventually Ingres itself were all being sold as offshoots to the original INGRES product in the 1980s. Even Microsoft SQL Server is actually a re-built version of Sybase, and thus, INGRES. Only Larry Ellison's Oracle started from a different chain, based on IBM's papers on System R, and beat IBM to market when the first version was released in 1978.

Stonebraker went on to apply the lessons from INGRES to develop a new database, Postgres, which is now known as PostgreSQL. PostgreSQL is often used for global mission critical applications (the .org and .info domain name registries use it as their primary data store, as do many large companies and financial institutions).

In Sweden, Codd's paper was also read and Mimer SQL was developed from the mid-70s at Uppsala University. In 1984, this project was consolidated into an independent enterprise. In the early 1980s, Mimer introduced transaction handling for high robustness in applications, an idea that was subsequently implemented on most other DBMS.

DBMS building blocks

A DBMS includes four main parts: modeling language, data structure, database query language, and transaction mechanisms:

Components of DBMS

- **DBMS Engine** accepts logical request from the various other DBMS subsystems, converts them into physical equivalent, and actually accesses the database and data dictionary as they exist on a storage device.
- **Data Definition Subsystem** helps user to create and maintain the data dictionary and define the structure of the files in a database.
- **Data Manipulation Subsystem** helps user to add, change, and delete information in a database and query it for valuable information. Software tools within the data manipulation subsystem are most often the primary interface between user and the information contained in a database. It allows user to specify its logical information requirements.
- **Application Generation Subsystem** contains facilities to help users to develop transactions-intensive applications. It usually requires that user perform a detailed series of tasks to process a transaction. It facilities easy-to-use data entry screens, programming languages, and interfaces.
- **Data Administration Subsystem** helps users to manage the overall database environment by providing facilitates for backup and recovery, security management, query optimization, concurrency control, and change management.

Modeling language

A data modeling language is used to define the schema of each database hosted in the DBMS, according to the DBMS database model. The four most common types of models are the:

- hierarchical model,
- network model,
- relational model, and
- object model.

Inverted lists and other methods are also used. A given database management system may provide one or more of the four models. The optimal structure depends on the natural organization of the application's data, and on the application's requirements (which include transaction rate (speed), reliability, maintainability, scalability, and cost).

The dominant model in use today is the ad hoc one embedded in SQL, despite the objections of purists who believe this model is a corruption of the relational model, since it violates several of its fundamental principles for the sake of practicality and performance. Many DBMSs also support the Open Database Connectivity API that supports a standard way for programmers to access the DBMS.

Before the database management approach, organizations relied on file processing systems to organize, store, and process data files. End users became aggravated with file processing because data is stored in many different files and each organized in a different way. Each file was specialized to be used with a specific application. Needless to say, file processing was bulky, costly and nonflexible when it came to supplying needed data accurately and promptly. Data redundancy is an issue with the file processing system because the independent data files produce duplicate data so when updates were needed each separate file would need to be updated. Another issue is the lack of data integration. The data is dependent on other data to organize and store it. Lastly, there was not any consistency or standardization of the data in a file processing system which makes maintenance difficult. For all these reasons, the database management approach was produced. Database management systems (DBMS) are designed to use one of five database structures to provide simplistic access to information stored in databases. The five database structures are hierarchical, network, relational, multidimensional and object-oriented models.

The hierarchical structure was used in early mainframe DBMS. Records' relationships form a treelike model. This structure is simple but nonflexible because the relationship is confined to a one-to-many relationship. IBM's IMS system and the RDM Mobile are examples of a hierarchical database system with multiple hierarchies over the same data. RDM Mobile is a newly designed embedded database for a mobile computer system. The hierarchical structure is used primary today for storing geographic information and file systems.

The network structure consists of more complex relationships. Unlike the hierarchical structure, it can relate to many records and accesses them by following one of several paths. In other words, this structure allows for many-to-many relationships.

The relational structure is the most commonly used today. It is used by mainframe, midrange and microcomputer systems. It uses two-dimensional rows and columns to store data. The tables of records can be connected by common key values. While working for IBM, E.F. Codd designed this structure in 1970. The model is not easy for the end user to run queries with because it may require a complex combination of many tables.

The multidimensional structure is similar to the relational model. The dimensions of the cube looking model have data relating to elements in each cell. This structure gives a spreadsheet like view of data. This structure is easy to maintain because records are stored as fundamental attributes, the same way they're viewed and the structure is easy to understand. Its high performance has made it the most popular database structure when it comes to enabling online analytical processing (OLAP).

The object oriented structure has the ability to handle graphics, pictures, voice and text, types of data, without difficultly unlike the other database structures. This structure is popular for multimedia Web-based applications. It was designed to work with object-oriented programming languages such as Java.

Data structure

Data structures (fields, records, files and objects) optimized to deal with very large amounts of data stored on a permanent data storage device (which implies relatively slow access compared to volatile main memory).

Database query language

A database query language and report writer allows users to interactively interrogate the database, analyze its data and update it according to the users previleges on data. It also controls the security of the database. Data security prevents unauthorized users from viewing or updating the database. Using passwords, users are allowed access to the entire database or subsets of it called *subschemas*. For example, an employee database can contain all the data about an individual employee, but one group of users may be authorized to view only payroll data, while others are allowed access to only work history and medical data.

If the DBMS provides a way to interactively enter and update the database, as well as interrogate it, this capability allows for managing personal databases. However, it may not leave an audit trail of actions or provide the kinds of controls necessary in a multi-user organization. These controls are only available when a set of application programs are customized for each data entry and updating function.

Transaction mechanism

A database transaction mechanism ideally guarantees ACID properties in order to ensure data integrity despite concurrent user accesses (concurrency control), and faults (fault tolerance). It also maintains the integrity of the data in the database. The DBMS can maintain the integrity of the database by not allowing more than one user to update the same record at the same time. The DBMS can help prevent duplicate records via unique index constraints; for example, no two customers with the same customer numbers (key fields) can be entered into the database. See ACID properties for more information (Redundancy avoidance).

External, Logical and Internal view

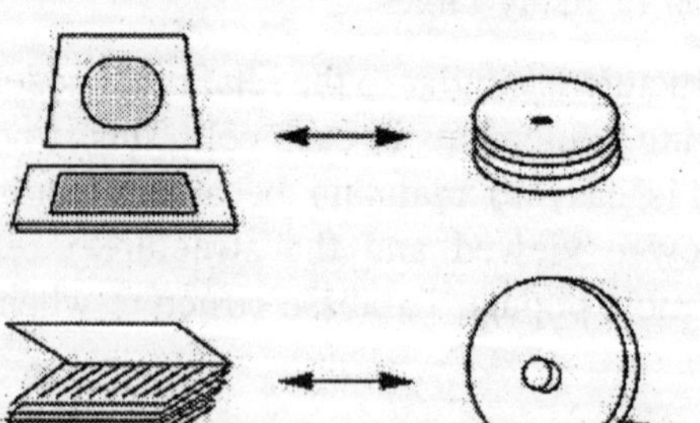

External Schema
-User view-

Internal Schema
-Computer View

Traditional View of Data

A database management system provides the ability for many different users to share data and process resources. But as there can be many different users, there are many different database needs. The question now is: How can a single, unified database meet the differing requirement of so many users?

A DBMS minimizes these problems by providing two views of the database data: an external view (or User view), logical view (or conceptual view) and physical (or internal) view. The user's view, of a database program represents data in a format that is meaningful to a user and to the software programs that process those data. That is, the logical view tells the user, in user terms, what is in the database. The physical view deals with the actual, physical arrangement and location of data in the direct access storage devices (DASDs). Database specialists use the physical view to make efficient use of storage and processing resources. With the logical view users can see data differently from how they are stored, and they do not want to know all the technical details of physical storage. After all, a business user is primarily interested in using the information, not in how it is stored.

One strength of a DBMS is that while there is typically only one conceptual (or logical) and physical (or Internal) view of the data, there can be an endless number of different External views. This feature allows users to see database information in a more business-related way rather than from a technical, processing viewpoint. Thus the logical view refers to the way user views data, and the physical view to the way the data are physically stored and processed.

DBMS features and capabilities

Alternatively, and especially in connection with the relational model of database management, the relation between attributes drawn from a specified set of domains can be seen as being primary. For instance, the database might indicate that a car that was originally "red" might fade to "pink" in time, provided it was of some particular "make" with an inferior paint job. Such higher parity relationships provide information on all of the underlying domains at the same time, with none of them being privileged above the others.

DBMS simple definition

Database management system is the system in which related data is stored in an "efficient" and "compact" manner. Efficient means that the data which is stored in the DBMS is accessed in very quick time and compact means that the data which is stored in DBMS covers very less space in computer's memory. In above definition the phrase "related data" is used which means that the data which is stored in DBMS is about some particular topic.

Throughout recent history specialized databases have existed for scientific, geospatial, imaging, document storage and like uses. Functionality drawn from such applications has lately begun appearing in mainstream DBMSs as well. However, the main focus there, at least when aimed at the commercial data processing market, is still on descriptive attributes on repetitive record structures.

Thus, the DBMSs of today roll together frequently needed services or features of attribute management. By externalizing such functionality to the DBMS, applications effectively share code with each other and are relieved of much internal complexity. Features commonly offered by database management systems include:

Query ability

Querying is the process of requesting attribute information from various perspectives and combinations of factors. Example: "How many 2-door cars in Texas are green?" A database query language and report writer allow users to interactively interrogate the database, analyze its data and update it according to the users previleges on data.

Backup and replication

Copies of attributes need to be made regularly in case primary disks or other equipment fails. A periodic copy of attributes may also be created for a distant organization that cannot readily access the original. DBMS usually provide utilities to facilitate the process of extracting and disseminating attribute sets. When data is replicated between database servers, so that the information remains consistent throughout the database system and users cannot tell or even know which server in the DBMS they are using, the system is said to exhibit replication transparency.

Rule enforcement

Often one wants to apply rules to attributes so that the attributes are clean and reliable. For example, we may have a rule that says each car can have only one engine associated with it (identified by Engine Number). If somebody tries to associate a second engine with a given car, we want the DBMS to deny such a request and display an error message. However, with changes in the model specification such as, in this example, hybrid gas-electric cars, rules may need to change. Ideally such rules should be able to be added and removed as needed without significant data layout redesign.

Security

Often it is desirable to limit who can see or change which attributes or groups of attributes. This may be managed directly by individual, or by the assignment of individuals and privileges to groups, or (in the most elaborate models) through the assignment of individuals and groups to roles which are then granted entitlements.

Computation

There are common computations requested on attributes such as counting, summing, averaging, sorting, grouping, cross-referencing, etc. Rather than have each computer application implement these from scratch, they can rely on the DBMS to supply such calculations.

Change and access logging

Often one wants to know who accessed what attributes, what was changed, and when it was changed. Logging services allow this by keeping a record of access occurrences and changes.

Automated optimization

If there are frequently occurring usage patterns or requests, some DBMS can adjust themselves to improve the speed of those interactions. In some cases the DBMS will merely provide tools to monitor performance, allowing a human expert to make the necessary adjustments after reviewing the statistics collected.

Meta-data repository

Metadata is data describing data. For example, a listing that describes what attributes are allowed to be in data sets is called "meta-information". The meta-data is also known as data about data.

Current trends

In 1998, database management was in need of new style databases to solve current database management problems. Researchers realized that the old trends of database management were becoming too complex and there was a need for automated configuration and management. Surajit Chaudhuri, Gerhard Weikum and Michael Stonebraker, were the pioneers that dramatically affected the thought of database management systems. They believed that database management needed a more modular approach and that there are so many specifications needs for various users. Since this new development process of database management we currently have endless possibilities. Database management is no longer limited to "monolithic entities". Many solutions have developed to satisfy individual needs of users. Development of numerous database options has created flexible solutions in database management. Today there are several ways database management has affected the technology world as we know it. Organizations demand for directory services has become an extreme necessity as organizations grow. Businesses are now able to use directory services that provide prompt searches for their company information. Mobile devices are not only able to store contact information of users but also have grown to bigger capabilities. Mobile technology is able to cache large information that is used for computers and is able to display it on smaller devices. Web searches have even been affected with database management. Search engine queries are able to locate data within the World Wide Web. Retailers have also benefited from the developments with data warehousing. These companies are able to record customer transactions made within their business. Online transactions have become tremendously popular with the e-business world. Consumers and businesses are able to make payments securely on company websites. None of these current developments would have been possible without the evolution of database management. Even with all the progress and current trends of database management, there will always be a need for new development as specifications and needs grow.

Relational Databases

The most common category of database is called "relational". Relational databases store information in tables (occasionally called "files"). Each table is composed of rows (a.k.a. "records") and columns (a.k.a. "fields"), just as you might find in a spreadsheet. Unlike spreadsheets, these tables are related to one another in very specific ways, and this relationship is defined by placing some of the column values from one table into columns of the related table. We won't trouble ourselves over the details of these relationships, but we do want to understand what they imply.

Relational Database Rules

There are a few rules laid down by the inventors of relational databases (a fellow by the name of E.F. Codd did most of the groundbreaking work) that should be followed by every database that you run into. Of course, for every rule, there are bound to be an exception or two.

- Every table in a database must have a unique name.
- Every column within a single table must have a unique name (but the same column name can be used in a different table).
- All of the values in a single column must be of the same datatype (e.g. numbers, strings of letters, dates, true/false).
- Each cell in a table must contain a single value. That is, no cell should contain a list of values.
- Each table must have one or more columns that uniquely identify each row in that table. This unique identifier is called a "primary key".
- A side-effect of the previous rule is that no two rows in a table may be identical.
- The order of columns in a table does not matter.
- The order of rows in a table does not matter.

There's much, much more theory underlying relational databases than just these few rules, but we can safely ignore the rest.

Relationships Between Tables

As mentioned earlier, tables are related to one another. Take, for instance, three tables named Student, Transcript, and Address (table names do not contain spaces). Each row in the Student table describes a single student enrolled in Yukon College, each row in the Transcript table describes a single student transcript, and each row of the Address table describes a single mailing address that might be used by a student, but perhaps by other people within the College as well.

These three tables will be related to one another in one of two ways:

- A one-to-one (sometimes written "1:1") relationship means that one row from table A can be related to, at most, one row from table B.
- A one-to-many ("1:M") relationship means that one row from table C and be related to one or more rows from table D. As it turns out, one-to-many relationships are *far* more common than the one-to-one variety.

Our college table relationships will then be as follows:

- There is a one-to-one relationship between Student and Address because each student can have at most one mailing address, and each mailing address corresponds to exactly one student.

- There is a one-to-many relationship between Student and Transcript because a student will receive many transcripts throughout their College program, and each transcript is issued to exactly one student.

Of course, you can think up scenarios where a student may have more than one mailing address, or where a single mailing address is used by more than one student, or even where a student doesn't have a mailing address (or the address is unknown). These sorts of issues plague the designers of relational databases.

An interesting offshoot of these types of relationships is that relational database theory doesn't recognize any numbers other than zero, one, or many (anywhere between zero and infinity).

NULL Values

Relational databases all make use of an interesting concept called a NULL value. NULLs can appear in certain columns and are usually interpreted to mean either "does not apply" or "unknown". For instance, if the Student table had a column called "Birthdate" and the student's birthdate was not known, this special NULL value would be used instead. NULLs can lead to unexpected behaviour if you're not used to them, so we'll try to give them a wide berth.

Microsoft Access

Microsoft Access is a relational database product shipped with some of the more expensive versions of Microsoft Office. It comes with an impressive list of features that make it relatively easy for non-programmers to create little database-enabled applications.

Access databases are stored in files that use the .mdb extension (for Microsoft DataBase). When the Access program is running, you will also see a temporary file with the same name as the database but with the extension .ldb. You can safely ignore that file.

One thing you'll notice when you use Access is that you do not save the file as you might in Word or Excel. Instead, every change made to the data in the database is saved immediately (although changes to the objects in Access sometimes require you to click the Save icon).

Access Objects

Access includes many types of "objects" in each database. These are listed on the left-hand side of Access's main window. We can explore all of them, but Tables are the most interesting to us.

Object	Description
Tables	These are the relational tables, containing columns and rows, and the data values in each cell.
Queries	Queries are like stored questions that you often wish to ask the database. This is where the true power of relational databases comes to light as you can retrieve a limitless variety of information stored in the tables.
Forms	Forms are the input screens used by a custom application that uses the underlying database.

Reports	Reports are just the results of Queries, but nicely formatted for printing. Reports are defined by people writing custom applications.
Pages	Pages or "Data Access Pages" as they're more formally known, are also written for custom applications and can be used to generate a web-based interface for the database.
Macros	Macros are little bits of programming that enable a person to quickly complex repetitive tasks.
Modules	Modules are made up of software code (written in a language called Visual Basic for Applications) used to implement the most complex parts of a custom application.

Viewing Table Relationships

Access can be used to diagram the relationships between tables. Choose **Relationships** from the **Tools** menu to view these relationships. Access uses **1** to show the "one" side of a one-to-one or a one-to-many relationship, and **“** (infinity, or the "sideways eight") to show the "many" side of a one-to-many relationship.

Column Datatypes

One of the relational database rules from above stated that each column must use a single "datatype" for its values. A datatype (sometimes called "domain") is simply a type of restriction on the sorts of values that can appear in a column. The most common datatypes in Access are shown below.

Datatype	Description
Text	Up to 255 characters of text, including: letters, punctuation, and numerical digits.
Memo	Up to 65,536 characters of text.
Number	Any sort of numerical values, including: integers, negative and positive numbers, and floating-point numbers (decimals).
Date/Time	Date and time values.
Currency	Monetary numerical values. The Currency datatype actually uses 4 decimal points to record each number (100ths of a penny) for accuracy. For technical reasons involving binary math, the Currency datatype is preferred over Number when dealing with money.
AutoNumber	The AutoNumber datatype is just like a Number column that stores integer values, but AutoNumber also "invents" these sequential numbers on its own, starting at 1 and increasing by 1 every time a new row is added to the table.
Yes/No	Columns using the Yes/No datatype can only represent one of two values (e.g. yes/no, true/false, on/off, 1/0, white/black).

Questions

(1) What are the different ways to create a word document? Explain each?

(2) What is print layout view?

(3) What is the difference web layout view and print layout view?

(4) What are headers and footers?

(5) How do we create a formula in a worksheet?

(6) Explain the types of formula in brief?

(7) What is a presentation? How is power point useful in presentations?

(8) Name the three different panes in normal view.

(9) What is database and name the database objects?

(10) What are the different ways of creating a table? Bring out their differences?

(11) What is DBMS? Differentiate b/w RDBMS & DBMS.

❐ ❐ ❐

Unit III

CHAPTER 4

Computer Network

BASIC OF NETWORKING

A computer network consists of a collection of computers, printers and other equipment that is connected together so that they can communicate with each other (see Advice Sheet 17 on the ICT Planning for schools pack). Fig. 1 gives an example of a network in a school comprising of a local area network or LAN connecting computers with each other, the internet, and various servers.

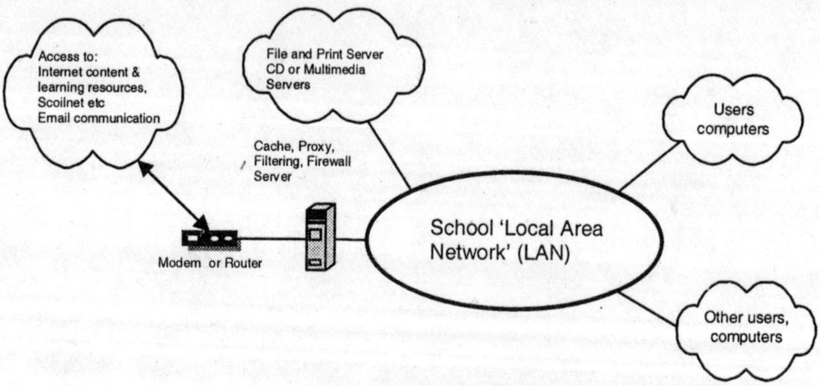

Fig. 1: Representation of Network in a school.

Broadly speaking, there are two types of network configuration, peer-to-peer networks and client/server networks.

Peer-to-peer networks are more commonly implemented where less then ten computers are involved and where strict security is not necessary. All computers have the same status, hence the term 'peer', and they communicate with each other on an equal footing. Files, such as word processing or spreadsheet documents, can be shared across the network and all the computers on the network can share devices, such as printers or scanners, which are connected to any one computer.

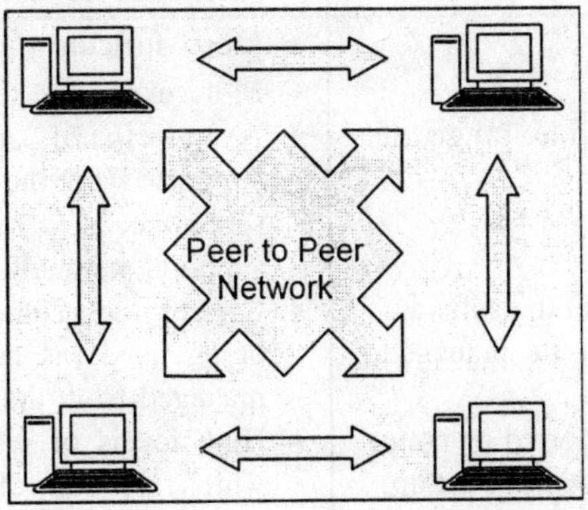

Fig. 2: Peer to Peer Networking

Client/server networks are more suitable for larger networks. A central computer, or 'server', acts as the storage location for files and applications shared on the network. Usually the server is a higher than average performance computer. The server also controls the network access of the other computers which are referred to as the 'client' computers. Typically, teachers and students in a school will use the client computers for their work and only the network administrator (usually a designated staff member) will have access rights to the server.

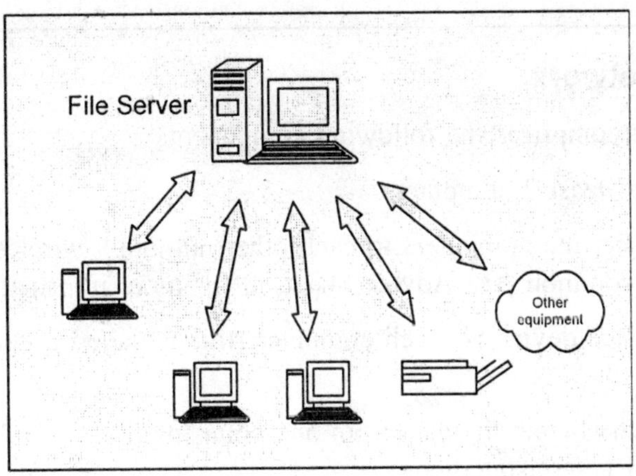

Fig. 3: Client - Server Networking

Table 1 provides a summary comparison between Peer-to-Peer and Client/Server Networks.

Peer-to-Peer Networks vs Client/Server Networks	
Peer-to-Peer Networks	**Client/Server Networks**
• Easy to set up	• More difficult to set up
• Less expensive to install	• More expensive to install
• Can be implemented on a wide range of operating systems	• A variety of operating systems can be supported on the client computers, but the server needs to run an operating system that supports networking
• More time consuming to maintain the software being used (as computers must be managed individually)	• Less time consuming to maintain the software being used (as most of the maintenance is managed from the server)
• Very low levels of security supported or none at all. These can be very cumbersome to set up, depending on the operating system being used	• High levels of security are supported, all of which are controlled from the server. Such measures prevent the deletion of essential system files or the changing of settings
• Ideal for networks with less than 10 computers	• No limit to the number of computers that can be supported by the network
• Does not require a server	• Requires a server running a server operating system
• Demands a moderate level of skill to administer the network	• Demands that the network administrator has a high level of IT skills with a good working knowledge of a server operating system

Components of a Network

A computer network comprises the following components:

- A minimum of at least 2 computers
- Cables that connect the computers to each other, although wireless communication is becoming more common (see Advice Sheet 20 for more information)
- A network interface device on each computer (this is called a network interface card or NIC)
- A 'Switch' used to switch the data from one point to another. Hubs are outdated and are little used for new installations.
- Network operating system software

Structured Cabling

The two most popular types of structured network cabling are **twisted-pair** (also known as **10BaseT**) and **thin coax** (also known as **10Base2**). 10BaseT cabling looks like ordinary telephone wire, except that it has 8 wires inside instead of 4. Thin coax looks like the copper coaxial cabling that's often used to connect a Video Recorder to a TV.

10 BaseT Cabling

When 10BaseT cabling is used, a strand of cabling is inserted between each computer and a hub. If you have 5 computers, you'll need 5 cables. Each cable cannot exceed 325 feet in length. Because the cables from all of the PCs converge at a common point, a 10BaseT network forms a **star configuration**.

Fig. 4a shows a Cat5e cable, with a standard connector, known as an RJ-45 connector.

Fig. 4b shows a standard Cat5e Wall Outlet socket which the cables are connected to.

Fig. 4c shows a standard Cat5e Patch Panel Wall Outlet socket which is used to terminate the cables from various points in the school bank to a central point.

Fig. 4d shows a wall mounted cabinet used to house and protect patch panel cables and connectors.

Fig. 4a: Cat5e Cable and a close up of RJ-45 connector

Fig. 4b: Cat5e Wall Outlets

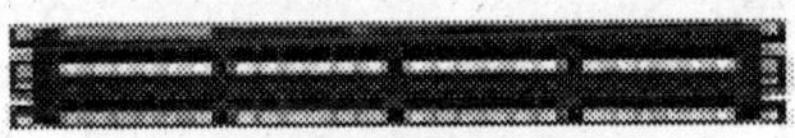

Fig. 4c: Cat5e Patch Panel

Fig. 4d: Wall Mounted Cabinet

10BaseT cabling is available in different grades or **categories**. Some grades, or "cats", are required for Fast Ethernet networks, while others are perfectly acceptable for standard 10Mbps networks—and less expensive, too. All new networks use a minimum of standard **unshielded twisted-pair (UTP) Category 5e** 10BaseT cabling because it offers a performance advantage over lower grades.

Network Interface Card (NIC)

A NIC (pronounced 'nick') is also known as a network card. It connects the computer to the cabling, which in turn links all of the computers on the network together. Each computer on a network must have a network card. Most modern network cards are 10/100 NICs and can operate at either 10Mbps or 100Mbps.

Only NICs supporting a minimum of 100Mbps should be used in new installations schools.

Computers with a wireless connection to a network also use a network card (see Advice Sheet 20 for more information on wireless networking).

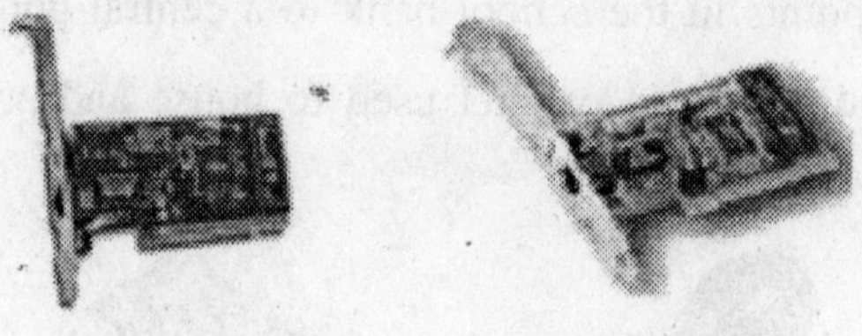

Fig. 5: Network Interface Cards (NICs)

Hub and Switch

A hub is a device used to connect a PC to the network. The function of a hub is to direct information around the network, facilitating communication between all connected devices. However in new installations switches should be used instead of hubs as they are more effective and provide better performance. A switch, is often termed as a 'smart hub'.

Switches and hubs are technologies or 'boxes' to which computers, printers, and other networking devices are connected. Switches are the more recent technology and the accepted way of building today's networks. With switching, each connection gets "dedicated bandwidth" and can operate at full speed. In contrast, a hub shares bandwidth across multiple connections such that activity from one PC or server can slow down the effective speed of other connections on the hub.

Now more affordable than ever, Dual-speed 10/100 autosensing switches are recommended for all school networks. Schools may want to consider upgrading any hub based networks with switches to improve network performance – i.e. speed of data on the network.

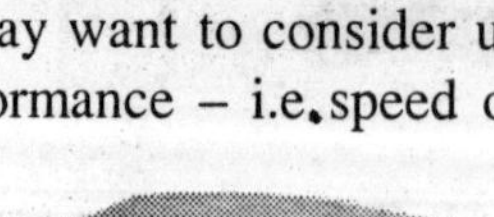

Fig. 6a: An 8 port Hub

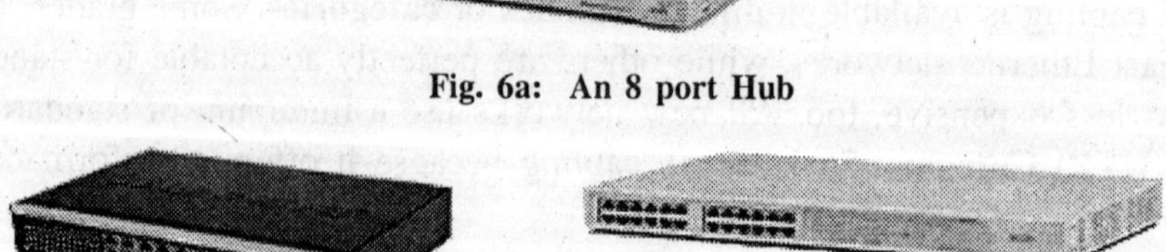

Fig. 6b: 2 Examples of 24 port Switches

Wireless Networks

The term 'wireless network' refers to two or more computers communicating using standard network rules or protocols, but without the use of cabling to connect the computers together. Instead, the computers use wireless radio signals to send information from one to the other. A wireless local area network (WLAN) consists of two key components: an access point (also called a base station) and a wireless card. Information can be transmitted between these two components as long as they are fairly close together (up to 100 metres indoors or 350 metres outdoors).

Fig. 7a: Wireless Access point or Wireless Basestation

Suppliers would need to visit the schools and conduct a site survey. This will determine the number of base stations you need and the best place(s) to locate them. A site survey will also enable each supplier to provide you with a detailed quote. It is important to contact a number of different suppliers as prices, equipment and opinions may vary. When the term 'wireless network' is used today, it usually refers to a wireless local area network or WLAN. A WLAN can be installed as the sole network in a school or building. However, it can also be used to extend an existing wired network to areas where wiring would be too difficult or too expensive to implement, or to areas located away from the main network or main building. Wireless networks can be configured to provide the same network functionality as wired networks, ranging from simple peer-to-peer configurations to large-scale networks accommodating hundreds of users.

Fig. 7b: Desktop PC Wireless LAN card

Fig. 7c: Laptop PC Wireless LAN card

What are the advantages and disadvantages of a Wireless LAN?

Wireless LANs have advantages and disadvantages when compared with wired LANs. A wireless LAN will make it simple to add or move workstations, and to install access points to provide connectivity in areas where it is difficult to lay cable. Temporary or semi-permanent buildings that are in range of an access point can be wirelessly connected to a LAN to give these buildings connectivity. Where computer labs are used in schools, the computers (laptops) could be put on a mobile cart and wheeled from classroom to classroom, provided they are in range of access points. Wired network points would be needed for each of the access points.

A WLAN has some specific advantages:

- It is easier to add or move workstations
- It is easier to provide connectivity in areas where it is difficult to lay cable
- Installation can be fast and easy and can eliminate the need to pull cable through walls and ceilings
- Access to the network can be from anywhere in the school within range of an access point
- Portable or semi-permanent buildings can be connected using a wireless LAN
- Where laptops are used, the 'computer suite' can be moved from classroom to classroom on mobile carts
- While the initial investment required for wireless LAN hardware can be similar to the cost of wired LAN hardware, installation expenses can be significantly lower
- Where a school is located on more than one site (such as on two sides of a road), it is possible with directional antennae, to avoid digging trenches under roads to connect the sites
- In historic buildings where traditional cabling would compromise the façade, a wireless LAN can avoid drilling holes in walls
- Long-term cost benefits can be found in dynamic environments requiring frequent moves and changes
- They allow the possibility of individual pupil allocation of wireless devices that move around the school with the pupil.

WLANs also have some disadvantages:

- As the number of computers using the network increases, the data transfer rate to each computer will decrease accordingly
- As standards change, it may be necessary to replace wireless cards and/or access points
- Lower wireless bandwidth means some applications such as video streaming will be more effective on a wired LAN
- Security is more difficult to guarantee, and requires configuration
- Devices will only operate at a limited distance from an access point, with the distance determined by the standard used and buildings and other obstacles between the access point and the user

- A wired LAN is most likely to be required to provide a backbone to the wireless LAN; a wireless LAN should be a supplement to a wired LAN and not a complete solution
- Long-term cost benefits are harder to achieve in static environments that require few moves and changes
- It is easier to make a wired network 'future proof' for high data transfer.

Wireless Network Components

There are certain parallels between the equipment used to build a WLAN and that used in a traditional wired LAN. Both networks require network interface cards or network adapter cards. A wireless LAN PC card, which contains an in-built antenna, is used to connect notebook computers to a wireless network. Usually, this is inserted into the relevant slot in the side of the notebook, but some may be internal to the notebook. Desktop computers can also connect to a wireless network if a wireless network card is inserted into one of its internal PCI slots.

In a wireless network, an 'access point' has a similar function to the hub in wired networks. It broadcasts and receives signals to and from the surrounding computers via their adapter card. It is also the point where a wireless network can be connected into an existing wired network.

The most obvious difference between wireless and wired networks, however, is that the latter uses some form of cable to connect computers together. A wireless network does not need cable to form a physical connection between computers.

Wireless Network Configurations

Wireless networks can be configured in an ad hoc/peer-to-peer arrangement or as a local area network.

Ad Hoc/Peer-to-Peer Configuration

This is the most basic wireless network configuration. It relies on the wireless network adapters installed in the computers that are communicating with each other. A computer within range of the transmitting computer can connect to it. However, if a number of computers are networked in this way, they must remain within range of each other. Even though this configuration has no real administration overhead, it should only be a consideration for very small installations.

Benefits and Educational Uses

The installation of cables is time consuming and expensive. The advantages of not doing so are apparent:

- the amount of work required and the time taken to complete it are significantly reduced.
- the network is accessible in places where wiring would have been difficult or impossible.
- with no cables linking computers together, cable-related faults and network downtime are minimised.

Where a wireless network is in place, teachers or students can have continuous access to the network, even as they move with their equipment from class to class.

The space over which a wireless network operates is not planar but spherical. Therefore, in a multi-level site, network access is available in rooms above or below the access point, without the need for additional infrastructure.

In a location within a school where network access is required occasionally, desktop computers fitted with wireless network cards can be placed on trolleys and moved from location to location. They can also be located in areas where group work is taking place. As they are connected to the network, documents and files can be shared, and access to the Internet is available, enhancing group project work.

As the range of the wireless network extends outside the building, students and teachers can use wireless devices to gather and record data outside, e.g., as part of a science experiment or individual performance data as part of a PE class.

Technical and Purchasing Considerations

Network interface cards for wireless networks are more expensive than their wired counterparts. The cost of the access points also has to be considered.

Wireless networks work at up top 54Mbps, whereas wired networks normally work at 100Mbps (Fast Ethernet). This data transmission rate is dependant on the number of users, the distance from the access point and the fabric of the building (metal structures in walls may have an impact). A wireless network will be noticeably slow when a group of users are transferring large files. This should be considered if multimedia applications are to be delivered over the network to a significant number of users.

As the range of the network may extend beyond the walls of the building, it can be accessed from outside. Consideration should be given to what security features the equipment provides to ensure that only valid users have access to the network and that data is protected.

Advantages of Networking schools

Speed.

Networks provide a very rapid method for sharing and transferring files. Without a network, files are shared by copying them to floppy disks, then carrying or sending the disks from one computer to another. This method of transferring files in this manner is very time-consuming.

Cost.

The network version of most software programs are available at considerable savings when compared to buying individually licensed copies. Besides monetary savings, sharing a program on a network allows for easier upgrading of the program. The changes have to be done only once, on the file server, instead of on all the individual workstations.

Centralized Software Management

One of the greatest benefits of installing a network at a school is the fact that all of the software can be loaded on one computer (the file server). This eliminates that need to spend time and energy installing updates and tracking files on independent computers throughout the building.

Resource Sharing.

Sharing resources is another area in which a network exceeds stand-alone computers. Most schools cannot afford enough laser printers, fax machines, modems, scanners, and CD-ROM players for each computer. However, if these or similar peripherals are added to a network, they can be shared by many users.

Flexible Access.

School networks allow students to access their files from computers throughout the school. Students can begin an assignment in their classroom, save part of it on a public access area of the network, then go to the media center after school to finish their work. Students can also work cooperatively through the network.

Security.

Files and programs on a network can be designated as "copy inhibit," so that you do not have to worry about illegal copying of programs. Also, passwords can be established for specific directories to restrict access to authorized users.

Main challenges of installing a School Network

Costs.

Although a network will generally save money over time, the initial costs can be substantial, and the installation may require the services of a technician.

Requires Administrative Time

Proper maintenance of a network requires considerable time and expertise. Many schools have installed a network, only to find that they did not budget for the necessary administrative support.

File Server May Fail

Although a file server is no more susceptible to failure than any other computer, when the files server "goes down," the entire network may come to a halt. When this happens, the entire school may lose access to necessary programs and files.

SHARING RESOURCES

The fundamental purpose of computer networks is to provide access to shared resources, most notably printers and data storage (both disk drives and tape drives). Local Area Networks (LANs) involve several primary components:

- Network interconnection (for example, copper wire, fiber optic cable, infrared, or radio).
- Network Interface Circuitry (NIC) in the individual personal computers, connected to the network. This circuitry may be part of the system motherboard or it may be on a separate plug-in card.
- The shared resources themselves, each with their own NIC connected to the network.
- Software on the individual personal computers that uses the NIC to access the shared resources. This software is typically arranged to present the appearance to the rest of the operating system that these resources are directly connected. In the jargon, "emulating local disks and printers."
- Software on the shared resource that coordinates with the software on the individual machines to provide access to the shared resources for the users of the multiple individual personal computers. This software is typically running on a computer system ("the server") to which the shared resources are directly attached, and is a multi-user operating system.

The most common case is for the server to be the same sort of personal computer hardware as the individual personal computers on the network (Intel or Macintosh). In this case, the operating system is called a "network operating system" to emphasize the difference from the single-user operating system of the personal computer. Novell is perhaps the most striking example of this approach.

Alternatives include a laser printer with a microprocessor-controlled NIC that runs software to manage the printer as a shared resource (e.g., the JetDirect cards for HP laser printers), and using a full-blown general-purpose multi-user server, with an operating system like VMS or unix. Windows NT Server is perhaps more accurately described as an example of this latter class.

NETWORK INTERCONNECTIONS

The network interconnection can be described in several ways:

- **Speed:** how many bits/sec can be transmitted through the network.
- **Topology:** Bus, Ring, or Star. Some networks provide a logical bus or ring topology with a physical star topology (Token Ring is, as you might suspect, a logical ring, but is a physical star; twisted-pair ("10baseT") ethernet is logically a bus, but is usually a physical star, although Farallon "etherwave" devices permit daisy-chaining).
- **Arbitration mechanism:** token-passing, collision-detection, guaranteed data rate, etc.

Network Protocols

The software on the individual personal computers and the software on the server have to cooperate with each other to provide access to the shared resources. This is done by designing the software to use an agreed set of conventions (a "protocol") that is standardized so that multiple vendors can provide interoperable systems.

There are several different network protocols in use, and they can co-exist on the same network interconnection if they are properly designed. For example, an ethernet network can simultaneously support general-purpose protocols, such as LAN Manager, DECnet, TCP/IP, AppleTalk, Novell, and at the same time special-purpose protocols, such as LAT and XNS.

Protocols specify, for example, that each data packet will have a header that includes agreed numbers of bits specifying

- the sender's address
- the intended recipient's address
- the type of packet
- the length of the data segment in the packet

and so on. The protocols also specify the circumstances, if any, under which the recipient is to send an acknowledgment of receipt of the data packet. Some protocols include a sequence number that permits the recipient to re-assemble a longer message that has been split into parts, even if those parts are not delivered in the same order that they were sent. (This can easily happen in an overloaded local-area network, or in a complex wide-area network that includes alternative pathways connecting the two machines.)

NETWORK INFRASTRUCTURE

In addition to the servers and their clients, a network will usually include other electronic devices connected to the network signal cabling.

- Some of this infrastructure is concerned with moving the data through the network, from the source machine to its destination.
  - o Hubs
  - o Routers
  - o Gateways
  - o Bridges
  - o Switches
  - o Terminal Servers
- Some of this infrastructure is concerned with maintaining dedicated databases of network information and providing that information to the clients and servers so that they can communicate.
  - o Domain Name Server
  - o DHCP Server
  - o WINS Server to support Microsoft Network Clients (like DNS)

ISO-OSI 7-LAYER NETWORK ARCHITECTURE

This lecture introduces the ISO-OSI layered architecture of Networks. According to the ISO standards, networks have been divided into 7 layers depending on the complexity of the fucntionality each of these layers provide. The detailed description of each of these layers is given in the notes below. We will first list the layers as defined by the standard in the increasing order of function complexity:

1. Physical Layer
2. Data Link Layer
3. Network Layer
4. Transport Layer
5. Session Layer
6. Presentation Layer
7. Application Layer

Physical Layer

This layer is the lowest layer in the OSI model. It helps in the transmission of data between two machines that are communicating through a physical medium, which can be optical fibres,copper wire or wireless etc. The following are the main functions of the physical layer:

1. **Hardware Specification:** The details of the physical cables, network interface cards, wireless radios, etc are a part of this layer.

These electronics may be provided with their own front panel with control switches or keypad, or they may have dedicated connections for a dumb terminal to be used as a control console. More and more, however, they are designed for remote control, through the network. The standard protocol for accomplishing remote management of network infrastructure is called SNMP, "Simple Network Management Protocol."

Coaxial Cable	Hybrid Cable	Wireless Card	Network Card
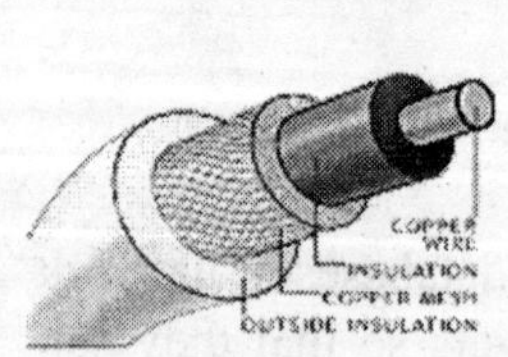			

2. **Encoding and Signalling:** How are the bits encoded in the medium is also decided by this layer. For example, on the copper wire medium, we can use different voltage levels for a certain time interval to represent '0' and '1'. We may use +5mV for 1nsec to represent '1' and -5mV for 1nsec to represent '0'. All the issues of modulation is dealt within this layer. For e.g.,

we may use Binary phase shift keying for the representation of '1' and '0' rather than using different volatage levels if we have to transfer in RF waves.

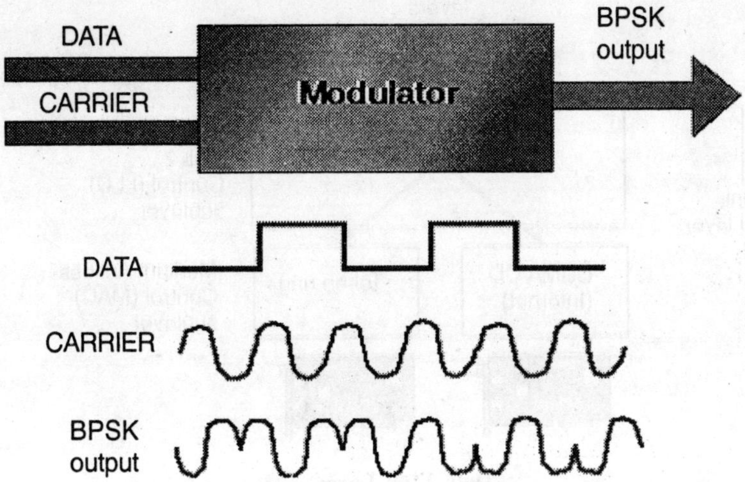

Binary Phase Shift Keying

3. Data Transmission and Reception: The transfer of each bit of data is the responsibility of this layer. This layer assures the transmissoin of each bit with a *high probability*. The transmission of the bits is not completely reliable as there is no error correction in this layer.

4. Topology and Network Design: The network design is the integral part of the physical layer. Which part of the network is the router going to be placed, where the switches will be used, where we will put the hubs, how many machines is each switch going to handle, what server is going to be placed where and many such concerns are to be taken care of by the physical layer. The various kinds of netopologies that we decide to use may be ring, bus, star or a hybrid of these topologies depending on our requirements.

DATA LINK LAYER

This layer provides reliable transmission of a packet by using the services of the physical layer which transmits bits over the medium in an unrcliable fashion. This layer is concerned with:

1. **Framing :** Breaking input data into frames (typically a few hundred bytes) and caring about the frame boundaries and the size of each frame.

2. **Acknowledgement :** Sent by the receiving end to inform the source that the frame was received without any error.

3. **Sequence Numbering :** To acknowledge which frame was received.

4. **Error Detection :** The frames may be damaged, lost or duplicated leading to errors.The error control is on **link to link** basis.

5. **Retransmission :** The packet is retransmitted if the source fails to receive acknowledgment.

6. **Flow Control :** Necessary for a fast transmitter to keep pace with a slow receiver.

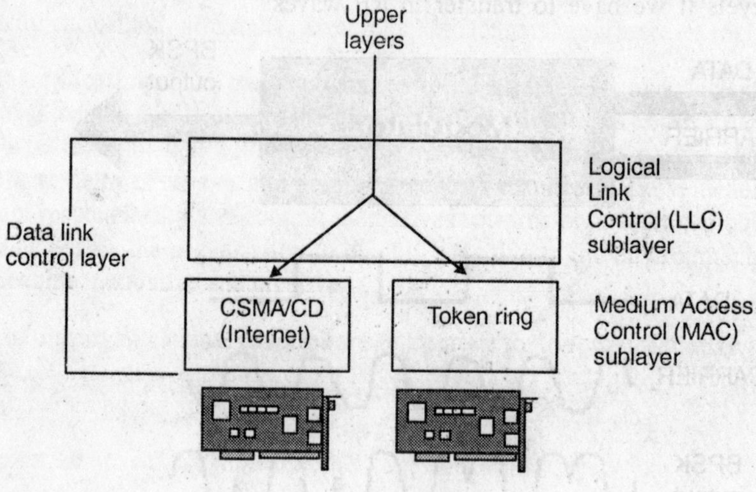

Data Link Layer

Network Layer

Its basic functions are routing and congestion control.

Routing: This deals with determining how packets will be routed (transferred) from source to destination. It can be of three types :

- **Static :** Routes are based on static tables that are "wired into" the network and are rarely changed.
- **Dynamic :** All packets of one application can follow different routes depending upon the topology of the network, the shortest path and the current network load.
- **Semi-Dynamic :** A route is chosen at the start of each conversation and then all the packets of the application follow the same route.

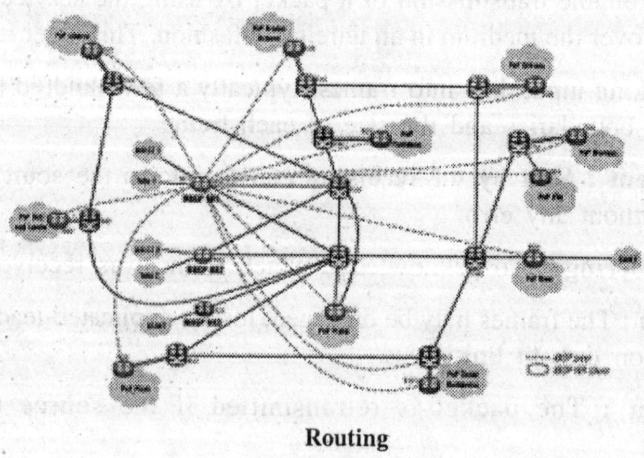

Routing

The services provided by the network can be of two types:

- **Connection less service:** Each packet of an application is treated as an independent entity. On each packet of the application the destination address is provided and the packet is routed.
- **Connection oriented service:** Here, first a connection is established and then all packets of the application follow the same route. To understand the above concept, we can also draw an analogy from the real life. Connection oriented service is modeled after the telephone system. All voice packets go on the same path after the connection is established till the connection is hung up. It acts like a tube; the sender pushes the objects in at one end and the receiver takes them out in the same order at the other end. Connection less service is modeled after the postal system. Each letter carries the destination address and is routed independent of all the others. Here, it is possible that the letter sent first is delayed so that the second letter reaches the destination before the first letter.

Congestion Control: A router can be connected to 4-5 networks. If all the networks send packet at the same time with maximum rate possible then the router may not be able to handle all the packets and may drop some/all packets. In this context the dropping of the packets should be minimized and the source whose packet was dropped should be informed. The control of such congestion is also a function of the network layer. Other issues related with this layer are transmitting time, delays, jittering.

Inter-Networking: Inter-Networks are multiple networks that are connected in such a way that they act as one large network, connecting multiple office or department networks. Inter-networks are connected by networking hardware such as routers, switches, and bridges.Inter-networking is a solution born of three networking problems: isolated LANs, duplication of resources, and the lack of a centralized network management system. With connected LANs, companies no longer have to duplicate programs or resources on each network. This in turn gives way to managing the network from one central location instead of trying to manage each separate LAN. We should be able to transmit any packet from one network to any other network even if they follow different protocols or use different addressing modes.

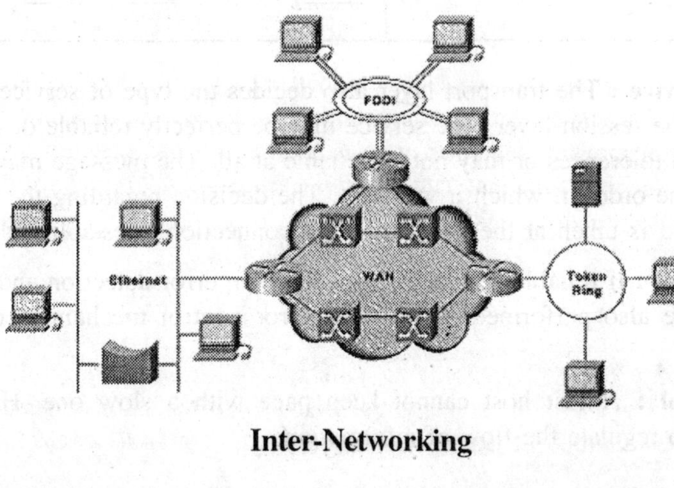

Inter-Networking

Network Layer **does not** guarantee that the packet will reach its intended destination. There are no reliability guarantees.

Transport Layer

Its functions are:

- **Multiplexing/Demultiplexing :** Normally the transport layer will create distinct network connection for each transport connection required by the session layer. The transport layer may either create multiple network connections (to improve throughput) or it may multiplex several transport connections onto the same network connection (because creating and maintaining networks may be expensive). In the latter case, demultiplexing will be required at the receiving end. A point to note here is that communication is always carried out between two processes and not between two machines. This is also known as process-to-process communication.

- **Fragmentation and Re-assembly :** The data accepted by the transport layer from the session layer is split up into smaller units (fragmentation) if needed and then passed to the network layer. Correspondingly, the data provided by the network layer to the transport layer on the receiving side is re-assembled.

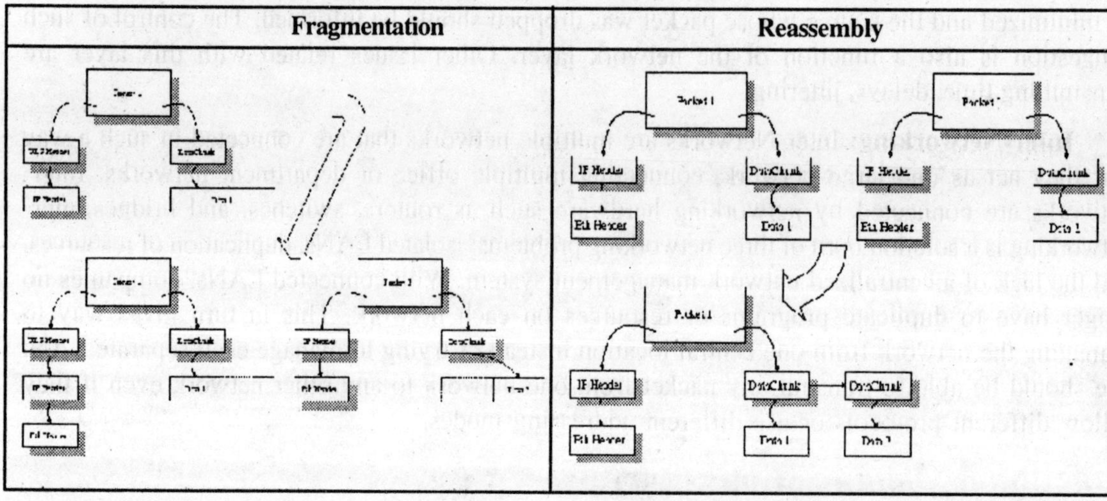

- **Types of service :** The transport layer also decides the type of service that should be provided to the session layer. The service may be perfectly reliable or may be reliable within certain tolerances or may not be reliable at all. The message may or may not be received in the order in which it was sent. The decision regarding the type of service to be provided is taken at the time when the connection is established.

- **Error Control :** If reliable service is provided then error detection and error recovery operations are also performed. It provides error control mechanism on **end to end** basis.

- **Flow Control :** A fast host cannot keep pace with a slow one. Hence, this is a mechanism to regulate the flow of information.

- **Connection Establishment/Release:** The transport layer also establishes and releases the connection across the network. This requires some sort of naming mechanism so that a process on one machine can indicate with whom it wants to communicate.

Session Layer

It deals with the concept of **Sessions** i.e. when a user logins to a remote server he should be **authenticated** before getting access to the files and application programs. Another job of session layer is to establish and maintain sessions. If during the transfer of data between two machines the session breaks down, it is the session layer which re-establishes the connection. It also ensures that the data transfer starts from where it breaks keeping it transparent to the end user. e.g., In case of a session with a database server, this layer introduces **check points** at various places so that in case the connection is broken and re-established, the transition running on the database is not lost even if the user has not committed. This activity is called **Synchronization**. Another function of this layer is **Dialogue Control** which determines whose turn is it to speak in a session. It is useful in video conferencing.

Presentation Layer

This layer is concerned with the syntax and semantics of the information transmitted. In order to make it possible for computers with different data representations to communicate, data structures to be exchanged can be defined in abstract way alongwith standard encoding. It also manages these abstract data structures and allows higher level of data structures to be defined an exchange. It encodes the data in standard agreed way(network format). Suppose there are two machines A and B one follows 'Big Endian' and other 'Little Endian' for data representation. This layer ensures that the data transmitted by one gets converted in the form compatibale to other machine. This layer is concerned with the syntax and semantics of the information transmitted. In order to make it possible for computers with different data representations to communicate, data structures to be exchanged can be defined in an abstract way alongwith standard encoding. It also manages these abstract data structures and allows higher level of data structures to be defined in exchange. Other functions include compression, encryption etc.

Application Layer

The seventh layer contains the application protocols with which the user gains access to the network. The choice of which specific protocols and their associated functions are to be used at the application level is up to the individual user. Thus the boundary between the presentation layer and the application layer represents a separation of the protocols imposed by the network designers from those being selected and implemented by the network users. For example commonly used protocols are HTTP(for web browsing), FTP(for file transfer) etc.

Network Layers as in Practice

In most of the networks today, we do not follow the OSI model of seven layers. What is actually implemented is as follows. The functionality of Application layer and Presentation layer is merged into one and is called as the Application Layer. Functionalities of Session Layer is not implemented in most networks today. Also, the Data Link layer is split theoretically into **MAC (Medium Access Control) Layer** and **LLC (Link Layer Control)**. But again in practice, the LLC layer is not implemented by most networks. So as of today, the network architecture is of 5 layers only.

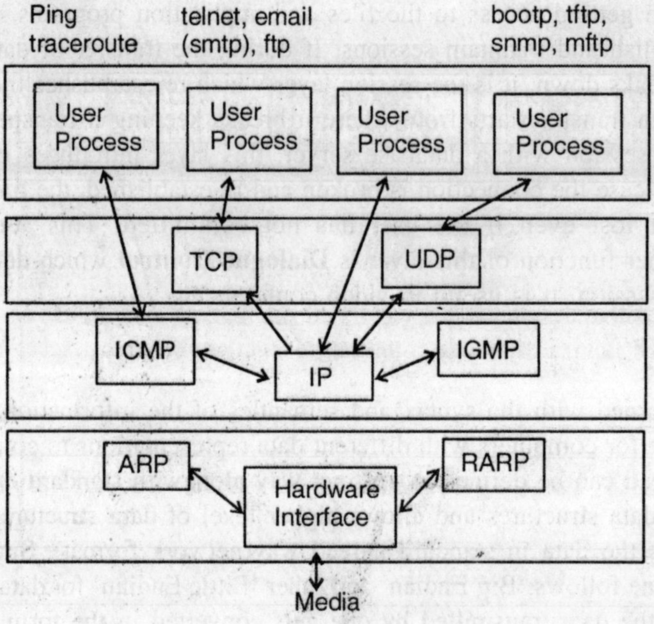

Network Layers in Internet Today

PHYSICAL LAYER

Physical layer is concerned with transmitting raw bits over a communication channel. The design issues have to do with making sure that when one side sends a bit, it is recieved by the other side as 1 bit and not as 0 bit. In physical layer we deal with the communication medium used for transmission.

Types of Medium

Medium can be classified into 2 categories:

1. **Guided Media :** Guided media means that signals are guided by the presence of physical media i.e. signals are under control and remain in the physical wire. For e.g., copper wire.
2. **Unguided Media :** Unguided Media means that there is no physical path for the signal to propogate. Unguided media are essentially electro-magnetic waves. There is no control on flow of signal. For eg. radio waves.

Communication Links

In a nework, nodes are connected through links. The communication through links can be classified as:

1. **Simplex :** Communication can take place only in one direction. e.g., T.V broadcasting.
2. **Half-duplex :** Communication can take place in one direction at a time. Suppose node A and B are connected then half-duplex communication means that at a time data can flow from A to B or from B to A but not simultaneously. e.g., two persons talking to each other such that when one speaks the other listens and vice versa.
3. **Full-duplex :** Communication can take place simultaneously in both directions. e.g., A discussion in a group without discipline.

Links can be further classified as:

1. **Point to Point :** In this communication only two nodes are connected to each other. When a node sends a packet then it can be recieved only by the node on the other side and no one else.
2. **Multipoint** : It is a kind of sharing communication, in which signal can be recieved by all nodes. This is also called broadcast.

Generally two kind of problems are associated in transmission of signals:

1. **Attenuation :** When a signal transmitts in a network then the quality of signal degrades as the signal travels longer distances in the wire. This is called attenuation. To improve quality of signal, amplifiers are used at regular distances.
2. **Noise :** In a communication channel many signals transmit simultaneously. Certain random signals are also present in the medium. Due to interference of these signals our signal gets disrupted a bit.

Bandwidth

Bandwidth simply means how many bits can be transmitted per second in the communication channel. In technical terms it indicates the width of frequency spectrum.

Transmission Media

Guided Transmission Media

In Guided transmission media generally two kind of materials are used:

1. Copper

o Coaxial Cable

o Twisted Pair

2. Optical Fiber

1. Coaxial Cable: Coaxial cable consists of an inner conductor and an outer conductor which are seperated by an insulator. The inner conductor is usually copper. The outer conductor is covered by a plastic jacket. It is named coaxial because the two conductors are coaxial. Typical diameter of coaxial cable lies between 0.4 inch to 1 inch. The most application of coaxial cable is cable T.V. The coaxial cable has high bandwidth, attenuation is less.

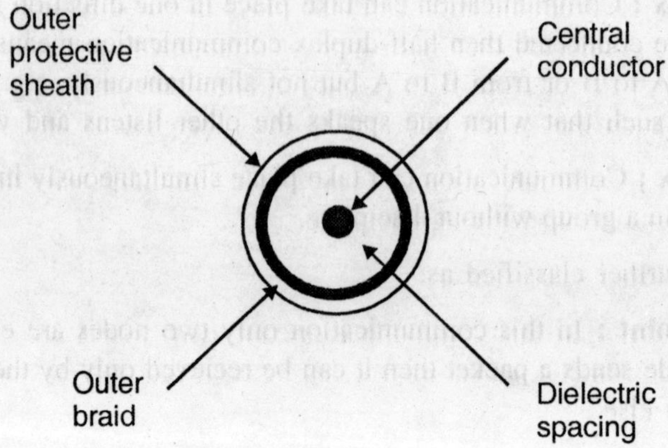

2. Twisted Pair: A Twisted pair consists of two insulated copper wires, typically 1mm thick. The wires are twisted together in a helical form. The purpose of twisting is to reduce cross talk interference between several pairs. Twisted Pair is much cheaper then coaxial cable but it is susceptible to noise and electromagnetic interference and attenuation is large.

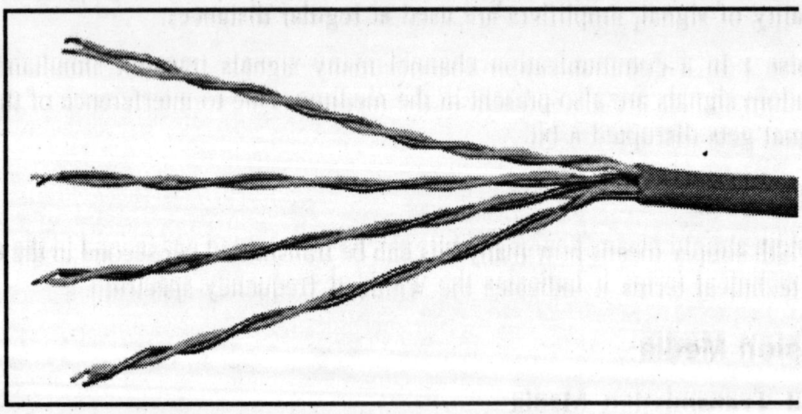

Twisted Pair can be further classified into two categories:

Unshielded twisted pair: In this no insulation is provided, hence they are susceptible to interference.

Shielded twisted pair: In this a protective thick insulation is provided but shielded twisted pair is expensive and not commonly used.

The most common application of twisted pair is the telephone system. Nearly all telephones are connected to the telephone company office by a twisted pair. Twisted pair can run several kilometers without amplification, but for longer distances repeaters are needed. Twisted pairs can be used for both analog and digital transmission. The bandwidth depends on the thickness of wire and the distance travelled. Twisted pairs are generally limited in distance, bandwidth and data rate.

1. Optical Fiber: In optical fiber light is used to send data. In general terms prescence of light is taken as bit 1 and its absence as bit 0. Optical fiber consists of inner core of either glass or plastic. Core is surrounded by cladding of the same material but of different refrective index. This cladding is surrounded by a plastic jacket which prevents optical fiber from electromagnetic interferrence and harshy environments. It uses the principle of total internal reflection to transfer data over optical fibers. Optical fiber is much better in bandwidth as compared to copper wire, since there is hardly any attenuation or electromagnetic interference in optical wires. Hence there is less requirement to improve quality of signal, in long distance transmission. Disadvantage of optical fiber is that end points are fairly expensive. (e.g., switches)

Differences between different kinds of optical fibers:

1. Depending on material
   - Made of glass
   - Made of plastic
2. Depending on radius
   - Thin optical fiber
   - Thick optical fiber
3. Depending on light source
   - LED (for low bandwidth)
   - Injection lased diode (for high bandwidth)

Wireless Transmission

1. Radio: Radio is a general term that is used for any kind of frequency. But higher frequencies are usually termed as microwave and the lower frequency band comes under radio frequency. There are many applications of radio. For e.g., cordless keyboard, wireless LAN, wireless ethernet. but it is limited in range to only a few hundred meters. Depending on frequency radio offers different bandwidths.

2. Terrestrial microwave: In terrestrial microwave two antennae are used for communication. A focused beam emerges from an antenna and is recieved by the other antenna, provided that both antennae should be facing each other with no obstacle in between. For this reason antennae are situated on high towers. Due to curvature of earth terristrial microwave can be used for long distance communication with high bandwidth. Telecom department is also using this for long distance communication. An advantage of wireless communication is that it is not required to lay down wires in the city, hence no permissions are required.

3. **Satellite communication:** Satellite acts as a switch in sky. On earth VSAT(Very Small Aperture Terminal) are used to transmit and recieve data from satellite. Generally one station on earth transmitts signal to satellite and it is recieved by many stations on earth. Satellite communication is generally used in those places where it is very difficult to obtain line of sight i.e. in highly irregular terrestrial regions. In terms of noise, wireless media is not as good as the wired media. There are frequency band in wireless communication and two stations should not be allowed to transmit simultaneously in a frequency band. The most promising advantage of satellite is broadcasting. If satellites are used for point to point communication then they are expensive as compared to wired media.

DATA ENCODING

Digital data to analog signals:

A modem (modulator-demodulator) converts digital data to analog signal. There are 3 ways to modulate a digital signal on an analog carrier signal.

1. **Amplitude shift keying (ASK):** is a form of modulation which represents digital data as variations in the amplitude of a carrier wave. Two different amplitudes of carrier frequency represent '0', '1'.

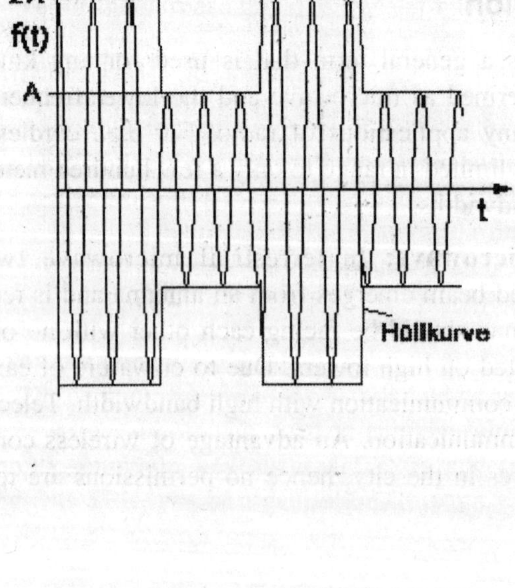

2. **Frequency shift keying (FSK):** In Frequency Shift Keying, the change in frequency define different digits. Two different frequencies near carrier frequency represent '0', '1'.

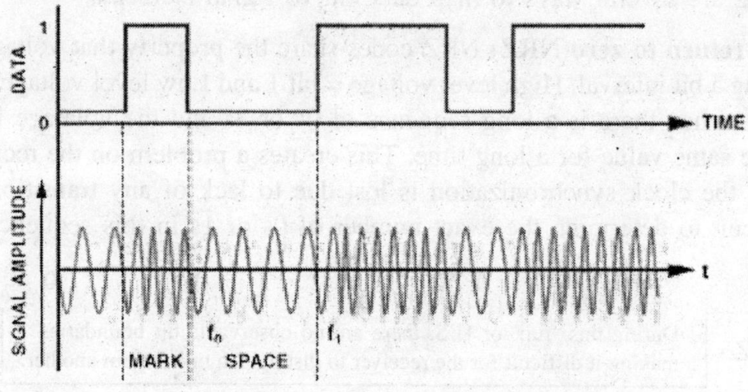

3. **Phase shift keying (PSK):** The phase of the carrier is discretely varied in relation either to a reference phase or to the phase of the immediately preceding signal element, in accordance with data being transmitted. Phase of carrier signal is shifted to represent '0', '1'.

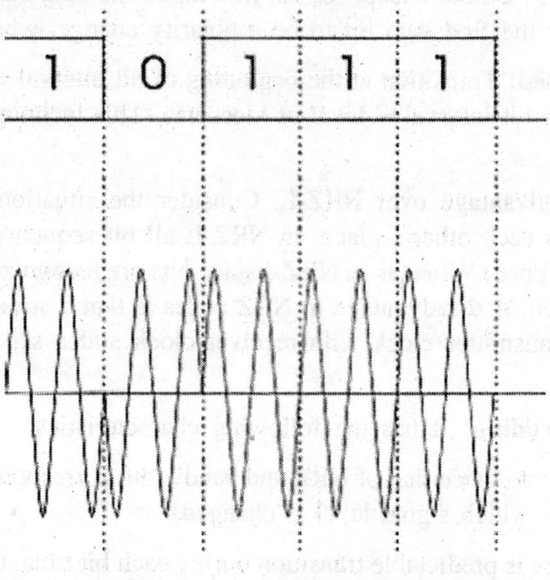

Digital data to digital signals:

A digital signal is a sequence of discrete, discontinuous voltage pulse. Each pulse is a signal element. Encoding scheme is an important factor in how successfully the receiver interprets the incoming signal.

Encoding Techniques

Following are several ways to map data bits to signal elements.

- **Non return to zero(NRZ)** NRZ codes share the property that voltage level is constant during a bit interval. High level voltage = bit 1 and Low level voltage = bit 0. A problem arises when there is a long sequence of 0s or 1s and the volatage level is maintained at the same value for a long time. This creates a problem on the recieving end because now, the clock synchronization is lost due to lack of any transitions and hence, it is difficult to determine the exact number of 0s or 1s in this sequence.

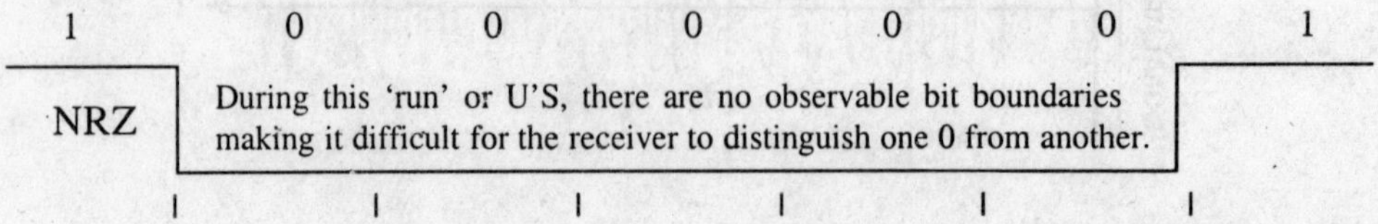

The two variations are as follows:

1. **NRZ-Level:** In NRZ-L encoding, the polarity of the signal changes only when the incoming signal changes from a 1 to a 0 or from a 0 to a 1. NRZ-L method looks just like the NRZ method, except for the first input one data bit. This is because NRZ does not consider the first data bit to be a polarity change, where NRZ-L does.

2. **NRZ-Inverted:** Transition at the beginning of bit interval = bit 1 and No Transition at beginning of bit interval = bit 0 or vicecersa. This technique is known as differential encoding.

NRZ-I has an advantage over NRZ-L. Consider the situation when two data wires are wrongly connected in each other's place. In NRZ-L all bit sequences will get reversed (B'coz voltage levels get swapped).Whereas in NRZ-I since bits are recognized by transition the bits will be correctly interpreted. A disadvantage in NRZ codes is that a string of 0's or 1's will prevent synchronization of transmitter clock with receiver clock and a separate clock line need to be provided.

- **Biphase encoding:** It has the following characteristics:

1. Modulation rate twice that of NRZ and bandwidth correspondingly greater. (Modulation is the rate at which signal level is changed).

2. Because there is predictable transition during each bit time, the receiver can synchronize on that transition i.e. clock is extracted from the signal itself.

3. Since there can be transition at the beginning as well as in the middle of the bit interval the clock operates at twice the data transfer rate.

Types of Encoding —>

- o **Biphase-manchester:** Transition from high to low in middle of interval = 1 and transition from low to high in middle of interval = 0

o **Differential-manchester:** Always a transition in middle of interval. No transition at beginning of interval = 1 and Transition at beginning of interval = 0

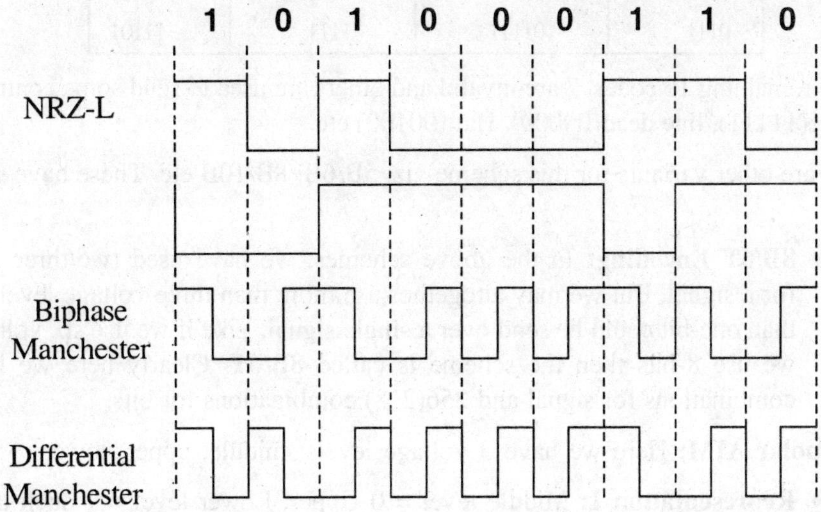

o **4B/5B Encoding:** In Manchester encoding scheme, there is a transition after every bit. It means that we must have clocks with double the speed to send same amount of data as in NRZ encodings. In other words, we may say that only 50% of the data is sent. This performance factor can be significantly improved if we use a better encoding scheme. This scheme may have a transition after fixed number of bits instead of every other bit. Like if we have a transition after every four bits, then we will be sending 80% data of actual capacity. This is a significant improvement in the performance.

This scheme is known as **4B/5B**. So here we convert 4-bits to 5-bits, ensuring at least one transition in them. The basic idea here is that 5-bit code selected must have:

- one leading 0
- no more than two trailing 0s

Thus it is ensured that we can never have more than three consecutive 0s. Now these 5-bit codes are transmitted using NRZ-I coding thus problem of consecutive 1s is solved.

The exact transformation is as follows:

4-bit Data	5-bit code	4-bit Data	5-bit code
0000	11110	1000	10010
0001	01001	1001	10011
0010	10100	1010	10110
0011	10101	1011	10111

0100	01010	1100	11010
0101	01011	1101	11011
0110	01110	1110	11100
0111	01111	1111	11101

Of the remaining 16 codes, 7 are invalid and others are used to send some control information like line idle(11111), line dead(00000), Halt(00100) etc.

There are other variants for this scheme viz. 5B/6B, 8B/10B etc. These have self suggesting names.

- **8B/6T Encoding:** In the above schemes, we have used two/three voltage levels for a signal. But we may altogether use more than three voltage levels so that more than one-bit could be send over a single signal. Like if we use six voltage levels and we use 8-bits then the scheme is called **8B/6T**. Clearly here we have 729(3^6) combinations for signal and 256(2^8) combinations for bits.

Bipolar AIM: Here we have 3 voltage levels: middle, upper, lower

- **Representation 1:** Middle level = 0 Upper, Lower level = 1 such that successive 1's will be represented alternately on upper and lower levels.
- **Representation 2 (pseudoternary):** Middle level = 1 Upper, Lower level = 0

Analog data to digital signal:

The process is called digitization. Sampling frequency must be at least twice that of highest frequency present in the the signal so that it may be fairly regenerated. Quantization - Max. and Min values of amplitude in the sample are noted. Depending on number of bits (say n) we use we divide the interval (min,max) into 2(^n) number of levels. The amplitude is then approximated to the nearest level by a 'n' bit integer. The digital signal thus consists of blocks of n bits.On reception the process is reversed to produce analog signal. But a lot of data can be lost if fewer bits are used or sampling frequency not so high.

- **Pulse code modulation(PCM):** Here intervals are equally spaced. 8 bit PCB uses 256 different levels of amplitude. In non-linear encoding levels may be unequally spaced.
- **Delta Modulation(DM):** Since successive samples do not differ very much we send the differences between previous and present sample. It requires fewer bits than in PCM.

Digital Data Communication Techniques

For two devices linked by a transmission medium to exchange data, a high degree of co-operation is required. Typically data is transmitted one bit at a time. The timing (rate, duration,spacing) of these bits must be same for transmitter and receiver. There are two options for transmission of bits:

1. **Parallel** All bits of a byte are transferred simultaneously on separate parallel wires. Synchronization between multiple bits is required which becomes difficult over large distance. Gives large band width but expensive. Practical only for devices close to each other.

2. **Serial** Bits transferred serially one after other.Gives less bandwidth but cheaper. Suitable for transmission over long distances.

Transmission Techniques:

1. **Asynchronous:** Small blocks of bits(generally bytes) are sent at a time without any time relation between consecutive bytes. when no transmission occurs a default state is maintained corresponding to bit 1. Due to arbitrary delay between consecutive bytes,the time occurrences of the clock pulses at the receiving end need to be synchronized for each byte. This is achieved by providing 2 extra bits start and stop.

Start bit: It is prefixed to each byte and equals 0. Thus it ensures a transition from 1 to 0 at onset of transmission of byte. The leading edge of start bit is used as a reference for generating clock pulses at required sampling instants. Thus each onset of a byte results in resynchronization of receiver clock.

Stop bit: To ensure that transition from 1 to 0 is always present at beginning of a byte it is necessary that default state be 1. But there may be two bytes one immediately following the other and if last bit of first byte is 0, transition from 1 to 0 will not occur. Therefore a stop bit is suffixed to each byte equaling 1. It's duration is usually 1,1.5,2 bits.

Asynchronous transmission is simple and cheap but requires an overhead of 3 bits i.e. for 7 bit code 2 (start, stop bits)+1 parity bit implying 30% overhead.However % can be reduced by sending larger blocks of data but then timing errors between receiver and sender can not be tolerated beyond [50/no. of bits in block] % (assuming sampling is done at middle of bit interval). It will not only result in incorrect sampling but also misaligned bit count i.e. a data bit can be mistaken for stop bit if receiver's clock is faster.

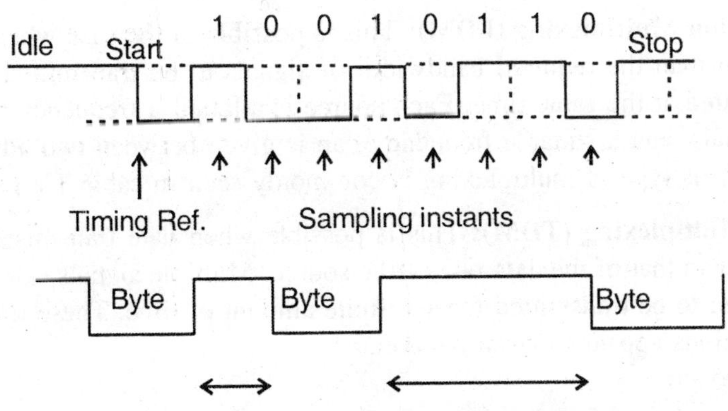

2. **Synchronous** - Larger blocks of bits are successfully transmitted. Blocks of data are either treated as sequence of bits or bytes. To prevent timing drift, clocks at two ends need to be synchronized. This can done in two ways:

   1. Provide a separate clock line between receiver and transmitter. **OR**

   2. Clocking information is embedded in data signal i.e. biphase coding for digital signals.

Still another level of synchronization is required so that receiver determines beginning or end of block of data. Hence each block begins with a start code and ends with a stop code. These are in general same known as flag that is unique sequence of fixed no. of bits. In addition some control characters encompass data within these flags. **Data+control information** is called a frame. Since any arbitrary bit pattern can be transmitted there is no assurance that bit pattern for flag will not appear inside the frame thus destroying frame level synchronization. So to avoid this we use bit stuffing

Bit Stuffing: Suppose our flag bits are 01111110 (six 1's). So the transmitter will always insert an extra 0 bit after each occurrence of five 1's (except for flags). After detecting a starting flag the receiver monitors the bit stream. If pattern of five 1's appear, the sixth is examined and if it is 0 it is deleted else if it is 1 and next is 0, the combination is accepted as a flag. Similarly byte stuffing is used for byte oriented transmission. Here we use an escape sequence to prefix a byte similar to flag and 2 escape sequences if byte is itself a escape sequence.

Start code	control chars.	DATA	control chars.	Stop code

Multiplexing

When two communicating nodes are connected through a media, it generally happens that bandwidth of media is several times greater than that of the communicating nodes. Transfer of a single signal at a time is both slow and expensive. The whole capacity of the link is not being utilized in this case. This link can be further exploited by sending several signals combined into one. This combining of signals into one is called multiplexing.

Frequency Division Multiplexing (FDM): This is possible in the case where transmission media has a bandwidth than the required bandwidth of signals to be transmitted. A number of signals can be transmitted at the same time. Each source is allotted a frequency range in which it can transfer it's signals, and a suitable frequency gap is given between two adjescent signals to avoid overlapping. This type of multiplexing is commonly seen in cable TV networks.

Time Division Multiplexing (TDM): This is possible when data transmission rate of the media is much higher than that of the data rate of the source. Multiple signals can be transmitted if each signal is allowed to be transmitted for a definite amount of time. These time slots are so small that all transmissions appear to be in parallel.

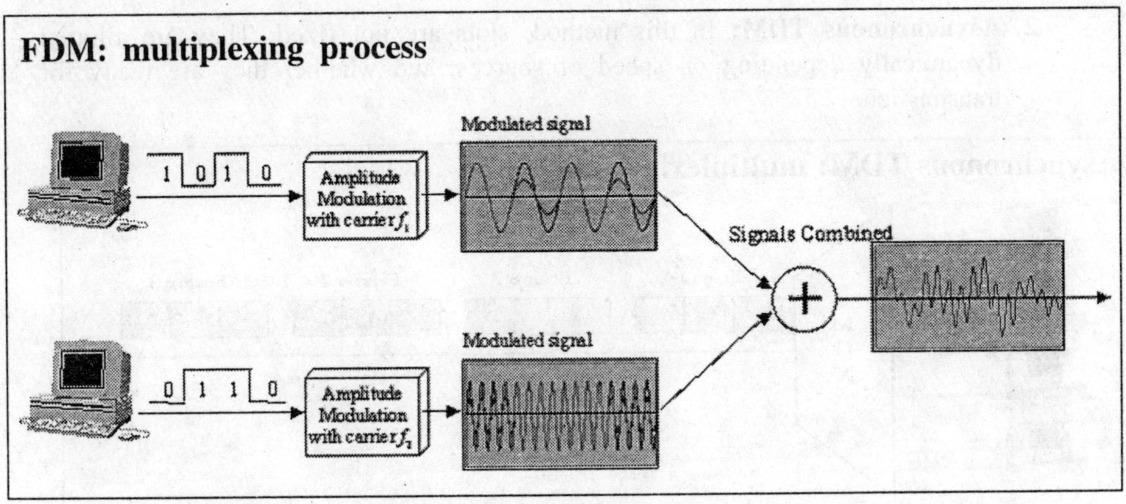

1. **Synchronous TDM:** Time slots are preassigned and are fixed. Each source is given it's time slot at every turn due to it. This turn may be once per cycle, or several turns per cycle, if it has a high data transfer rate or may be once in a no. of cycles if it is slow. This slot is given even if the source is not ready with data. So this slot is transmitted empty.

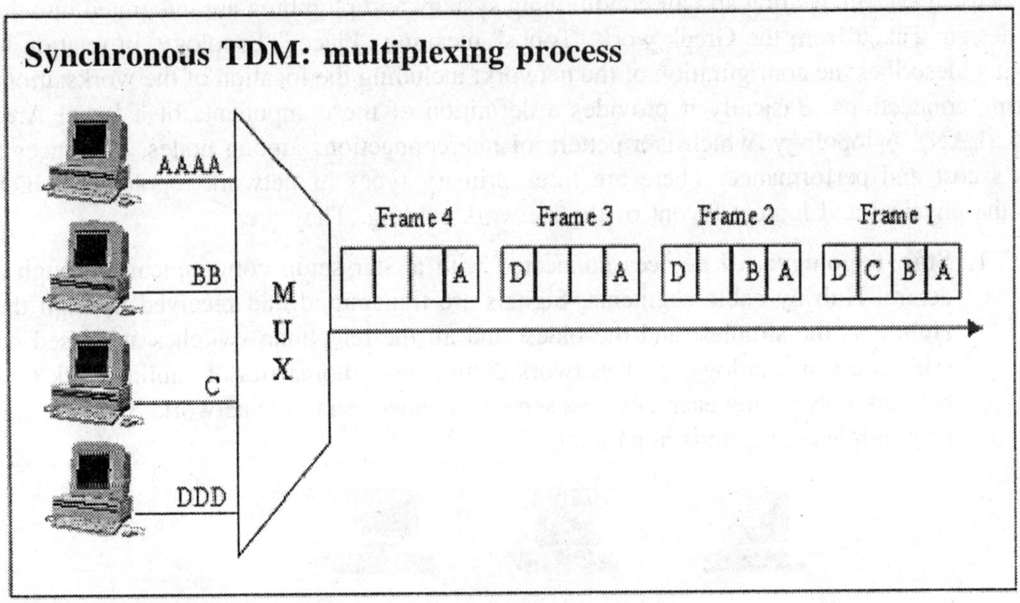

2. **Asynchronous TDM:** In this method, slots are not fixed. They are allotted dynamically depending on speed of sources, and whether they are ready for transmission.

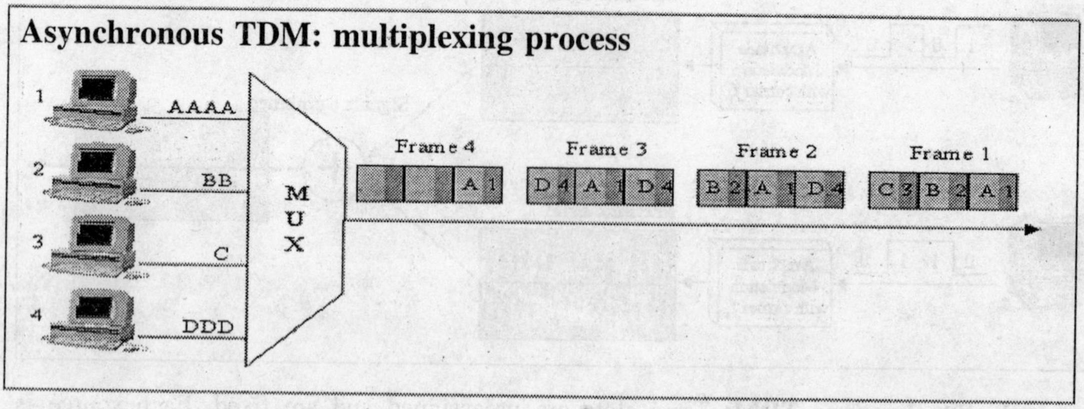

Network Topologies

A network topology is the basic design of a computer network. It is very much like a map of a road. It details how key network components such as nodes and links are interconnected. A network's topology is comparable to the blueprints of a new home in which components such as the electrical system, heating and air conditioning system, and plumbing are integrated into the overall design. Taken from the Greek work "Topos" meaning "Place," Topology, in relation to networking, describes the configuration of the network; including the location of the workstations and wiring connections. Basically it provides a definition of the components of a Local Area Network (LAN). A topology, which is a pattern of interconnections among nodes, influences a network's cost and performance. There are three primary types of network topologies which refer to the physical and logical layout of the Network cabling. They are:

1. **Star Topology:** All devices connected with a Star setup communicate through a central Hub by cable segments. Signals are transmitted and received through the Hub. It is the simplest and the oldest and all the telephone switches are based on this. In a star topology, each network device has a home run of cabling back to a network hub, giving each device a separate connection to the network. So, there can be multiple connections in parallel.

Advantages

- Network administration and error detection is easier because problem is isolated to central node
- Networks runs even if one host fails
- Expansion becomes easier and scalability of the network increases
- More suited for larger networks

Disadvantages

- Broadcasting and multicasting is not easy because some extra functionality needs to be provided to the central hub
- If the central node fails, the whole network goes down; thus making the switch some kind of a bottleneck
- Installation costs are high because each node needs to be connected to the central switch

2. Bus Topology: The simplest and one of the most common of all topologies, Bus consists of a single cable, called a Backbone, that connects all workstations on the network using a single line. All transmissions must pass through each of the connected devices to complete the desired request. Each workstation has its own individual signal that identifies it and allows for the requested data to be returned to the correct originator. In the Bus Network, messages are sent in both directions from a single point and are read by the node (computer or peripheral on the network) identified by the code with the message. Most Local Area Networks (LANs) are Bus Networks because the network will continue to function even if one computer is down. This topology works equally well for either peer to peer or client server.

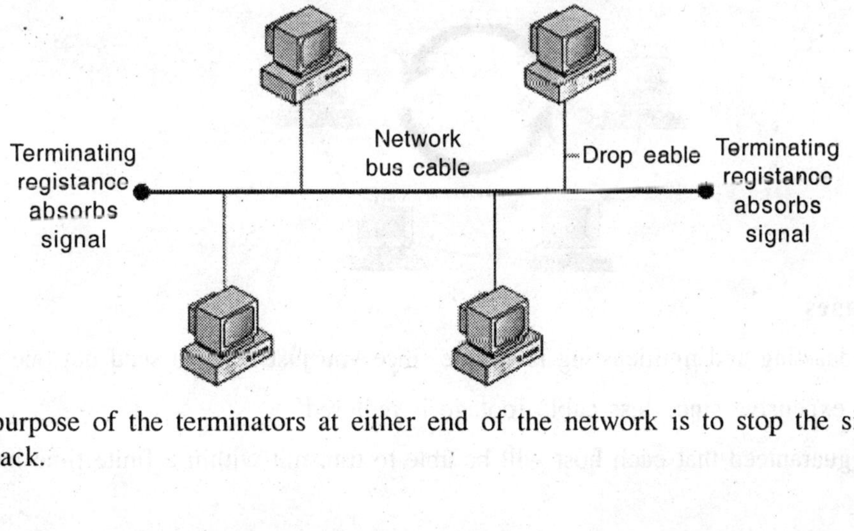

The purpose of the terminators at either end of the network is to stop the signal being reflected back.

Advantages

- Broadcasting and multicasting is much simpler
- Network is redundant in the sense that failure of one node doesn't effect the network. The other part may still function properly
- Least expensive since less amount of cabling is required and no network switches are required
- Good for smaller networks not requiring higher speeds

Disadvantages

- Trouble shooting and error detection becomes a problem because, logically, all nodes are equal
- Less secure because sniffing is easier
- Limited in size and speed

3. **Ring Topology:** All the nodes in a Ring Network are connected in a closed circle of cable. Messages that are transmitted travel around the ring until they reach the computer that they are addressed to, the signal being refreshed by each node. In a ring topology, the network signal is passed through each network card of each device and passed on to the next device. Each device processes and retransmits the signal, so it is capable of supporting many devices in a somewhat slow but very orderly fashion. There is a very nice feature that everybody gets a chance to send a packet and it is guaranteed that every node gets to send a packet in a finite amount of time.

Advantages

- Broadcasting and multicasting is simple since you just need to send out one message
- Less expensive since less cable footage is required
- It is guaranteed that each host will be able to transmit within a finite time interval

- Very orderly network where every device has access to the token and the opportunity to transmit
- Performs better than a star network under heavy network load

Disadvantages

- Failure of one node brings the whole network down
- Error detection and network administration becomes difficult
- Moves, adds and changes of devices can effect the network
- It is slower than star topology under normal load

Generally, a BUS architecture is preferred over the other topologies - ofcourse, this is a very subjective opinion and the final design depends on the requirements of the network more than anything else. Lately, most networks are shifting towards the STAR topology. Ideally we would like to design networks, which physically resemble the STAR topology, but behave like BUS or RING topology.

DATA LINK LAYER

Data link layer can be characterized by two types of layers:

1. Medium Access Layer (MAL)
2. Logical Link Layer

Aloha Protocols

History

The Aloha protocol was designed as part of a project at the University of Hawaii. It provided data transmission between computers on several of the Hawaiian Islands using radio transmissions.

- Communications was typically between remote stations and a central sited named Menehune or vice versa.
- All message to the Menehune were sent using the same frequency.
- When it received a message intact, the Menehune would broadcast an ack on a distinct outgoing frequency.
- The outgoing frequency was also used for messages from the central site to remote computers.
- All stations listened for message on this second frequency.

Pure Aloha

Pure Aloha is an unslotted, fully-decentralized protocol. It is extremely simple and trivial to implement. The ground rule is - "when you want to talk, just talk!". So, a node which wants to transmits, will go ahead and send the packet on its broadcast channel, with no consideration whatsoever, as to if anybody else is transmitting or not.

One serious drawback here is that, you dont know whether what you are sending has been received properly or not (so as to say, "whether you've been heard and understood?"). To resolve this, in Pure Aloha, when one node finishes speaking, it expects an acknowledgement in a finite amount of time – otherwise it simply retransmits the data. This scheme works well in small networks where the load is not high. But in large, load intensive networks where many nodes may want to transmit at the same time, this scheme fails miserably. This led to the development of Slotted Aloha.

Slotted Aloha

This is quite similar to Pure Aloha, differing only in the way transmissions take place. Instead of transmitting right at demand time, the sender waits for some time. This delay is specified as follows - the timeline is divided into equal slots and then it is required that transmission should take place only at slot boundaries. To be more precise, the slotted-Aloha makes the following assumptions:

- All frames consist of exactly L bits.
- Time is divided into slots of size L/R seconds (i.e., a slot equals the time to transmit one frame).
- Nodes start to transmit frames only at the beginnings of slots.
- The nodes are synchronized so that each node knows when the slots begin.
- If two or more frames collide in a slot, then all the nodes detect the collision event before the slot ends.

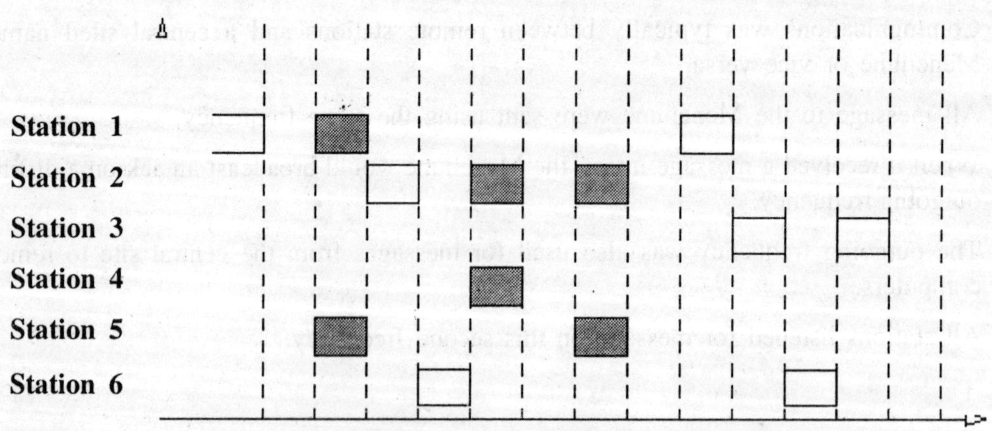

Time (shaded slots indicate collisions)

In this way, the number of collisions that can possibly take place is reduced by a huge margin. And hence, the performance become much better compared to Pure Aloha. Collisions may only take place with nodes that are ready to speak at the same time. But nevertheless, this is a substantial reduction.

Carrier Sense Mutiple Access Protocols

In both slotted and pure ALOHA, a node's decision to transmit is made independently of the activity of the other nodes attached to the broadcast channel. In particular, a node neither pays attention to whether another node happens to be transmitting when it begins to transmit, nor stops transmitting if another node begins to interfere with its transmission. As humans, we have human protocols that allow us to not only behave with more civility, but also to decrease the amount of time spent "colliding" with each other in conversation and consequently increasing the amount of data we exchange in our conversations. Specifically, there are two important rules for polite human conversation:

1. **Listen before speaking:** If someone else is speaking, wait until they are done. In the networking world, this is termed carrier sensing - a node listens to the channel before transmitting. If a frame from another node is currently being transmitted into the channel, a node then waits ("backs off") a random amount of time and then again senses the channel. If the channel is sensed to be idle, the node then begins frame transmission. Otherwise, the node waits another random amount of time and repeats this process.
2. **If someone else begins talking at the same time, stop talking:** In the networking world, this is termed collision detection - a transmitting node listens to the channel while it is transmitting. If it detects that another node is transmitting an interfering frame, it stops transmitting and uses some protocol to determine when it should next attempt to transmit.

It is evident that the end-to-end channel propagation delay of a broadcast channel - the time it takes for a signal to propagate from one channel to another - will play a crucial role in determining its performance. The longer this propagation delay, the larger the chance that a carrier-sensing node is not yet able to sense a transmission that has already begun at another node in the network.

CSMA- Carrier Sense Multiple Access

This is the simplest version CSMA protocol as described above. It does not specify any collision detection or handling. So collisions might and WILL occur and clearly then, this is not a very good protocol for large, load intensive networks.

So, we need an improvement over CSMA - this led to the development of CSMA/CD.

CSMA/CD- CSMA with Collision Detection

In this protocol, while transmitting the data, the sender simultaneously tries to receive it. So, as soon as it detects a collission (it doesn't receive its own data) it stops transmitting. Thereafter, the node waits for some time interval before attempting to transmit again. Simply put, **"listen while you talk"**. But, how long should one wait for the carrier to be freed? There are three schemes to handle this:

1. **1-Persistent:** In this scheme, transmission proceeds immediately if the carrier is idle. However, if the carrier is busy, then sender continues to sense the carrier until it becomes idle. The main problem here is that, if more than one transmitters are ready to send, a collision is GUARANTEED!!
2. **Non-Persistent:** In this scheme, the broadcast channel is not monitored continuously. The sender polls it at random time intervals and transmits whenever the carrier is idle. This decreases the probability of collisions. But, it is not efficient in a low load situation, where number of collisions are anyway small. The problems it entail are:
   - o If back-off time is too long, the idle time of carrier is wasted in some sense
   - o It may result in long access delays
3. **p-Persistent:** Even if a sender finds the carrier to be idle, it uses a probabilistic distribution to determine whether to transmit or not. Put simply, "toss a coin to decide". If the carrier is idle, then transmission takes place with a probability p and the sender waits with a probability 1-p. This scheme is a good trade off between the Non-persistent and 1-persistent schemes. So, for low load situations, p is high (example: 1-persistent); and for high load situations, p may be lower. Clearly, the value of p plays an important role in determining the performance of this protocol. Also the same p is likely to provide different performance at different loads.

CSMA/CD doesn't work in some wireless scenarios called **"hidden node"** problems. Consider a situation, where there are 3 nodes - A, B and C communicating with each other using a wireless protocol. Morover, B can communicate with both A and C, but A and C lie outside each other's range and hence can't communicate directly with each other. Now, suppose both A and C want to communicate with B simultaneously. They both will sense the carrier to be idle and hence will begin transmission, and even if there is a collision, neither A nor C will ever detect it. B on the other hand will receive 2 packets at the same time and might not be able to understand either of them. To get around this problem, a better version called CSMA/CA was developed, specially for wireless applications.

CSMA with Collision Avoidance

We have observed that CSMA/CD would break down in wireless networks because of hidden node and exposed node problems. We will have a quick recap of these two problems through examples.

Hidden Node Problem

In the case of wireless network it is possible that A is sending a message to B, but C is out of its range and hence while "listening" on the network it will find the network to be free and might try to send packets to B at the same time as A. So, there will be a collision at B. The problem can be looked upon if A and C are hidden from each other. Hence it is called the "hidden node problem".

Exposed Node Problem

If C is transmitting a message to D and B wants to transmit a message to A, B will find the network to be busy as B hears C transmitting. Even if B would have transmitted to A, it would not have been a problem at A or D. CSMA/CD would not allow it to transmit message to A, while the two transmissions could have gone in parallel.

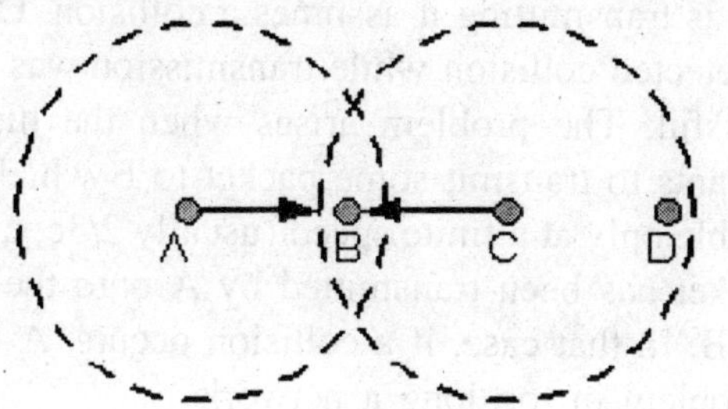

Hidden node problem

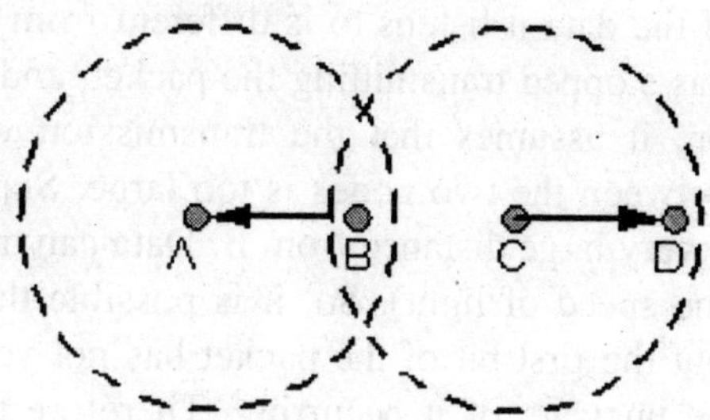

Exposed node problem

Addressing hidden node problem (CSMA/CA)

Consider the figure above. Suppose A wants to send a packet to B. Then it will first send a small packet to B called **"Request to Send" (RTS)**. In response, B sends a small packet to A called **"Clear to Send" (CTS)**. Only after A receives a CTS, it transmits the actual data. Now, any of the nodes which can hear either CTS or RTS assume the network to be busy. Hence even if some other node which is out of range of both A and B and sends an RTS to C (which can hear at least one of the RTS or CTS between A and B), C would not send a CTS to it and hence the communication would not be established between C and D.

One issue that needs to be addressed is how long the rest of the nodes should wait before they can transmit data over the network. The answer is that the RTS and CTS would carry some information about the size of the data that B intends to transfer. So, they can calculate time that would be required for the transmission to be over and assume the network to be free after that. Another interesting issue is what a node should do if it hears RTS but not a corresponding CTS. One possibility is that it assumes the recipient node has not responded and hence no transmission is going on, but there is a catch in this. It is possible that the node hearing RTS is just on the boundary of the node sending CTS. Hence, it does hear CTS but the signal is so deteriorated that it fails to recognize it as a CTS. Hence to be on the safer side, a node will not start transmission if it hears either an RTS or a CTS.

The assumption made in this whole discussion is that if a node X can send packets to a node Y, it can also receive a packet from Y, which is a fair enough assumption given the fact that we are talking of a local network where standard instruments would be used. If that is not the case additional complexities would get introduced in the system.

Does CSMA/CD work universally in the wired networks ?

The problem of range is there in wired networks as well in the form of deterioration of signals. Normally to counter this, we use repeaters, which can regenerate the original signal from a deteriorated one. But does that mean that we can build as long networks as we want with repeaters. The answer, unfortunately, is NO! The reason is the beyond a certain length CSMA/CD will break down.

The mechanism of collision detection which CSMA/CD follows is through listening while talking. What this means is so long as a node is transmitting the packet, it is listening on the cable. If the data it listens to is different from the data it is transmitting it assumes a collision. Once it has stopped transmitting the packet, and has not detected collision while transmission was going on, it assumes that the transmission was successful. The problem arises when the distance between the two nodes is too large. Suppose A wants to transmit some packet to B which is at a very large distance from B. Data can travel on cable only at a finite speed (usually 2/3c, c being the speed of light). So, it is possible that the packet has been transmitted by A onto the cable but the first bit of the packet has not yet reached B. In that case, if a collision occurs, A would be unaware of it occurring. Therefore there is problem in too long a network.

Let us try to parametrize the above problem. Suppose "t" is the time taken for the node A to transmit the packet on the cable and "T" is the time, the packet takes to reach from A to B. Suppose transmission at A starts at time t0. In the worst case the collision takes place just when the first packet is to reach B. Say it is at t0+T-e (e being very small). Then the collision information will take T-e time to propagate back to A. So, at t0+2(T-e) A should still be transmitting. Hence, for the correct detection of collision (ignoring e)

$$t > 2T$$

t increases with the number of bits to be transferred and decreases with the rate of transfer (bits per second). T increases with the distance between the nodes and decreases with the speed of the signal (usually 2/3c). We need to either keep t large enough or T as small. We do not want to live with lower rate of bit transfer and hence slow networks. We can not do anything about the speed of the signal. So what we can rely on is the minimum size of the packet and the distance between the two nodes. Therefore, we fix some minimum size of the packet and if the size is smaller than that, we put in some extra bits to make it reach the minimum size. Accordingly we fix the maximum distance between the nodes. Here too, there is a tradeoff to be made. We do not want the minimum size of the packets to be too large since that wastes lots of resources on cable. At the same time we do not want the distance between the nodes to be too small. Typical minimum packet size is 64 bytes and the corresponding distance is 2-5 kilometers.

COLLISION FREE PROTOCOLS

Although collisions do not occur with CSMA/CD once a station has unambigously seized the channel, they can still occur during the contention period. These collisions adversely affect the efficiency of transmission. Hence some protocols have been developed which are contention free.

Bit-Map Method

In this method, there are N slots. If node 0 has a frame to send, it transmits 1 bit during the first slot. No other node is allowed to transmit during this period. Next node 1 gets a chance to transmit 1 bit if it has something to send, regardless of what node 0 had transmitted. This is done for all the nodes. In general node j may declare the fact that it has a frame to send by inserting a 1 into slot j. Hence after all nodes have passed, each node has complete knowledge of who wants to send a frame. Now they begin transmitting in numerical order. Since everyone knows who is transmitting and when, there could never be any collision.

The basic problem with this protocol is its inefficiency during low load. If a node has to transmit and no other node needs to do so, even then it has to wait for the bitmap to finish. Hence the bitmap will be repeated over and over again if very few nodes want to send wasting valuable bandwidth.

Binary Countdown

In this protocol, a node which wants to signal that it has a frame to send does so by writing its address into the header as a binary number. The arbitration is such that as soon as a node sees that a higher bit position that is 0 in its address has been overwritten with a 1, it gives up. The final result is the address of the node which is allowed to send. After the node has transmitted the whole process is repeated all over again. Given below is an example situation.

Nodes	Addresses
A	0010
B	0101
C	1010
D	1001
	——
	1010

Node C having higher priority gets to transmit. The problem with this protocol is that the nodes with higher address always wins. Hence this creates a priority which is highly unfair and hence undesirable.

LIMITED CONTENTION PROTOCOLS

Both the type of protocols described above - Contention based and Contention - free has their own problems. Under conditions of light load, contention is preferable due to its low delay. As the load increases, contention becomes increasingly less attractive, because the overload associated with channel arbitration becomes greater. Just the reverse is true for contention - free protocols. At low load, they have high delay, but as the load increases, the channel efficiency improves rather than getting worse as it does for contention protocols.

Obviously it would be better if one could combine the best properties of the contention and contention - free protocols, that is, protocol which used contention at low loads to provide low delay, but used a contention-free technique at high load to provide good channel efficiency. Such protocols do exist and are called Limited contention protocols.

It is obvious that the probablity of some station aquiring the channel could only be increased by decreasing the amount of competition. The limited contention protocols do exactly that. They first divide the stations up into (not necessarily disjoint) groups. Only the members of group 0 are permitted to compete for slot 0. The competition for aquiring the slot within a group is contention based. If one of the members of that group succeeds, it aquires the channel and transmits a frame. If there is collision or no node of a particular group wants to send then the members of the next group compete for the next slot. The probablity of a particular node is set to a particular value (optimum).

Adaptive Tree Walk Protocol

The following is the method of adaptive tree protocol. Initially all the nodes are allowed to try to aquire the channel. If it is able to aquire the channel, it sends its frame. If there is collision then the nodes are divided into two equal groups and only one of these groups compete for slot 1. If one of its member aquires the channel then the next slot is reserved for the other group. On the other hand, if there is a collision then that group is again subdivided and the same process is followed. This can be better understood if the nodes are thought of as being organised in a binary tree as shown in the following figure.

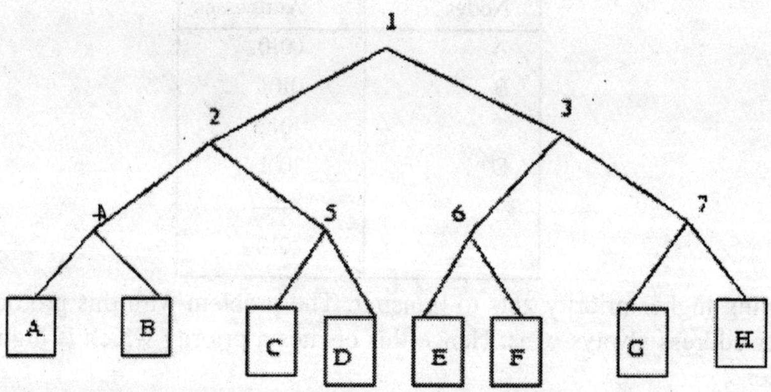

Fig. 8: Adaptive Tree Walk abstraction of nodes in binary tree.

Many improvements could be made to the algorithm. For example, consider the case of nodes G and H being the only ones wanting to transmit. At slot 1 a collision will be detected and so 2 will be tried and it will be found to be idle. Hence it is pointless to probe 3 and one should directly go to 6,7.

IEEE 802.3 and Ethernet

- Very popular LAN standard.
- Ethernet and IEEE 802.3 are distinct standards but as they are very similar to one another these words are used interchangeably.
- A standard for a 1-persistent CSMA/CD LAN.
- It covers the physical layer and MAC sublayer protocol.

Ethernet Physical Layer

A Comparison of Various Ethernet and IEEE 802.3 Physical-Layer Specifications

Characteristic	Ethernet Value	IEEE 802.3 Values					
		10Base5	**10Base2**	**10BaseT**	**10BaseF**	**10 Base -TX**	**100Base T4**
Data rate (Mbps)	10	10	10	10	10	100	100
Signaling method	Baseband	Baseband	Baseband	Baseband	Baseband	Baseband	Baseband
Maximum segment length (m)	500	500	185	100	2,000	100	100
Media	50-ohm coax (thick)	50-ohm coax (thick)	50-ohm coax (thin)	Unshielded twisted-pair cable	Fiber-optic	Cat 5 UTP	Unshielded twisted-pair cable
Nodes /segment	100	100	30	1024	1024		
Topology	Bus	Bus	Bus	Star	Point-to-point	Bus	Bus

10Base5 means it operates at 10 Mbps, uses baseband signaling and can support segments of up to 500 meters. The 10Base5 cabling is popularly called the Thick Ethernet. Vampire taps are used for their connections where a pin is carefully forced halfway into the co-axial cable's core as shown in the figure below. The 10Base2 or Thin Ethernet bends easily and is connected using standard BNC connectors to form T junctions (shown in the figure below). In the 10Base-T scheme a different kind of wiring pattern is followed in which all stations have a twisted-pair cable running to a central hub (see below). The difference between the different physical connections is shown below:

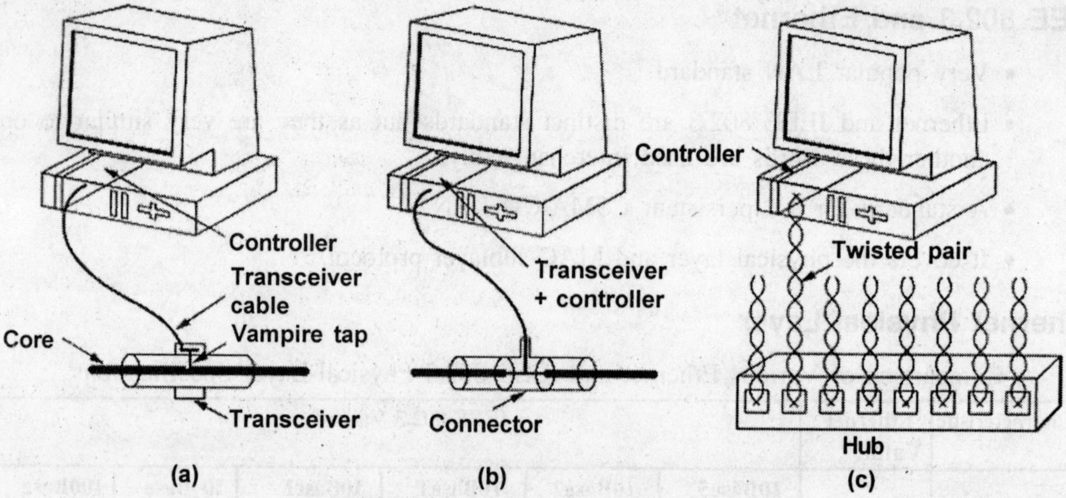

(a) 10Base5 (b)10Base2 (c)10Base-T

All 802.3 baseband systems use Manchester encoding, which is a way for receivers to unambiguously determine the start, end or middle of each bit without reference to an external clock. There is a restriction on the minimum node spacing (segment length between two nodes) in 10Base5 and 10Base2 and that is 2.5 meter and 0.5 meter respectively. The reason is that if two nodes are closer than the specified limit then there will be very high current which may cause trouble in detection of signal at the receiver end. Connections from station to cable of 10Base5 (i.e. Thick Ethernet) are generally made using vampire taps and to 10Base2 (i.e. Thin Ethernet) are made using industry standard BNC connectors to form T junctions. To allow larger networks, multiple segments can be connected by repeaters as shown. A repeater is a physical layer device. It receives, amplifies and retransmits signals in either direction.

Note: To connect multiple segments, amplifier is not used because amplifier also amplifies the noise in the signal, whereas repeater regenerates signal after removing the noise.

IEEE 802.3 Frame Structure

Preamble (7 bytes)	Start of Frame Delimiter (1 byte)	Dest. Address (2/6 bytes)	Source Address (2/6 bytes)	Length (2 bytes)	802.2 Header+Data (46-1500 bytes)	Frame Checksum (4 bytes)

A brief description of each of the fields

- **Preamble :** Each frame starts with a preamble of 7 bytes, each byte containing the bit pattern 10101010. Manchester encoding is employed here and this enables the receiver's clock to synchronize with the sender's and initialise itself.
- **Start of Frame Delimiter :** This field containing a byte sequence 10101011 denotes the start of the frame itself.

- **Dest. Address :** The standard allows 2-byte and 6-byte addresses. Note that the 2-byte addresses are always local addresses while the 6-byte ones can be local or global.
- **2-Byte Address-Manually assigned address**

Individual(0)/Group(1)(1 bit)	Address of the machine(15 bits)

- **6-Byte Address-Every Ethernet card with globally unique address**

Individual(0)/Group(1) (1 bit)	Universal(0)/Local(1) (1 bit)	Address of the machine (46 bits)

- **Multicast :** Sending to group of stations. This is ensured by setting the first bit in either 2-byte/6-byte addresses to 1.
- **Broadcast :** Sending to all stations. This can be done by setting all bits in the address field to 1. All Ethernet cards(Nodes) are a member of this group.
- **Source Address :** Refer to Dest. Address. Same holds true over here.
- **Length :** The Length field tells how many bytes are present in the data field, from a minimum of 0 to a maximum of 1500. The Data and padding together can be from 46bytes to 1500 bytes as the valid frames must be at least 64 bytes long, thus if data is less than 46 bytes the amount of padding can be found out by length field.
- **Data :** Actually this field can be split up into two parts - Data(0-1500 bytes) and Padding(0-46 bytes).

Reasons for having a minimum length frame:

1. To prevent a station from completing the transmission of a short frame before the first bit has even reached the far end of the cable, where it may collide with another frame. Note that the transmission time ought to be greater than twice the propagation time between two farthest nodes.

   transmission time for frame > 2*propagation time between two farthest nodes

2. When a transceiver detects a collision, it truncates the current frame, which implies that stray bits and pieces of frames appear on the cable all the time. Hence to distinguish between valid frames from garbage, 802.3 states that the minimum length of valid frames ought to be 64 bytes (from Dest. Address to Frame Checksum).

   - **Frame Checksum :** It is a 32-bit hash code of the data. If some bits are erroneously received by the destination (due to noise on the cable), the checksum computed by the destination wouldn't match with the checksum sent and therefore the error will be detected. The checksum algorithm is a cyclic redundancy checksum (CRC) kind. The checksum includes the packet from Dest. Address to Data field.

Ethernet Frame Structure

Preamble (8 bytes)	Dest. Address (2/6 bytes)	Source Address (2/6 bytes)	Type(2 bytes)	Data (46-1500 bytes)	Frame Checksum (4 bytes)

A brief description of the fields which differ from IEEE 802.3

- **Preamble:** The *Preamble* and *Start of Frame Delimiter* are merged into one in Ethernet standard. However, the contents of the first 8 bytes remains the same in both.
- **Type:** The length field of IEEE 802.3 is replaced by Type field, which denotes the type of packet being sent viz. IP, ARP, RARP, etc. If the field indicates a value less than 1500 bytes then it is length field of 802.3 else it is the type field of Ethernet packet.

Truncated Binary Exponential Back off

In case of collision the node transmitting backs off by a random number of slots, each slot time being equal to transmission time of 512 bits (64 Byte- minimum size of a packet) in the following fashion:

No of Collision	Random No of slots
1st	0-1
2nd	0-3
3rd	0-7
|	|
|	|
10th	0-1023
11th	0-1023
12th	0-1023
|	|
16th	0-1023

In general after i collisions a random number between 0-2^i-1 is chosen , and that number of slots is skipped. However, after 10 collisions have been reached the randomization interval is frozen at maximum of 1023 slots. After 16 collisions the controller reports failure back to the computer.

5-4-3 Rule

Each version of 802.3 has a maximum cable length per segment because long propagation time leads to difficulty in collision detection. To compensate for this the transmission time has to be increased which can be achieved by slowing down the transmission rate or increasing the packet size, neither of which is desirable. Hence to allow for large networks, multiple cables are connected via **repeaters**. Between any two nodes on an Ethernet network, there can be at most five segments, four repeaters and three populated segments (non-populated segments are those which do not have any machine connected between the two repeaters). This is known as the **5-4-3 Rule**.

IEEE 802.5: TOKEN RING NETWORK

- Token Ring is formed by the nodes connected in ring format as shown in the diagram below. The principle used in the token ring network is that a token is circulating in the ring and whichever node grabs that token will have right to transmit the data.
- Whenever a station wants to transmit a frame it inverts a single bit of the 3-byte token which instantaneously changes it into a normal data packet. Because there is only one token, there can atmost be one transmission at a time.
- Since the token rotates in the ring it is guarenteed that every node gets the token with in some specified time. So there is an upper bound on the time of waiting to grab the token so that starvation is avoided.
- There is also an upper limit of 250 on the number of nodes in the network.
- To distinguish the normal data packets from token (control packet) a special sequence is assigned to the token packet. When any node gets the token it first sends the data it wants to send, then recirculates the token.

If a node transmits the token and nobody wants to send the data the token comes back to the sender. If the first bit of the token reaches the sender before the transmission of the last bit, then error situation araises. So to avoid this we should have:

propogation delay + transmission of n-bits (1-bit delay in each node) > transmission of the token time

A station may hold the token for the token-holding time. which is 10 ms unless the installation sets a different value. If there is enough time left after the first frame has been transmitted to send more frames, then these frames may be sent as well. After all pending frames have been transmitted or the transmission frame would exceed the token-holding time, the station regenerates the 3-byte token frame and puts it back on the ring.

Modes of Operation

1. **Listen Mode:** In this mode the node listens to the data and transmits the data to the next node. In this mode there is a one-bit delay associated with the transmission.

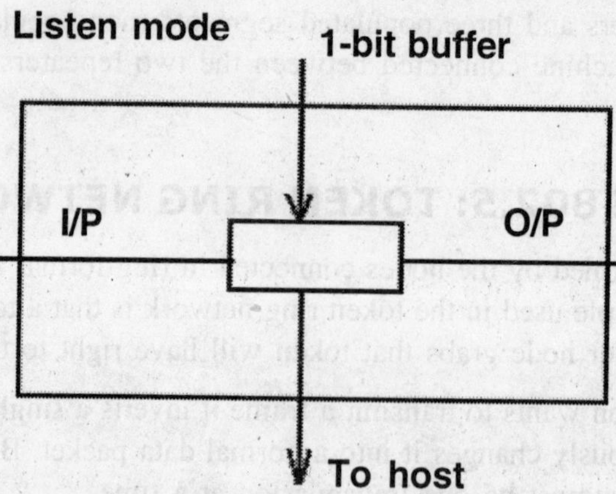

2. **Transmit Mode:** In this mode the node just discards the any data and puts the data onto the network.

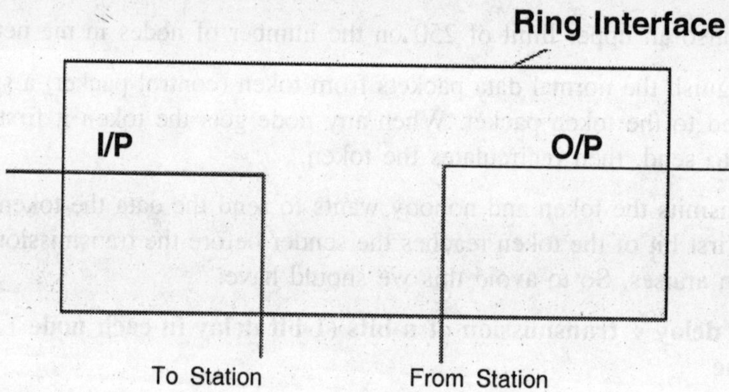

3. **By-pass Mode:** In this mode reached when the node is down. Any data is just bypassed. There is no one-bit delay in this mode.

Token Ring Using Ring Concentrator

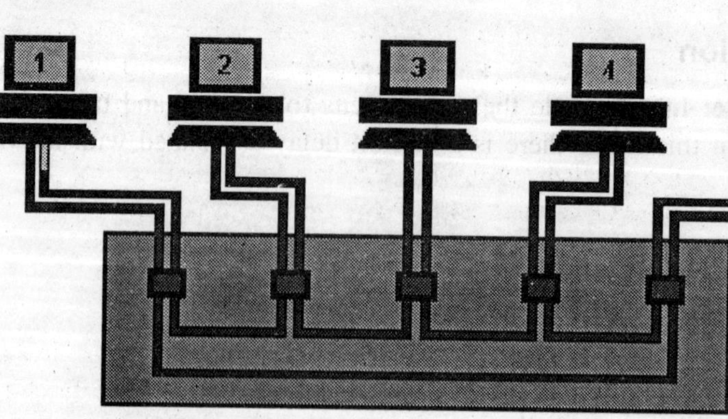

One problem with a ring network is that if the cable breaks somewhere, the ring dies. This problem is elegantly addressed by using a ring concentrator. A Token Ring concentrator simply changes the topology from a physical ring to a star wired ring. But the network still remains a ring logically. Physically, each station is connected to the ring concentrator (wire center) by a cable containing at least two twisted pairs, one for data to the station and one for data from the station. The Token still circulates around the network and is still controlled in the same manner, however, using a hub or a switch greatly improves reliability because the hub can automatically bypass any ports that are disconnected or have a cabling fault. This is done by having bypass relays inside the concentrator that are energized by current from the stations. If the ring breaks or station goes down, loss of the drive current will release the relay and bypass the station. The ring can then continue operation with the bad segment bypassed.

Who should remove the packet from the ring?

There are 3 possibilities-

1. **The source itself removes the packet after one full round in the ring.**
2. **The destination removes it after accepting it:** This has two potential problems. Firstly, the solution won't work for broadcast or multicast, and secondly, there would be no way to acknowledge the sender about the receipt of the packet.
3. **Have a specialized node only to discard packets:** This is a bad solution as the specialized node would know that the packet has been received by the destination only when it receives the packet the second time and by that time the packet may have actually made about one and half (or almost two in the worst case) rounds in the ring.

Thus the first solution is adopted with the source itself removing the packet from the ring after a full one round. With this scheme, broadcasting and multicasting can be handled as well as the destination can acknowledge the source about the receipt of the packet (or can tell the source about some error).

Token Format

The token is the shortest frame transmitted (24 bit)

MSB (Most Significant Bit) is always transmitted first - as opposed to Ethernet

SD	AC	ED

SD = Starting Delimiter (1 Octet)

AC = Access Control (1 Octet)

ED = Ending Delimiter (1 Octet)

Starting Delimiter Format:

J	K	0	J	K	0	0	0

J = Code Violation

K = Code Violation

Access Control Format:

P	P	P	T	M	R	R	R

T=Token

T = 0 for Token

T = 1 for Frame

When a station with a Frame to transmit detects a token which has a priority equal to or less than the Frame to be transmitted, it may change the token to a start-of-frame sequence and transmit the Frame

P = Priority

Priority Bits indicate tokens priority, and therefore, which stations are allowed to use it. Station can transmit if its priority is at least as high as that of the token.

M = Monitor

The monitor bit is used to prevent a token whose priority is greater than 0 or any frame from continuously circulating on the ring. If an active monitor detects a frame or a high priority token with the monitor bit equal to 1, the frame or token is aborted. This bit shall be transmitted as 0 in all frame and tokens. The active monitor inspects and modifies this bit. All other stations shall repeat this bit as received.

R = Reserved bits

The reserved bits allow station with high priority Frames to request that the next token be issued at the requested priority.

Ending Delimiter Format:

J	K	1	J	K	1	1	E

J = Code Violation

K = Code Violation

I = Intermediate Frame Bit

E = Error Detected Bit

Frame Format:

MSB (Most Significant Bit) is always transmitted first - as opposed to Ethernet

SD	AC	FC	DA	SA	DATA	CRC	ED	FS

SD=Starting Delimiter(1 octet)

AC=Access Control(1 octet)

FC = Frame Control (1 Octet)

DA = Destination Address (2 or 6 Octets)

SA = Source Address (2 or 6 Octets)

DATA = Information 0 or more octets up to 4027

CRC = Checksum(4 Octets)

ED = Ending Delimiter (1 Octet)

FS=Frame Status

Starting Delimiter Format:

J	K	0	J	K	0	0	0

J = Code Violation

K = Code Violation

Access Control Format:

P	P	P	T	M	R	R	R

T=Token

T= ?0? for Token,

T = ?1? for Frame.

When a station with a Frame to transmit detects a token which has a priority equal to or less than the Frame to be transmitted, it may change the token to a start-of-frame sequence and transmit the Frame.

P = Priority

Bits Priority Bits indicate tokens priority, and therefore, which stations are allowed to use it. Station can transmit if its priority as at least as high as that of the token.

M = Monitor

The monitor bit is used to prevent a token whose priority is greater than 0 or any frame from continuously circulating on the ring. if an active monitor detects a frame oı a high priority token with the monitor bit equal to 1, the frame or token is aborted. This bit shall be transmitted as 0 in all frame and tokens. The active monitor inspects and modifies this bit. All other stations shall repeat this bit as received.

R = Reserved bits

The reserved bits allow station with high priority Frames to request that the next token be issued at the requested priority.

Frame Control Format:

F	F CONTROL BITS (6 BITS)

FF = Type of Packet-Regular data packet or MAC layer packet

Control Bits = Used if the packet is for MAC layer protocol itself

Source and Destination Address Format:

The addresses can be of 2 bytes (local address) or 6 bytes (global address).

local address format:

I/G (1 BIT)	NODE ADDRESS (15 BITS)

alternatively

I/G (1 BIT)	RING ADDRESS	(7 BITS) NODE ADDRESS (8 BITS)

The first bit specifies individual or group address.

universal (global) address format:

I/G (1 BIT)	L/U (1 BIT)	RING ADDRESS (14 BITS)	NODE ADDRESS (32 BITS)

The first bit specifies individual or group address.

The second bit specifies local or global (universal) address.

local group addresses (16 bits):

I/G (1 BIT)	T/B(1 BIT)	GROUP ADDRESS (14 BITS)

The first bit specifies an individual or group address.

The second bit specifies traditional or bit signature group address.

Traditional Group Address: 2Exp14 groups can be defined.

Bit Signature Group Address: 14 groups are defined. A host can be a member of none or any number of them. For multicasting, those group bits are set to which the packet should go. For broadcasting, all 14 bits are set. A host receives a packet only if it is a member of a group whose corresponding bit is set to 1.

universal group addresses (16 bits):

I/G (1 BIT)	RING NUMBER	T/B (1 BIT)	GROUP ADDRESS (14 BITS)

The description is similar to as above.

Data Format:

No upper limit on amount of data as such, but it is limited by the token holding time.

Checksum:

The source computes and sets this value. Destination too calculates this value. If the two are different, it indicates an error, otherwise the data may be correct.

Frame Status:

It contains the A and C bits.

A bit set to 1: destination recognized the packet.

C bit set to 1: destination accepted the packet.

This arrangement provides an automatic acknowledgement for each frame. The A and C bits are present twice in the Frame Status to increase reliability in as much as they are not covered by the checksum.

Ending Delimiter Format:

J	K	1	J	K	1	I	E

J = Code Violation

K = Code Violation

I = Intermediate Frame Bit

If this bit is set to 1, it indicates that this packet is an intermediate part of a bigger packet, the last packet would have this bit set to 0.

E = Error Detected Bit

This bit is set if any interface detects an error.

This concludes our description of the token ring frame format.

Phase Jitter Compensation :

In a token ring the source starts discarding all it's previously transmitted bits as soon as they circum-navigate the ring and reach the source. Hence, it's not desirable that while a token is being sent some bits of the token which have already been sent become available at the incoming end of the source. This behavior though is desirable in case of data packets which ought to be drained from the ring once they have gone around the ring. To achieve the aforesaid behavior with respect to tokens, we would like the ring to hold at least 24 bits at a time. How do we ensure this?

Each node in a ring introduces a 1 bit delay. So, one approach might be to set the minimum limit on the number of nodes in a ring as 24. But, this is not a viable option. The actual solution is as follows. We have one node in the ring designated as **"monitor"**. The monitor maintains a 24 bits buffer with help of which it introduces a 24 bit delay. The catch here is what if the clocks of nodes following the source are faster than the source? In this case the 24 bit delay of the monitor would be less than the 24 bit delay desired by the host. To avoid this situation the monitor maintains 3 extra bits to compensate for the faster bits. The 3 extra bits suffice even if bits are 10 % faster. This compensation is called Phase Jitter Compensation.

Handling multiple priority frames

Each node or packet has a priority level. We don't concern ourselves with how this priority is decided. The first 3 bits of the Access Control byte in the token are for priority and the last 3 are for reservation.

P	P	P	T	M	R	R	R

Initially the reservation bits are set to 000. When a node wants to transmit a priority n frame, it must wait until it can capture a token whose priority is less than or equal to n. Furthermore, when a data frame goes by, a station can try to reserve the next token by writing the priority of the frame it wants to send into the frame's Reservation bits. However, if a higher priority has already been reserved there, the station cannot make a reservation. When the current frame is finished, the next token is generated at the priority that has been reserved.

A slight problem with the above reservation procedure is that the reservation priority keeps on increasing. To solve this problem, the station raising the priority remembers the reservation priority that it replaces and when it is done it reduces the priority to the previous priority.

Note that in a token ring, low priority frames may starve.

Ring Maintenance

Each token ring has a monitor that oversees the ring. Among the monitor's responsibilities are seeing that the token is not lost, taking action when the ring breaks, cleaning the ring when garbled frames appear and watching out for orphan frames. An orphan frame occurs when a station transmits a short frame in it's entirety onto a long ring and then crashes or is powered down before the frame can be removed. If nothing is done, the frame circulates indefinitely.

- **Detection of orphan frames:** The monitor detects orphan frames by setting the monitor bit in the Access Control byte whenever it passes through. If an incoming frame has this bit set, something is wrong since the same frame has passed the monitor twice. Evidently it was not removed by the source, so the monitor drains it.

- **Lost Tokens:** The monitor has a timer that is set to the longest possible tokenless interval : when each node transmits for the full token holding time. If this timer goes off, the monitor drains the ring and issues a fresh token.

- **Garbled frames:** The monitor can detect such frames by their invalid format or checksum, drain the ring and issue a fresh token.

The token ring control frames for maintenance are:

Control field	Name	Meaning
00000000	Duplicate address test	Test if two stations have the same address
00000010	Beacon	Used to locate breaks in the ring
00000011	Claim token	Attempt to become monitor
00000100	Purge	Reinitialize the ring
00000101	Active monitor present	Issued periodically by the monitor
00000110	Standby monitor present	Announces the presence of potential monitors

The monitor periodically issues a message "Active Monitor Present" informing all nodes of its presence. When this message is not received for a specific time interval, the nodes detect a monitor failure. Each node that believes it can function as a monitor broadcasts a "Standby Monitor Present" message at regular intervals, indicating that it is ready to take on the monitor's job. Any node that detects failure of a monitor issues a "Claim" token. There are 3 possible outcomes:

1. If the issuing node gets back its own claim token, then it becomes the monitor.
2. If a packet different from a claim token is received, apparently a wrong guess of monitor failure was made. In this case on receipt of our own claim token, we discard it. Note that our claim token may have been removed by some other node which has detected this error.
3. If some other node has also issued a claim token, then the node with the larger address becomes the monitor.

In order to resolve errors of duplicate addresses, whenever a node comes up it sends a **"Duplicate Address Detection"** message (with the destination = source) across the network. If the address recognize bit has been set on receipt of the message, the issuing node realizes a duplicate address and goes to standby mode. A node informs other nodes of removal of a packet from the ring through a **"Purge"** message. One maintenance function that the monitor cannot handle is locating breaks in the ring. If there is no activity detected in the ring (e.g., Failure of monitor to issue the **Active Monitor Present** token...), the usual procedures of sending a claim token are followed. If the claim token itself is not received besides packets of any other kind, the node then sends **"Beacons"** at regular intervals until a message is received indicating that the broken ring has been repaired.

Other Ring Networks

The problem with the token ring system is that large rings cause large delays. It must be made possible for multiple packets to be in the ring simultaneously. The following ring networks resolve this problem to some extent:-

Slotted Ring

In this system, the ring is slotted into a number of fixed size frames which are continuously moving around the ring. This makes it necessary that there be enough number of nodes (large ring size) to ensure that all the bits can stay on the ring at the same time. The frame header contains information as to whether the slots are empty or full. The usual disadvantages of overhead/wastage associated with fixed size frames are present.

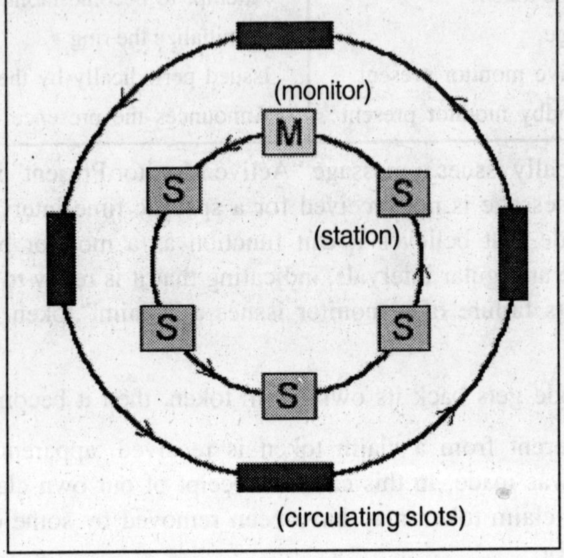

Register Insertion Rings

This is an improvement over slotted ring architecture. The network interface consists of two registers : a shift register and an output buffer. At startup, the input pointer points to the rightmost bit position in the input shift register .When a bit arrives it is in the rightmost empty position (the one indicated by the input pointer). After the node has detected that the frame is not addressed to it, the bits are transmitted one at time (by shifting). As new bits come in, they are inserted at the position indicated by the pointer and then the contents are shifted. Thus :he pointer is not moved. Once the shift register has pushed out the last bit of a frame, it checks to see if it has an output frame waiting. In case yes, then it checks that if the number of empty slots in the shift register is at least equal to the number of bits in the output frame. After this the output connection is switched to this second register and after the register has emptied its contents, the output line is switched back to the shift register. Thus, no single node can hog the bandwidth. In a loaded system, a node can transmit a k-bit frame only if it has saved up a k-bits of inter frame gaps.

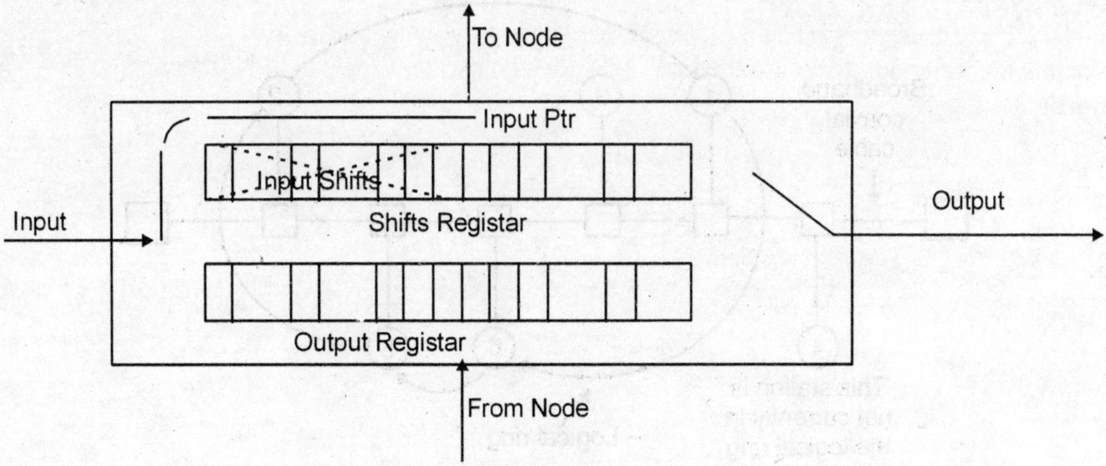

Register Insertion Ring

Two major disadvantages of this topology are complicated hardware and difficulty in the detection of start/end of packets.

Contention Ring

The token ring has primarily two problems:

- On light loads, huge overhead is incurred for token passing.
- Nodes with low priority data may starve if there is always a node with high priority data.

A contention ring attempts to address these problems. In a contention ring, if there is no communication in the ring for a while, a sender node will send its data immediately, followed by a token. If the token comes back to the sender without any data packet in between, the sender removes it from the ring. However under heavy load the behavior is that of a normal token ring. In case a collision, each of the sending nodes will remove the others' data packet from the ring, back off for a random period of time and then resend their data.

IEEE 802.4: Token Bus Network

In this system, the nodes are physically connected as a bus, but logically form a ring with tokens passed around to determine the turns for sending. It has the robustness of the 802.3 broadcast cable and the known worst case behavior of a ring. The structure of a token bus network is as follows:

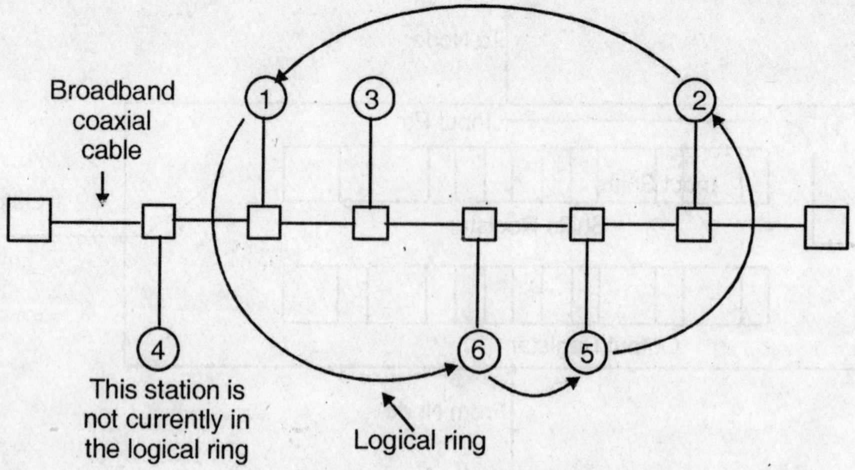

Frame Structure

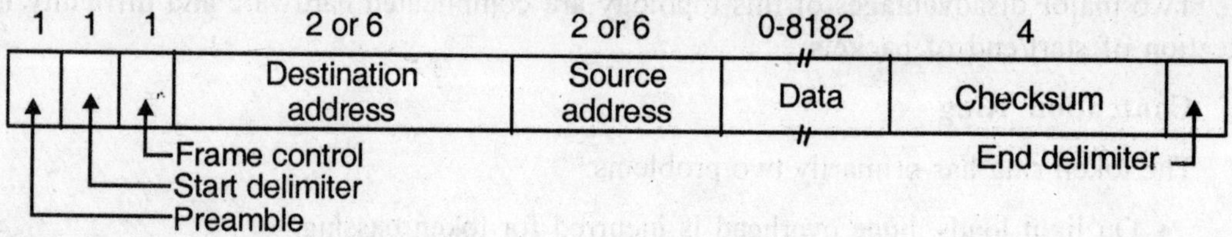

IEEE 802.4 Frame Format

A 802.4 frame has the following fields:

- **Preamble:** The Preamble is used to synchronize the receiver's clock.
- **Starting Delimiter (SD) and End Delimiter (ED):** The Starting Delimiter and Ending Delimiter fields are used to mark frame boundaries. Both of them contain analog encoding of symbols other than 1 or 0 so that they cannot occur accidentally in the user data. Hence no length field is needed.
- **Frame Control (FC):** This field is used to distinguish data frames from control frames. For data frames, it carries the frame's priority as well as a bit which the destination can set as an acknowledgement. For control frames, the Frame Control field is used to specify the frame type. The allowed types include token passing and various ring maintenance frames.
- **Destination and Source Address:** The Destination and Source address fields may be 2 bytes (for a local address) or 6 bytes (for a global address).
- **Data:** The Data field carries the actual data and it may be 8182 bytes when 2 byte addresses are used and 8174 bytes for 6 byte addresses.
- **Checksum:** A 4-byte checksum calculated for the data. Used in error detection.

Ring Maintenance

When the first node on the token bus comes up, it sends a **Claim_token** packet to initialize the ring. If more than one station send this packet at the same time, there is a collision. Collision is resolved by a contention mechanism, in which the contending nodes send random data for 1, 2, 3 and 4 units of time depending on the first two bits of their address. The node sending data for the longest time wins. If two nodes have the same first two bits in their addresses, then contention is done again based on the next two bits of their address and so on.

After the ring is set up, new nodes which are powered up may wish to join the ring. For this a node sends **Solicit_successor_1** packets from time to time, inviting bids from new nodes to join the ring. This packet contains the address of the current node and its current successor, and asks for nodes in between these two addresses to reply. If more than one nodes respond, there will be collision. The node then sends a **Resolve_contention** packet, and the contention is resolved using a similar mechanism as described previously. Thus at a time only one node gets to enter the ring. The last node in the ring will send a **Solicit_successor_2** packet containing the addresses of it and its successor. This packet asks nodes not having addresses in between these two addresses to respond.

A question arises that how frequently should a node send a Solicit_successor packet? If it is sent too frequently, then overhead will be too high. Again if it is sent too rarely, nodes will have to wait for a long time before joining the ring. If the channel is not busy, a node will send a Solicit_successor packet after a fixed number of token rotations. This number can be configured by the network administrator. However if there is heavy traffic in the network, then a node would defer the sending of bids for successors to join in.

There may be problems in the logical ring due to sudden failure of a node. What happens when a node goes down along with the token? After passing the token, a node, say node A, listens to the channel to see if its successor either transmits the token or passes a frame. If neither happens, it resends a token. Still if nothing happens, A sends a **Who_follows** packet, containing the address of the down node. The successor of the down node, say node C, will now respond with a **Set_successor** packet, containing its own address. This causes A to set its successor node to C, and the logical ring is restored. However, if two successive nodes go down suddenly, the ring will be dead and will have to be built afresh, starting from a **Claim_token** packet.

When a node wants to shutdown normally, it sends a **Set_successor** packet to its predecessor, naming its own successor. The ring then continues unbroken, and the node goes out of the ring.

The various control frames used for ring maintenance are shown below:

Frame Control Field	Name	Meaning
00000000	Claim_token	Claim token during ring maintenance
00000001	Solicit_successor_1	Allow stations to enter the ring
00000010	Solicit_successor_2	Allow stations to enter the ring
00000011	Who_follows	Recover from lost token
00000100	Resolve_contention	Used when multiple stations want to enter
00001000	Token	Pass the token
00001100	Set_successor	Allow the stations leave the ring

Priority Scheme

Token bus supports four distinct priority levels: 0, 2, 4 and 6.

0 is the lowest priority level and 6 the highest. The following times are defined by the token bus:

- THT: Token Holding Time. A node holding the token can send priority 6 data for a maximum of this amount of time.
- TRT_4: Token Rotation Time for class 4 data. This is the maximum time a token can take to circulate and still allow transmission of class 4 data.
- TRT_2 and TRT_0: Similar to TRT_4.

When a station receives data, it proceeds in the following manner:

- It transmits priority 6 data for at most THT time, or as long as it has data.
- Now if the time for the token to come back to it is less than TRT_4, it will transmit priority 4 data, and for the amount of time allowed by TRT_4. Therefore the maximum time for which it can send priority 4 data is = Actual TRT - THT - TRT_4
- Similarly for priority 2 and priority 0 data.

This mechanism ensures that priority 6 data is always sent, making the system suitable for real time data transmission. In fact this was one of the primary aims in the design of token bus.

What is DLL(Data Link Layer)

The Data Link Layer is the second layer in the OSI model, above the Physical Layer, which ensures that the error free data is transferred between the adjacent nodes in the network. It breaks the datagrams passed down by above layers and convert them into frames ready for transfer. This is called Framing. It provides two main functionalities

- Reliable data transfer service between two peer network layers
- Flow Control mechanism which regulates the flow of frames such that data congestion is not there at slow receivers due to fast senders.

What is Framing?

Since the physical layer merely accepts and transmits a stream of bits without any regard to meaning or structure, it is upto the data link layer to create and recognize frame boundaries. This can be accomplished by attaching special bit patterns to the beginning and end of the frame. If these bit patterns can accidentally occur in data, special care must be taken to make sure these patterns are not incorrectly interpreted as frame delimiters. The four framing methods that are widely used are

- Character count
- Starting and ending characters, with character stuffing

- Starting and ending flags, with bit stuffing
- Physical layer coding violations

Character Count

This method uses a field in the header to specify the number of characters in the frame. When the data link layer at the destination sees the character count,it knows how many characters follow, and hence where the end of the frame is. The disadvantage is that if the count is garbled by a transmission error, the destination will lose synchronization and will be unable to locate the start of the next frame. So, this method is rarely used.

Character stuffing

In the second method, each frame starts with the ASCII character sequence DLE STX and ends with the sequence DLE ETX.(where DLE is Data Link Escape, STX is Start of TeXt and ETX is End of TeXt.) This method overcomes the drawbacks of the character count method. If the destination ever loses synchronization, it only has to look for DLE STX and DLE ETX characters. If however, binary data is being transmitted then there exists a possibility of the characters DLE STX and DLE ETX occurring in the data. Since this can interfere with the framing, a technique called character stuffing is used. The sender's data link layer inserts an ASCII DLE character just before the DLE character in the data. The receiver's data link layer removes this DLE before this data is given to the network layer. However character stuffing is closely associated with 8-bit characters and this is a major hurdle in transmitting arbitrary sized characters.

Bit stuffing

The third method allows data frames to contain an arbitrary number of bits and allows character codes with an arbitrary number of bits per character. At the start and end of each frame is a flag byte consisting of the special bit pattern 01111110. Whenever the sender's data link layer encounters five consecutive 1s in the data, it automatically stuffs a zero bit into the outgoing bit stream. This technique is called bit stuffing. When the receiver sees five consecutive 1s in the incoming data stream, followed by a zero bit, it automatically destuffs the 0 bit. The boundary between two frames can be determined by locating the flag pattern.

Physical layer coding violations

The final framing method is physical layer coding violations and is applicable to networks in which the encoding on the physical medium contains some redundancy. In such cases normally, a 1 bit is a high-low pair and a 0 bit is a low-high pair. The combinations of low-low and high-high which are not used for data may be used for marking frame boundaries.

Error Control

The bit stream transmitted by the physical layer is not guaranteed to be error free. The data link layer is responsible for error detection and correction. The most common error control method is to compute and append some form of a checksum to each outgoing frame at the sender's data link layer and to recompute the checksum and verify it with the received checksum at the receiver's side. If both of them match, then the frame is correctly received; else it is erroneous. The checksums may be of two types:

Error detecting : Receiver can only detect the error in the frame and inform the sender about it. # Error detecting and correcting : The receiver can not only detect the error but also correct it.

Examples of Error Detecting methods:

- **Parity bit:**

Simple example of error detection technique is parity bit. The parity bit is chosen that the number of 1 bits in the code word is either even(for even parity) or odd (for odd parity). For example when 10110101 is transmitted then for even parity an 1 will be appended to the data and for odd parity a 0 will be appended. This scheme can detect only single bits. So if two or more bits are changed then that can not be detected.

- **Longitudinal Redundancy Checksum:**

Longitudinal Redundancy Checksum is an error detecting scheme which overcomes the problem of two erroneous bits. In this conceptof parity bit is used but with slightly more intelligence. With each byte we send one parity bit then send one additional byte which have the parity corresponding to the each bit position of the sent bytes. So the parity bit is set in both horizontal and vertical direction. If one bit get flipped we can tell which row and column have error then we find the intersection of the two and determine the erroneous bit. If 2 bits are in error and they are in the different column and row then they can be detected. If the error are in the same column then the row will differentiate and vice versa. Parity can detect the only odd number of errors. If they are even and distributed in a fashion that in all direction then LRC may not be able to find the error.

- **Cyclic Redundancy Checksum (CRC):**

We have an n-bit message. The sender adds a k-bit Frame Check Sequence (FCS) to this message before sending. The resulting (n+k) bit message is divisible by some (k+1) bit number. The receiver divides the message ((n+k)-bit) by the same (k+1)-bit number and if there is no remainder, assumes that there was no error. How do we choose this number?

For example, if k = 12 then 1000000000000 (13-bit number) can be chosen, but this is a pretty crappy choice. Because it will result in a zero remainder for all (n+k) bit messages with the last 12 bits zero. Thus, any bits flipping beyond the last 12 go undetected. If k = 12, and we take 1110001000110 as the 13-bit number (incidentally, in decimal representation this turns out to be 7238). This will be unable to detect errors only if the corrupt message and original message have a difference of a multiple of 7238. The probablilty of this is low, much lower than the probability that anything beyond the last 12-bits flips. In practice, this number is chosen after analyzing common network transmission errors and then selecting a number which is likely to detect these common errors.

How to detect source errors?

In order ensure that the frames are delivered correctly, the receiver should inform the sender about incoming frames using positive or negative acknowledgements. On the sender's side the receipt of a positive acknowledgement implies that the frame has arrived at the destination safely while the receipt of a negative acknowledgement means that an error has occurred in the frame and it needs to be retransmitted. However, this scheme is too simplistic because if a noise burst causes the frame to vanish completely, the receiver will not respond at all and the sender would hang forever waiting for an acknowledgement. To overcome this drawback, timers are introduced into the data link layer. When the sender transmits a frame it also simultaneously starts a timer. The timer is set to go off after a interval long enough for the frame to reach the destination, be processed there, and have the acknowledgement propogate back to the sender. If the frame is received correctly the positive acknowledgment arrives before the timer runs out and so the timer is canceled. If however either the frame or the acknowledgement is lost the timer will go off and the sender may retransmit the frame. Since multiple transmission of frames can cause the receiver to accept the same frame and pass it to the network layer more than once, sequence numbers are generally assigned to the outgoing frames.

The types of acknowledgements that are sent can be classified as follows:

- Cumulative acknowledgements: A single acknowledgement informing the sender that all the frames upto a certain number have been received.
- Selective acknowledgements: Acknowledgement for a particular frame.

They may be also classified as:

- Individual acknowledgements: Individual acknowledgement for each frame.
- Group acknowledgements: A bit-map that specifies the acknowledgements of a range of frame numbers.

Flow Control

Consider a situation in which the sender transmits frames faster than the receiver can accept them. If the sender keeps pumping out frames at high rate, at some point the receiver will be completely swamped and will start losing some frames. This problem may be solved by introducing flow control. Most flow control protocols contain a feedback mechanism to inform the sender when it should transmit the next frame.

Mechanisms For Flow Control:

- **Stop and Wait Protocol:** This is the simplest file control protocol in which the sender transmits a frame and then waits for an acknowledgement, either positive or negative, from the receiver before proceeding. If a positive acknowledgement is received, the sender transmits the next packet; else it retransmits the same frame. However, this protocol has one major flaw in it. If a packet or an acknowledgement is completely destroyed in transit due to a noise burst, a deadlock will occur because the sender cannot proceed until it receives an acknowledgement.

This problem may be solved using timers on the sender's side. When the frame is transmitted, the timer is set. If there is no response from the receiver within a certain time interval, the timer goes off and the frame may be retransmitted.

- **Sliding Window Protocols:** Inspite of the use of timers, the stop and wait protocol still suffers from a few drawbacks. Firstly, if the receiver had the capacity to accept more than one frame, its resources are being underutilized. Secondly, if the receiver was busy and did not wish to receive any more packets, it may delay the acknowledgement. However, the timer on the sender's side may go off and cause an unnecessary retransmission. These drawbacks are overcome by the sliding window protocols.

In sliding window protocols the sender's data link layer maintains a 'sending window' which consists of a set of sequence numbers corresponding to the frames it is permitted to send. Similarly, the receiver maintains a 'receiving window' corresponding to the set of frames it is permitted to accept. The window size is dependent on the retransmission policy and it may differ in values for the receiver's and the sender's window. The sequence numbers within the sender's window represent the frames sent but as yet not acknowledged. Whenever a new packet arrives from the network layer, the upper edge of the window is advanced by one. When an acknowledgement arrives from the receiver the lower edge is advanced by one. The receiver's window corresponds to the frames that the receiver's data link layer may accept. When a frame with sequence number equal to the lower edge of the window is received, it is passed to the network layer, an acknowledgement is generated and the window is rotated by one. If however, a frame falling outside the window is received, the receiver's data link layer has two options. It may either discard this frame and all subsequent frames until the desired frame is received or it may accept these frames and buffer them until the appropriate frame is received and then pass the frames to the network layer in sequence.

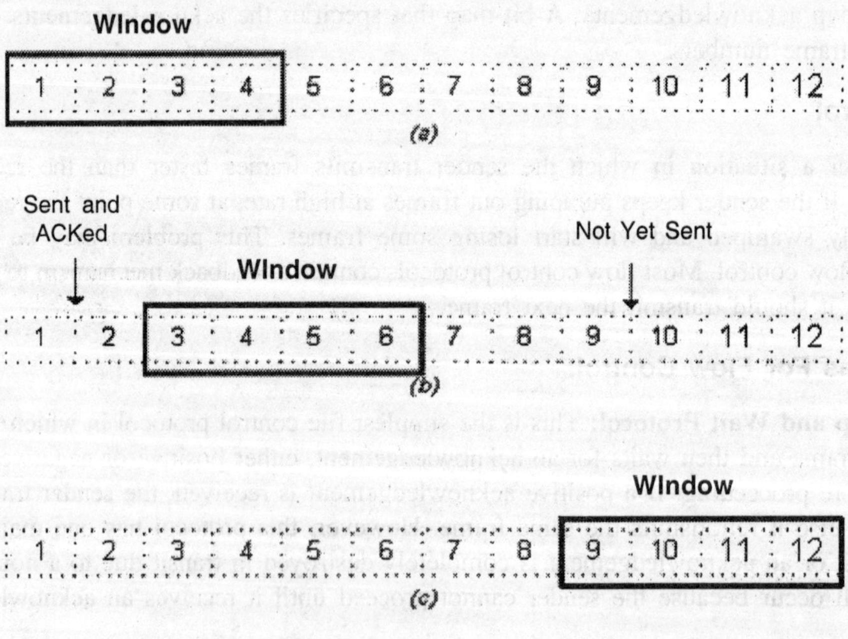

In this simple example, there is a 4-byte sliding window. Moving from left to right, the window "slides" as bytes in the stream are sent and acknowledged.

Most sliding window protocols also employ ARQ (Automatic Repeat reQuest) mechanism. In ARQ, the sender waits for a positive acknowledgement before proceeding to the next frame. If no acknowledgement is received within a certain time interval it retransmits the frame. ARQ is of two types:

1. Go Back 'n': If a frame is lost or received in error, the receiver may simply discard all subsequent frames, sending no acknowledgments for the discarded frames. In this case the receive window is of size 1. Since no acknowledgements are being received the sender's window will fill up, the sender will eventually time out and retransmit all the unacknowledged frames in order starting from the damaged or lost frame. The maximum window size for this protocol can be obtained as follows. Assume that the window size of the sender is n. So the window will initially contain the frames with sequence numbers from 0 to (w-1). Consider that the sender transmits all these frames and the receiver's data link layer receives all of them correctly. However, the sender's data link layer does not receive any acknowledgements as all of them are lost. So the sender will retransmit all the frames after its timer goes off. However the receiver window has already advanced to w. Hence to avoid overlap , the sum of the two windows should be less than the sequence number space.

w-1 + 1 < Sequence Number Space

i.e., w < Sequence Number Space

Maximum Window Size = Sequence Number Space - 1

2. Selective Repeat: In this protocol rather than discard all the subsequent frames following a damaged or lost frame, the receiver's data link layer simply stores them in buffers. When the sender does not receive an acknowledgement for the first frame it's timer goes off after a certain time interval and it retransmits only the lost frame. Assuming error - free transmission this time, the sender's data link layer will have a sequence of a many correct frames which it can hand over to the network layer. Thus there is less overhead in retransmission than in the case of Go Back n protocol.

In case of selective repeat protocol the window size may be calculated as follows. Assume that the size of both the sender's and the receiver's window is w. So initially both of them contain the values 0 to (w-1). Consider that sender's data link layer transmits all the w frames, the receiver's data link layer receives them correctly and sends acknowledgements for each of them. However, all the acknowledgemnets are lost and the sender does not advance it's window. The receiver window at this point contains the values w to (2w-1). To avoid overlap when the sender's data link layer retransmits, we must have the sum of these two windows less than sequence number space. Hence, we get the condition.

Maximum Window Size = Sequence Number Space / 2

THE MEDIUM ACCESS SUBLAYER

The **MAC** (Medium Access Control) sublayer is between the physical layer and the data link layer. The MAC sublayer is especially important in LANs, nearly all of which use a **multiaccess** (or broadcast) channel as the basis of their networks.

This chapter mainly deals with LANs, other broadcast networks and their protocols. The **key issue:** how to determine who gets to use the channel when there is competition for it?

Subsections

- The channel allocation problem
- Multiple access protocols
- IEEE standard 802 for LANs and MANs
- Bridges
- High-speed LANs
- Satellite networks

THE CHANNEL ALLOCATION PROBLEM

Static channel allocation in LANs and MANs

FDM (Frequency-Division Multiplexing): Divide the bandwidth into equal sized portions so that each user can be assigned one portion.

Under what circumstances FDM is efficient?

When there is only a small and fixed number of users, and each of which has a heavy (buffered) load of traffic (e.g., carriers' switching offices).

What's the problem with FDM?

- If fewer than users are currently interested in communication, some portions of spectrum will be wasted.
- If more than users want to communicate, some of them will be denied permission even if some users with allocated frequency hardly ever transmit anything.
- Even the number of users is and constant, when some users are quiescent, no one else can use their bandwidth so it is simply wasted.
- For bursty data traffic (peak traffic to mean traffic ratio of 1000:1), the allocated small subchannel will be idle most of the time but unable to handle the peak traffic.

Queueing theory calculation

Let be the mean time delay for a channel of bandwidth bps, with an frame arrival rate of per sec, each frame having a mean length of bits. From the queuing theory, we have where is the mean number of frames transmitted per sec by the channel.

Suppose the single channel is divided up into independent subchannels, each with capacity of bps. The frame arrival rate for each subchannel will be. Then the mean time delay for a subchannel:

Conclusion: the mean delay using FDM is times worse than if all the frames were transited in a big central channel.

The same arguments are also applicable to synchronous time-division multiplexing.

Dynamic channel allocation in LANs and MANs

Five key assumptions:

1. **Station model:**
   - o independent stations for generating frames.
   - o The probability of generating a frame in an interval of is (is the arrival rate of new frames).
   - o Once a frame has been generated, the station is blocked until the frame has been transmitted.
2. **Single channel assumption**. A single channel for all communication (send and receive), and all stations are equivalent.
3. **Collision assumption**. If the transmission of two frames overlap in time, a **collision** occurs. All stations can detect collisions. A collided frame must be retransmitted.
4. **Time assumption:**
   - o **Continuous time**. Frame transmission can begin at any instant.
   - o **Slotted time**. Frame transmission always begin at the start of a slot (a discrete intervals), controlled by a master clock.
5. **Sense assumption:**
   - o **Carrier sense**. Stations can tell if the channel is in use before trying to use it.
   - o **No carrier sense**. Stations cannot sense the channel before trying to use it.

MULTIPLE ACCESS PROTOCOLS

ALOHA

The ALOHA system was used for ground-based radio broadcasting, but the basic idea is applicable to any system in which uncoordinated users are competing for the use of a single shared channel.

Pure ALOHA

Basic idea:

- Let users transmit whenever they have data to be sent.
- A sender can always find out whether or not its frame was destroyed by listening to the channel output (due to the feedback property of broadcasting).
- If the frame was destroyed, the sender just waits a random amount of time and sends it again.

Systems in which multiple users share a common channel in a way that can lead to conflicts are known as **contention** systems.

Whenever two frames try to occupy the channel at the same time there will be a collision.

What fraction of all transmitted frames escape collisions under these chaotic circumstances?

Assumptions and definitions:

- **Infinite population**: there are an infinite number of users (stations) in the system.
- **T**: the amount of time needed to transmit a standard, fixed-length frame.
- **S**: the mean number of frames **generated** within one T. Normally, What happens if?

  At equilibrium (a balanced situation), S represents the number of successful transmissions (or throughput) of the network.
- **G**: the mean number of frames **transmitted** within one T. G includes the number of new frames and retransmissions and it represents the traffic load.
- where is the probability of a transmission being successful.

A frame will not suffer a collision if no other frames are sent within one frame time of its start.

The vulnerable period in which the transmitted frame will be destroyed is.

In an interval of, the mean number of frames transmitted is.

The probability that frames are generated during a given period of time is (by the assumption of Poisson distribution):

where is the mean number of frames transmitted within the given period of time.

The probability that frame is generated during a given period of time is:

The probability of no other traffic being initiated during the entire vulnerable period () is

Using, we get

At, (18% channel utilization)

Slotted ALOHA system:

- Time is divided up into discrete intervals, each interval corresponding to one frame.
- A terminal is not permitted to send until the beginning of the next slot.

The vulnerable period is reduced in half (instead of), the number of transmitted frames in this period is (instead of), leading to

Slotted ALOHA peaks at, with, twice that of pure ALOHA.

The main reason for poor channel utilization of ALOHA (pure or slotted) is that all stations can transmit at will, without paying attention to what the other stations are doing.

In LANs, it is possible for stations to detect what other stations are doing, and adapt their behavior accordingly, achieving a much better channel utilization.

Carrier sense multiple access protocols

Protocols in which stations listen for a carrier (i.e., a transmission) and act accordingly are called **carrier sense protocols**.

Persistent and nonpersistent CSMA

1-persistent CSMA (Carrier Sense Multiple Access):

- To send data, a station first listens to the channel to see if anyone else is transmitting.
- If so, the station waits (keeps sensing it) until the channel becomes idle. Otherwise, it transmits a frame.
- If a collision occurs (how?), the station waits a random amount of time and starts all over again.

It is called 1-persistent because the station transmits with a probability of 1 whenever it starts sensing the channel and finds the channel idle.

How could collisions happen in CSMA?

Whenever more than one station detect a idle channel and their transmission times overlap.

Discussions:

- What's the effect of signal propagation delay?

The longer the delay, the more the collisions, and the worse the performance of the protocol.

- How about zero propagation delay?

There still exist chances of collisions.

- Is this protocol any better than ALOHA (both pure and slotted)?

Yes, because both stations have the decency to desist from interfering with the third station's frame.

Nonpersistent CSMA

- To send data, a station first listens to the channel to see if anyone else is transmitting.
- If so, the station waits a random period of time (instead of keeping sensing until the end of the transmission) and repeats the algorithm. Otherwise, it transmits a frame.
- If a collision occurs, the station waits a random amount of time and starts all over again.

This protocol has better channel utilization and longer delays than 1-persistent CSMA.

P-persistent CSMA(applied to slotted channels):

- To send data, a station first listens to the channel to see if anyone else is transmitting.
- If the channel is idle, it transmits with a probability. With a probability it defers until the next slot.

If the next slot is also idle, it either transmits or defers again, with probabilities and.

This process is repeated until either the frame has been transmitted or another station has begun transmitting. In the latter case, it waits a random time and starts again.

- If a collision occurs, the station waits a random amount of time and starts all over again.
- If the channel is (initially) busy, it waits until the next slot and apply the above algorithm.

CSMA with collision detection

Persistent and nonpersistent CSMA protocols improve ALOHA by ensuring that no station begins to transmit when it senses the channel busy.

CSMA/CD (Carrier Sense Multiple Access with Collision Detection) protocol further improves ALOHA by aborting transmissions as soon as a collision is detected.

The conceptual model:

- To send data, a station first listens to the channel to see if anyone else is transmitting.
- If so, the station waits until the end of the transmission (1-persistent) or wait a random period of time and repeats the algorithm (nonpersistent). Otherwise, it transmits a frame.
- If a collision occurs, the station will detect the collision, abort its transmission, waits a random amount of time, and starts all over again.

The model for CSMA/CD consists of alternating contention and transmission periods, with idle periods occurring when all stations are quiet.

When two stations both begin transmitting at exactly the same time, how long will it take them to realize that there has been a collision?

The minimum time to detect the collision is the time it takes the signal to propagate from one station to the other.

How long could the transmitting station be sure it has seized the network? (or? where is time equal to the full cable propagation).

The contention interval can be modeled as a slotted ALOHA system with slot width.

Collision detection is an *analog* process the signal encoding must allow collisions to be detected Manchester encoding.

It is worth noting that no MAC-sublayer protocol guarantees reliable delivery. Even in the absence of collisions, the receiver may not have copied the frame correctly due to various reasons (e.g., lack of buffer space or a missed interrupt).

Collision-free protocols

Can we avoid collision all together, even during the contention period?

Yes. But how?

One assumption: there are stations, each with a unique address from 0 to "wired" into it.

Which station gets the channel after a successful transmission?

A basic bit-map protocol:

- Each contention period consists of exactly slots, with one slot time being at least.
- If station has a frame to send, it transmits 1 bit during the th slot; otherwise, it transmits 0 bit during the th slot.
- After all slots have passed by, stations begin transmitting in numerical order.
- After the last ready station has transmitted its frame, another -bit contention period is begun.

Protocols like this in which the desire to transmit is broadcast before the actual transmission are called **reservation protocols.**

Low load situation: the bit map repeats over and over.

Assume one contention bit slot as one time unit, and a data frame consists of time units.

For a low-numbered station, when it's ready to send, the "current" slot may be somewhere in the middle of the bit map.

Therefore, it has to wait slots (on the average) for the current scan to finish and another full slots for the following scan to complete before it may begin transmitting.

For a high-numbered station, it will have to wait half a scan (bit slots) before starting to transmit.

The mean waiting bit slots for all station is slots.

The channel efficiency is at low load, but at high load.

Binary countdown

A problem with the basic bit-map protocol is that overhead is 1 contention bit slot per station. We can do better than that by using binary station addresses.

- Each station has a binary address. All addresses are the same length.
- To transmit, a station broadcasts its address as a binary bit string, starting with high-order bit.
- The bits in each address position from different stations are BOOLEAN ORed together (so called **Binary countdown**).
- As soon as a station sees that a high-order bit position that is 0 in its address has been overwritten with a 1, it gives up.
- After the winning station has transmitted its frame, there is no information available telling how many other stations to send, so the algorithm begins all over with the next frame.

The channel efficiency of this method is.

Limited-contention protocols

Two basic channel acquisition strategies studied:

1. Contention methods. E.g., ALOHA, CSMA.
2. Collision-free methods. E.g., basic bit map.

Two performance measures:

1. Delay at low load. Contention methods are preferable.
2. Channel efficiency at high load. Collision-free methods are preferable.

Could we combine the best properties of both the contention and collision-free protocols?

Yes. Such new protocols, called **limited contention protocols**, use a contention method at low loads, but use a collision-free technique at high loads.

Analysis of symmetric contention protocols

Assumption: all stations attempt to acquire the channel with the same probability .

The probability for a station to successfully acquire the channel during a given slot if there are stations contending for it:

Basic idea

- Stations are divided into groups.
- Each group is allocated a slot for transmission.
- Members of one group compete for one slot only.

Special cases

- Each group with only one member (e.g., basic bit-map). Collision-free.
- Each group with two stations. The probability that both will try to transmit during a slot is, which for small is negligible.
- A single group containing all stations (i.e., slotted ALOHA). Zero delay at low load but very high collisions at high load.

What we need is a way to assign stations to slots dynamically, with many stations per slot when the load is low and few station per slot when the load is high.

The adaptive tree walk protocol

The algorithm devised by US Army for testing soldiers for syphilis during WW II:

- The Army took a blood sample from soldiers.
- A portion of each sample was poured into a single test tube. The mixed sample was then tested for antibodies.
- If none were found, all the soliders in the group were declared healthy.
- Otherwise, two new mixed samples were prepared, one for soldiers 1 through and one from the rest.
- The process was repeated recursively until the infected soldiers were determined.

The computer version of this algorithm organizes the stations in a binary tree, as illustrated in Fig.

Each bit slot (group) is associated with a particular node in the tree, with the root node corresponding to slot 0 for all stations in one group.

- Starting from the root node: all stations are permitted to try to acquire the channel.
- If a collision occurs, the search continues recursively with the left and right children of that node.
- If a bit slot goes idle or if there is exactly one station that transmits into it, the searching of its node can stop.

Is it worthwhile to dedicate slot 0 to the root node for all stations to compete?

At what level in the tree the search should begin?

The heavier the load, the deeper level the search should begin.

Assumption: each station has a good estimate of the number of ready station, and the ready stations are uniformly distributed.

The levels of the tree are numbered as follows: the level of the root node is numbered 0. For a level, the level below it is numbered as.

Each node at level has a fraction of of the total stations below it. The number of ready stations below a specific node at level is.

Therefore, the optimal level to begin searching the tree should be the one at which the mean number of contending stations per slot is 1, i.e., so.

IEEE standard 802 for LANs and MANs

IEEE 802 standards include CSMA/CD, token bus, and token ring.

IEEE standard 802.3 and Ethernet

This standard is for a 1-persistent CSMA/CD LAN:

- When a station wants to transmit, it listens to the cable.
- If the cable is busy, the station waits until it goes idle, otherwise it transmits immediately.
- If a collision occurs, all colliding stations terminate their transmission, wait a random time, and repeat the whole process all over again.

802.3 Cabling

Detecting cable breaks, bad taps, or loose connectors can be a major problem with both 10Base5 and 10Base2, which has driven systems using 10Base-T based on twisted pairs.

Connection device: transceiver.

- Contact the cable.
- Handle carrier detection and collision detection.
- Issue invalid signals.

A transceiver cable (up to 50 m) connects the transceiver to an interface board in the computer.

The interface board contains a controller chip that transmits frames to, and receives frames from, the transceiver. The controller is responsible for

- assembling the data into the proper frame format,
- computing checksums on outgoing frames and verifying them on incoming frames, and
- (optionally) managing a pool of buffers for incoming frames, a queue of buffers for frames to be transmitted.

The controller contact the computer by means of interrupts, DMA, and I/O commands.

Repeaters are used to connect multiple cables together. It receives, amplifies, and retransmits signals in both directions. Repeaters are physical layer devices.

No two transceivers may be more than 2.5 km apart, and no path between any two transceivers may traverse more than four repeaters.

Manchester encoding

None of the versions of 802.3 use straight binary encoding because it leads to ambiguities: it cannot tell the difference between an idle sender (0 volts) and a 0 bit (0 volts).

What is needed is a way for receivers to unambiguously determine the start, end, or middle of each bit without reference to an external clock.

All 802.3 baseband systems use Manchester encoding due to its simplicity. The high signal is volts and the low signal is volts, giving a DC value of 0 volts.

The 802.3 MAC sublayer protocol

Preamble of 7 bytes, each with the bit pattern 10101010. For synchronization between the sender and the receiver.

Start of frame byte contains 10101011 to denote the start of the frame.

Destination and source addresses, each with 2-6 bytes.

- Ordinary address: the high-order bit value is 0.
- Multicast address: the high-order bit value is 1.
- Broadcast address: all bits have a value of 1.
- Local address: assigned by local network administrator, distinguished by the second high-order bit (46) value 0.
- Global address ( ): assigned by IEEE to ensure world wide uniqueness, distinguished by the second high-order bit value 1.

Length: 0 (46) - 1500 bytes. To make it easier to distinguish valid frames from garbage, 802.3 states that valid frames must be at least 64 bytes.

Another more important reason for having a minimum length frame is to prevent a station from completing the transmission of a short frame before the first bit has even reached the far end of the cable, which it may collide with another frame.

After a collision, the station waits for a random time and try again. How the randomization is done?

The **binary exponential backoff** algorithm:

Time is divided into discrete slots whose length is equal to the worst case round trip propagation time ().

- After the first collision, each station waits either 0 or 1 slot time at random.
- After the second collision, each station waits either 0, 1, 2, or 3 slot times at random.
- After collisions, a random number between 0 and is chosen, and that number of slots is skipped.

- After 10 collisions have been reached, the randomization interval is frozen at 1023 slots.
- After 16 collisions, the controller gives up and reports failure.

What happens if the randomization interval for all collisions is always 1023? Think about the average delay when only a few stations collide.

What happens if the randomization interval for all collisions is always 2? Think about the time needed to resolve the collision when 100 stations try to send at once.

For reliable communication, the first contention slot following successful transmission can be reserved for the destination to acknowledge the source.

802.3 performance

Conditions: heavy and constant load, i.e., stations always ready to transmit.

If the mean frame takes sec to transmit, when many stations have frames to send,

Channel efficiency = What is the?

If each station transmits during a contention slot with probability , the probability that only one station transmits during that slot is

is maximized when, with as.

The probability that the contention interval has exactly slots in it is , so the mean number of slots per contention is Since each slot has a duration, the *mean-contention-interval* is. So

Channel efficiency = The longer the cable, the longer the contention interval (the larger the), and the lower the channel efficiency.

Let be the frame length, the network bandwidth, the cable length, and the speed of signal propagation. With , , and (the optimal case), we have,

Channel efficiency = Increasing the frame length () raises the channel efficiency.

Increasing network bandwidth () and/or distance () reduces channel efficiency for a given frame size. So 802.3 is not suitable for networks with high bandwidth over long distances (e.g., fiber optic MANs).

The channel efficiency is plotted versus number of ready stations for sec and a data rate of 10 Mbps using.

Channel efficiency (Mbps) = With 64-byte frames and a 64-byte slot time, the efficiency is very low (with 0.5 being the best).

With 1024-byte frames and an asymptotic value of slots per contention interval, the efficiency is 0.85.

Switched 802.3 LANs

The heart of the system is a switch containing a high-speed (typically over 1 Gbps) backplane and room for multiple plug-in cards (typically 4 to 32), with one to eight connectors in each card.

- To transmit, a station outputs a standard 802.3 frame to a plug-in card in the switch.
- The plug-in card checks to see if the frame is destined for one of the other stations connected to the same card.

If so, the frame is copied there. If not, the frame is sent over the high-speed backplane to the destination station's card.

What happens if two machines attached to the same plug-in card transmit frames at the same time?

In case that all the ports on the card are wired together to form a local on-card LAN:

- Collisions on this on-card LAN will be detected and handled the same as any other collisions on a CSMA/DC network.
- Only one transmission per card is possible at any instant, but all the cards can be transmitting in parallel.

In case that each input port is buffered, so incoming frames are stored in the card's on-board RAM as they arrive:

- Once a frame has been completely received, the card checks to see if the frame is destined for another port on the same card, or for a distant port.

  In the former case it can be transmitted directly to the destination.

  In the latter case, it must be transmitted over the backplane to the proper card.
- All input ports can receive (and transmit) frames at the same time, for parallel, full-duplex operation.

If all the input ports are connected to hubs, rather than to individual stations, the switch just becomes an 802.3 to 802.3 bridge (to be discussed later).

IEEE standard 802.4: token bus

Two problems with 802.3:

1. The worst case is unbounded: a station might have to wait arbitrarily long to send a frame. Unsuitable for factory automation applications (e.g, GM).
2. Frames do not have priorities. Unsuitable for real time systems.

- Physically, it is a linear or tree-shaped cable onto which the stations are attached.

  The 75-ohm broadband coaxial cable is used at the physical layer. Analog modulation schemes are used to transmit digital signals. Speeds of 1, 5, 10 Mbps are possible.

- Logically, the stations are organized into a ring, with each station knowing the address of the station to its "left" and "right".
  - o When the logical ring is initialized, the highest numbered station may send the first frame.
  - o Then, it passes to its immediate neighbor a special frame called a **token**.
  - o The token propagates around the logical ring, with only the token holder being permitted to transmit.

Since only one station at a time holds the token, collisions do not occur.

If there are stations and each station can hold the token for a maximum sec, no station will ever have to wait more than sec to get a chance.

When a station is first powered on, it is not in the ring. Provisions are provided for adding to, and deleting stations from the ring.

The token bus MAC sublayer protocol

Token propagation direction: from high address to low address.

The priority scheme:

- Each station conceptually consists of four substations, with each substation in one of the four traffic priority classes: 0, 2, 4, and 6 (the highest).

  As input comes into the MAC sublayer from above, the data are routed to one of the substations according to their priority.
- When a token comes in, it is passed internally to the priority 6 substation, which may transmit until its queue is empty or its timer expires and then pass the token to the next priority substation, and so on.
- Each station may hold the token for certain amount of time (quantum), then it must pass the token on (preemptive).

  The priority 6 substation is guaranteed for a fraction of the total quantum (by setting its timer properly), the lower priorities will live with what is left over.

For a network of 50 stations, if 1/3 of its bandwidth 10 Mbps is allocated to priority 6 traffic, then each station has a guaranteed kbps for priority 6 substation.

The frame format

Preamble field (1 byte) is used to synchronize the receiver's clock.

Starting and ending delimiters fields contain analog encoding of symbols other than 0s and 1s. As a result, no length field is needed.

Frame control field distinguishes data frames from control frames.

- For data frames, it carries the frame's priority and an indicator for whether an acknowledgement is required.
- For control frames, it carries the frame's type: token passing, entering the ring, leaving the ring, and so on.

Destination and source addresses fields are the same as in 802.3.

Data field may be up to 8182 bytes - five times the maximum 802.3 frame.

Logical ring maintenance

Each station interface contains the following infrastructures:

- Addresses of the predecessor and successor stations. Initialized after joining a ring.
- Two random bits used to distinguish 4 time slots for resolving collisions (combined with the binary countdown protocol). Regenerated periodically or after use.
- A number of timers.

Joining the ring

- The token holder periodically (timer) broadcasts a frame which contains the holder's address and its successor's.
- Only stations with addresses in that range are allowed to bid to enter.
- If no one bids to enter within a slot time (), the token holder continues with its normal business.
- If exactly one station bids to enter, it is inserted into the ring, and becomes the token holder's successor.
- If two or more stations bid to enter, a collision occurs. The token holder runs an arbitration algorithm (a variation of binary countdown), starting with the broadcast of a frame. Only one station may enter at each solicitation.

Leaving the ring

- Suppose the leaving station, has successor and predecessor.
- It leaves the ring by sending a frame telling it that henceforth its successor is instead of.

The should also be informed that its new predecessor is.

- stops transmitting.

Initializing the ring

- When the first station comes on line, it notices that there is no traffic for a certain period (timer). Then it sends a frame.
- Not hearing any competitors contending for the token, it creates a token and sets up a ring containing only itself.

If two or more stations are powered on simultaneously, an arbitration algorithm is used to resolve the collision. Only one of the stations may create a token.

- Periodically (timer), it solicits bids for new stations to join.

What happens if a station tries to pass the token to its successor that has gone down?

- After passing the token, a station listens to see if its successor either transmits a frame or passes the token.
- If the successor does neither, the token is passed a second time.
- If that also fails, the station the successor has gone down, and transmits a frame specifying the address of its successor.
- When the failed station's successor sees this frame naming its predecessor, it responds by sending a frame to the station whose successor failed, naming itself as the new successor.
- If a station fails to pass the token to its successor and also fails to locate the successor's successor, which may also be down, it sends a frame to see if else is still alive so all alive stations will re-join the ring.

What happens if the token holder goes down and takes the token with it?

- Each station has a timer that is reset whenever a frame appears on network.
- When this timer hits a threshold value, the station issues a frame to reinitialize the ring.

What happens if there are multiple tokens in the ring?

- If a station holding the token notices a transmission from another station, it discards its token.
- If, by accident, all the tokens are discarded, the lack of activity will cause one or more stations to try to claim the token.

IEEE standard 802.5: token ring

A ring network is not really a broadcast medium, but a collection of point-to-point links that happen to form a circle. Main attractive features:

- Point-to-point links can run on different transmission media.
- Ring engineering is almost entirely digital (Ethernet has a substantial analog component for collision detection).
- A ring is fair and has a known upper bound on channel access.

The concept of "physical length" of a bit:

- If the data rate of the ring is Mbps, a bit is emitted every sec.
- With a typical signal propagation speed of 200 m/sec, each bit occupies meters on the ring.

For a 1-Mbps ring whose circumference is 1000 meters can contain only 5 bits on it at once.

Each bit arriving at an interface is copied into a 1-bit buffer, inspected, possibly modified, and then copied out onto the ring again, causing a so called 1-bit delay at each interface.

In a token ring,

- A special bit pattern, called the **token,** circulates whenever all stations are idle.
- When a station wants to transmit, it is required to seize the token and remove it from the ring before transmitting.
- After a station has finished transmitting the last bit of its last frame, it must regenerate the token.

The ring must have a sufficient delay (the 1-bit delay plus the signal propagation delay) to contain a complete token to circulate when all stations are idle.

Ring interfaces have two operating modes:

- In **listen mode**, the input bits are copied to output. The input may be copied into the station if it is the destination.
- In **transmit mode**, which is entered only after the token has been seized, the interface breaks the connection between input and output, entering its own data onto the ring.

When the last bit of the frame has gone around and come back, the interface must switch back into listen mode.

As bits have propagated around the ring and come back, they are removed from the ring by the sender. So there is no limit on the size of the frames.

Acknowledgement handling:

- The frame includes a 1-bit, initially zero.
- When the destination has received a frame, it inverts the bit.
- For broadcast, a more complicated scheme is needed.

The network efficiency can approach 100% under conditions of heavy load.

802.5 standard:

- Shielded twisted pairs running at 1 or 4 Mbps.
- Signals are encoded using differential Manchester encoding.

Wire center: to improve the ring's reliability and maintainability.

The token ring MAC sublayer protocol

The basic operation:

- When no traffic on the ring, a 3-byte token circulates endlessly.

- When the token is seized, a specific 0 bit in the second byte is converted into 1. This action converts the first two bytes of the token into the start-of-frame sequence.
- The station then outputs the rest of a normal data frame.

A station may hold the token for the token-holding time (10 msec).

Starting and ending delimiters mark the boundaries of the frame using invalid differential Machester patterns (HH and LL).

Access control byte contains the token bit, and Monitor bit, Priority bits, and Reservation bits.

Frame control byte distinguishes data frames from various control frames.

Destination and source addresses are the same as in 802.3 and 802.4.

Data field may be as long as necessary but must be transmitted within a token holding time.

Checksum field is also the same as 802.3 and 802.4.

Frame status byte contains the and bits, which may be modified by the destination station. When the source station drains the frame from the ring, it examines the two bits:

1. and : destination not present or not powered up.
2. and : destination present but frame not accepted.
3. and : destination present and frame copied.

Priority handling:

- The 3-byte token frame contains a field in the middle byte giving the priority of the token.
- When a station wants to transmit a priority frame, it must wait until it can capture a token with a priority less than or equal to.
- When a data frame goes by, a station can reserve the next token by writing the priority of the frame it want to send into the passing frame's *Reservation bits* if there is no higher priority already reserved there.
- When the current frame is finished, the next token is generated at the the priority reserved.

Ring maintenance

Centralized monitoring: One of the stations acts as a **monitor station** which oversees the ring. If the monitor goes down, a contention protocol insures that another station is elected monitor.

Monitor generation

- When the ring comes up or any station notices that there is no monitor, it transmits a control frame.

- If this frame circumnavigates the ring before any other frames are sent, the sender becomes the new monitor.

Monitor's responsibilities

- Checking whether the token is lost.

  A timer is set to the longest possible tokenless interval, i.e., each station transmitting for the full token-holding time. If this timer goes off, the monitor drains the ring and issues a new token.

- Taking action when the ring breaks.

  Locating breaks in the ring is not done by the monitor. Any station may transmit a frame to locate and delete its presumably dead neighbors, without human intervention.

- Keeping the ring longer than 24 bits.

  If the 1-bit delays in the stations plus the cable length add up to less than 24 bits (the length of a token), the monitor inserts extra delay bits so that a token can circulate.

- Cleaning the ring up when garbled frames appear.

  When a garbled frame appears, the monitor can detect it by its invalid format or checksum, and then open the ring to drain it, issuing a new token when the ring has been cleaned up.

- Watching out for orphan frames.

  An orphan frame occurs when a station transmits a short frame in its entirety onto a long ring and then crashes or is powered down before the frame can be drained.

  The monitor detects orphan frames by setting the *monitor* bit in the *Access control* byte whenever it passes through. If an incoming frame has this bit set, it is treated as an orphan (drained).

Comparison of 802.3, 802.4, and 802.5

Which LAN would you like to choose?

Three LAN standards use roughly similar technology and get roughly similar performance.

Advanteges of 802.3 (Ethernet)

- The most widely used type.
- Simple algorithm.
- Stations can be installed on the fly, without taking the network down.
- A passive cable is used and modems are not required.
- The delay at low load is very low.

Limitations and problems of 802.3 (Ethernet):

- It has a substantial analog component to detect collision.
- The minimum frame is 64 bytes, a substantial overhead when the data is just a single character.
- It is nondeterministic, without upper bound for delay.
- It has no priorities.
- The cable length is limited to 2.5 km because the round trip cable length determines the slot time.
- It is very difficult to run at high speed because when the speed increase, the frame transmission times drop but the contention interval does not (alway), resulting in low efficiency.
- At high load, collisions become a major problem (low throughput).
- It is not well suited to fiber optics due to the difficulty of installing taps.

Advantages of 802.4 (token bus):

- It uses highly reliable, off-the-shelf cable TV equipment.
- It is more deterministic than 802.3. (what about the repeated losses of the token at critical moments?).
- It can handle short minimum frames.
- It supports priorities and provides a guaranteed fraction of the bandwidth to high-priority traffic.
- Excellent throughput and efficiency at high load (effectively TDM).
- Broadband cable can support multiple channels.

Limitations and problems of 802.4 (token bus):

- Broadband systems use analog engineering (modems and amplifiers).
- Extremely complex protocol and substantial delay at low load (wait for the token).
- Poorly suited for fiber optic implementation.

Advantages of 802.5 (token ring):

- Point-to-point connections mean easy engineering and fully digital.
- Rings can be built using any transmission medium.
- The standard twisted pair is cheap and simple to install.
- The use of wire centers makes the token ring the only LAN that can detect and eliminate cable failures automatically.

- Priorities are possible (using not so fair scheme).
- Short frames are possible.
- The length of large frames is limited only by the token-holding time.
- Excellent throughput and efficiency at high load.

Limitations and problems of 802.4 (token bus):

- The centralized monitor introduces a critical component.
- Large delay at low load..

The principle conclusion we can draw from these studies is that we can draw no conclusion from them.

One inarguable general statement: an overloaded 802.3 LAN will collapse totally, but an overloaded token-based system will have an efficiency approaching 100 per cent.

The convergence of three LANs is an unlikely event, so the issue of interconnecting (by bridges and gateways) different LANs is an important one, which will be discussed later.

IEEE standard 802.6: Distributed Queue Dual Bus

For networks covering an entire city with thousands of stations, IEEE defined one MAN, called **DQDB (Distributed Queue Dual Bus)**, as standard 802.6.

- Two unidirectional buses.
- Each bus has a head-end, which generates a steady stream of 53-byte cells. Each cell travels downstream from the head-end, carring a 44-byte payload field. When it reaches the end, it falls off the bus.
- Each cell also holds two protocol bits, *Busy*, set to indicate that a cell is occupied, and *Request*, which can be set when a station wants to make a request.
- Data traffic to the right uses the upper bus (but the lower bus is used for making a request).
- Traffic to the left uses the lower bus (but the upper bus is used for making a request).

Stations in a DQDB queue up in the order they became ready to send and transmit in FIFO order.

DQDB systems typically run for up to 160 km at speed 44.736 Mbps (T3).

How does DQDB achieve FIFO order without having a central queue?

IEEE standard 802.2: Logical Link Control

The LLC (Logical Link Control) layer offers three types of services to the network layer:

- connectionless (type 1),

- connection-oriented (type 2),
- and acknowledged connectless (type 3).

The LLC header is based on the older HDLC protocol.

Bridges

LANs can be connected by devices called **bridges**, which operate in the data link layer. This means that bridges do not examine the network layer header and can thus copy IP, IPX, and OSI packets equally well.

Most bridges connect 802 LANs, so we will concentrate primarily on 802 bridges.

Reasons why a single organization may end up with multiple LANs and bridges are needed:

1. Different goals of different departments.
2. Geographical distance (cheaper and shorter delay).
3. Accommodation of the heavy load

Bridges from 802.x to 802.y

General problems:

- Different frame formats.

  Solution: reformatting.
- Different data rates (802.3 10Mbps, 802.4 10Mbps, and 802.5 4Mbps).

  Solution: buffering.
- Different maximum frame length (802.3 1518 bytes, 802.4 8191 bytes, and 802.5 no upper limit (token holding time 10 msec 5000 bytes)).

  Solution: None.

IEEE 802 committee produced incompatible bridge designs to cope with their incompatible LAN standards.

Transparent bridges

The CSMA/CD and token bus people chose the transparent bridges.

Multiple LANs connected by **transparent bridges** do not need any change on their hardware and software.

Transparent bridges operate in promiscuous mode, accepting every frame transmitted on all the LANs to which it is attached.

When a frame arrives, a bridge must decide whether to discard or forward it, and if the latter, on which LAN to put the frame.

A bridge maintains a big (hash) table of destination addresses.

- Initially all the hash tables are empty.
- Every incoming frame for an unknown destination is output on all the LANs to which the bridge is connected except the one it arrived on (flooding).
- By looking at the incoming frame's source address (backward learning), a bridge is able to know which machine is accessible on which LAN, so it make an entry in its hash table linking the source machine with the incoming LAN.
- To handle dynamic topologies, whenever a hash table entry is made, the arrival time of the frame is noted in the entry.

The entry time is updated whenever a frame from the address in that entry arrives.

Periodically, a process in the bridge scans the hash table and purges all entries more than a few minutes old.

Routing procedure:

1. If destination and source LANs are the same, discard the frame.
2. If the destination and source LANs are different, forward the frame.
3. If the destination LAN is unknown, use flooding.

Special purpose VLSI chips exist to do the lookup and update the table entry, all in a few microsecond.

To increase reliability, some sites use two or more bridges in parallel between pairs of LANs.

This arrangement creates loops in the topology.

What happens if a frame with an unknow destination arrives?

The solution is for the bridges to communicate with each other and overlay the actual topology with a spanning tree that reaches every LAN.

Large networks can be partitioned into multiple communicating spanning trees.

Source routing bridges

The ring people (with encouragement from IBM) preferred a scheme called **source routing**:

- The sender of each frame is assumed to know whether or not the destination is on its own LAN.
- When sending a frame to a different LAN, the source machine sets the high-order bit of the destination address to 1 and includes in the frame header the exact path that the frame is to follow.
- Each LAN has a unique 12-bit number, and each bridge has a 4-bit number that uniquely identify it in its LANs.

A route is a sequence of bridge, LAN, bridge, LAN, ..., numbers.

- Only those frames with the high-order bit of the destination set to 1 are interested by the source routing bridge.

The source routing bridge scans the route looking for the number of the LAN on which the frame arrived.

If this LAN number is followed by its own bridge number, the bridge forwards the frame onto the LAN those number follows its bridge number in the route.

Otherwise, the frame is discarded.

Three possible implementations:

1. Software: the bridge copies all frames to its memory to see if they have the high-order destination bit set to 1. If so, the frame is inspected further, otherwise it is not.
2. Hybrid: the bridge's LAN interface inspects the high-order bit and only gives it frames with the bit set.
3. Hardware: the LAN interface checks the high-order bit and scan the route and only gives the bridge the frames that must be forwarded.

How can each machine in the internetwork know the exact path to every other machine ?

- If a destination is unknown, the source issues a broadcast frame asking where it is.
- This **discovery frame** is copied by every bridge so that it reaches every LAN on the internetwork.
- When the reply comes back, the bridges record their identity in it, so that the original sender can see the exact route taken and ultimately choose the best route.
- Once a host has discovered a route to a certain destination, it stores the route in a cache.

Comparison of 802 bridges

Remote bridges

Distant LANs can be connected by bridges to form one large LAN.

Distant bridges are connected by point-to-point lines, which can be regarded as hostless LANs.

High-speed LANs

High speed LANs often use fiber. Advantages of fiber optics:

- High bandwidth.
- Thin and lightweight.

- Not affected by electromagnetic interference from heavy machinery, power surges, or lightning.
- Excellent security.

FDDI

FDDI (Fiber Distributed Data Interface) is a high-performance fiber optic token ring LAN running at 100 Mbps over distance up to 200 km with up to 1000 stations connected.

Used as normal LANs, or as a backbone to connect copper LANs

The basic FDDI protocols are closely model on the 802.5 protocols:

- To transmit data, a station must first capture the token.
- Then it tranmits a frame and removes it when it comes around again.
- A new token can be put back onto the ring as soon as it has finished transmitting its frames.

FDDI data frames are very similar to the 802.5 data frames,

Fast Ethernet

The **Fast Ethernet** (IEEE 802.3u) is backward compatible with but faster than the existing 802.3 standard.

All the 802.3 packet formats, interfaces, and procedural rules are kept, but the bit time is reduced from 100 (10 Mbps) nsec to 10 nsec (100 Mbps).

Fast Ethernet is based entirely on twisted pair or fiber wiring,

100Base-T4 uses four twisted pairs (three for traffic from the station to the hub, one for the reverse traffic). Each pair runs at a signaling speed of 25 MHz. 4 bits (by the 8B6T scheme) are transmitted per clock cycle via three twisted pairs (to give 100Mbps), and another twisted pair provides a reverse channel at 33.3 Mbps.

100Base-TX uses two twisted pairs (one for each direction), each running at a signaling speed of 125 MHz. The **4B5B** scheme is used to transmit 4 bits per 5 clock cycles via each twisted pair (to give a full-duplex 100 Mbps).

100Base F uses two strands of multimode fiber, one for each direction, to give full duplex 100 Mbps. The distance between the station and the hub can be up to 2 km.

Two kinds of hubs are possible with 100Base-T4 and 100Base-TX:

- In a shared hub, all the incoming lines are logically connected, forming a single collision domain. Only one station at a time can be transmitting.
- In a switched hub, each incoming frame is buffered on a plug-in line card. Multiple stations can transmit and receive at the same time, increasing the total bandwidth of the system by an order of magnitude or more.

SATELLITE NETWORKS

Channel allocation in broadcast WANs.

Two basic facts:

1. Stations send frames to the satellite on the uplink frequency, and the satellite shifts these frames to the downlink frequency and **rebroadcasts** them.
2. The end-to-end propagation delay is about 270 msec (compared to a few microsec in coaxial cable-based LANs).
   - o Carrier sensing is impossible.
   - o A token based protocol is unattractive (27 sec is needed to pass a token around a 100 station ring/bus).

FDM and DTM

Satellites are used to connect a limited number of telephone switching offices, each of which has a continuous flow of data to transmit FDM or TDM.

- FDM: The transponder channel is divided into disjoint subchannels at different frequencies. When a call is placed, a subchannel is allocated and dedicated to it until the call is terminated. If no subchannel is available, the caller gets a busy signal and has to try again later.
- TDM: The transponder channel is divided into time slots, which are grouped into frames. Each frame time is 125 sec. When a call is placed, a slot in very frame is allocated and dedicated to it until the call is terminated. If no slot is available, the caller gets a busy signal and has to try again later.

Is there any difference between FDM and TDM?

- FDM requires guard bands to keep the signals well separated, but DTM does not.
- FDM can be used for broadcasting, but TDM cannot.
- TDM needs careful time slot synchronization, but FDM does not.

An example of FDM: the **SPADE** system.

Each transponder has a 50 Mbps bandwidth for the uplink portion, and another 50 Mbps bandwidth for the downlink portion.

Each transponder portion is divided into 794 simplex (64 kps) PCM channels, along with a 128 kbps common signaling channel.

The PCM channels are used in pairs to provide full duplex service. The common signaling channel is divided into units of 50 msec (TDM).

- A unit contains 50 slots of 1 msec (128 bits).

- Each slot is "owned" by one of 50 ground stations.
- When a ground station has data to send, it picks a currently unused channel at random and writes the number of that channel in its next 128-bit slot.
- If the selected channel is still unused when the request is seen on the downlink, the channel is considered allocated.
- If two or more stations try to allocate the same channel in the same unit, the first one wins.
- When a station is finished using its channel, it sends a deallocation message in its slot on the common channel.

ALOHA revisited

TDM, FDM, or SPADE are suitable for small and static number of stations, and all of them have continuous traffic.

ALOHA is a serious candidate for satellite broadcasting networks when there are hundreds stations with bursty traffic.

Can we improve ALOHA's channel efficiency at low load?

Analysis of the rebroadcasting cost of a slotted ALOHA satellite system:

- The satellite bandwidth is bps, which is equally allocated to the uplink channel and the downlink channel.
- The throughput is ().
- The channel efficiency is or

What happens if we use a system with two (independent slotted ALOHA) uplink channels but one downlink channel?

- A station chooses one of the two uplink channels at random for transmision each time.
- For each uplink channel, under the optimal condition , the probability of an empty slot is 0.368, the probability of successful transmission is 0.368, and the probability of a collision is 0.264.
- The probability of exactly one success:
- The probability of two successes (but one of them is rebroadcasted by the downlink channel): 0.135.
- The utilization of the downlink:
- The throughput: , so the efficiency is . 9% better.

Reservation ALOHA

Basic idea: using slotted ALOHA at low load, but using some kind of TDM as the channel load grows.

In TDM, each slot is permanently reserved for a specific station.

One common feature of all methods: some slots are reserved for specific stations.

Binder's method: A slot is owned by a station but available to others if the owner does not need it.

- Initially, TDM is used. So consecutive slots are grouped into a group, with one station "owning" one slot.
- If there is no transmitting during a slot time in the current group as the owner of a slot has no traffic or the slot is an extra not assigned to anyone, it is a signal to all others that this slot is free for contention.
- In the next group, free slots are available to everyone (including the owner), on a contention basis.
- If there is a collision in a slot, everyone except the owner must give up. So the owner can always begin transmitting within two group times in the worst case.

What's the problem with Binder's method?

Crowther's method: a dynamic mix of slotted ALOHA and TDM and applicable even when the number of stations is unknown and varying dynamically.

- Slots do not have permanent owners.
- All slots are free initially.
- Free slots are available for all users, on contention basis.
- Whenever a transmission is successful, the station is entitled to that slot in the next group until it finishes.

Assumption: the probability that all stations will have long runs of data to send simultaneously is very low.

Roberts' method and its variations (e.g., **PODA**, and **Distributed Reservation Control**): making advance requests before transmitting.

ARRA (Annouced Retransmission Random Access method: use the reservation slots not for reserving channel time for the frames, but for their retransmissions in the event of a collision.

NETWORK LAYER

What is Network Layer?

The network layer is concerned with getting packets from the source all the way to the destination. The packets may require to make many hops at the intermediate routers while reaching the destination. This is the lowest layer that deals with end to end transmission. In order to achieve its goals, the network layer must know about the topology of the communication network. It must also take care to choose routes to avoid overloading of some of the communication lines while leaving others idle. The network layer-transport layer interface frequently is the interface between the carrier and the customer, that is the boundary of the subnet. The functions of this layer include:

1. **Routing -** The process of transferring packets received from the Data Link Layer of the source network to the Data Link Layer of the correct destination network is called routing. Involves decision making at each intermediate node on where to send the packet next so that it eventually reaches its destination. The node which makes this choice is called a router. For routing we require some mode of addressing which is recognized by the Network Layer. This addressing is different from the MAC layer addressing.
2. **Inter-networking -** The network layer is the same across all physical networks (such as Token-Ring and Ethernet). Thus, if two physically different networks have to communicate, the packets that arrive at the Data Link Layer of the node which connects these two physically different networks, would be stripped of their headers and passed to the Network Layer. The network layer would then pass this data to the Data Link Layer of the other physical network..
3. **Congestion Control -** If the incoming rate of the packets arriving at any router is more than the outgoing rate, then congestion is said to occur. Congestion may be caused by many factors. If suddenly, packets begin arriving on many input lines and all need the same output line, then a queue will build up. If there is insufficient memory to hold all of them, packets will be lost. But even if routers have an infinite amount of memory, congestion gets worse, because by the time packets reach to the front of the queue, they have already timed out (repeatedly), and duplicates have been sent. All these packets are dutifully forwarded to the next router, increasing the load all the way to the destination. Another reason for congestion are slow processors. If the router's CPUs are slow at performing the bookkeeping tasks required of them, queues can build up, even though there is excess line capacity. Similarly, low-bandwidth lines can also cause congestion.

We will now look at these function one by one.

Addressing Scheme

IP addresses are of 4 bytes and consist of:

(i) The network address, followed by

(ii) The host address

The first part identifies a network on which the host resides and the second part identifies the particular host on the given network. Some nodes which have more than one interface to a network must be assigned separate internet addresses for each interface. This multi-layer addressing makes it easier to find and deliver data to the destination. A fixed size for each of these would lead to wastage or under-usage that is either there will be too many network addresses and few hosts in each (which causes problems for routers who route based on the network address) or there will be very few network addresses and lots of hosts (which will be a waste for small network requirements). Thus, we do away with any notion of fixed sizes for the network and host addresses.

We classify networks as follows:

1. **Large Networks :** 8-bit network address and 24-bit host address. There are approximately 16 million hosts per network and a maximum of 126 (2^7 - 2) Class A networks can be defined. The calculation requires that 2 be subtracted because 0.0.0.0 is reserved for use as the default route and 127.0.0.0 be reserved for the loop back function. Moreover each Class A network can support a maximum of 16,777,214 (2^24 - 2) hosts per network. The host calculation requires that 2 be subtracted because all 0's are reserved to identify the network itself and all 1s are reserved for broadcast addresses. The reserved numbers may not be assigned to individual hosts.
2. **Medium Networks :** 16-bit network address and 16-bit host address. There are approximately 65000 hosts per network and a maximum of 16,384 (2^14) Class B networks can be defined with up to (2^16-2) hosts per network.
3. **Small networks :** 24-bit network address and 8-bit host address. There are approximately 250 hosts per network.

You might think that Large and Medium networks are sort of a waste as few corporations/ organizations are large enough to have 65000 different hosts. (By the way, there are very few corporations in the world with even close to 65000 employees, and even in these corporations it is highly unlikely that each employee has his/her own computer connected to the network.) Well, if you think so, you're right. This decision seems to have been a mistak.

Address Classes

The IP specifications divide addresses into the following classes:

- Class A - For large networks

0	7	bits of the network address	24 bits of host address

- Class B - For medium networks

1	0	14 bits of the network address	16 bits of host address

- Class C - For small networks

1	1	0	21 bits of the network address	8 bits of host address

- Class D - For multi-cast messages (multi-cast to a "group" of networks)

1	1	1	0	28 bits for some sort of group address

- Class E - Currently unused, reserved for potential uses in the future

1	1	1	1	28 bits

Internet Protocol

Special Addresses: There are some special IP addresses:

1. Broadcast Addresses They are of two types:

   (i) Limited Broadcast : It consists of all 1's, i.e., the address is 255.255.255.255 . It is used only on the LAN, and not for any external network.

   (ii) Directed Broadcast : It consists of the network number + all other bits as1's. It reaches the router corresponding to the network number, and from there it broadcasts to all the nodes in the network. This method is a major security problem, and is not used anymore. So now if we find that all the bits are 1 in the host no. field, then the packet is simply dropped. Therefore, now we can only do broadcast in our own network using Limited Broadcast.

2. Network ID = 0

It means we are referring to this network and for local broadcast we make the host ID zero.

3. Host ID = 0

This is used to refer to the entire network in the routing table.

4. Loop-back Address

Here we have addresses of the type 127.x.y.z It goes down way upto the IP layer and comes back to the application layer on the same host. This is used to test network applications before they are used commercially.

Subnetting

Sub netting means organizing hierarchies within the network by dividing the host ID as per our network. For example consider the network ID : 150.29.x.y

We could organize the remaining 16 bits in any way, like:

4 bits - department

4 bits - LAN

8 bits - host

This gives some structure to the host IDs. This division is not visible to the outside world. They still see just the network number, and host number (as a whole). The network will have an internal routing table which stores information about which router to send an address to. Now consider the case where we have : 8 bits - subnet number, and 8 bits - host number. Each router on the network must know about all subnet numbers. This is called the subnet mask. We put the network number and subnet number bits as 1 and the host bits as 0. Therefore, in this example the subnet mask becomes : 255.255.255.0 . The hosts also need to know the subnet mask when they send a packet. To find if two addresses are on the same subnet, we can AND source address with subnet mask, and destination address with with subnet mask, and see if the two results are the same. The basic reason for sub netting was avoiding broadcast. But if at the lower level, our switches are smart enough to send directed messages, then we do not need sub netting. However, sub netting has some security related advantages.

Supernetting

This is moving towards class-less addressing. We could say that the network number is 21 bits (for 8 class C networks) or say that it is 24 bits and 7 numbers following that. For example : a.b.c.d / 21 This means only look at the first 21 bits as the network address.

Addressing on IITK Network

If we do not have connection with the outside world directly then we could have Private IP addresses (172.31) which are not to be publicised and routed to the outside world. Switches will make sure that they do not broadcast packets with such addressed to the outside world. The basic reason for implementing subnetting was to avoid broadcast. So in our case we can have some subnets for security and other reasons although if the switches could do the routing properly, then we do not need subnets. In the IITK network we have three subnets -CC, CSE building are two subnets and the rest of the campus is one subset

Packet Structure

Version Number (4 bits)	Header Length (4 bits)	Type of Service (8 bits)	Total Length (16 bits)
	ID (16 bits)	Flags (3bits)	Flag Offset (13 bits)
Time To Live (8 bits)	Protocol (8 bits)	Header Checksum (16 bits)	
	Source (32 bits)		
	Destination (32 bits)		
	Options		

Version Number : The current version is Version 4 (0100).

1. **Header Length :** We could have multiple sized headers so we need this field. Header will always be a multiple of 4bytes and so we can have a maximum length of the field as 15, so the maximum size of the header is 60 bytes (20 bytes are mandatory).
2. **Type Of Service (ToS) :** This helps the router in taking the right routing decisions. The structure is:

First three bits : They specify the precedences i.e. the priority of the packets.

Next three bits :

- o D bit - D stands for delay. If the D bit is set to 1, then this means that the application is delay sensitive, so we should try to route the packet with minimum delay.
- o T bit - T stands for throughput. This tells us that this particular operation is throughput sensitive.
- o R bit - R stands for reliability. This tells us that we should route this packet through a more reliable network.

Last two bits: The last two bits are never used. Unfortunately, no router in this world looks at these bits and so no application sets them nowadays. The second word is meant for handling fragmentations. If a link cannot transmit large packets, then we fragment the packet and put sufficient information in the header for recollection at the destination.

3. **ID Field :** The source and ID field together will represent the fragments of a unique packet. So each fragment will have a different ID.
4. **Offset :** It is a 13 bit field that represents where in the packet, the current fragment starts. Each bit represents 8 bytes of the packet. So the packet size can be at most 64 kB. Every fragment except the last one must have its size in bytes as a multiple of 8 in order to ensure compliance with this structure. The reason why the position of a fragment is given as an offset value instead of simply numbering each packet is because refragmentation may occur somewhere on the path to the other node. Fragmentation, though supported by IPv4 is not encouraged. This is because if even one fragment is lost the entire packet needs to be discarded. A quantity M.T.U (Maximum Transmission Unit) is defined for each link in the route. It is the size of the largest packet that can be handled by the link. The Path-M.T.U is then defined as the size of the largest packet that can be handled by the path. It is the smallest of all the MTUs along the path. Given information about the path MTU we can send packets with sizes smaller than the path MTU and thus prevent fragmentation. This will not completely prevent it because routing tables may change leading to a change in the path.
5. **Flags :**It has three bits -
   - o M bit : If M is one, then there are more fragments on the way and if M is 0, then it is the last fragment
   - o DF bit : If this bit is sent to 1, then we should not fragment such a packet.
   - o Reserved bit : This bit is not used.

   Reassembly can be done only at the destination and not at any intermediate node. This is because we are considering Datagram Service and so it is not guaranteed that all the fragments of the packet will be sent thorough the node at which we wish to do reassembly.
6. **Total Length :** It includes the IP header and everything that comes after it.
7. **Time To Live (TTL) :** Using this field, we can set the time within which the packet should be delivered or else destroyed. It is strictly treated as the number of hops. The

packet should reach the destination in this number of hops. Every router decreases the value as the packet goes through it and if this value becomes zero at a particular router, it can be destroyed.

8. **Protocol :** This specifies the module to which we should hand over the packet (UDP or TCP). It is the next encapsulated protocol.

Value	Protocol
0	Pv6 Hop-by-Hop Option.
1	ICMP, Internet Control Message Protocol.
2	IGMP, Internet Group Management Protocol. RGMP, Router-port Group Management Protocol.
3	GGP, Gateway to Gateway Protocol.
4	IP in IP encapsulation.
5	ST, Internet Stream Protocol.
6	TCP, Transmission Control Protocol.
7	UCL, CBT.
8	EGP, Exterior Gateway Protocol.
9	IGRP.
10	BBN RCC Monitoring.
11	NVP, Network Voice Protocol.
12	PUP.
13	ARGUS.
14	EMCON, Emission Control Protocol.
15	XNET, Cross Net Debugger.
16	Chaos.
17	UDP, User Datagram Protocol.
18	TMux, Transport Multiplexing Protocol.
19	DCN Measurement Subsystems.
255	

9. **Header Checksum :** This is the usual checksum field used to detect errors. Since the TTL field is changing at every router so the header checksum (upto the options field) is checked and recalculated at every router.

10. **Source :** It is the IP address of the source node.

11. Destination : It is the IP address of the destination node.

12. IP Options : The options field was created in order to allow features to be added into IP as time passes and requirements change. Currently 5 options are specified although not all routers support them. They are:

- o **Securtiy:** It tells us how secret the information is. In theory a military router might use this field to specify not to route through certain routers. In practice no routers support this field.

Source Routing: It is used when we want the source to dictate how the packet traverses the network. It is of 2 types

-> **Loose Source Record Routing (LSRR):** It requires that the packet traverse a list of specified routers, in the order specified but the packet may pass though some other routers as well.

-> **Strict Source Record Routing (SSRR):** It requires that the packet traverse only the set of specified routers and nothing else. If it is not possible, the packet is dropped with an error message sent to the host.

0	8	16	24
CODE(137)	LENGTH	POINTER	
IP ADDRESS OF FIRST HOP			
IP ADDRESS OF SECOND HOP			
....			

The format of Source Route options in an IP Datagram

The above is the format for SSRR. For LSRR the code is 131.

- o **Record Routing :**

0	8	16	24
CODE(7)	LENGTH	POINTER	
FIRST IP ADDRESS			
SECOND IP ADDRESS			
....			

Format of the Record Route option in an IP Datagram

In this the intermediate routers put there IP addresses in the header, so that the destination knows the entire path of the packet. Space for storing the IP address is specified by the source itself. The pointer field points to the position where the next IP address has to be written. Length field gives the number of bytes reserved by the source for writing the IP addresses. If the space provided for storing the IP addresses of the routers visited, falls short while storing these addresses, then the subsequent routers do not write their IP addresses.

o **Time Stamp Routing :**

0	8	16	24	31
CODE	LENGTH	POINTER	OVERFLOW	FLAGS
FIRST IP ADDRESS (IP_1)				
FIRST TIME STAMP (TS_1)				
SECOND IP ADDRESS (IP_2)				
SECOND TIME STAMP (TS_2)				

Format Of Timestamp Option

It is similar to record route option except that nodes also add their timestamps to the packet. The new fields in this option are

-> **Flags:** It can have the following values

- 0 - Enter only timestamp.
- 1 - The nodes should enter Timestamp as well as their IP.
- 3 - The source specifies the IPs that should enter their timestamp. A special point of interest is that only if the IP is the same as that at the pointer then the time is entered. Thus if the source specifies IP1 and IP2 but IP2 is first in the path then the field IP2 is left empty, even after having reached IP2 but before reaching IP1.

-> **Overflow:** It stores the number of nodes that were unable to add their timestamps to the packet. The maximum value is 15.

o **Format of the type/code field**

Copy Bit	Type of option	Option Number.

- **Copy bit:** It says whether the option is to be copied to every fragment or not. a value of 1 stands for copying and 0 stands for not copying.
- **Type:** It is a 2 bit field. Currently specified values are 0 and 2.0 means the option is a control option while 2 means the option is for measurement.
- **Option Number:** It is a 5 bit field which specifies the option number.

For all options a length field is put in order that a router not familiar with the option will know how many bytes to skip. Thus every option is of the form.

o **TLV: Type/Length/Value.** This format is followed in not only in IP but in nearly all major protocols.

The network layer is concerned with getting packets from the source all the way to the destnation. The packets may require to make many hops at the intermediate routers while reaching the destination. This is the lowest layer that deals with end to end transmission. In order to achieve its goals, the network later must know about the topology of the communication network. It must also take care to choose routes to avoid overloading of some of the communication lines while leaving others idle. The main functions performed by the network layer are as follows:

- Routing
- Congestion Control
- Internetwokring

Routing

Routing is the process of forwarding of a packet in a network so that it reaches its intended destination. The main goals of routing are:

1. **Correctness:** The routing should be done properly and correctly so that the packets may reach their proper destination.
2. **Simplicity:** The routing should be done in a simple manner so that the overhead is as low as possible. With increasing complexity of the routing algorithms the overhead also increases.
3. **Robustness:** Once a major network becomes operative, it may be expected to run continuously for years without any failures. The algorithms designed for routing should be robust enough to handle hardware and software failures and should be able to cope with changes in the topology and traffic without requiring all jobs in all hosts to be aborted and the network rebooted every time some router goes down.
4. **Stability:** The routing algorithms should be stable under all possible circumstances.
5. **Fairness:** Every node connected to the network should get a fair chance of transmitting their packets. This is generally done on a first come first serve basis.
6. **Optimality:** The routing algorithms should be optimal in terms of throughput and minimizing mean packet delays. Here there is a trade-off and one has to choose depending on his suitability.

Classification of Routing Algorithms

The routing algorithms may be classified as follows:

1. **Adaptive Routing Algorithm:** These algorithms change their routing decisions to reflect changes in the topology and in traffic as well. These get their routing information from adjacent routers or from all routers. The optimization parameters are the distance, number of hops and estimated transit time. This can be further classified as follows:

    1. **Centralized:** In this type some central node in the network gets entire information about the network topology, about the traffic and about other nodes. This then

transmits this information to the respective routers. The advantage of this is that only one node is required to keep the information. The disadvantage is that if the central node goes down the entire network is down, i.e. single point of failure.

2. **Isolated:** In this method the node decides the routing without seeking information from other nodes. The sending node does not know about the status of a particular link. The disadvantage is that the packet may be send through a congested route resulting in a delay. Some examples of this type of algorithm for routing are:

   - **Hot Potato:** When a packet comes to a node, it tries to get rid of it as fast as it can, by putting it on the shortest output queue without regard to where that link leads. A variation of this algorithm is to combine static routing with the hot potato algorithm. When a packet arrives, the routing algorithm takes into account both the static weights of the links and the queue lengths.

   - **Backward Learning:** In this method the routing tables at each node gets modified by information from the incoming packets. One way to implement backward learning is to include the identity of the source node in each packet, together with a hop counter that is incremented on each hop. When a node receives a packet in a particular line, it notes down the number of hops it has taken to reach it from the source node. If the previous value of hop count stored in the node is better than the current one then nothing is done but if the current value is better then the value is updated for future use. The problem with this is that when the best route goes down then it cannot recall the second best route to a particular node. Hence all the nodes have to forget the stored informations periodically and start all over again.

3. **Distributed:** In this the node receives information from its neighbouring nodes and then takes the decision about which way to send the packet. The disadvantage is that if in between the the interval it receives information and sends the paket something changes then the packet may be delayed.

2. **Non-Adaptive Routing Algorithm:** These algorithms do not base their routing decisions on measurements and estimates of the current traffic and topology. Instead the route to be taken in going from one node to the other is computed in advance, off-line, and downloaded to the routers when the network is booted. This is also known as static routing. This can be further classified as:

   1. **Flooding:** Flooding adapts the technique in which every incoming packet is sent on every outgoing line except the one on which it arrived. One problem with this method is that packets may go in a loop. As a result of this a node may receive several copies of a particular packet which is undesirable. Some techniques adapted to overcome these problems are as follows:

      - **Sequence Numbers:** Every packet is given a sequence number. When a node receives the packet it sees its source address and sequence number. If the node finds that it has sent the same packet earlier then it will not transmit the packet and will just discard it.

- **Hop Count:** Every packet has a hop count associated with it. This is decremented (or incremented) by one by each node which sees it. When the hop count becomes zero (or a maximum possible value) the packet is dropped.
- **Spanning Tree:** The packet is sent only on those links that lead to the destination by constructing a spanning tree routed at the source. This avoids loops in transmission but is possible only when all the intermediate nodes have knowledge of the network topology.

  Flooding is not practical for general kinds of applications. But in cases where high degree of robustness is desired such as in military applications, flooding is of great help.

2. **Random Walk:** In this method a packet is sent by the node to one of its neighbours randomly. This algorithm is highly robust. When the network is highly interconnected, this algorithm has the property of making excellent use of alternative routes. It is usually implemented by sending the packet onto the least queued link.

Delta Routing

Delta routing is a hybrid of the centralized and isolated routing algorithms. Here each node computes the cost of each line (i.e some functions of the delay, queue length, utilization, bandwidth etc) and periodically sends a packet to the central node giving it these values which then computes the **k** best paths from node **i** to node **j**. Let **Cij1** be the cost of the best **i-j** path, **Cij2** the cost of the next best path and so on.If **Cijn - Cij1 < delta**, (**Cijn** - cost of **n'th** best **i-j** path, **delta** is some constant) then path **n** is regarded equivalent to the best **i-j** path since their cost differ by so little. When **delta -> 0** this algorithm becomes centralized routing and when **delta -> infinity** all the paths become equivalent.

Multipath Routing

In the above algorithms it has been assumed that there is a single best path between any pair of nodes and that all traffic between them should use it. In many networks however there are several paths between pairs of nodes that are almost equally good. Sometimes in order to improve the performance multiple paths between single pair of nodes are used. This technique is called multipath routing or bifurcated routing. In this each node maintains a table with one row for each possible destination node. A row gives the best, second best, third best, etc outgoing line for that destination, together with a relative weight. Before forwarding a packet, the node generates a random number and then chooses among the alternatives, using the weights as probabilities. The tables are worked out manually and loaded into the nodes before the network is brought up and not changed thereafter.

Hierarchical Routing

In this method of routing the nodes are divided into regions based on hierarchy. A particular node can communicate with nodes at the same hierarchial level or the nodes at a lower level and directly under it. Here, the path from any source to a destination is fixed and is exactly one if the heirarchy is a tree.

ROUTING ALGORITHMS

Non-Hierarchical Routing

In this type of routing, interconnected networks are viewed as a single network, where bridges, routers and gateways are just additional nodes.

- Every node keeps information about every other node in the network
- In case of adaptive routing, the routing calculations are done and updated for all the nodes.

The above two are also the disadvantages of non-hierarchical routing, since the table sizes and the routing calculations become too large as the networks get bigger. So this type of routing is feasible only for small networks.

Hierarchical Routing

This is essentially a 'Divide and Conquer' strategy. The network is divided into different regions and a router for a particular region knows only about its own domain and other routers. Thus, the network is viewed at two levels:

1. The Sub-network level, where each node in a region has information about its peers in the same region and about the region's interface with other regions. Different regions may have different 'local' routing algorithms. Each local algorithm handles the traffic between nodes of the same region and also directs the outgoing packets to the appropriate interface.
2. The Network Level, where each region is considered as a single node connected to its interface nodes. The routing algorithms at this level handle the routing of packets between two interface nodes, and is isolated from intra-regional transfer,

Networks can be organized in hierarchies of many levels; e.g., local networks of a city at one level, the cities of a country at a level above it, and finally the network of all nations.

In Hierarchical routing, the interfaces need to store information about:

- All nodes in its region which are at one level below it.
- Its peer interfaces.
- At least one interface at a level above it, for outgoing packages.

Advantages of Hierarchical Routing:

- Smaller sizes of routing tables.
- Substantially lesser calculations and updates of routing tables.

Disadvantage:

- Once the hierarchy is imposed on the network, it is followed and possibility of direct paths is ignored. This may lead to sub optimal routing.

Source Routing

Source routing is similar in concept to virtual circuit routing. It is implemented as under:

- Initially, a path between nodes wishing to communicate is found out, either by flooding or by any other suitable method.
- This route is then specified in the header of each packet routed between these two nodes. A route may also be specified partially, or in terms of some intermediate hops.

Advantages:

- Bridges do not need to lookup their routing tables since the path is already specified in the packet itself.
- The throughput of the bridges is higher, and this may lead to better utilization of bandwidth, once a route is established.

Disadvantages:

- Establishing the route at first needs an expensive search method like flooding.
- To cope up with dynamic relocation of nodes in a network, frequent updates of tables are required, else all packets would be sent in wrong direction. This too is expensive.

Policy Based Routing

In this type of routing, certain restrictions are put on the type of packets accepted and sent. e.g. The IIT- K router may decide to handle traffic pertaining to its departments only, and reject packets from other routes. This kind of routing is used for links with very low capacity or for security purposes.

Shortest Path Routing

Here, the central question dealt with is 'How to determine the optimal path for routing?' Various algorithms are used to determine the optimal routes with respect to some predetermined criteria. A network is represented as a graph, with its terminals as nodes and the links as edges. A 'length' is associated with each edge, which represents the cost of using the link for transmission. Lower the cost, more suitable is the link. The cost is determined depending upon the criteria to be optimized. Some of the important ways of determining the cost are:

- **Minimum number of hops:** If each link is given a unit cost, the shortest path is the one with minimum number of hops. Such a route is easily obtained by a breadth first search method. This is easy to implement but ignores load, link capacity etc.
- **Transmission and Propagation Delays:** If the cost is fixed as a function of transmission and propagation delays, it will reflect the link capacities and the geographical distances. However these costs are essentially static and do not consider the varying load conditions.
- **Queuing Delays:** If the cost of a link is determined through its queuing delays, it takes care of the varying load conditions, but not of the propagation delays.

Ideally, the cost parameter should consider all the above mentioned factors, and it should be updated periodically to reflect the changes in the loading conditions. However, if the routes are changed according to the load, the load changes again. This feedback effect between routing and load can lead to undesirable oscillations and sudden swings.

Routing Algorithms

As mentioned above, the shortest paths are calculated using suitable algorithms on the graph representations of the networks. Let the network be represented by graph G (V, E) and let the number of nodes be 'N'. For all the algorithms discussed below, the costs associated with the links are assumed to be positive. A node has zero cost w.r.t itself. Further, all the links are assumed to be symmetric, i.e. if $d_{i,j}$ = cost of link from node i to node j, then $d_{i,j} = d_{j,i}$. The graph is assumed to be complete. If there exists no edge between two nodes, then a link of infinite cost is assumed. The algorithms given below find costs of the paths from all nodes to a particular node; the problem is equivalent to finding the cost of paths from a source to all destinations.

Bellman-Ford Algorithm

This algorithm iterates on the number of edges in a path to obtain the shortest path. Since the number of hops possible is limited (cycles are implicitly not allowed), the algorithm terminates giving the shortest path.

Notation:

$d_{i,j}$ = Length of path between nodes i and j, indicating the cost of the link.

h = Number of hops.

D[i,h] = Shortest path length from node i to node 1, with upto 'h' hops.

D[1,h] = 0 for all h.

Algorithm :

Initial condition : D[i, 0] = infinity, for all i (i != 1)

Iteration : D[i, h+1] = min { $d_{i,j}$ + D[j,h] } over all values of j .

Termination : The algorithm terminates when

D[i, h] = D [i, h+1] for all i .

Principle

For zero hops, the minimum length path has length of infinity, for every node. For one hop the shortest-path length associated with a node is equal to the length of the edge between that node and node 1. Hereafter, we increment the number of hops allowed, (from h to h+1) and find out whether a shorter path exists through each of the other nodes. If it exists, say through node 'j', then its length must be the sum of the lengths between these two nodes (i.e., $d_{i,j}$) and the shortest path between j and 1 obtainable in upto h paths. If such a path doesn't exist, then the path length remains the same. The algorithm is guaranteed to terminate, since there are utmost N nodes, and so N-1 paths. It has time complexity of O (N^3).

Dijkstra's Algorithm

Notation:

D_i = Length of shortest path from node 'i' to node 1.

$d_{i,j}$ = Length of path between nodes i and j .

Algorithm

Each node j is labeled with Dj, which is an estimate of cost of path from node j to node 1. Initially, let the estimates be infinity, indicating that nothing is known about the paths. We now iterate on the length of paths, each time revising our estimate to lower values, as we obtain them. Actually, we divide the nodes into two groups; the first one, called set P contains the nodes whose shortest distances have been found, and the other Q containing all the remaining nodes. Initially P contains only the node 1. At each step, we select the node that has minimum cost path to node 1. This node is transferred to set P. At the first step, this corresponds to shifting the node closest to 1 in P. Its minimum cost to node 1 is now known. At the next step, select the next closest node from set Q and update the labels corresponding to each node using :

$$D_j = \min [\ D_j\ ,\ D_i + d_{j,i}\ ]$$

Finally, after N-1 iterations, the shortest paths for all nodes are known, and the algorithm terminates.

Principle

Let the closest node to 1 at some step be i. Then i is shifted to P. Now, for each node j , the closest path to 1 either passes through i or it doesn't. In the first case Dj remains the same. In the second case, the revised estimate of D_j is the sum $D_i + d_{i,j}$. So we take the minimum of these two cases and update D_j accordingly. As each of the nodes get transferred to set P, the estimates get closer to the lowest possible value. When a node is transferred, its shortest path length is known. So finally all the nodes are in P and the D_j 's represent the minimum costs. The algorithm is guaranteed to terminate in N-1 iterations and its complexity is O(N^2).

The Floyd Warshall Algorithm

This algorithm iterates on the set of nodes that can be used as intermediate nodes on paths. This set grows from a single node (say node 1) at start to finally all the nodes of the graph. At each iteration, we find the shortest path using given set of nodes as intermediate nodes, so that finally all the shortest paths are obtained.

Notation

$D_{i,j}$ [n] = Length of shortest path between the nodes i and j using only the nodes 1,2,....n as intermediate nodes.

Initial Condition

$D_{i,j}[0] = d_{i,j}$ for all nodes i,j .

Algorithm

Initially, n = 0. At each iteration, add next node to n. i.e. For n = 1,2, ...N-1 ,

$D_{i,j}[n + 1] = \min \{ D_{i,j}[n], D_{i,n+1}[n] + D_{n+1,j}[n]\}$

Principle

Suppose the shortest path between i and j using nodes 1,2,...n is known. Now, if node n+1 is allowed to be an intermediate node, then the shortest path under new conditions either passes through node n+1 or it doesn't. If it does not pass through the node n+1, then $D_{i,j}[n+1]$ is same as $D_{i,j}[n]$. Else, we find the cost of the new route, which is obtained from the sum, $D_{i,n+1}[n] + D_{n+1,j}[n]$. So we take the minimum of these two cases at each step. After adding all the nodes to the set of intermediate nodes, we obtain the shortest paths between all pairs of nodes together. The complexity of Floyd-Warshall algorithm is O (N^3).

It is observed that all the three algorithms mentioned above give comparable performance, depending upon the exact topology of the network.

ARP,RARP,ICMP PROTOCOLS

Address Resolution Protocol

If a machine talks to another machine in the same network, it requires its physical or MAC address. But, since the application has given the destination's IP address it requires some mechanism to bind the IP address with its MAC address.This is done through Address Resolution protocol (ARP). IP address of the destination node is broadcast and the destination node informs the source of its MAC address.

1. Assume broadcast nature of LAN
2. Broadcast IP address of the destination
3. Destination replies it with its MAC address.
4. Source maintains a cache of IP and MAC address bindings

But this means that every time machine A wants to send packets to machine B, A has to send an ARP packet to resolve the MAC address of B and hence this will increase the traffic load too much, so to reduce the communication cost computers that use ARP maintains a cache of recently acquired IP_to_MAC address bindings, i.e. they dont have to use ARP repeatedly. ARP Refinements Several refinements of ARP are possible: When machine A wants to send packets to macine B, it is possible that machine B is going to send packets to machine A in the near future.So to avoid ARP for machine B, A should put its IP_to_MAC address binding in the special packet while requesting for the MAC address of B. Since A broadcasts its initial request for the MAC address of B, every machine on the network should extract and store in its cache the IP_to_MAC address binding of A When a new machine appears on the network (e.g., when an operating system reboots) it can broadcast its IP_to_MAC address binding so that all other machines can store it in their caches. This will eliminate a lot of ARP packets by all other machines, when they want to communicate with this new machine.

Example displaying the use of Address Resolution Protocol:

Consider a scenario where a computer tries to contact some remote machine using ping program, assuming that there has been no exchange of IP datagrams previously between the two machines and therefore arp packet must be sent to identify the MAC address of the remote machine.

The arp request message (who is A.A.A.A tell B.B.B.B where the two are IP addresses) is broadcast on the local area network with an Ethernet protocol type 0x806. The packet is discarded by all the machines except the target machine which responds with an arp response message (A.A.A.A is hh:hh:hh:hh:hh:hh where hh:hh:hh:hh:hh:hh is the Ethernet source address). This packet is unicast to the machine with IP address B.B.B.B. Since the arp request message included the hardware address (Ethernet source address) of the requesting computer, target machine doesn't require another arp message to figure it out.

Reverse Address Resolution Protocol

RARP is a protocol by which a physical machine in a local area network can request to learn its IP address from a gateway server's Address Resolution Protocol table or cache. This is needed since the machine may not have permanently attacded disk where it can store its IP address permanently. A network administrator creates a table in a local area network's gateway router that maps the physical machine (or Medium Access Control - MAC) addresses to corresponding Internet Protocol addresses. When a new machine is set up, its RARP client program requests from the RARP server on the router to be sent its IP address. Assuming that an entry has been set up in the router table, the RARP server will return the IP address to the machine which can store it for future use.

Detailed Mechanism

Both the machine that issues the request and the server that responds use physical network addresses during their brief communication. Usually, the requester does not know the physical address. So, the request is broadcasted to all the machines on the network. Now, the requester must identify istelf uniquely to the server. For this either CPU serial number or the machine's physical network address can be used. But using the physical address as a unique id has two advantages.

- These addresses are always available and do not have to be bound into bootstrap code.
- Because the identifying information depends on the network and not on the CPU vendor, all machines on a given network will supply unique identifiers.

Request

Like an ARP message, a RARP message is sent from one machine to the another encapsulated in the data portion of a network frame. An ethernet frame carrying a RARP request has the usual preamle, Ethernet source and destination addresses, and packet type fields in front of the frame. The frame conatins the value 8035 (base 16) to identify the contents of the frame as a RARP message. The data portion of the frame contains the 28-octet RARP message. The sender braodcasts a RARP request that specifies itself as both the sender and target machine, and supplies its physical network address in the target hardware address field. All machines on the network receive the request, but only those authorised to supply the RARP services process the request and send a reply, such machines are known informally as RARP servers. For RARP to succeed, the network must contain at least one RARP server.

Reply

Servers answers request by filling in the target protocol address field, changing the message type from request to reply, and sending the reply back directly to the machine making the request.

Timing RARP Transactions

Since RARP uses the physical network directly, no other protocol software will time the response or retransmit the request. RARP software must handle these tasks. Some workstations that rely on RARP to boot, choose to retry indefinitely until the receive a response. Other implementations announce failure after only a few tries to avoid flooding the network with unnecessary broadcast.

Mulitple RARP Servers

Advantage: More reliability. Diadvantage: Overloading may result when all servers respond. So, to get away with disadvantage we have primary and secondary servers. Each machine that makes RARP request is assigned a primary server. Normally, the primary server responds but if it fails, then requester may time out and rebroadcast the request.Whenever a secondary server receives a second copy of the request within a short time of the first, it responds. But, still there might be a problem that all secondary servers respond, thus overloading the network. So, the solution adopted is to avoid having all secondary servers transmit responses simultaneously. Each secondary server that receives the request computes a random delay and then sends a response.

Drawbacks of RARP

- Since it operates at low level, it requires direct addresss to the network which makes it difficult for an application programmer to build a server.
- It doesn't fully utilizes the capability of a network like ethernet which is enforced to send a minimum packet size since the reply from the server contains only one small piece of information, the 32-bit internet address.

RARP is formally described in RFC903.

ICMP

This protocol discusses a mechanism that gateways and hosts use to communicate control or error information.The Internet protocol provides unreliable,connectionless datagram service,and that a datagram travels from gateway to gateway until it reaches one that can deliver it directly to its final destination. If a gateway cannot route or deliver a datagram, or if the gateway detects an unusual condition, like network congestion, that affects its ability to forward the datagram, it needs to instruct the original source to take action to avoid or correct the problem. The Internet Control Message Protocol allows gateways to send error or control messages to other gateways or hosts; ICMP provides communication between the Internet Protocol software on one machine and the Internet Protocol software on another. This is a special purpose message mechanism added by the designers to the TCP/IP protocols. This is to allow gateways in an internet to report errors or provide information about unexpecter circumstances. The IP protocol itself contains nothing to help the sender test connectivity or learn about failures.

Error Reporting vs Error Correction

ICMP only reports error conditions to the original source; the source must relate errors to individual application programs and take action to correct problems. It provides a way for gateway to report the error It does not fully specify the action to be taken for each possible error. ICMP is restricted to communicate with the original source but not intermediate sources.

ICMP Message Delivery

ICMP messages travel across the internet in the data portion of an IP datagram,which itself travels across the internet in the data portion of an IP datagram,which itself travels across each physical network in the data portion of a frame.Datagrams carryin ICMP messages are routed exactly like datagrams carrying information for users;there is no additional reliability or priority.An exception is made to the error handling procedures if an IP datagram carrying an ICMP messages are not generated for errors that result from datagrams carrying ICMP error messages.

ICMP Message Format

It has three fields; an 8-bit integer message TYPE field that identifies the message, an 8-bit CODE field that provides further information about the message type, and a 16-bit CHECKSUM field (ICMP uses the same additive checksum algorithm as IP, but the ICMP checksum only covers the ICMP message). In addition , ICMP messages that report errors always include the header and first 64 data bits of the datagram causing the problem. The ICMP TYPE field defines the meaning of the message as well as its format.

The Types include :

TYPE FIELD	ICMP MESSAGE TYPE
0	ECHO REPLY
3	DESTINATION UNREACHABLE
4	SOURCE QUENCH

5 REDIRECT(CHANGE A ROUTE)

8 ECHO REQUEST

11 TIME EXCEEDED FOR A DATAGRAM

12 PARAMETER PROBLEM ON A DATAGRAM

13 TIMESTAMP REQUEST

14 TIMESTAMP REPLY

15 INFORMATION REQUEST(OBSOLETE)

16 INFORMATION REPLY(OBSOLETE)

17 ADDRESS MASK REQUEST

18 ADDRESS MASK REPLY TESTING DESTINATION

Reachabilty and Status

TCP/IP protocols provide facilities to help network managers or users identify network problems.One of the most frequently used debugging tools invokes the ICMP echo request and echo reply messages. A host or gateway sends an ICMP echo request message to a specified destination.Any machine that receives an echo request formulates an echo reply and returns to the original sender. The request contains an optional data area; the reply contains a copy of the data sent in the request. The echo request and associated reply can be used to test whether a destination is reachable and responding.Because both the request and reply travel in IP datagrams, successful receipt of a reply verifies that major pieces of the transport system work.

1.1 : IP software on the source must route the datagram

2.2 : Intermediate gateways between the source and destination must be operating and must route datagram correctly.

3.3 : The destination machine must be running , and both ICMP and IP software must be working.

4.4 : Routes in gateways along the return path must be correct.

Echo Request and Reply

The field listed OPTIONAL DATA is a variable length field that contains data to be returned to the sender. An echo reply always returns exactly the same data as was received in the request.Fields IDENTIFIER and SEQUENCE NUMBER are used by the sender to match replies to request. The value of the TYPE field specifies whether the message is a request(8) or a reply(0).

Reports of Unreachable Destinations

The Code field in a destination unreachable message contains an integer that further describes th problem.Possible values are:

CODE VALUE	MEANING
0	NETWORK UNREACHABLE
1	HOST UNREACHABLE
2	PROTOCOL UNREACHABLE
3	PORT UNREACHABLE
4	FRAGMENTATION NEEDED AND DF SET
5	SOURCE ROOT FAILED
6	DESTINATION NETWORK UNKNOWN
7	DESTINATION HOST UNKNOWN
8	SOURCE HOST ISOLATED
9	COMMUNICATION WITH DESTINATION NETWORK ADMINISTRATIVELY PROHIBITED
10	COMMUNICATION WTTH DESTINATION HOST ADMINISTRATIVELY PROHIBITED
11	NETWORK UNREACHABLE FOR TYPE OF SERVICE
12	HOST UNREACHABLE FOR TYPE OF SERVICE

Whenever an error prevents a gateway from routing or delivering a datagram, the gateway sends a destination unreachable message back to the source and then drops the datagram.Network unreachable errors usually imply roting failures; host unreachable errors imply delivery failures.Because the message contains a short prefix of the datagram that caused the problem, the source will know exactly which address is unreachable. Destinations may be unreachable because hardware is temporarily out of service, because the sender specified a nonexistent destination address, or because the gateway does not have a route to the destination network. Although gateways send destination unreachable messages if they cannot route or deliver datagrams, not all such errors can be detected.If the datagram contains the source route option with an incorrect route, it may trigger a source route failure message. If a gateway needs to fragment adatagram but the "don't fragment" bit is set, the gateway sends a fragmentation needed message back to the source.

Congestion and Datagram Flow Control:

Gateways cannot reserve memory or communication resources in advance of receiving datagrams because IP is connectionless. The result is, gateways can overrun with traffic, a condition known as congestion. Congestion arises due to two reasons:

1. A high speed computer may be able to generate traffic faster than a network can transfer it.
2. If many computers sumultaneously need to send datagrams through a single gateway, the gateway can experience congestion, even though no single source causes the problem.

When datagrams arrive too quickly for a host or a gateway to process, it enqueues them in memory temporarily.If the traffic continues, the host or gateway eventually exhausts menory ans must discard additional datagrams that arrive. A machine uses ICMP source quench messages to releive congestion. A source quench message is a request for the source to reduce its current rate of datagram transmission.

There is no ICMP messages to reverse the effect of a source quench.

Source Quench

Source quench messages have a field that contains a datagram prefix in addition to the usual ICMP TYPE,CODE,CHECKSUM fields.Congested gateways send one source quench message each time they discard a datagram; the datagram prefix identifies the datagram that was dropped.

Route Change Requests From Gateways

Internet routing tables are initialized by hosts from a configuration file at system startup, and system administrators seldom make routing changes during normal operations.Gateways exchange routing information periodically to accomadate network changes and keep their routes up-to-date.The general rule is, Gateways are assumed to know correct routes; host begin wint minimal routing information and learn new routes from gateways. The GATEWAY INTERNET ADDRESS field contains the address of a gateway that the host is to use to reach the destination mentioned in the datagram header. The INTERNET HEADER field contains IP header plus the next 64 bits of the datagram that triggered the message.The CODE field of an ICMP redirect message further specifies how to interpret the destination address, based on values assigned as follows:

Code Value	Meaning
0	REDIRECT DATAGRAMS FOR THE NET
1	REDIRECT DATAGRAMS FOR THE HOST
2	REDIRECT DATAGRAMS FOR THE TYPE OF SERVICE AND NET
3	REDIRECT DATAGRAMS FOR THE TYPE OF SERVICE AND HOST

Gateways only send ICMP redirect requests to hosts and not to other gateways.

Detecting Circular or Excessively Long Routes

Internet gateways compute a next hop using local tables, errors in routing tables can produce a routing cycle for some destination. A routing cycle can consist of two gateways that each route a datagram for a particular destination to other, or it can consist of several gateways. To prevent datagrams from circling forever in a TCP/IP internet, each IP datagram contains a time-to-live counter, sometimes called a hop count. A gateway decrements the time-to-live counter whenever it processes the datagram and discards the datagram when the count reaches zero. Whenever a gateway discards a datagram because its hop count has reached zero or because a timeout occured while waiting for fragments of a datagram, it sends an ICMP time exceeded message back to the datagram's source, A gateway sends this message whenever a datagram is discarded because the time-to-live field in the datagram header has reached zero or because its reassembly timer expired while waiting for fragments.

The code field explains the nature of the timeout:

Code Value	Meaning
0	TIME-TO-LIVE COUNT EXCEEDED
1	FRAGMENT REASSEMBLY TIME EXCEEDED

Fragment reassembly refers to the task of collecting all the fragments from a datagram.

Reprting Other Problems: When a gateway or host finds problems with a datagram not covered by previous ICMP error messages it sends a parameter problem message to the original source. To make the message unambigous, the sender uses the POINTER field in the message header to identify the octet in the datagram that caused the problem. Code 1 is used to report that a required option is missing; the POINTER field is not used for code 1.

Clock Synchronization nd Transmit the estimation: ICMP messages are used to obtain the time from another machine.A requesting machine sends an ICMP timestamp request message to another machine, asking that the second machine return its current value of the time of day. The receiving machine returns a timestamp reply back to the machine making the request. TCP/IP protocol suite includes several protocols that can be used to synchronize clocks. This is one of the simplest techniques used by TCP/IP. The TYPE field idintifies the message as a request (13) or a reply (14); the IDENTIFIER and SEQUENCE NUMBER fields are used by the source to associate replies with requests.The ORIGINATE TIMESTAMP filed is filled in by the original sendet just before the packet is transmitted, the RECEIVE TIMESTAMP field is filled immediately upon receipt of a request, and the TRANSMIT TIMESTAMP field is filled immediately before the reply is transmitted. Hosts use the three timestamp fields to compute estimates of the delay time between them and to synchronize their clock.A host can compute the total time required for a request to travel to a destination, be transformed into a reply, and return. In practice, accurate estimation of round-trip delay can be difficult and substantially restirct the utility of ICMP timestanp messages. To obtain an accurate estimate to round trip delay one must take many measurements and average them.

Obtaining a Subnet Mask: Subnet addressing is used by the hosts to extract some bits in the hostid portion of their IP address to identify a physical network. To participate in subnet addressing, hosts need to know which bits of the 32-bit internet address correspond to the physical network and which correspond to host identifiers. The information needed to interpret the address is represented in a 32-bit quatity called the subnet mask. To learn the subnet mask used for the local network, a machine can send an address mask request message to a gateway and receive an address mask reply. The TYPE field in an address mask message specifies whether the message is a request (17) or a reply (18). A reply contains the nework's subnet address mask in the ADDRESS MASK field. The IDENTIFIER and SEQUENCE NUMBER fields allow a machine to associate replies with requests.

Questions

(1) What is network? Explain how has old computer system been replaced by computer networks today?

(2) Explain different types of computer networks?

(3) Define classification of different networks?

(4) Define network technology used by different networks?

(5) What are the two industry wide standards for more broadly based local area netwoks?

(6) What is key distinction between a computer network and distributed system?

(7) Why do many companys use network now a days?

(8) What is the benefit of using computer networks?

(9) Define the Network Topology?

(10) Describe the ways by which network can be classified?

(11) Describe different types of Network topology? Can string topology be used for Wide Area Network (WAN)?

(12) How can a network be connected?

(13) Describe the Network terminology: channel, protocol, Bridges, Routers, Gateways, Modems, Repeater, Hub, Multiplexers?

CHAPTER
5

Internet

INTRODUCTION

The **Internet** is a global system of interconnected computer networks that use the standardized Internet Protocol Suite (TCP/IP). It is a *network of networks* that consists of millions of private and public, academic, business, and government networks of local to global scope that are linked by copper wires, fiber-optic cables, wireless connections, and other technologies.

The Internet carries a vast array of information resources and services, most notably, the inter-linked hypertext documents of the World Wide Web (WWW) and the infrastructure to support electronic mail, in addition to popular services such as online chat, file transfer and file sharing, online gaming, and Voice over Internet Protocol (VoIP) person-to-person communication via voice and video.

The origins of the Internet reach back to the 1960s when the United States funded research projects of its military agencies to build robust, fault-tolerant and distributed computer networks. This research and a period of civilian funding of a new U.S. backbone by the National Science Foundation spawned worldwide participation in the development of new networking technologies and led to the commercialization of an international network in the mid 1990s, and resulted in the following popularization of countless applications in virtually every aspect of modern human life. By 2009, an estimated quarter of Earth's population uses the services of the Internet (see Growth).

TERMINOLOGY

The terms *Internet* and *World Wide Web* are often used in everyday speech without much distinction. However, the Internet and the World Wide Web are not one and the same. The Internet is a global data communications system. It is a hardware and software infrastructure that provides connectivity between computers. In contrast, the Web is one of the services communicated via the Internet. It is a collection of interconnected documents and other resources, linked by hyperlinks and URLs.

The term *Internet*, when referring to the Internet, has traditionally been treated as a proper noun and written with an initial capital letter. There is a trend to regard it as a generic term or common noun and thus write it as "the internet", without the capital.

HISTORY

Creation

The USSR's launch of Sputnik spurred the United States to create the Advanced Research Projects Agency, known as ARPA, in February 1958 to regain a technological lead. ARPA created the Information Processing Technology Office (IPTO) to further the research of the Semi Automatic Ground Environment (SAGE) program, which had networked country-wide radar systems together for the first time. J. C. R. Licklider was selected to head the IPTO.

Licklider moved from the Psycho-Acoustic Laboratory at Harvard University to MIT in 1950, after becoming interested in information technology. At MIT, he served on a committee that established Lincoln Laboratory and worked on the SAGE project. In 1957 he became a Vice President at BBN, where he bought the first production PDP-1 computer and conducted the first public demonstration of time-sharing.

At the IPTO, Licklider got Lawrence Roberts to start a project to make a network, and Roberts based the technology on the work of Paul Baran, who had written an exhaustive study for the U.S. Air Force that recommended packet switching (as opposed to circuit switching) to make a network highly robust and survivable. After much work, the first two nodes of what would become the ARPANET were interconnected between UCLA and SRI International (SRI) in Menlo Park, California, on October 29, 1969. The ARPANET is one of the "eve" networks of today's Internet.

Following on from the demonstration that packet switching worked on the ARPANET, the British Post Office, Telenet, DATAPAC and TRANSPAC collaborated to create the first international packet-switched network service. In the UK, this was referred to as the International Packet Switched Service (IPSS), in 1978. The collection of X.25-based networks grew from Europe and the US to cover Canada, Hong Kong and Australia by 1981. The X.25 packet switching standard was developed in the CCITT (now called ITU-T) around 1976.

Birth of the Internet plaque at Stanford University

X.25 was independent of the TCP/IP protocols that arose from the experimental work of DARPA on the ARPANET, Packet Radio Net and Packet Satellite Net during the same period. Vinton Cerf and Robert Kahn developed the first description of the TCP protocols during 1973 and published a paper on the subject in May 1974. Use of the term "Internet" to describe a single global TCP/IP network originated in December 1974 with the publication of RFC 675, the first full specification of TCP that was written by Vinton Cerf, Yogen Dalal and Carl Sunshine, then at Stanford University. During the next nine years, work proceeded to refine the protocols and to implement them on a wide range of operating systems.

The first TCP/IP-based wide-area network was operational by January 1, 1983 when all hosts on the ARPANET were switched over from the older NCP protocols. In 1985, the United State's National Science Foundation (NSF) commissioned the construction of the NSFNET, a university 56 kilobite/second network backbone using computers called "fuzzballs" by their inventor, David L. Mills. The following year, NSF sponsored the conversion to a higher-speed 1.5 megabite/second network. A key decision to use the DARPA TCP/IP protocols was made by Dennis Jennings, then in charge of the Supercomputer program at NSF.

The opening of the network to commercial interests began in 1988. The US Federal Networking Council approved the interconnection of the NSFNET to the commercial MCI Mail system in that year and the link was made in the summer of 1989. Other commercial electronic e-mail services were soon connected, including OnTyme, Telemail and Compuserve. In that same year, three commercial Internet service providers (ISPs) were created: UUNET, PSINet and CERFNET. Important, separate networks that offered gateways into, then later merged with, the Internet include Usenet and BITNET. Various other commercial and educational networks, such as Telenet, Tymnet, Compuserve and JANET were interconnected with the growing Internet. Telenet (later called Sprintnet) was a large privately funded national computer network with free dial-up access in cities throughout the U.S. that had been in operation since the 1970s. This network was eventually interconnected with the others in the 1980s as the TCP/IP became increasingly popular.

The ability of TCP/IP to work over virtually any pre-existing communication networks allowed for a great ease of growth, although the rapid growth of the Internet was due primarily to the availability of an array of standardized commercial routers from many companies, the availability of commercial Ethernet equipment for local-area networking, and the widespread implementation and rigorous standardization of TCP/IP on UNIX and virtually every other common operating system.

Growth

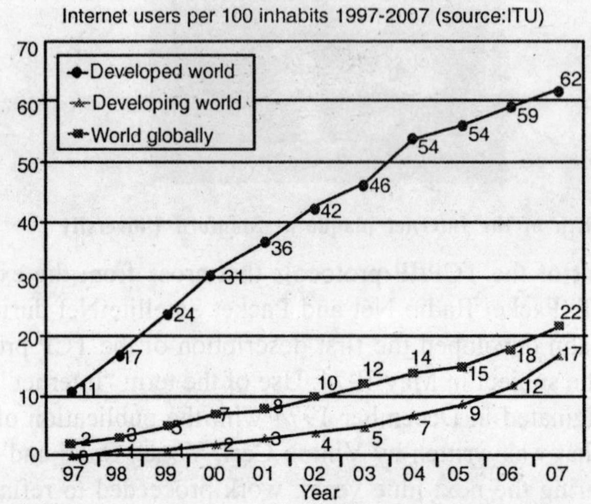

Graph of Internet users per 100 inhabitants between 1997 and 2007 by International Telecommunication Union

Although the basic applications and guidelines that make the Internet possible had existed for almost two decades, the network did not gain a public face until the 1990s. On 6 August 1991, CERN, a pan European organisation for particle research, publicized the new World Wide Web project. The Web was invented by English scientist Tim Berners-Lee in 1989.

An early popular web browser was ViolaWWW, patterned after HyperCard and built using the X Window System. It was eventually replaced in popularity by the Mosaic web browser. In 1993, the National Center for Supercomputing Applications at the University of Illinois released version 1.0 of Mosaic, and by late 1994 there was growing public interest in the previously academic, technical Internet. By 1996 usage of the word *Internet* had become commonplace, and consequently, so had its use as a synecdoche in reference to the World Wide Web.

Meanwhile, over the course of the decade, the Internet successfully accommodated the majority of previously existing public computer networks (although some networks, such as FidoNet, have remained separate). During the 1990s, it was estimated that the Internet grew by 100 per cent per year, with a brief period of explosive growth in 1996 and 1997. This growth is often attributed to the lack of central administration, which allows organic growth of the network, as well as the non-proprietary open nature of the Internet protocols, which encourages vendor interoperability and prevents any one company from exerting too much control over the network.

Using various statistics, Advanced Micro Devices estimated the population of Internet users to be 1.5 billion as or January 2009.

TECHNICAL FOUNDATION

The complex communications infrastructure of the Internet consists of its hardware components and a system of software layers that control various aspects of the architecture. While the hardware can often be used to support other software systems, it is the design and the rigorous standardization process of the software architecture that characterises the Internet and provides the foundation for its scalability and success.

The responsibility for the architectural design of the Internet software systems has been delegated to the Internet Engineering Task Force (IETF). The IETF conducts standard-setting work groups, open to any individual, about the various aspects of Internet architecture. Resulting discussions and final standards are published in a series of publications each of which is called a Request for Comment (RFC), freely available on the IETF web site. The principal methods of networking that enable the Internet are contained in specially designated RFCs that constitute the Internet Standards.

These standards describe a framework known as the Internet Protocol Suite. This is a model architecture that divides methods into a layered system of protocols (RFC 1122, RFC 1123). The layers correspond to the environment or scope in which their services operate. At the top is the Application Layer, the space for the application-specific networking methods used in software applications, e.g., a web browser program, and just below it is the Transport Layer which connects applications on *different hosts* via the network (e.g., client-server model) with appropriate data exchange methods. Underlying these layers are the actual networking technologies, consisting of two layers. The Internet Layer enables computers to identify and locate each other via Internet Protocol (IP) addresses, and allows them to connect to one-another via intermediate (transit) networks. Lastly, at the bottom of the architecture, is a software layer that provides connectivity between hosts on the same local network link (therefore called Link Layer), such as a local area network (LAN) or a dial-up connection. The model, also known as TCP/IP, is designed to be independent of the underlying hardware which the model therefore does not concern itself with in any detail. Other models have been developed, such as the Open Systems Interconnection (OSI) model, but they are not compatible in the details of description, nor implementation, but many similarities exist and the TCP/IP protocols are usually included in the discussion of OSI networking.

The most prominent component of the Internet model is the Internet Protocol (IP) which provides addressing systems (IP addresses) for computers on the Internet. IP enables internetworking and essentially establishes the Internet itself. IP Version 4 (IPv4) is the initial version used on the first generation of the today's Internet and is still in dominant use. It was designed to address up to ~4.3 billion (10^9) Internet hosts. However, the explosive growth of the Internet has led to the exhaustion of IPv4 address which is estimated to enter its final stage in approximately 2011. A new protocol version, IPv6, was developed which provides vastly larger addressing capabilities and more efficient routing of Internet traffic. IPv6 is currently in commercial deployment phase around the world and Internet address registries (RIRs) have begun to urge all resource managers to plan rapid adoption and conversion.

IPv6 is not interoperable with IPv4. It essentially establishes a "parallel" version of the Internet not directly accessible with IPv4 software. This means software upgrades or translator facilities are necessary for every networking device that needs to communicate on the IPv6 Internet. Most modern computer operating systems are already converted to operate with both versions of the Internet Protocol. Network infrastructures, however, are still lagging in this development.

Apart from the complex physical connections that make up its infrastructure, the Internet is facilitated by bi- or multi-lateral commercial contracts (e.g., peering agreements), and by technical specifications or protocols that describe how to exchange data over the network. Indeed, the Internet is defined by its interconnections and routing policies.

TODAY'S INTERNET

Internet structure

The Internet and its structure have been studied extensively. For example, it has been determined that both the IP routing structure and hypertext links of the World Wide Web are examples of scale-free networks.

Similar to the way the commercial Internet providers connect via Internet exchange points, research networks tend to interconnect into large subnetworks such as GEANT, GLORIAD, Internet2 (successor of the Abilene Network), and the UK's national research and education network JANET. These in turn are built around smaller networks (see also the list of academic computer network organizations).

Many computer scientists describe the Internet as a "prime example of a large-scale, highly engineered, yet highly complex system". The Internet is extremely heterogeneous; for instance, data transfer rates and physical characteristics of connections vary widely. The Internet exhibits "emergent phenomena" that depend on its large-scale organization. For example, data transfer rates exhibit temporal self-similarity. Further adding to the complexity of the Internet is the ability of more than one computer to use the Internet through only one node, thus creating the possibility for a very deep and hierarchical sub-network that can theoretically be extended infinitely (disregarding the programmatic limitations of the IPv4 protocol). Principles of this architecture date back to the 1960s and it might not be a solution best suited to modern needs. Thus, the possibility of developing alternative structures is currently being looked into.

According to a June 2007 article in *Discover* magazine, the combined weight of all the electrons moved within the Internet in a day is 0.2 millionths of an ounce. Others have estimated this at nearer 2 ounces (50 grams).

Computer network diagrams often represent the Internet using a cloud symbol from which network communications pass in and out.

ICANN

ICANN headquarters in Marina Del Rey, California, United States

The Internet Corporation for Assigned Names and Numbers (ICANN) is the authority that coordinates the assignment of unique identifiers on the Internet, including domain names, Internet Protocol (IP) addresses, protocol port and parameter numbers. A globally unified name space (i.e., a system of names in which there is at most one holder for each possible name) is essential for the Internet to function. ICANN is headquartered in Marina del Rey, California, but is overseen by an international board of directors drawn from across the Internet technical, business, academic, and non-commercial communities. The US government continues to have the primary role in approving changes to the root zone file that lies at the heart of the domain name system. Because the Internet is a distributed network comprising many voluntarily interconnected networks, the Internet has no governing body. ICANN's role in coordinating the assignment of unique identifiers distinguishes it as perhaps the only central coordinating body on the global Internet, but the scope of its authority extends only to the Internet's systems of domain names, IP addresses, protocol ports and parameter numbers.

On November 16, 2005, the World Summit on the Information Society, held in Tunis, established the Internet Governance Forum (IGF) to discuss Internet-related issues.

Language

The prevalent language for communication on the Internet is English. This may be a result of the origin of the Internet, as well as English's role as a lingua franca. It may also be related to the poor capability of early computers, largely originating in the United States, to handle characters other than those in the English variant of the Latin alphabet.

After English (28.6% of Web visitors) the most requested languages on the World Wide Web are Chinese (20.3%), Spanish (8.2%), Japanese (5.9%), French and Portuguese (4.6%), German (4.1%), Arabic (2.6%), Russian (2.4%), and Korean (2.3%).

By region, 41% of the world's Internet users are based in Asia, 25% in Europe, 16% in North America, 11% in Latin America and the Caribbean, 3% in Africa, 3% in the Middle East and 1% in Australia.

The Internet's technologies have developed enough in recent years, especially in the use of Unicode, that good facilities are available for development and communication in most widely used languages. However, some glitches such as *mojibake* (incorrect display of foreign language characters, also known as *kryakozyabry*) still remain.

Internet and the workplace

The Internet is allowing greater flexibility in working hours and location, especially with the spread of unmetered high-speed connections and Web Applications.

The Internet viewed on mobile devices

The Internet can now be accessed virtually anywhere by numerous means. Mobile phones, datacards, handheld game consoles and cellular routers allow users to connect to the Internet from anywhere, where there is a cellular network supporting that device's technology.

Within the limitations imposed by the small screen and other limited facilities of such a pocket-sized device, all the services of the Internet, including email and web browsing, may be available in this way. Service providers may restrict the range of these services and charges for data access may be significant, compared to home usage.

COMMON USES

E-mail

The concept of sending electronic text messages between parties in a way analogous to mailing letters or memos predates the creation of the Internet.

Today it can be important to distinguish between internet and internal e-mail systems. Internet e-mail may travel and be stored unencrypted on many other networks and machines out of both the sender's and the recipient's control. During this time it is quite possible for the content to be read and even tampered with by third parties, if anyone considers it important enough. Purely internal or intranet mail systems, where the information never leaves the corporate or organization's network, are much more secure, although in any organization there will be IT and other personnel whose job may involve monitoring, and occasionally accessing, the e-mail of other employees not addressed to them.

Pictures, documents and other files can be sent as e-mail attachments. E-mails can be cc-ed to multiple e-mail addresses.

The World Wide Web

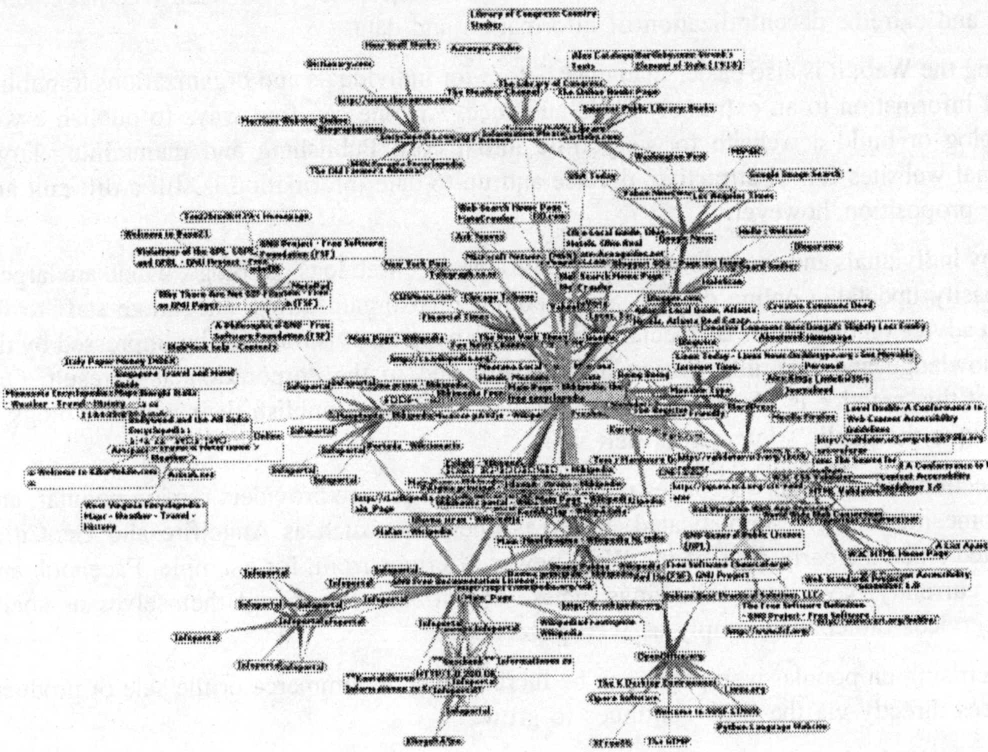

Graphic representation of a minute fraction of the WWW, demonstrating hyperlinks

Many people use the terms *Internet* and *World Wide Web* (or just the *Web*) interchangeably. But, as discussed above, the two terms are not synonymous.

The World Wide Web is a huge set of interlinked documents, images and other resources, linked by hyperlinks and URLs. These hyperlinks and URLs allow the web servers and other machines that store originals, and cached copies of these resources to deliver them as required using HTTP (Hypertext Transfer Protocol). HTTP is only one of the communication protocols used on the Internet.

Web services also use HTTP to allow software systems to communicate in order to share and exchange business logic and data.

Software products that can access the resources of the Web are correctly termed *user agents*. In normal use, web browsers, such as Internet Explorer, Firefox, Opera, Apple Safari, and Google Chrome, access web pages and allow users to navigate from one to another via hyperlinks. Web documents may contain almost any combination of computer data including graphics, sounds, text, video, multimedia and interactive content including games, office applications and scientific demonstrations.

Through keyword-driven Internet research using search engines like Yahoo! and Google, millions of people worldwide have easy, instant access to a vast and diverse amount of online information. Compared to encyclopedias and traditional libraries, the World Wide Web has enabled a sudden and extreme decentralization of information and data.

Using the Web, it is also easier than ever before for individuals and organizations to publish ideas and information to an extremely large audience. Anyone can find ways to publish a web page, a blog or build a website for very little initial cost. Publishing and maintaining large, professional websites full of attractive, diverse and up-to-date information is still a difficult and expensive proposition, however.

Many individuals and some companies and groups use "web logs" or blogs, which are largely used as easily updatable online diaries. Some commercial organizations encourage staff to fill them with advice on their areas of specialization in the hope that visitors will be impressed by the expert knowledge and free information and be attracted to the corporation as a result. One example of this practice is Microsoft, whose product developers publish their personal blogs in order to pique the public's interest in their work.

Collections of personal web pages published by large service providers remain popular, and have become increasingly sophisticated. Whereas operations such as Angelfire and GeoCities have existed since the early days of the Web, newer offerings from, for example, Facebook and MySpace currently have large followings. These operations often brand themselves as social network services rather than simply as web page hosts.

Advertising on popular web pages can be lucrative and e-commerce or the sale of products and services directly via the Web continues to grow.

In the early days, web pages were usually created as sets of complete and isolated HTML text files stored on a web server. More recently, websites are more often created using content management or wiki software with initially very little content. Contributors to these systems, who may be paid staff, members of a club or other organization or members of the public, fill underlying databases with content using editing pages designed for that purpose, while casual visitors view and read this content in its final HTML form. There may or may not be editorial, approval and security systems built into the process of taking newly entered content and making it available to the target visitors.

Remote access

The Internet allows computer users to connect to other computers and information stores easily, wherever they may be across the world. They may do this with or without the use of security, authentication and encryption technologies, depending on the requirements.

These are encouraging new ways of working from home, collaboration and information sharing in many industries. An accountant sitting at home can audit the books of a company based in another country, on a server situated in a third country that is remotely maintained by IT specialists in a fourth. These accounts could have been created by home-working bookkeepers, in other remote locations, based on information e-mailed to them from offices all over the world.

Some of these things were possible before the widespread use of the Internet, but the cost of private leased lines would have made many of them infeasible in practice.

An office worker away from their desk, perhaps on the other side of the world on a business trip or a holiday, can open a remote desktop session into his normal office PC using a secure Virtual Private Network (VPN) connection via the Internet. This gives the worker complete access to all of his or her normal files and data, including e-mail and other applications, while away from the office.

This concept is also referred to by some network security people as the Virtual Private Nightmare, because it extends the secure perimeter of a corporate network into its employee's homes.

Collaboration

The low cost and nearly instantaneous sharing of ideas, knowledge, and skills has made collaborative work dramatically easier. Not only can a group cheaply communicate and share ideas, but the wide reach of the Internet allows such groups to easily form in the first place. An example of this is the free software movement, which has produced Linux, Mozilla Firefox, OpenOffice.org etc.

Internet "chat", whether in the form of IRC chat rooms or channels or via instant messaging systems, allow colleagues to stay in touch in a very convenient way when working at their computers during the day. Messages can be exchanged even more quickly and conveniently than via e-mail. Extensions to these systems may allow files to be exchanged, "whiteboard" drawings to be shared or voice and video contact between team members.

Version control systems allow collaborating teams to work on shared sets of documents without either accidentally overwriting each other's work or having members wait until they get "sent" documents to be able to make their contributions.

Business and project teams can share calendars as well as documents and other information. Such collaboration occurs in a wide variety of areas including scientific research, software development, conference planning, political activism and creative writing.

Social and political collaboration is also becoming more widespread as both Internet access and computer literacy grow. From the flash mob 'events' of the early 2000s to the use of social networking in the 2009 Iranian election protests, the Internet allows people to work together more effectively and in many more ways than was possible without it.

File sharing

A computer file can be e-mailed to customers, colleagues and friends as an attachment. It can be uploaded to a website or FTP server for easy download by others. It can be put into a "shared location" or onto a file server for instant use by colleagues. The load of bulk downloads to many users can be eased by the use of "mirror" servers or peer-to-peer networks.

In any of these cases, access to the file may be controlled by user authentication, the transit of the file over the Internet may be obscured by encryption, and money may change hands for access to the file. The price can be paid by the remote charging of funds from, for example, a credit card whose details are also passed—hopefully fully encrypted—across the Internet. The origin and authenticity of the file received may be checked by digital signatures or by MD5 or other message digests.

These simple features of the Internet, over a worldwide basis, are changing the production, sale and distribution of anything that can be reduced to a computer file for transmission. This includes all manner of print publications, software products, news, music, film, video, photography, graphics and the other arts. This in turn has caused seismic shifts in each of the existing industries that previously controlled the production and distribution of these products.

Streaming media

Many existing radio and television broadcasters provide Internet "feeds" of their live audio and video streams (for example, the BBC). They may also allow time-shift viewing or listening such as Preview, Classic Clips and Listen Again features. These providers have been joined by a range of pure Internet "broadcasters" who never had on-air licenses. This means that an Internet-connected device, such as a computer or something more specific, can be used to access on-line media in much the same way as was previously possible only with a television or radio receiver. The range of material is much wider, from pornography to highly specialized, technical webcasts. Podcasting is a variation on this theme, where—usually audio—material is downloaded and played back on a computer or shifted to a portable media player to be listened to on the move. These techniques using simple equipment allow anybody, with little censorship or licensing control, to broadcast audio-visual material on a worldwide basis.

Webcams can be seen as an even lower-budget extension of this phenomenon. While some webcams can give full-frame-rate video, the picture is usually either small or updates slowly. Internet users can watch animals around an African waterhole, ships in the Panama Canal, traffic at a local roundabout or monitor their own premises, live and in real time. Video chat rooms and video conferencing are also popular with many uses being found for personal webcams, with and without two-way sound.

YouTube was founded on 15th February 2005 and is now the leading website for free streaming video with a vast number of users. It uses a flash-based web player to stream and show video files. Registered users may upload an unlimited amount of video and build their own personal profile. YouTube claims that its users watch hundreds of millions, and upload hundreds of thousands of videos daily.

Internet Telephony (VoIP)

VoIP stands for Voice-over-Internet Protocol, referring to the protocol that underlies all Internet communication. The idea began in the early 1990s with walkie-talkie-like voice applications for personal computers. In recent years many VoIP systems have become as easy to use and as convenient as a normal telephone. The benefit is that, as the Internet carries the voice traffic, VoIP can be free or cost much less than a traditional telephone call, especially over long distances and especially for those with always-on Internet connections such as cable or ADSL.

VoIP is maturing into a competitive alternative to traditional telephone service. Interoperability between different providers has improved and the ability to call or receive a call from a traditional telephone is available. Simple, inexpensive VoIP network adapters are available that eliminate the need for a personal computer.

Voice quality can still vary from call to call but is often equal to and can even exceed that of traditional calls.

Remaining problems for VoIP include emergency telephone number dialling and reliability. Currently, a few VoIP providers provide an emergency service, but it is not universally available. Traditional phones are line-powered and operate during a power failure; VoIP does not do so without a backup power source for the phone equipment and the Internet access devices.

VoIP has also become increasingly popular for gaming applications, as a form of communication between players. Popular VoIP clients for gaming include Ventrilo and Teamspeak. Wii, PlayStation 3, and Xbox 360 also offer VoIP chat features.

INTERNET BY REGION

Internet access

Common methods of home access include dial-up, landline broadband (over coaxial cable, fiber optic or copper wires), Wi-Fi, satellite and 3G technology cell phones.

Public places to use the Internet include libraries and Internet cafes, where computers with Internet connections are available. There are also Internet access points in many public places such as airport halls and coffee shops, in some cases just for brief use while standing. Various terms are used, such as "public Internet kiosk", "public access terminal", and "Web payphone". Many hotels now also have public terminals, though these are usually fee-based. These terminals are widely accessed for various usage like ticket booking, bank deposit, online payment etc. Wi-Fi provides wireless access to computer networks, and therefore can do so to the Internet itself. Hotspots providing such access include Wi-Fi cafes, where would-be users need to bring their own wireless-enabled devices such as a laptop or PDA. These services may be free to all, free to customers only, or fee-based. A hotspot need not be limited to a confined location. A whole campus or park, or even an entire city can be enabled. Grassroots efforts have led to wireless community networks. Commercial Wi-Fi services covering large city areas are in place in London, Vienna, Toronto, San Francisco, Philadelphia, Chicago and Pittsburgh. The Internet can then be accessed from such places as a park bench.

Apart from Wi-Fi, there have been experiments with proprietary mobile wireless networks like Ricochet, various high-speed data services over cellular phone networks, and fixed wireless services.

High-end mobile phones such as smartphones generally come with Internet access through the phone network. Web browsers such as Opera are available on these advanced handsets, which can also run a wide variety of other Internet software. More mobile phones have Internet access than PCs, though this is not as widely used. An Internet access provider and protocol matrix differentiates the methods used to get online.

[hide]Internet access								
Network type	Wired					Wireless		
	Optical	Coaxial cable	Ethernet cable	Phone line	Power line	Unlicensed terrestrial band	Licensed terrestrial band	Satellite
LAN	1000BASE-X	G.hn	Ethernet · G.hn	Home PNA	G.hn	Wi-Fi · Bluetooth · DECT · Wireless USB		
WAN	PON	DOCSIS		Dial-up · ISDN · DSL	BPL	Muni Wi-Fi	GPRS · iBurst · WiBro/WiMAX · UMTS-TDD, HSPA · EVDO · LTE	Satellite

Social impact

Chris Young was voted into the 2007 Major League Baseball All-Star Game on the Internet via the All-Star Final Vote.

The Internet has made possible entirely new forms of social interaction, activities and organizing, thanks to its basic features such as widespread usability and access.

Social networking websites such as Facebook and MySpace have created a new form of socialization and interaction. Users of these sites are able to add a wide variety of items to their personal pages, to indicate common interests, and to connect with others. It is also possible to find a large circle of existing acquaintances, especially if a site allows users to utilize their real names, and to allow communication among large existing groups of people.

Sites like meetup.com exist to allow wider announcement of groups which may exist mainly for face-to-face meetings, but which may have a variety of minor interactions over their group's site at meetup.org, or other similar sites.

Digital Natives

The first generation is now being raised with widespread availability of Internet connectivity, with consequences for privacy, identity, and copyright concerns. These "Digital Natives" face a variety of concerns that were not present for prior generations.

Political organization and censorship

In democratic societies, the Internet has achieved new relevance as a political tool. The presidential campaign of Howard Dean in 2004 in the United States became famous for its ability to generate donations via the Internet. Many political groups use the Internet to achieve a whole new method of organizing, in order to carry out Internet activism.

Some governments, such as those of Iran, North Korea, Myanmar, the People's Republic of China, and Saudi Arabia, restrict what people in their countries can access on the Internet, especially political and religious content. This is accomplished through software that filters domains and content so that they may not be easily accessed or obtained without elaborate circumvention.

In Norway, Denmark, Finland and Sweden, major Internet service providers have voluntarily (possibly to avoid such an arrangement being turned into law) agreed to restrict access to sites listed by police. While this list of forbidden URLs is only supposed to contain addresses of known child pornography sites, the content of the list is secret.

Many countries, including the United States, have enacted laws making the possession or distribution of certain material, such as child pornography, illegal, but do not use filtering software.

There are many free and commercially available software programs with which a user can choose to block offensive websites on individual computers or networks, such as to limit a child's access to pornography or violence. See *Content-control software.*

Leisure activities

The Internet has been a major source of leisure since before the World Wide Web, with entertaining social experiments such as MUDs and MOOs being conducted on university servers, and humor-related Usenet groups receiving much of the main traffic. Today, many Internet forums have sections devoted to games and funny videos; short cartoons in the form of Flash movies are also popular. Over 6 million people use blogs or message boards as a means of communication and for the sharing of ideas.

The pornography and gambling industries have both taken full advantage of the World Wide Web and often provide a significant source of advertising revenue for other websites. Although many governments have attempted to put restrictions on both industrie's use of the Internet, this has generally failed to stop their widespread popularity.

One main area of leisure on the Internet is multiplayer gaming. This form of leisure creates communities, bringing people of all ages and origins to enjoy the fast-paced world of multiplayer games. These range from MMORPG to first-person shooters, from role-playing games to online gambling. This has revolutionized the way many people interact and spend their free time on the Internet.

While online gaming has been around since the 1970s, modern modes of online gaming began with services such as GameSpy and MPlayer, to which players of games would typically subscribe. Non-subscribers were limited to certain types of game play or certain games.

Many use the Internet to access and download music, movies and other works for their enjoyment and relaxation. As discussed above, there are paid and unpaid sources for all of these, using centralized servers and distributed peer-to-peer technologies. Some of these sources take more care over the original artists' rights and over copyright laws than others.

Many use the World Wide Web to access news, weather and sports reports, to plan and book holidays and to find out more about their random ideas and casual interests.

People use chat, messaging and e-mail to make and stay in touch with friends worldwide, sometimes in the same way as some previously had pen pals. Social networking websites like MySpace, Facebook and many others like them also put and keep people in contact for their enjoyment.

The Internet has seen a growing number of Web desktops, where users can access their files, folders, and settings via the Internet.

Cyberslacking has become a serious drain on corporate resources; the average UK employee spends 57 minutes a day surfing the Web at work, according to a study by Peninsula Business Services.[21]

Market

The Internet has also become a large market for companies; some of the biggest companies today have grown by taking advantage of the efficient nature of low-cost advertising and commerce through the Internet, also known as e-commerce. It is the fastest way to spread information to a vast number of people simultaneously. The Internet has also subsequently revolutionized shopping—for example; a person can order a CD online and receive it in the mail within a couple of days, or download it directly in some cases. The Internet has also greatly facilitated personalized marketing which allows a company to market a product to a specific person or a specific group of people more so than any other advertising medium.

Examples of personalized marketing include online communities such as MySpace, Friendster, Orkut, Facebook and others which thousands of Internet users join to advertise themselves and make friends online. Many of these users are young teens and adolescents ranging from 13 to 25 years old. In turn, when they advertise themselves they advertise interests and hobbies, which online marketing companies can use as information as to what those users will purchase online, and advertise their own companies products to those users.

WORLD WIDE WEB

The **World Wide Web** (commonly abbreviated as the "**Web**") is a system of interlinked hypertext documents accessed via the Internet. With a Web browser, one can view Web pages that may contain text, images, videos, and other multimedia and navigate between them using hyperlinks. Using concepts from earlier hypertext systems, the World Wide Web was invented in 1989 by the English physicist Sir Tim Berners-Lee, now the Director of the World Wide Web Consortium, and later assisted by Robert Cailliau, a Belgian computer scientist, while both were working at CERN in Geneva, Switzerland. In 1990, they proposed building a "web of nodes" storing "hypertext pages" viewed by "browsers" on a network, and released that web in December. Connected by the existing Internet, other websites were created, around the world, adding international standards for domain names and the HTML language. Since then, Berners-Lee has played an active role in guiding the development of Web standards (such as the markup languages in which Web pages are composed), and in recent years has advocated his vision of a Semantic Web.

The World Wide Web enabled the spread of information over the Internet through an easy-to-use and flexible format. It thus played an important role in popularizing use of the Internet.[3] Although the two terms are sometimes conflated in popular use, *World Wide Web* is not synonymous with *Internet*. The Web is an application built on top of the Internet.

History

This NeXT Computer used by Sir Tim Berners-Lee at CERN became the first Web server.

In March 1989, Berners Lee wrote a proposal that referenced ENQUIRE, a database and software project he had built in 1980, and described a more elaborate information management system. With help from Robert Cailliau, he published a more formal proposal (on November 12, 1990) to build a "Hypertext project" called "WorldWideWeb" (one word, also "W3") as a "web of nodes" with "hypertext documents" to store data. That data would be viewed in "hypertext pages" (webpages) by various "browsers" (line-mode or full-screen) on the computer network, using an "access protocol" connecting the "Internet and DECnet protocol worlds".

This NeXT Computer used by Sir Tim Berners-Lee at CERN became the first Web server.

In March 1989, Berners Lee wrote a proposal that referenced ENQUIRE, a database and software project he had built in 1980, and described a more elaborate information management system. With help from Robert Cailliau, he published a more formal proposal (on November 12, 1990) to build a "Hypertext project" called "WorldWideWeb" (one word, also "W3") as a "web of nodes" with "hypertext documents" to store data. That data would be viewed in "hypertext pages" (webpages) by various "browsers" (line-mode or full-screen) on the computer network, using an "access protocol" connecting the "Internet and DECnet protocol worlds".

The proposal had been modeled after EBT's (Electronic Book Technology, a spin-off from the Institute for Research in Information and Scholarship at Brown University) Dynatext SGML reader that CERN had licensed. The Dynatext system, although technically advanced (a key player in the extension of SGML ISO 8879:1986 to Hypermedia within HyTime), was considered too expensive and with an inappropriate licensing policy for general HEP (High Energy Physics) community use: a fee for each document and each time a document was changed.

A NeXT Computer was used by Berners-Lee as the world's first Web server and also to write the first Web browser, WorldWideWeb, in 1990. By Christmas 1990, Berners-Lee had built all the tools necessary for a working Web: the first Web browser (which was a Web editor as well), the first Web server, and the first Web pages[7] which described the project itself.

On August 6, 1991, he posted a short summary of the World Wide Web project on the alt.hypertext newsgroup. This date also marked the debut of the Web as a publicly available service on the Internet.

The first server outside Europe was set up at SLAC in December 1991.

The crucial underlying concept of hypertext originated with older projects from the 1960s, such as the Hypertext Editing System (HES) at Brown University— among others Ted Nelson and Andries van Dam— Ted Nelson's Project Xanadu and Douglas Engelbart's On-Line System (NLS). Both Nelson and Engelbart were in turn inspired by Vannevar Bush's microfilm-based "memex," which was described in the 1945 essay "As We May Think".

Lee's breakthrough was to marry hypertext to the Internet. In his book *Weaving The Web*, he explains that he had repeatedly suggested that a marriage between the two technologies was possible to members of *both* technical communities, but when no one took up his invitation, he finally tackled the project himself. In the process, he developed a system of globally unique identifiers for resources on the Web and elsewhere: the Uniform Resource Identifier.

The World Wide Web had a number of differences from other hypertext systems that were then available. The Web required only unidirectional links rather than bidirectional ones. This made it possible for someone to link to another resource without action by the owner of that resource.

It also significantly reduced the difficulty of implementing Web servers and browsers (in comparison to earlier systems), but in turn presented the chronic problem of link rot. Unlike predecessors such as HyperCard, the World Wide Web was non-proprietary, making it possible to develop servers and clients independently and to add extensions without licensing restrictions.

On April 30, 1993, CERN announced[10] that the World Wide Web would be free to anyone, with no fees due. Coming two months after the announcement that the Gopher protocol was no longer free to use, this produced a rapid shift away from Gopher and towards the Web. An early popular Web browser was ViolaWWW, which was based upon HyperCard.

Scholars generally agree that a turning point for the World Wide Web began with the introduction of the Mosaic Web browser in 1993, a graphical browser developed by a team at the National Center for Supercomputing Applications at the University of Illinois at Urbana-Campaign (NCSA-UIUC), led by Marc Andreessen. Funding for Mosaic came from the U.S. *High-Performance Computing and Communications Initiative*, a funding program initiated by the *High Performance Computing and Communication Act of 1991*, one of several computing developments initiated by U.S. Senator Al Gore. Prior to the release of Mosaic, graphics were not commonly mixed with text in Web pages, and its popularity was less than older protocols in use over the Internet, such as Gopher and Wide Area Information Servers (WAIS). Mosaic's graphical user interface allowed the Web to become, by far, the most popular Internet protocol.

The World Wide Web Consortium (W3C) was founded by Tim Berners-Lee after he left the European Organization for Nuclear Research (CERN) in October, 1994. It was founded at the Massachusetts Institute of Technology Laboratory for Computer Science (MIT/LCS) with support from the Defense Advanced Research Projects Agency (DARPA)—which had pioneered the Internet—and the European Commission.

By the end of 1994, while the total number of websites was still minute compared to present standards, quite a number of notable websites were already active, many of whom are the precursors or inspiration for today's most popular services.

How it works

The terms Internet and World Wide Web are often used in every-day speech without much distinction. However, the Internet and the World Wide Web are not one and the same. The Internet is a global data communications system. It is a hardware and software infrastructure that provides connectivity between computers. In contrast, the Web is one of the services communicated via the Internet. It is a collection of interconnected documents and other resources, linked by hyperlinks and URLs. In short, the Web is an application running on the Internet.

Viewing a Web page on the World Wide Web normally begins either by typing the URL of the page into a Web browser, or by following a hyperlink to that page or resource. The Web browser then initiates a series of communication messages, behind the scenes, in order to fetch and display it.

First, the server-name portion of the URL is resolved into an IP address using the global, distributed Internet database known as the domain name system, or DNS. This IP address is necessary to contact the Web server. The browser then requests the resource by sending an HTTP request to the Web server at that particular address. In the case of a typical Web page, the HTML text of the page is requested first and parsed immediately by the Web browser, which then makes additional requests for images and any other files that form parts of the page.

Statistics measuring a website's popularity are usually based either on the number of 'page views' or associated server 'hits' (file requests) that take place.

Having received the required files from the Web server, the browser then renders the page onto the screen as specified by its HTML, CSS, and other Web languages. Any images and other resources are incorporated to produce the on-screen Web page that the user sees.

Most Web pages will themselves contain hyperlinks to other related pages and perhaps to downloads, source documents, definitions and other Web resources. Such a collection of useful, related resources, interconnected via hypertext links, is what was dubbed a "web" of information. Making it available on the Internet created what Tim Berners-Lee first called the **WorldWideWeb** (in its original CamelCase, which was subsequently discarded) in November 1990.

Ajax updates

JavaScript is a scripting language that was initially developed in 1995 by Brendan Eich, then of Netscape, for use within Web pages. The standardized version is ECMAScript. To overcome some of the limitations of the page-by-page model described above, some web applications also use Ajax (asynchronous JavaScript and XML). JavaScript is delivered with the page that can make additional HTTP requests to the server, either in response to user actions such as mouse-clicks, or based on lapsed time. The server's responses are used to modify the current page rather than creating a new page with each response. Thus the server only needs to provide limited, incremental information. Since multiple Ajax requests can be handled at the same time, users can interact with a page even while data is being retrieved. Some web applications regularly poll the server to ask if new information is available.[*citation needed*]

WWW prefix in Web addresses

Many Web addresses begin with *www*, because of the long-standing practice of naming Internet hosts (servers) according to the services they provide. So, the host name for a web server is often *www* as it is *ftp* for an FTP server, and *news* or *nntp* for a USENET news server etc. These host names then appear as DNS subdomain names, as in "www.example.com".

The use of such subdomain names is not required by any technical or policy standard; indeed, the first ever web server was called "nxoc01.cern.ch", and many web sites exist without a *www* subdomain prefix, or with some other prefix such as "www2", "secure" etc. These subdomain prefixes have no consequence; they are simply chosen names. Many web servers are set up such that both the domain by itself (e.g., example.com) and the *www* subdomain (e.g., www.example.com) refer to the same site, others require one form or the other, or they may map to different web sites.

When a single word is typed into the address bar and the return key is pressed, some web browsers automatically try adding "www." to the beginning of it and possibly ".com", ".org" and ".net" at the end. For example, typing 'microsoft<return>' may resolve to *http://www.microsoft.com* and 'openoffice<return>' to *http://www.openoffice.org*. This feature was beginning to be included in early versions of Mozilla Firefox (when it still had the working title 'Firebird') in early 2003. It is reported that Microsoft was granted a US patent for the same idea in 2008, but only with regard to mobile devices.

The 'http://' or 'https://' part of web addresses *do* have meaning: These refer to Hypertext Transfer Protocol and to HTTP Secure and so define the communication protocol that will be used to request and receive the page and all its images and other resources. The HTTP network protocol is fundamental to the way the World Wide Web works, and the encryption involved in HTTPS adds an essential layer if confidential information such as passwords or bank details are to be exchanged over the public internet. Web browsers often prepend this 'scheme' part to URLs too, if it is omitted. In overview, RFC 2396 defined web URLs to have the following form: <scheme>://<path>?<query>#<fragment>.

Pronunciation of "www"

In English, *www* is pronounced by individually pronouncing the name of characters (*double-u double-u double-u*). Although some technical users pronounce it *dub-dub-dub* this is not widespread. The English writer Douglas Adams once quipped:

The World Wide Web is the only thing I know of whose shortened form takes three times longer to say than what it's short for.

– Douglas Adams, *The Independent on Sunday, 1999*

It is also interesting that in Mandarin Chinese, *World Wide Web* is commonly translated via a phono-semantic matching to *wàn wéi wÎng* (Nô~Qn), which satisfies *www* and literally means "myriad dimensional net", a translation that very appropriately reflects the design concept and proliferation of the World Wide Web.

Tim Berners-Lee's web-space states that *World Wide Web* is officially spelled as three separate words, each capitalized, with no intervening hyphens. Additionally, *Web* (with a capital *W*) is used to indicate its status as an abbreviation.

Standards

Many formal standards and other technical specifications define the operation of different aspects of the World Wide Web, the Internet, and computer information exchange. Many of the documents are the work of the World Wide Web Consortium (W3C), headed by Berners-Lee, but some are produced by the Internet Engineering Task Force (IETF) and other organizations.

Usually, when Web standards are discussed, the following publications are seen as foundational:

- Recommendations for markup languages, especially HTML and XHTML, from the W3C. These define the structure and interpretation of hypertext documents.
- Recommendations for stylesheets, especially CSS, from the W3C.
- Standards for ECMAScript (usually in the form of JavaScript), from Ecma International.
- Recommendations for the Document Object Model, from W3C.

Additional publications provide definitions of other essential technologies for the World Wide Web, including, but not limited to, the following:

- *Uniform Resource Identifier* (URI), which is a universal system for referencing resources on the Internet, such as hypertext documents and images. URIs, often called URLs, are defined by the IETF's RFC 3986 / STD 66: *Uniform Resource Identifier (URI): Generic Syntax*, as well as its predecessors and numerous URI scheme-defining RFCs;
- *HyperText Transfer Protocol (HTTP)*, especially as defined by RFC 2616: *HTTP/1.1* and RFC 2617: *HTTP Authentication*, which specify how the browser and server authenticate each other.

Privacy

Computer users, who save time and money, and who gain conveniences and entertainment, may or may not have surrendered the right to privacy in exchange for using a number of technologies including the Web.[21] Worldwide, more than a half billion people have used a social network service,[22] and of Americans who grew up with the Web, half created an online profile[23] and are part of a generational shift that could be changing norms.[24][25] Facebook progressed from U.S. college students to a 70% non-U.S. audience and estimates that only 20% of its members use privacy settings.

Privacy representatives from 60 countries have resolved to ask for laws to complement industry self-regulation, for education for children and other minors who use the Web, and for default protections for users of social networks. They also believe data protection for personally identifiable information benefits business more than the sale of that information. Users can opt-in to features in browsers to clear their personal histories locally and block some cookies and advertising networks but they are still tracked in website's server logs, and particularly Web beacons. Berners-Lee and colleagues see hope in accountability and appropriate use achieved by extending the Web's architecture to policy awareness, perhaps with audit logging, reasoners and appliances.

Among services paid for by advertising, Yahoo! could collect the most data about users of commercial websites, about 2,500 bits of information per month about each typical user of its site and its affiliated advertising network sites. Yahoo! was followed by MySpace with about half that potential and then by AOL-TimeWarner, Google, Facebook, Microsoft, and eBay.

Security

The Web has become criminal's preferred pathway for spreading malware. Cybercrime carried out on the Web can include identity theft, fraud, espionage and intelligence gathering. Web-based vulnerabilities now outnumber traditional computer security concerns, and as measured by Google, about one in ten Web pages may contain malicious code. Most Web-based attacks take place on legitimate websites, and most, as measured by Sophos, are hosted in the United States, China and Russia.

The most common of all malware threats is SQL injection attacks against websites. Through HTML and URIs the Web was vulnerable to attacks like cross-site scripting (XSS) that came with the introduction of JavaScript and were exacerbated to some degree by Web 2.0 and Ajax web design that favors the use of scripts. Today by one estimate, 70% of all websites are open to XSS attacks on their users.

Proposed solutions vary to extremes. Large security vendors like McAfee already design governance and compliance suites to meet post-9/11 regulations, and some, like Finjan have recommended active real-time inspection of code and all content regardless of its source. Some have argued that for enterprise to see security as a business opportunity rather than a cost center, "ubiquitous, always-on digital rights management" enforced in the infrastructure by a handful of organizations must replace the hundreds of companies that today secure data and networks. Jonathan Zittrain has said users sharing responsibility for computing safety is far preferable to locking down the Internet.

Accessibility

Access to the Web is for everyone regardless of disability including visual, auditory, physical, speech, cognitive, and neurological. Accessibility features also help others with temporary disabilities like a broken arm and an aging population as their abilities change. The Web is used for receiving information as well as providing information and interacting with society, making it essential that the Web be accessible in order to provide equal access and equal opportunity to people with disabilities.

The power of the Web is in its universality. Access by everyone regardless of disability is an essential aspect. —Tim Berners-Lee

Many countries regulate web accessibility as a requirement for websites. International cooperation in the W3C Web Accessibility Initiative led to simple guidelines that Web content authors as well as software developers can use to make the Web accessible to persons who may or may not be using assistive technology.

Internationalization

The W3C Internationalization Activity assures that Web technology will work in all languages, scripts, and cultures. Beginning in 2004 or 2005, Unicode gained ground and eventually in December 2007 surpassed both ASCII and Western European as the Web's most frequently used character encoding. Originally RFC 3986 allowed resources to be identified by URI in a subset of US-ASCII. RFC 3987 allows more characters—any character in the Universal Character Set—and now a resource can be idenfified by IRI in any language.

Statistics

According to a 2001 study, there were massively more than 550 billion documents on the Web, mostly in the invisible Web or deep Web. A 2002 survey of 2,024 million Web pages determined that by far the most Web content was in English: 56.4%; next were pages in German (7.7%), French (5.6%), and Japanese (4.9%). A more recent study, which used Web searches in 75 different languages to sample the Web, determined that there were over 11.5 billion Web pages in the publicly indexable Web as of the end of January 2005. As of March 2009[update], the indexable web contains at least 25.21 billion pages. On July 25, 2008, Google software engineers Jesse Alpert and Nissan Hajaj announced that Google Search had discovered one trillion unique URLs.

As of May 2009[update], over 109.5 million websites operated. Of these 74% were commercial or other sites operating in the.com generic top-level domain.

Speed issues

Frustration over congestion issues in the Internet infrastructure and the high latency that results in slow browsing has led to an alternative, pejorative name for the World Wide Web: the *World Wide Wait*. Speeding up the Internet is an ongoing discussion over the use of peering and QoS technologies. Other solutions to reduce the World Wide Wait can be found at W3C.

Standard guidelines for ideal Web response times are:

- 0.1 second (one tenth of a second). Ideal response time. The user doesn't sense any interruption.
- 1 second. Highest acceptable response time. Download times above 1 second interrupt the user experience.
- 10 seconds. Unacceptable response time. The user experience is interrupted and the user is likely to leave the site or system.

Caching

If a user revisits a Web page after only a short interval, the page data may not need to be re-obtained from the source Web server. Almost all Web browsers cache recently-obtained data, usually on the local hard drive. HTTP requests sent by a browser will usually only ask for data that has changed since the last download. If the locally-cached data are still current, it will be reused.

Caching helps reduce the amount of Web traffic on the Internet. The decision about expiration is made independently for each downloaded file, whether image, stylesheet, JavaScript, HTML, or whatever other content the site may provide. Thus even on sites with highly dynamic content, many of the basic resources only need to be refreshed occasionally. Web site designers find it worthwhile to collate resources such as CSS data and JavaScript into a few site-wide files so that they can be cached efficiently. This helps reduce page download times and lowers demands on the Web server.

There are other components of the Internet that can cache Web content. Corporate and academic firewalls often cache Web resources requested by one user for the benefit of all. (See also Caching proxy server.) Some search engines, such as Google or Yahoo!, also store cached content from websites.

Apart from the facilities built into Web servers that can determine when files have been updated and so need to be re-sent, designers of dynamically-generated Web pages can control the HTTP headers sent back to requesting users, so that transient or sensitive pages are not cached. Internet banking and news sites frequently use this facility.

Data requested with an HTTP 'GET' is likely to be cached if other conditions are met; data obtained in response to a 'POST' is assumed to depend on the data that was POSTed and so is not cached.

Link rot and Web archival

> This article **is missing citations or needs footnotes**. Please help add inline citations to guard against copyright violations and factual inaccuracies. *(May 2009)*

Over time, many Web resources pointed to by hyperlinks disappear, relocate, or are replaced with different content. This phenomenon is referred to in some circles as "link rot" and the hyperlinks affected by it are often called "dead links".

The ephemeral nature of the Web has prompted many efforts to archive Web sites. The Internet Archive is one of the best-known efforts; it has been active since 1996.

Introduction

A **web browser** is a software application for retrieving, presenting and traversing information resources on the World Wide Web. An information resource is identified by a Uniform Resource Identifier (URI) and may be a web page, image, video or other piece of content. Hyperlinks present in resources enable users to easily navigate their browsers to related resources.

Although browsers primarily intended to access the World Wide Web, they can also be used to access information provided by web servers in private networks or files in file systems.

The major web browsers are Windows Internet Explorer, Mozilla Firefox, Apple Safari, Google Chrome, and Opera.

History

The history of the web browser dates back to late 1980s, when a variety of technologies laid the foundation for the first web browser, WorldWideWeb, by Tim Berners-Lee in 1991. That browser brought together a variety of existing and new software and hardware technologies.

The introduction of the NCSA Mosaic web browser in 1993 – one of the first graphical web browsers – led to an explosion in web use. Marc Andreessen, the leader of the Mosaic team at NCSA, soon started his own company, named Netscape, and released the Mosaic-influenced Netscape Navigator in 1994, which quickly became the world's most popular browser, accounting for 90% of all web use at its peak (see usage share of web browsers).

Microsoft responded with its browser Internet Explorer in 1995 (also heavily influenced by Mosaic), initiating the industry's first browser war. By bundling Internet Explorer with Windows, Microsoft was able to leverage its dominance in the operating system market to take over the web browser market; Internet Explorer usage share peaked at over 95% by 2002.

In 1998, Netscape launched what was to become the Mozilla Foundation in an attempt to produce a competitive browser using the open source software model. That browser would eventually evolve into Firefox, which developed a respectable following while still in the beta stage of development; shortly after the release of Firefox 1.0 in late 2004, Firefox (all versions) accounted for 7.4% of browser use. As of February 2009, Firefox has a 21.77% usage share.

Opera debuted in 1996; although it has never achieved widespread use, having less than 1% browser usage share as of February 2009 according to Net Applications,[5] it has a substantial share of the fast-growing mobile phone web browser market, being preinstalled on over 40 million phones. It is also available on several other embedded systems, including Nintendo's Wii video game console.

Apple's Safari had its first beta release in January 2003; as of February 2009, it has a dominant share of Apple-based web browsing, accounting for just over 8% of the entire browser market.

The most recent major entrant to the browser market is Google's Chrome, first released in September 2008. As of February 2009, it has a 1.15% usage share.

Function

The primary purpose of a web browser is to display resources to the user. This process begins when the user inputs a Uniform Resource Identifier (URI), for example *http://en.wikipedia.org/*, into the browser. The prefix of the URI determines how the URI will be interpreted. The most commonly used kind of URI starts with *http:* and identifies a resource to be retrieved over the Hypertext Transfer Protocol (HTTP). Many browsers also support a variety of other prefixes, such as *https:* for HTTPS, *ftp:* for the File Transfer Protocol, and *file:* for local files. Prefixes that the web browser cannot directly handle are often handed off to another application entirely. For example, *mailto:* URIs are usually passed to the user's default e-mail application, and *news:* URIs are passed to the user's default newsgroup reader.

In the case of *http*, *https*, *file*, and others, once the resource has been retrieved the web browser sets about displaying it. HTML is handed off to the browser's layout engine to be transformed from markup to an interactive document. Aside from HTML, web browsers can generally display any kind of content that can be part of a web page. Most browsers can display images, audio, video, and XML files, and often have plug-ins to support Flash applications and Java applets. Upon encountering a file of an unsupported type or a file that is set up to be downloaded rather than displayed, the browser prompts the user to save the file to disk.

Information resources may contain hyperlinks to other information resources. Each link indicates the URI of a resource to go to. When a link is clicked, the browser navigates to the resource indicated by the link's target URI and the process of bringing content to the user begins again.

Features

Available web browsers range in features from minimial, text-based user interfaces with bare-bones support for HTML to rich user interfaces supporting a wide variety of file formats and protocols. Browsers which include additional components to support e-mail, Usenet news, and Internet Relay Chat (IRC), are sometimes referred to as "Internet suites" rather than merely "web browsers".

All major web browsers allow the user to open multiple information resources at the same time, either in different browser windows or in different tabs of the same window. Major browsers also include pop-up blockers to prevent unwanted windows from "popping up" without the user's consent.

Most web browsers can display a list of web pages that the user has *bookmarked* so that the user can quickly return to them. Bookmarks are also called "Favorites" in Internet Explorer. In addition, all major web browsers have some form of built-in web feed aggregator. In Mozilla Firefox, web feeds are formatted as "live bookmarks" and behave like a folder of bookmarks corresponding to recent entries in the feed. In Opera, a more traditional feed reader is included which stores and displays the contents of the feed.

Furthermore, most browsers can be extended via plug-ins, downloadable components that provide additional features.

User interface

Most major web browsers have these user interface elements in common:

- *Back* and *forward* buttons to go back to the previous resource and forward again.
- A *refresh* or *reload* button to reload the current resource.
- A *stop* button to cancel loading the resource. In some browsers, the stop button is often merged with the reload button.
- A *home* button to return to the user's home page
- An address bar to input the Uniform Resource Identifier (URI) of the desired resource and display it.
- A search bar to input terms into a search engine
- A status bar to display progress in loading the resource and also the URI of links when the cursor hovers over them, and page zooming capability.

Major browsers also possess incremental find features to search within a web page.

Privacy and security

Most browsers support HTTP Secure and offer quick and easy ways to delete the web cache, cookies, and browsing history.

Standards support

Early web browsers supported only a very simple version of HTML. The rapid development of proprietary web browsers led to the development of non-standard dialects of HTML, leading to problems with interoperability. Modern web browsers support a combination of standards-based and *de facto* HTML and XHTML, which should be rendered in the same way by all browsers.

Introduction E-mail

Electronic mail, often abbreviated as **email** or **e-mail**, is a method of exchanging digital messages, designed primarily for human use. E-mail systems are based on a store-and-forward model in which e-mail computer server systems accept, forward, deliver and store messages on behalf of users, who only need to connect to the e-mail infrastructure, typically an e-mail server, with a network-enabled device (e.g., a personal computer) for the duration of message submission or retrieval. Rarely is e-mail transmitted directly from one user's device to another's.

An electronic mail message consists of two components, the message *header*, and the message *body*, which is the email's content. The message header contains control information, including, minimally, an originator's email address and one or more recipient addresses. Usually additional information is added, such as a subject header field.

Originally a text-only communications medium, email is extended to carry multi-media content attachments, which were standardized in with RFC 2045 through RFC 2049, collectively called, Multipurpose Internet Mail Extensions (MIME).

The foundation for today's global Internet e-mail service was created in the early ARPANET and standards for encoding of messages were proposed as early as, for example, in 1973 (RFC 561). An e-mail sent in the early 1970s looked very similar to one sent on the Internet today. Conversion from the ARPANET to the Internet in the early 1980s produced the core of the current service.

Network-based email was initially exchanged on the ARPANET in extensions to the File Transfer Protocol (FTP), but is today carried by the Simple Mail Transfer Protocol (SMTP), first published as Internet Standard 10 (RFC 821) in 1982. In the process of transporting email messages between systems, SMTP communicates delivery parameters using a message *envelope* separately from the message (headers and body) itself.

Spelling

The spelling variations *e-mail* and *email* are both common. Several prominent journalistic and technical style guides recommend *e-mail*, and the spelling *email* is also recognized in many dictionaries. In the original RFC neither spelling is used; the service is referred to as *mail*, and a single piece of electronic mail is called a *message*. The plural form "e-mails" (or emails) is also recognized.

Newer RFCs and IETF working groups require *email* for consistent capitalization, hyphenation, and spelling of terms. ARPANET users and early developers from Unix, CMS, AppleLink, eWorld, AOL, GEnie, and HotMail used *eMail* with the letter *M* capitalized. The authors of some of the original RFCs used *eMail* when giving their own addresses.

Donald Knuth considers the spelling "e-mail" to be archaic and notes that it is more often spelled "email" in the UK. In some other European languages (French, German, Dutch, Romanian), "email" (ignoring diacritics) is the word for "enamel".

Origin

E-mail predates the inception of the Internet, and was in fact a crucial tool in creating the Internet.

MIT first demonstrated the Compatible Time-Sharing System (CTSS) in 1961. It allowed multiple users to log into the IBM 7094 from remote dial-up terminals, and to store files online on disk. This new ability encouraged users to share information in new ways. E-mail started in 1965 as a way for multiple users of a time-sharing mainframe computer to communicate. Although the exact history is murky, among the first systems to have such a facility were SDC's Q32 and MIT's CTSS.

E-mail was quickly extended to become *network e-mail*, allowing users to pass messages between different computers by 1966 or earlier (it is possible that the SAGE system had something similar some time before).

The ARPANET computer network made a large contribution to the development of e-mail. There is one report that indicates experimental inter-system e-mail transfers began shortly after its creation in 1969. Ray Tomlinson initiated the use of the "@" sign to separate the names of the user and their machine in 1971. The ARPANET significantly increased the popularity of e-mail, and it became the killer app of the ARPANET.

Most other networks had their own email protocols and address formats; as the influence of the ARPANET and later the Internet grew, central sites often hosted email gateways that passed mail between the Internet and these other networks. Internet email addressing is still complicated by the need to handle mail destined for these older networks. Some well-known examples of these were UUCP (mostly Unix computers), BITNET (mostly IBM and VAX mainframes at universities), FidoNet (personal computers), and DECNET (various networks).

An example of an Internet email address that routed mail to a user at a UUCP host:

hubhost!middlehost!edgehost!user@uucpgateway.somedomain.example.com

This was necessary because in early years UUCP computers did not maintain (or consult servers for) information about the location of all hosts they exchanged mail with, but rather only knew how to communicate with a few network neighbors; email messages (and other data such as Usenet News) were passed along in a chain among hosts who had explicitly agreed to share data with each other.

Operation overview

The diagram to the right shows a typical sequence of events that takes place when Alice composes a message using her mail user agent (MUA). She enters the e-mail address of her correspondent, and hits the "send" button.

1. Her MUA formats the message in e-mail format and uses the Simple Mail Transfer Protocol (SMTP) to send the message to the local mail transfer agent (MTA), in this case smtp.a.org, run by Alice's Internet Service Provider (ISP).
2. The MTA looks at the destination address provided in the SMTP protocol (not from the message header), in this case bob@b.org. An Internet e-mail address is a string of the form localpart@exampledomain. The part **before** the @ sign is the **local part** of the address, often the username of the recipient, and the part **after** the @ sign is a domain name or a fully qualified domain name. The MTA resolves a domain name to determine the fully qualified domain name of the mail exchange server in the Domain Name System.

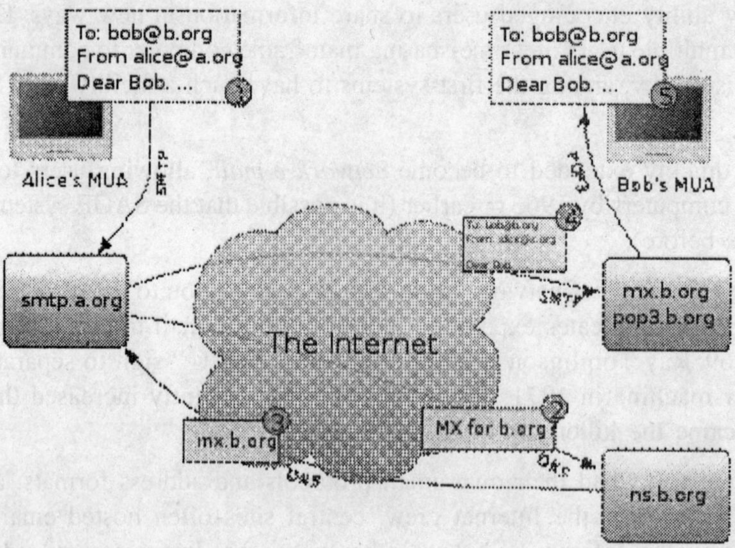

3. The DNS server for the b.org domain, ns.b.org, responds with any MX records listing the mail exchange servers for that domain, in this case mx.b.org, a server run by Bob's ISP.

4. smtp.a.org sends the message to mx.b.org using SMTP, which delivers it to the mailbox of the user bob.

5. Bob presses the "get mail" button in his MUA, which picks up the message using the Post Office Protocol (POP3).

That sequence of events applies to the majority of e-mail users. However, there are many alternative possibilities and complications to the e-mail system:

- Alice or Bob may use a client connected to a corporate e-mail system, such as IBM Lotus Notes or Microsoft Exchange. These systems often have their own internal e-mail format and their clients typically communicate with the e-mail server using a vendor-specific, proprietary protocol. The server sends or receives e-mail via the Internet through the product's Internet mail gateway which also does any necessary reformatting. If Alice and Bob work for the same company, the entire transaction may happen completely within a single corporate e-mail system.
- Alice may not have a MUA on her computer but instead may connect to a webmail service.
- Alice's computer may run its own MTA, so avoiding the transfer at step 1.
- Bob may pick up his e-mail in many ways, for example using the Internet Message Access Protocol, by logging into mx.b.org and reading it directly, or by using a webmail service.
- Domains usually have several mail exchange servers so that they can continue to accept mail when the main mail exchange server is not available.

- E-mail messages are not secure if e-mail encryption is not used correctly.

Many MTAs use to accept messages for any recipient on the Internet and do their best to deliver them. Such MTAs are called *open mail relays*. This was very important in the early days of the Internet when network connections were unreliable. If an MTA couldn't reach the destination, it could at least deliver it to a relay closer to the destination. The relay stood a better chance of delivering the message at a later time. However, this mechanism proved to be exploitable by people sending unsolicited bulk e-mail and as a consequence very few modern MTAs are open mail relays, and many MTAs don't accept messages from open mail relays because such messages are very likely to be spam.

Message format

The Internet e-mail message format is defined in RFC 5322 and a series of RFCs, RFC 2045 through RFC 2049, collectively called, *Multipurpose Internet Mail Extensions*, or *MIME*. Although as of July 13, 2005, RFC 2822 is technically a proposed IETF standard and the MIME RFCs are draft IETF standards, these documents are the standards for the format of Internet e-mail. Prior to the introduction of RFC 2822 in 2001, the format described by RFC 822 was the standard for Internet e-mail for nearly 20 years; it is still the official IETF standard. The IETF reserved the numbers 5321 and 5322 for the updated versions of RFC 2821 (SMTP) and RFC 2822, as it previously did with RFC 821 and RFC 822, honoring the extreme importance of these two RFCs. RFC 822 was published in 1982 and based on the earlier RFC 733.

Internet e-mail messages consist of two major sections:

- Header — Structured into fields such as summary, sender, receiver, and other information about the e-mail.
- Body — The message itself as unstructured text; sometimes containing a signature block at the end. This is exactly the same as the body of a regular letter.

The header is separated from the body by a blank line.

Message header

Each message has exactly one header, which is structured into fields. Each field has a name and a value. RFC 5322 specifies the precise syntax.

Informally, each line of text in the header that begins with a printable character begins a separate field. The field name starts in the first character of the line and ends before the separator character ":". The separator is then followed by the field value (the "body" of the field). The value is continued onto subsequent lines if those lines have a space or tab as their first character. Field names and values are restricted to 7-bit ASCII characters. Non-ASCII values may be represented using MIME encoded words.

Header fields

The message header should include at least the following fields:

- From: The e-mail address, and optionally the name of the sender. In many e-mail clients not changeable except through changing account settings.
- To: The e-mail address(es), and optionally name(s) of the message's recipient(s). Indicates primary recipients (multiple allowed), for secondary recipients see Cc: and Bcc: below.
- Subject: A brief summary of the contents of the message.
- Date: The local time and date when the message was written. Like the *From:* field, many email clients fill this in automatically.
- Message-ID: Also an automatically generated field; used to prevent multiple delivery and for reference in In-Reply-To: (see below).

Note that the "To:" field is not necessarily related to the addresses to which the message is delivered. The actual delivery list is supplied separately to the transport protocol, SMTP, which may or may not originally have been extracted from the header content. The "To:" field is similar to the addressing at the top of a conventional letter which is delivered according to the address on the outer envelope. Also note that the "From:" field does not have to be the real sender of the e-mail message. One reason is that it is very easy to fake the "From:" field and let a message seem to be from any mail address. It is possible to digitally sign e-mail, which is much harder to fake, but such signatures require extra programming and often external programs to verify. Some Internet service providers do not relay e-mail claiming to come from a domain not hosted by them, but very few (if any) check to make sure that the person or even e-mail address named in the "From:" field is the one associated with the connection. Some Internet service providers apply e-mail authentication systems to e-mail being sent through their MTA to allow other MTAs to detect forged spam that might appear to come from them.

Other common header fields include (see RFC 4021 or RFC 2076 for more):

- Bcc: Blind Carbon Copy; addresses added to the SMTP delivery list but not (usually) listed in the message data, remaining invisible to other recipients.
- Cc: Carbon copy; Many e-mail clients will mark e-mail in your inbox differently depending on whether you are in the To: or Cc: list.
- Content-Type: Information about how the message is to be displayed, usually a MIME type.
- In-Reply-To: Message-ID of the message that this is a reply to. Used to link related messages together.
- Precedence: commonly with values "bulk", "junk", or "list"; used to indicate that should automated "vacation" or "out of office" responses should not be returned for this mail, eg. to prevent vacation notices from being sent to all other subscribers of a mailinglist.

- Received: Tracking information generated by mail servers that have previously handled a message, in reverse order (last handler first).
- References: Message-ID of the message that this is a reply to, and the message-id of the message the previous was reply a reply to, etc.
- Reply-To: Address that should be used to reply to the sender.
- Sender: Address of the actual sender acting on order of the address-owner listed in the To: field (secretary, list manager, etc.).
- X-Face: Small icon.

IANA maintains a list of standard header fields.

Message body

Content encoding

E-mail was originally designed for 7-bit ASCII. Much e-mail software is 8-bit clean but must assume it will communicate with 8-bit servers and mail readers. The MIME standard introduced character set specifiers and two content transfer encodings to enable transmission of non-ASCII data: quoted printable for mostly 7 bit content with a few characters outside that range and base64 for arbitrary binary data. The 8BITMIME extension was introduced to allow transmission of mail without the need for these encodings but many mail transport agents still do not support it fully. In some countries, several encoding schemes coexist; as the result, by default, the message in a non-Latin alphabet language appears in non-readable form (the only exception is coincidence, when the sender and receiver use the same encoding scheme). Therefore, for international character sets, Unicode is growing in popularity.

Plain text and HTML

Both plain text and HTML are used to convey e-mail. While text is certain to be read by all users without problems, there is a perception[citation needed] that HTML-based e-mail has a higher aesthetic value, assuming the recipient uses an e-mail client that will properly show the HTML markup. This is not always the case, especially among the technological savvy and bandwidth-constrained users. Advantages of HTML include the ability to include inline links and images, set apart previous messages in block quotes, wrap naturally on any display, use emphasis such as underlines and italics, and change font styles. HTML e-mail messages often include an automatically-generated plain text copy as well, for compatibility reasons. Disadvantages include the increased size of the email, privacy concerns about web bugs, abuse of HTML email as a vector for phishing attacks and the spread of malicious software.

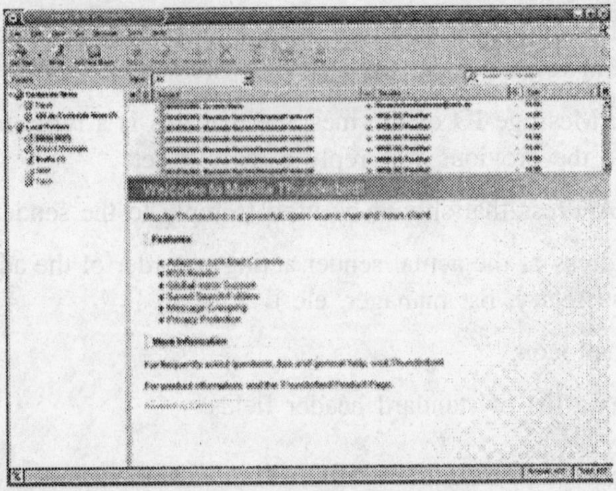

Servers and client applications

Messages are exchanged between hosts using the Simple Mail Transfer Protocol with software programs called mail transfer agents. Users can retrieve their messages from servers using standard protocols such as POP or IMAP, or, as is more likely in a large corporate environment, with a proprietary protocol specific to Lotus Notes or Microsoft Exchange Servers. Webmail interfaces allow users to access their mail with any standard web browser, from any computer, rather than relying on an e-mail client.

Mail can be stored on the client, on the server side, or in both places. Standard formats for mailboxes include Maildir and mbox. Several prominent e-mail clients use their own proprietary format and require conversion software to transfer e-mail between them.

Accepting a message obliges an MTA to deliver it, and when a message cannot be delivered, that MTA must send a bounce message back to the sender, indicating the problem.

Filename extensions

Upon reception of e-mail messages, e-mail client applications save message in operating system files in the filesystem. Some clients save individual messages as separate files, while others use various database formats, often proprietary, for collective storage. A historical standard of storage is the *mbox* format. The specific format used is often indicated by special filename extensions:

eml

This is the default e-mail file extension for Mozilla Thunderbird and Windows Mail. It is also used by Microsoft Outlook Express.

.emlx

Used by Apple Mail.

.msg

Used by Microsoft Office Outlook.

.mbx

Used by Opera Mail, KMail, and Apple Mail based on the mbox format.

Some applications (like Apple Mail) also encode attachments into messages for searching while also producing a physical copy of the files on a disk. Others separate attachments from messages by depositing them into designated folders on disk.

URI scheme *mailto:*

The URI scheme, as registered with the IANA, defines the mailto: scheme for SMTP email addresses. Though its use is not strictly defined, URLs of this form are intended to be used to open the new message window of the user's mail client when the URL is activated, with the address as defined by the URL in the "To:" field.

Use

In society

There are numerous ways in which people have changed the way they communicate in the last 50 years; e-mail is certainly one of them. Traditionally, social interaction in the local community was the basis for communication – face to face. Yet, today face-to-face meetings are no longer the primary way to communicate as one can use a landline telephone or any number of the computer mediated communications such as e-mail.

Research has shown that people actively use e-mail to maintain core social networks, particularly when alters live at a distance. However, contradictory to previous research, the results suggest that increase in Internet usage are associated with decrease in other modes of communication, with proficiency of Internet and e-mail use serving as a mediating factor in this relationship.

Flaming

Flaming occurs when a person sends a message with angry or antagonistic content. Flaming is assumed to be more common today because of the ease and impersonality of e-mail communications: confrontations in person or via telephone require direct interaction, where social norms encourage civility, whereas typing a message to another person is an indirect interaction, so civility may be forgotten.[citation needed] Flaming is generally looked down upon by Internet communities as it is considered rude and non-productive.

E-mail bankruptcy

Also known as "e-mail fatigue", e-mail bankruptcy is when a user ignores a large number of e-mail messages after falling behind in reading and answering them. The reason for falling behind is often due to information overload and in a general sense there is so much information that it is not possible to read it at all. As a solution, people occasionally send a boilerplate message explaining that the e-mail inbox is being cleared out. Stanford University law professor Lawrence Lessig is credited with coining this term, but he may only have popularized it.

In business

E-mail was widely accepted by the business community as the first broad electronic communication medium and was the first 'e-revolution' in business communication. E-mail is very simple to understand and like postal mail, e-mail solves two basic problems of communication: logistics and synchronization (see below). LAN based email is also an emerging form of usage for business. It not only allows the business user to download mail when *offline*, it also provides the small business user to have multiple users e-mail ID's with just *one e-mail connection.*

Pros

- **The problem of logistics**

Much of the business world relies upon communications between people who are not physically in the same building, area or even country; setting up and attending an in-person meeting, telephone call, or conference call can be inconvenient, time-consuming and costly. E-mail provides a way to exchange information between two or more people with no set-up costs and that is generally far less expensive than physical meetings or phone calls.

- **The problem of synchronization**

With real time communication by meetings or phone calls, participants have to work on the same schedule, and each participant must spend the same amount of time in the meeting or call. E-mail allows asynchrony: each participant may control their schedule independently.

Cons

Most business workers today spend from one to two hours of their working day on e-mail: reading, ordering, sorting, 're-contextualizing' fragmented information, and writing e-mail. The use of e-mail is increasing due to increasing levels of globalization—labour division and outsourcing amongst other things. E-mail can lead to some well-known problems:

- **Loss of Context:** which means that the context is lost forever; there is no way to get the text back.

Information in context (as in a newspaper) is much easier and faster to understand than unedited and sometimes unrelated fragments of information. Communicating in context can only be achieved when both parties have a full understanding of the context and issue in question.

- **Information overload:** E-mail is a push technology—the sender controls who receives the information. Convenient availability of mailing lists and use of "copy all" can lead to people receiving unwanted or irrelevant information of no use to them.

- **Inconsistency:** E-mail can duplicate information. This can be a problem when a large team is working on documents and information while not in constant contact with the other members of their team.

Despite these disadvantages, e-mail has become the most widely used medium of communication within the business world.

Challenges

Information overload

A December 2007 New York Times blog post described E-mail as "a $650 Billion Drag on the Economy", and the New York Times reported in April 2008 that "E-MAIL has become the bane of some people's professional lives" due to information overload, yet "none of the current wave of high-profile Internet start-ups focused on e-mail really eliminates the problem of e-mail overload because none helps us prepare replies".

Technology investors reflect similar concerns.

Spamming and computer viruses

The usefulness of e-mail is being threatened by four phenomena: e-mail bombardment, spamming, phishing, and e-mail worms.

Spamming is unsolicited commercial (or bulk) e-mail. Because of the very low cost of sending e-mail, spammers can send hundreds of millions of e-mail messages each day over an inexpensive Internet connection. Hundreds of active spammers sending this volume of mail results in information overload many computer users who receive voluminous unsolicited e-mail each day.

E-mail worms use e-mail as a way of replicating themselves into vulnerable computers. Although the first e-mail worm affected UNIX computers, the problem is most common today on the more popular Microsoft Windows operating system.

The combination of spam and worm programs results in users receiving a constant drizzle of junk e-mail, which reduces the usefulness of e-mail as a practical tool.

A number of anti-spam techniques mitigate the impact of spam. In the United States, U.S. Congress has also passed a law, the Can Spam Act of 2003, attempting to regulate such e-mail. Australia also has very strict spam laws restricting the sending of spam from an Australian ISP, but its impact has been minimal since most spam comes from regimes that seem reluctant to regulate the sending of spam.

E-mail spoofing

E-mail spoofing occurs when the header information of an email is altered to make the message appear to come from a known or trusted source. It is often used as a ruse to collect personal information.

E-mail bombing

E-mail bombing is the intentional sending of large volumes of messages to a target address. The overloading of the target email address can render it unusable and can even cause the mail server to crash.

Privacy concerns

E-mail privacy, without some security precautions, can be compromised because:

- e-mail messages are generally not encrypted;
- e-mail messages have to go through intermediate computers before reaching their destination, meaning it is relatively easy for others to intercept and read messages;
- many Internet Service Providers (ISP) store copies of e-mail messages on their mail servers before they are delivered. The backups of these can remain for up to several months on their server, despite deletion from the mailbox;
- the Received: fields and other information in the e-mail can often identify the sender, preventing anonymous communication.

There are cryptography applications that can serve as a remedy to one or more of the above. For example, Virtual Private Networks or the Tor anonymity network can be used to encrypt traffic from the user machine to a safer network while GPG, PGP, SMEmail, or S/MIME can be used for end-to-end message encryption, and SMTP STARTTLS or SMTP over Transport Layer Security/Secure Sockets Layer can be used to encrypt communications for a single mail hop between the SMTP client and the SMTP server.

Additionally, many mail user agents do not protect logins and passwords, making them easy to intercept by an attacker. Encrypted authentication schemes such as SASL prevent this.

Finally, attached files share many of the same hazards as those found in peer-to-peer filesharing. Attached files may contain trojans or viruses.

Tracking of sent mail

The original SMTP mail service provides limited mechanisms for tracking a transmitted message, and none for verifying that it has been delivered or read. It requires that each mail server must either deliver it onward or return a failure notice (bounce message), but both software bugs and system failures can cause messages to be lost. To remedy this, the IETF introduced Delivery Status Notifications (delivery receipts) and Message Disposition Notifications (return receipts); however, these are not universally deployed in production.

US Government

The US Government has been involved in e-mail in several different ways.

Starting in 1977, the US Postal Service (USPS) recognized that electronic mail and electronic transactions posed a significant threat to First Class mail volumes and revenue. Therefore, the USPS initiated an experimental e-mail service known as E-COM. Electronic messages were transmitted to a post office, printed out and delivered as hard copy. To take advantage of the service, an individual had to transmit at least 200 messages. The delivery time of the messages was the same as First Class mail and cost 26 cents. Both the Postal Regulatory Commission and the Federal Communications Commission opposed E-COM. The FCC concluded that E-COM constituted common carriage under its jurisdiction and the USPS would have to file a tariff. Three years after initiating the service, USPS canceled E-COM and attempted to sell it off.

The early ARPANET dealt with multiple e-mail clients that had various, and at times incompatible, formats. For example, in the system Multics, the "@" sign meant "kill line" and anything after the "@" sign was ignored. The Department of Defense DARPA desired to have uniformity and interoperability for e-mail and therefore funded efforts to drive towards unified interoperable standards. This led to David Crocker, John Vittal, Kenneth Pogran, and Austin Henderson publishing RFC 733, "Standard for the Format of ARPA Network Text Message" (November 21, 1977), which was apparently not effective. In 1979, a meeting was held at BBN to resolve incompatibility issues. Jon Postel recounted the meeting in RFC 808, "Summary of Computer Mail Services Meeting Held at BBN on 10 January 1979" (March 1, 1982), which includes an appendix listing the varying e-mail systems at the time. This, in turn, lead to the release of David Crocker's RFC 822, "Standard for the Format of ARPA Internet Text Messages" (August 13, 1982).

The National Science Foundation took over operations of the ARPANET and Internet from the Department of Defense, and initiated NSFNet, a new backbone for the network. A part of the NSFNet AUP forbade commercial traffic. In 1988, Vint Cerf arranged for an interconnection of MCI Mail with NSFNET on an experimental basis. The following year Compuserve e-mail interconnected with NSFNET. Within a few years the commercial traffic restriction was removed from NSFNETs AUP, and NSFNET was privatized.

In the late 1990s, the Federal Trade Commission grew concerned with fraud transpiring in e-mail, and initiated a series of procedures on spam, fraud, and phishing. In 2004, FTC jurisdiction over spam was codified into law in the form of the CAN SPAM Act.[47] Several other US Federal Agencies have also exercised jurisdiction including the Department of Justice and the Secret Service.

Introduction FTP-

File Transfer Protocol (FTP) is a standard network protocol used to exchange and manipulate files over an Internet Protocol computer network, such as the Internet. FTP is built on a client-server architecture and utilizes separate control and data connections between the client and server applications. Client applications were originally interactive command-line tools with a standardized command syntax, but graphical user interfaces have been developed for all desktop operating systems in use today. FTP is also often used as an application component to automatically transfer files for program internal functions. FTP can be used with user-based password authentication or with anonymous user access. The Trivial File Transfer Protocol (TFTP) is a similar, but simplified, not interoperable, and unauthenticated version of FTP.

Purpose

The objectives of FTP, as outlined by its RFC, are:

- To promote sharing of files (computer programs and/or data).

- To encourage indirect or implicit use of remote computers.
- To shield a user from variations in file storage systems among different hosts.
- To transfer data reliably and efficiently.

Connection methods

FTP runs over the Transmission Control Protocol (TCP). Usually FTP servers listen on the well-known port number 21 (IANA-reserved) for incoming connections from clients. A connection to this port from the FTP client forms the control stream on which commands are passed to the FTP server and responses are collected. FTP uses out-of-band control; it opens dedicated data connections on other port numbers. The parameters for the data streams depend on the specifically requested transport mode. Data connections usually use port number 20.

In **active mode**, the FTP client opens a dynamic port, sends the FTP server the dynamic port number on which it is listening over the control stream and waits for a connection from the FTP server. When the FTP server initiates the data connection to the FTP client it binds the source port to port 20 on the FTP server.

In order to use active mode, the client sends a PORT command, with the IP and port as argument. The format for the IP and port is "h1,h2,h3,h4,p1,p2". Each field is a decimal representation of 8 bits of the host IP, followed by the chosen data port. For example, a client with an IP of 192.168.0.1, listening on port 49154 for the data connection will send the command "PORT 192,168,0,1,192,2". The port fields should be interpreted as p1 × 256 + p2 = port, or, in this example, 192 × 256 + 2 = 49154.

In **passive mode**, the FTP server opens a dynamic port, sends the FTP client the server's IP address to connect to and the port on which it is listening (a 16-bit value broken into a high and low byte, as explained above) over the control stream and waits for a connection from the FTP client. In this case, the FTP client binds the source port of the connection to a dynamic port.

To use passive mode, the client sends the *PASV* command to which the server would reply with something similar to "227 Entering Passive Mode (127,0,0,1,192,52)". The syntax of the IP address and port are the same as for the argument to the PORT command.

In **extended passive mode**, the FTP server operates exactly the same as passive mode, however it only transmits the port number (not broken into high and low bytes) and the client is to assume that it connects to the same IP address that was originally connected to. Extended passive mode was added by RFC 2428 in September 1998.

While data is being transferred via the data stream, the control stream sits idle. This can cause problems with large data transfers through firewalls which time out sessions after lengthy periods of idleness. While the file may well be successfully transferred, the control session can be disconnected by the firewall, causing an error to be generated.

The FTP protocol supports resuming of interrupted downloads using the REST command. The client passes the number of bytes it has already received as argument to the REST command and restarts the transfer. In some commandline clients for example, there is an often-ignored but valuable command, "reget" (meaning "get again"), that will cause an interrupted "get" command to be continued, hopefully to completion, after a communications interruption.

Resuming uploads is not as easy. Although the FTP protocol supports the APPE command to append data to a file on the server, the client does not know the exact position at which a transfer got interrupted. It has to obtain the size of the file some other way, for example over a directory listing or using the SIZE command.

In ASCII mode (see below), resuming transfers can be troublesome if client and server use different *end of line* characters.

Security problems

The original FTP specification is an inherently unsecure method of transferring files because there is no method specified for transferring data in an encrypted fashion. This means that under most network configurations, user names, passwords, FTP commands and transferred files can be captured by anyone on the same network using a packet sniffer. This is a problem common to many Internet protocol specifications written prior to the creation of SSL, such as HTTP, SMTP and Telnet. The common solution to this problem is to use either SFTP (SSH File Transfer Protocol), or FTPS (FTP over SSL), which adds SSL or TLS encryption to FTP as specified in RFC 4217.

FTP return codes

FTP server return codes indicate their status by the digits within them. A brief explanation of various digit's meanings are given below:

- 1xx: Positive Preliminary reply. The action requested is being initiated but there will be another reply before it begins.
- 2xx: Positive Completion reply. The action requested has been completed. The client may now issue a new command.
- 3xx: Positive Intermediate reply. The command was successful, but a further command is required before the server can act upon the request.
- 4xx: Transient Negative Completion reply. The command was not successful, but the client is free to try the command again as the failure is only temporary.
- 5xx: Permanent Negative Completion reply. The command was not successful and the client should not attempt to repeat it again.
- x0x: The failure was due to a syntax error.
- x1x: This response is a reply to a request for information.
- x2x: This response is a reply relating to connection information.
- x3x: This response is a reply relating to accounting and authorization.
- x4x: Unspecified as yet.

- x5x: These responses indicate the status of the Server file system vis-a-vis the requested transfer or other file system action.

Anonymous FTP

A host that provides an FTP service may additionally provide anonymous FTP access. Users typically login to the service with an 'anonymous' account when prompted for user name. Although users are commonly asked to send their email address in lieu of a password, little to no verification is actually performed on the supplied data.

As modern FTP clients typically hide the anonymous login process from the user, the ftp client will supply dummy data as the password (since the user's email address may not be known to the application). For example, the following ftp user agents specify the listed passwords for anonymous logins:

- **Mozilla Firefox** (3.0.7) — mozilla@example.com
- **KDE Konqueror** (3.5) — anonymous@
- **wget** (1.10.2) — -wget@
- **lftp** (3.4.4) — lftp@

The Gopher protocol has been suggested as an alternative to anonymous FTP, as well as File Service Protocol.[citation needed]

Transfer parameters

According to the FTP standard RFC959, the transfer of data is determined by four main parameters:

- the data structure: stream-oriented, record-oriented or page-oriented
- the data type: the textual types of ASCII, EBCDIC, with subtypes for different carriage control disciplines; the binary types of byte-oriented, or arbitrary length word-oriented
- the vertical format control: for the textual types of ASCII and EBCDIC, whether vertical format control is specified using
- the transfer mode: stream-oriented transfer, uncompressed block-oriented transfer or compressed block-oriented transfer

By the 1990s, the usage of FTP centred on stream-oriented file structure and stream-oriented transfer mode; most FTP servers and clients from the 1990s onwards do not support other file structures or transfer modes.

Data structure

Data structure is specified using the STRU command. The following file structures are defined in section 3.1.1 of RFC959:

- **F** or FILE structure (stream-oriented). Files are viewed as an arbitrary sequence of bytes, characters or words. This is the usual file structure on Unix systems and other systems such as CP/M, MSDOS and Microsoft Windows. [Section 3.1.1.1]
- **R** or RECORD structure (record-oriented). Files are viewed as divided into records, which may be fixed or variable length. This file organization is common on mainframe and midrange systems, such as MVS, VM/CMS, OS/400 and VMS.
- **P** or PAGE structure (page-oriented). Files are divided into pages, which may either contain data or metadata; each page may also have a header giving various attributes. This file structure was specifically designed for TENEX systems, and is generally not supported on other platforms. RFC1123 section 4.1.2.3 recommends that this structure not be implemented.
- Data type

Data type is specified using the TYPE command. The following data types are defined:

- **A** (ASCII). Textual data transferred over the network in the NVT ASCII character set.
- **E** (EBCDIC). Textual data transferred over the network in the EBCDIC character set.
- **I** or **IMAGE** (byte-oriented). Binary data transferred as a stream of 8-bit bytes.
- **L** or **LOCAL** (word-oriented). Binary data transferred as a stream of words. The number of bits in the word is specified as an argument, e.g. L32 for 32-bit words, L36 for 36-bit words. The words are packed into

A common problem historically has been FTP clients and servers which default to ASCII type, but do not provide any protection against transferring binary files. As a result, the binary files are corrupted, through e.g. translation of newline characters. In most contemporary clients, this is avoided by automatically defaulting to image type. Another approach would be to choose the FTP TYPE based on the type of the file as recorded in the filesystem (for those filesystems which do this) or heuristically.

L8 is effectively equivalent to I, and most FTP servers or clients do not accept other word sizes, save for 36-bit platforms. The data is to be transferred in packed binary format for transfer.

Note the data type indicates the type for transfer, not the type in which the data is stored on the source or destination systems. The client and server are free to convert the data to a form which is most convenient on their platform. For example, the textual data types of A and E may be subjected to translation of character set (e.g. ASCII vs EBCDIC), translation of newline convention (e.g. CRLF vs LF), or translation of textual data between stream-oriented and record-oriented formats (i.e. one record per a line, possibly padded with spaces to the maximum line length v.s. stream-oriented with newline characters to separate the lines). Similarly, a 36-bit platform may choose to store an L32 format file sent or received as 36-bit words each padded with four zero bits. The I data type is the least likely to be converted, but even it may be subject to conversion on non-byte oriented platforms.

Frequently FTP clients use the word "MODE" to refer to the data type, although that is a misnomer, since the word "MODE" is already taken to refer to the transfer mode.

Vertical format control

Only applicable to the the textual data types (A and E), and indicated as the second parameter to the TYPE command (section 3.1.1.5):

- **N** for non-print, meaning no vertical format control is specified. This is the default if none is specified.
- **T** to indicate that vertical format control is specified using the ASCII/EBCDIC TELNET format control characters, i.e. CR, LF, NL, VT, FF
- **A** to indicate that ASA vertical format control is to be applied

Transfer mode

The transfer mode is specified by the MODE command (section 3.40. The following modes are defined:

- **S** or STREAM MODE: data is represented as a stream of 8-bit bytes. An escape mechanism is defined for record-oriented files, to explicitly indicate record boundaries and explicit end of file. For stream-oriented files, no escape mechanism is defined and end of file is represented by closing the connection.
- **B** or BLOCK MODE: data is represented as a stream of blocks. Each block has a header to indicate its length, and also flags to mark end-of-record and end-of-file. The flags can also be used to indicate a suspect data block, e.g., a block of data read from a magnetic tape which failed its checksum, but is being transferred anyway even though it may contain errors. Also supports restart markers, which enable restarting the data transmission from that point.
- **C** or COMPRESSED MODE: similar to stream mode, but adds support for run-length encoding and also the flags defined in block mode.

As of the 1990s, most FTP clients and servers only support STREAM mode.

FTP commands

Commands which begin with the letter X are generally reserved for experimental extensions, although one should use SITE subcommands instead for this purpose.

RFC959 defines the following FTP commands, which were also present in RFC765:

- **USER:** supplies the username for login.
- **PASS:** supplies the password for login.
- **ACCT:** supplies accounting information. For example, a user may work on multiple projects; the account can be used to ensure that the charges for the data storage are billed to the correct project. (Not commonly implemented).

- **CWD:** changes the working directory to that specified.
- **REIN:** removes all authentication information and parameter settings; must be followed by relogin via USER.
- **QUIT:** terminates the connection.
- **PORT:** host/port specification for data transfer.
- **PASV:** enter passive mode.
- **TYPE:** specify data type and vertical format control (see above).
- **STRU:** specify data structure (see above).
- **MODE:** specify transmission mode (see above).
- **RETR:** initiates a data transfer from server to client, specifying name of file to retrieve
- **STOR:** initiates a data transfer from client to server, specifying name file is to be stored in on server.
- **APPE:** similar to STOR, except if file already exists, append received data to end of it rather than create.
- **ALLO:** allocates space for a file. Optionally, specifies the maximum size of each record.
- **REST:** specifies the restart marker from which the transfer is to resume. Originally intended for use with restart markers sent by the server in B or C mode, but later extended in RFC3659 to byte offsets specified in S mode.
- **RNFR:** to rename a file, specify the file to be renamed.
- **RNTO:** to rename a file, specifies the new name for the file, and performs the rename. Often also used to implement moves.
- **DELE:** deletes a file.
- **PWD:** prints the current working directory.
- **LIST:** opens a data connection with A or E data type, to transfer a listing of files in the current directory. The format of data is system-specific, but intended to be human readable.
- **NLST:** similar to LIST, but transfer unadorned names of files with CRLF or NL.
- **SITE:** provides subcommands to perform system specific services. The nature of these services is undefined.
- **STAT:** without arguments, current status of connection. With argument, equivalent to LIST, but the listing is transfered over the control connection encapsulated in messages.
- **HELP:** provides HELP, optionally with an argument to specify the specific command on which help is requested.

- **NOOP:** does nothing.

RFC959 adds the following new commands which were not present in RFC765:

- **CDUP:** changes the working directory to the parent. Present since the notation for parent directory varies from platform to platform (although most commonly .. on systems descended from Unix or MS DOS).
- **SMNT:** mount a different file system or volume. Intended for systems such as DOS or VMS where there is a distinction between volume and directory in pathnames; but commonly unimplemented even on such systems.
- **STOU:** store unique - initiates a data transfer from client to server; server shall chose a unique name for file to be received
- **RMD:** removes a directory
- **MKD:** creates a directory
- **PWD:** prints the current directory
- **SYST:** identifies the operating system of the server

RFC765 described a number of commands which were removed in RFC959. These have not been part of FTP implementations since the early 1980s, since their functionality was later replaced (in part) by SMTP:

- **MLFL:** used to send email over the data connection
- **MAIL:** used to send email over the control connection
- **MSND:** like MAIL, but sends data directly to user's terminal rather than their mailbox
- **MSOM:** behaves as either MAIL or MSND — send to terminal if allowed, otherwise to mailbox
- **MSAM:** similar to MSOM — except that MSOM only sends to mailbox if delivery to terminal not possible; but MSAM sends to mailbox irrespective of whether terminal delivery is successfully attempted
- **MRSQ:** enables transmission of a single email to multiple users at the same host
- **MRCP:** subsequent to MRSQ, identifies one such recipient; repeated for each recipient

RFC2228 adds a number of commands related to encryption and message authentication:

- **AUTH:** identifies the authentication/security mechanism to be used
- **ADAT:** specifies security data specific to the chosen AUTH mechanism
- **PBSZ:** used to negotiate maximum buffer size for encrypted data
- **PROT:** specifies protection level for data channel. Following levels are defined:
    - o C (Clear) - data channel is subject neither to encryption nor integrity protection

  - o S (Safe) - integrity protection applied to data channel
  - o E (Confidential) - encryption applied to data channel
  - o P (Private) - both encryption and integrity protection applied to data channel
- **CCC:** disables integrity protection for subsequent commands on control channel
- **MIC:** sends a command with integrity protection
- **CONF:** sends a command with confidentiality protection
- **ENC:** sends a command with both integrity and confidentiality protection

RFC1639 ("FOOBAR"; succeeded RFC1545) adds support for FTP over arbitrary transport protocols, such as IPX/SPX or OSI. For this, it defines two new commands:

- **LPRT:** similar to PORT, but supports arbitrary address and port formats.
- **LPSV:** similar extension to PASV

RFC2389 defines two new commands used as a generic extension mechanism for FTP:

- **FEAT:** retrieves a listing of optional features supported by FTP server
- **OPTS:** a generic mechanism for the client to specify options to arbitrary FTP commands

RFC2428 adds two new commands, similar in principle to RFC1639 but differing in details:

- **EPRT:** similar to PORT, but supports arbitrary address families rather than only IPv4; specifically intended for IPv6.
- **EPSV:** similar extension to PASV

LPRT sends addresses as an arbitrary octet string (albeit decimal encoded), EPRT sends them as formatted strings, the format of the string being dependent upon the address format. EPRT assumes the use of TCP-style 16-bit port numbers, whereas LPRT is more flexible and supports transport protocols with greater than 16-bit port numbers.

RFC2640 adds one new command:

- **LANG:** used to choose the language for FTP messages

RFC3659 defines several new commands:

- **MDTM:** retrieve file modification time
- **SIZE:** retrieve file size
- **MLSD:** retrieve listing of files in a directory. Unlike NLST, this returns not only file names but also attributes; but unlike LIST, it returns the attributes in an extensible standardised format rather than an arbitrary platform-specific one. Unlike LIST or NLST, the data is transferred over the control rather than data connection.
- **MLST:** same as MLSD, but retrieves listing for an individual file rather than a directory. For directories, retrieves their own attributes rather than a listing of their members.

FTP and web browsers

Most recent web browsers and file managers can connect to FTP servers, although they may lack the support for protocol extensions such as FTPS. This allows manipulation of remote files over FTP through an interface similar to that used for local files. This is done via an FTP URL, which takes the form ftp(s)://*<ftpserveraddress>* (e.g., ftp://ftp.gimp.org/). A password can optionally be given in the URL, e.g.:

ftp(s)://*<login>*:*<password>*@*<ftpserveraddress>*:*<port>*.

Most web-browsers require the use of passive mode FTP, which not all FTP servers are capable of handling. Some browsers allow only the downloading of files, but offer no way to upload files to the server.

FTP and NAT devices

The representation of the IP addresses and port numbers in the PORT command and PASV reply poses another challenge for Network address translation (NAT) devices in handling FTP. The NAT device must alter these values, so that they contain the IP address of the NAT-ed client, and a port chosen by the NAT device for the data connection. The new address and port will probably differ in length in their decimal representation from the original address and port. This means that altering the values on the control connection by the NAT device must be done carefully, changing the TCP Sequence and Acknowledgment fields for all subsequent packets. Such translation is not usually performed in most NAT devices, but special application layer gateways exist for this purpose.

FTP over SSH (not SFTP)

FTP over SSH (not SFTP) refers to the practice of tunneling a normal FTP session over an SSH connection.

Because FTP uses multiple TCP connections (unusual for a TCP/IP protocol that is still in use), it is particularly difficult to tunnel over SSH. With many SSH clients, attempting to set up a tunnel for the *control channel* (the initial client-to-server connection on port 21) will protect only that channel; when data is transferred, the FTP software at either end will set up new TCP connections (*data channels*) which will bypass the SSH connection, and thus have no confidentiality, integrity protection, etc.

Otherwise, it is necessary for the SSH client software to have specific knowledge of the FTP protocol, and monitor and rewrite FTP control channel messages and autonomously open new forwardings for FTP data channels. Version 3 of SSH Communications Security's software suite, and the GPL licensed FONC are two software packages that support this mode.

FTP over SSH is sometimes referred to as **secure FTP**; this should not be confused with other methods of securing FTP, such as with SSL/TLS (FTPS). Other methods of transferring files using SSH that are not related to FTP include SFTP and SCP; in each of these, the entire conversation (credentials and data) is always protected by the SSH protocol.

Introduction of Telnet-

Telnet (Teletype network) is a network protocol used on the Internet or local area networks to provide a bidirectional interactive communications facility. Typically, telnet provides access to a command-line interface on a remote host via a virtual terminal connection which consists of an 8-bit byte oriented data connection over the Transmission Control Protocol (TCP). User data is interspersed in-band with TELNET control information.

Telnet was developed in 1969 beginning with RFC 15, extended in RFC 854, and standardized as Internet Engineering Task Force (IETF) Internet Standard STD 8, one of the first Internet standards.

The term *telnet* may also refer to the software that implements the client part of the protocol. Telnet client applications are available for virtually all computer platforms. Most network equipment and operating system with a TCP/IP stack support a Telnet service for remote configuration (including systems based on Windows NT). Because of security issues with Telnet, its use has waned in favor of SSH for remote access.

Telnet is also used as a verb. *To telnet* means to establish a connection with the Telnet protocol, either with command line client or with a programmatic interface. For example, a common directive might be: "*To change your password, telnet to the server, login and run the passwd command.*" Most often, a user will be *telnetting* to a Unix-like server system or a network device such as a router and obtain a login prompt to a command line text interface or a character-based full-screen manager.

On many systems, a Telnet client application may also be used to establish interactive raw-TCP sessions. It is commonly believed that a Telnet session which does not use the IAC (character 255) is functionally identical.[citation needed] This is not the case, however, because there are other *network virtual terminal* (NVT) rules, such as the requirement for a bare carriage return character (CR, ASCII 13) to be followed by a NULL (ASCII 0) character, that distinguish the telnet protocol from raw-TCP sessions.

Protocol details

Telnet is a client-server protocol, based on a reliable connection-oriented transport. Typically this protocol is used to establish a connection to Transmission Control Protocol (TCP) port number 23, where a Telnet server application (telnetd) is listening. Telnet, however, predates TCP/IP and was originally run over Network Control Program (NCP) protocols.

Before March 5th, 1973, Telnet was an ad-hoc protocol with no official definition. Essentially, it used an 8-bit channel to exchange 7-bit ASCII data. Any byte with the high bit set was a special Telnet character. On March 5th, 1973, a Telnet protocol standard was defined at UCLA with the publication of two NIC documents: Telnet Protocol Specification, NIC #15372, and Telnet Option Specifications, NIC #15373.

The protocol has many extensions, some of which have been adopted as Internet standards, IETF documents STD 27 through STD 32. Some extensions have been widely implemented and others are proposed standards on the IETF standards track.

Security

When Telnet was initially developed in 1969, most users of networked computers were in the computer departments of academic institutions, or at large private and government research facilities. In this environment, security was not nearly as much of a concern as it became after the bandwidth explosion of the 1990s. The rise in the number of people with access to the Internet, and by extension, the number of people attempting to crack other people's servers made encrypted alternatives much more of a necessity.

Experts in computer security, such as SANS Institute, recommend that the use of Telnet for remote logins should be discontinued under all normal circumstances, for the following reasons:

- Telnet, by default, does not encrypt any data sent over the connection (including passwords), and so it is often practical to eavesdrop on the communications and use the password later for malicious purposes; anybody who has access to a router, switch, hub or gateway located on the network between the two hosts where Telnet is being used can intercept the packets passing by and obtain login and password information (and whatever else is typed) with any of several common utilities like tcpdump and Wireshark.
- Most implementations of Telnet have no authentication that would ensure communication is carried out between the two desired hosts and not intercepted in the middle.
- Commonly used Telnet daemons have several vulnerabilities discovered over the years.

These security-related shortcomings have seen the usage of the Telnet protocol drop rapidly, especially on the public Internet, in favor of the Secure Shell (SSH) protocol, first released in 1995. SSH provides much of the functionality of telnet, with the addition of strong encryption to prevent sensitive data such as passwords from being intercepted, and public key authentication, to ensure that the remote computer is actually who it claims to be.

As has happened with other early Internet protocols, extensions to the Telnet protocol provide Transport Layer Security (TLS) security and Simple Authentication and Security Layer (SASL) authentication that address the above issues. However, most Telnet implementations do not support these extensions; and there has been relatively little interest in implementing these as SSH is adequate for most purposes. The main advantage of TLS-Telnet would be the ability to use certificate-authority signed server certificates to authenticate a server host to a client that does not yet have the server key stored. In SSH, there is a weakness in that the user must trust the first session to a host when it has not yet acquired the server key.

Telnet 5250

IBM 5250 or 3270 workstation emulation is supported via custom telnet clients, TN5250/TN3270, and IBM servers. Clients and servers designed to pass IBM 5250 data streams over Telnet generally do support SSL encryption, as SSH does not include 5250 emulation. Under OS/400, port 992 is the default port for secured telnet.

Current status

As of the mid-2000s, while the Telnet protocol itself has been mostly superseded for remote login, Telnet clients are still used, often when diagnosing problems, to manually "talk" to other services without specialized client software. For example, it is sometimes used in debugging network services such as SMTP, IRC, HTTP, FTP or POP3 servers, to issue commands to a server and examine the responses.

This approach has limitations, however, because Telnet clients do not use a raw character mode (due to terminal control handshaking and the special rules regarding \377 and \15). Thus, other software such as *nc* (netcat) or *socat* on Unix (or PuTTY on Windows) are popular among system administrators, as they can be called with arguments not to send any terminal control handshaking data.

Telnet is popular in various application areas:

- enterprise networks to access host applications, e.g., on IBM Mainframes.
- administration of network elements, e.g., in commissioning, integration and maintenance of core network elements in mobile communication networks, and many industrial control systems.
- MUD games played over the Internet, as well as talkers, MUSHes, MUCKs, MOOes, and the resurgent BBS community.
- Internet game clubs, like the Internet Chess Club, the Free Internet Chess Server and the Internet Go server.
- embedded systems
- Oxford University students and faculty members; it is still used as an interface for library catalogue searches, and many prefer it over more modern interfaces.

Related RFCs

- RFC 854, TELNET protocol specification
- RFC 855, TELNET option specifications
- RFC 856, TELNET binary transmission
- RFC 857, TELNET echo option
- RFC 858, TELNET suppress Go Ahead option
- RFC 859, TELNET status option
- RFC 860, TELNET timing mark option
- RFC 861, TELNET extended options - list option
- RFC 885, Telnet end of record option
- RFC 1041, Telnet 3270 regime option

- RFC 1073, Telnet Window Size Option
- RFC 1079, Telnet terminal speed option
- RFC 1091, Telnet terminal-type option
- RFC 1096, Telnet X display location option
- RFC 1184, Telnet linemode option
- RFC 1205, 5250 Telnet interface
- RFC 1372, Telnet remote flow control option
- RFC 1572, Telnet Environment Option
- RFC 2217, Telnet Com Port Control Option
- RFC 2941, Telnet Authentication Option
- RFC 2942, Telnet Authentication: Kerberos Version 5
- RFC 2943, TELNET Authentication Using DSA
- RFC 2944, Telnet Authentication: SRP
- RFC 2946, Telnet Data Encryption Option
- RFC 4248, The telnet URI Scheme
- RFC 4777, IBM's iSeries Telnet Enhancements

Telnet clients

- AbsoluteTelnet is a telnet client for Windows. It also supports SSH and SFTP,
- Host Explorer part of Hummingbird Connectivity; it implements the telnet, TN 3270, 5250, Ansi, and other protocols.
- IVT VT 220
- NCSA Telnet
- PowerTerm by Ericom — has integrated FTP client
- Bitvise Tunnelier
- TeraTerm
- PuTTY is a free, open source SSH, Telnet, rlogin, and raw TCP client for Windows, Linux, and Unix.
- Passport from Zephyr Corp, available as both regular executables and a web-based SSH/Telnet application
- SecureCRT and CRT from Van Dyke Software
- ZOC from EmTec

Introduction IRC-

Internet Relay Chat (**IRC**) is a form of real-time Internet text messaging (chat) or synchronous conferencing. It is mainly designed for group communication in discussion forums, called *channels*, but also allows one-to-one communication via private message as well as chat and data transfers via Direct Client-to-Client.

As of May 2009, the top 100 IRC networks served more than half a million users at a time, with hundreds of thousands of channels (the vast majority of which stand mostly vacant), operating on a total of roughly 1,500 servers worldwide.

IRC was created by Jarkko Oikarinen in August 1988 to replace a program called MUT (MultiUser Talk) on a BBS called OuluBox in Finland. Oikarinen found inspiration in a chat system known as Bitnet Relay, which operated on the BITNET.

IRC was used to report on the Soviet coup attempt of 1991 throughout a media blackout. It was previously used in a similar fashion during the Persian Gulf War. Logs of these and other events are kept in the ibiblio archive.

IRC client software is available for virtually every computer operating system that supports TCP/IP networking.

TECHNICAL INFORMATION

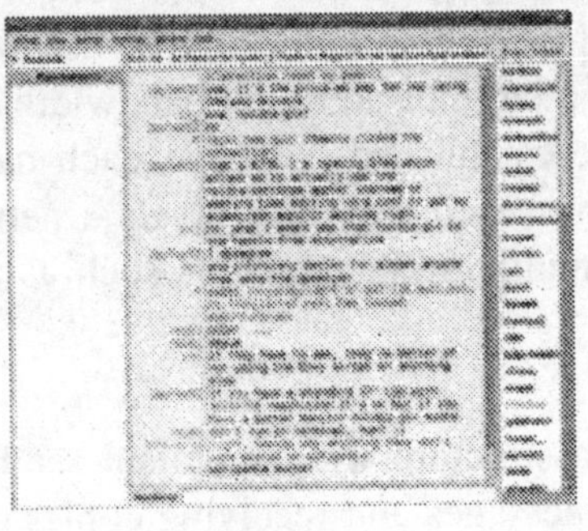

Xaric, a console based IRC client, in use on Mac OS X. Shown are two IRC channels and a private conversation with the software author.

IRC is an open protocol that uses TCP and optionally TLS. An IRC server can connect to other IRC servers to expand the IRC network. Users access IRC networks by connecting a client to a server. There are many client implementations such as mIRC or Xchat and server implementations, e.g. the original IRCd. Most IRC servers do not require users to register an account but a user will have to set a nickname before being connected.

IRC was originally a plain text protocol (although later extended), which on request was assigned port 194/TCP by IANA. However, the de facto has always been to run IRC on 6667/TCP and nearby port numbers (for example TCP ports 6112-6119) to avoid having to run the IRCd software with root privileges.

The protocol specified that characters were 8-bit but did not specify the character encoding the text was supposed to use. This can cause problems when users using different clients and/or different platforms want to converse.

All client-to-server IRC protocols in use today are descended from the protocol implemented in the irc2.4.0 version of the IRC2 server, and documented in RFC 1459. Since RFC 1459 was published, the new features in the irc2.10 implementation led to the publication of several revised protocol documents; RFC 2810, RFC 2811, RFC 2812 and RFC 2813, however these protocol changes have not been widely adopted among other implementations.[citation needed]

Although many specifications on the IRC protocol have been published, there is no official specification, as the protocol remains dynamic. Virtually no clients and very few servers rely strictly on the above RFCs as a reference.[citation neded]

Microsoft made an extension for IRC in 1998 via the proprietary IRCX. They later stopped distributing software supporting IRCX, instead developing the proprietary MSN.NET Messenger Service.

The standard structure of a network of IRC servers is a tree. Messages are routed along only necessary branches of the tree but network state is sent to every server and there is generally a high degree of implicit trust between servers. This architecture has a number of problems. A misbehaving or malicious server can cause major damage to the network and any changes in structure, whether intentional or a result of conditions on the underlying network, require a net-split and net-join. This results in a lot of network traffic and spurious quit/join messages to users and temporary loss of communication to users on the splitting servers. Adding a server to a large network means a large background bandwidth load on the network and a large memory load on the server. Once established however, each message to multiple recipients is delivered by multicast which means each message travels a network link exactly once. This is a strength in comparison to non-multicasting protocols such as SMTP or XMPP.

Commands and replies

IRC is based on a line-based structure with the client sending single-line messages to the server, receiving replies to those messages and receiving copies of some messages sent by other clients. In most clients users can enter commands by prefixing them with /. Depending on the command, these may either be handled entirely by the client, or (generally for commands the client does not recognize) passed directly to the server, possibly with some modification.[citation needed]

Due to the nature of the protocol automated systems cannot always correctly pair a sent command with its reply with full reliability and are subject to guessing.[citation needed]

Channels

The basic means of communication in an established IRC session is a *channel*. Channels in a server can be displayed using the IRC command *LIST* that lists all currently available channels.

Users can *join* to a channel using the *JOIN* command, in most clients available as */join #channelname*. Messages sent to the joined channels are then relayed to all other users.

Channels that are available across an entire IRC network are prepended with a '#', while those local to a server use '&'. Other non-standard and less common channel types include '+' channels — 'modeless' channels without operators — and '!' channels, a form of timestamped channel on normally non-timestamped networks.[32]

Modes

Users and channels may have *modes* which are represented by single case-sensitive letters and are set using the mode command. User modes and channel modes are separate and can use the same letter to mean different things (e.g. usermode "i" is invisible mode whilst channelmode "i" is invite only). Modes are usually set and unset using the mode command which takes a target (user or channel), a set of modes to set (+) or unset (-) and any parameters the modes need.

Some but not all channel modes take parameters and some channel modes apply to a user on a channel or add or remove a mask (e.g., a ban mask) from a list associated with the channel rather than applying to the channel as a whole. Modes that apply to users on a channel have an associated symbol which is used to represent the mode in names replies (sent to clients on first joining a channel and use of the names command) and in many clients also used to represent it in the client's displayed list of users in a channel or to display an own indicator for a user's modes.

In order to correctly parse incoming mode messages and track channel state the client must know which mode is of which type and for the modes that apply to a user on a channel which symbol goes with which letter. In early implementations of IRC this had to be hard-coded in the client but there is now a de-facto standard extension to the protocol which sends this information to the client at connect time.

There is a small design fault in IRC regarding modes that apply to users on channels, the names message used to establish initial channel state can only send one such mode per user on the channel, but multiple such modes can be set on a single user. For example, if a user holds both operator status (+o) and voice status (+v) on a channel, a new client will be unable to know the less precedented mode (voice). Workarounds for this are possible on both the client and server side but none are widely implemented.

Many IRCd programmers have added extra modes or modified the behavior of modes in the above list so it is strongly advisable to check the documentation of the IRC network or IRCd (though note that the network may have patched the IRCd) for more detailed information on what the modes do on a particular server or network.

Standard (RFC1459) modes					
User modes		**Channel modes**			
Letter	**Description**	**Letter**	**Symbol**	**Parameter**	**Description**
i	Invisible — cannot be seen without a common channel or knowing the exact name	**o**	@	Name of affected user	Channel operator — can change channel modes and kick users out of the channel among other things
s	Receives server notices	**p**	None	None	Private channel — listed in channel list as "prv" according to rfc1459
w	Receives wallops	**s**	None	None	Secret channel — not shown in channel list or user who is except to users already on the channel
o	User is an IRC operator (ircop)	**i**	None	None	Invite only — users can only join if invited by another user on that specific channel
		t	None	None	Topic only settable by channel operators
n			None	None	Users cannot send external messages from outside the channel
m			None	None	Channel is moderated (only those who hold operator or voice status on the channel can send messages to it)
l			None	Limit number	Limits number of users able to be on channel (when full, no new users can join)
b			None	Ban mask (nick!user @host with wildcards allowed)	Bans hostmasks from channel

	v	+.	Name of affected user	Gives a user voice status on channel (see +m above)
	k	None	New channel key	Sets a channel key such that only users knowing the key can enter

IRC operators

There are also users who maintain elevated rights on their local server, or the entire network; these are called IRC Operators, sometimes shortened to IRCops. On some IRC implementations, IRC operators are also given channel operator status in every channel, although many people believe[who?] that administration of channels, and administration of the network should be kept separate and that IRC operator status does not confer the right to interfere with a particular channel's operation[citation needed]. However in most networks, IRC operators usually do not interfere with channel administrations unless they violate the network's terms of service.

Challenges

Issues in the original design of IRC were the amount of shared state data being a limitation on its scalability, the absence of unique user identifications leading to the nickname collision problem, lack of protection from netsplits by means of cyclic routing, the trade-off in scalability for the sake of real-time user presence information, protocol weaknesses providing a platform for abuse, no transparent and optimizable message passing, no encryption. Some of these issues have been addressed in *Modern IRC.*

Attacks

Because IRC connections are usually unencrypted and typically span long time periods, they are an attractive target for malicious crackers. Because of this, careful security policy is necessary to ensure that an IRC network is not susceptible to an attack such as an IRC takeover war. IRC networks may also k-line or g-line users or networks that have a harming effect.

A small number of IRC servers support SSL connections for security purposes. This helps stop the use of packet sniffer programs to obtain the passwords of IRC users, but has little use beyond this scope due to the public nature of IRC channels. SSL connections require both client and server support (which may require the user to install SSL binaries and IRC client specific patches or modules on their computers).

IRC served as an early laboratory for many kinds of Internet attacks, such as using fake ICMP unreachable messages to break TCP-based IRC connections (nuking) to annoy users or facilitate takeovers.

Abuse prevention

One of the most contentious technical issues surrounding IRC implementations, which survives to this day, is the merit of "Nick/Channel Delay" vs. "Timestamp" protocols. Both methods exist to solve the problem of denial-of-service attacks, but take very different approaches.

The problem with the original IRC protocol as implemented was that when two servers split and rejoined, the two sides of the network would simply merge their channels. If a user could join on a "split" server, where a channel which existed on the other side of the network was empty, and gain operator status, they would become a channel operator of the "combined" channel after the netsplit ended; if a user took a nickname which existed on the other side of the network, the server would kill both users when rejoining (i.e., 'nick-collision').

This was often abused to "mass-kill" all users on a channel, thus creating "opless" channels where no operators were present to deal with abuse. Apart from causing problems within IRC, this encouraged people to conduct denial of service attacks against IRC servers in order to cause netsplits, which they would then abuse.

Nick/channel delay

The nick/channel delay (abbreviated ND/CD) solution to this problem was very simple. After a user signed off and the nickname became available or a channel ceased to exist because all its users left (as often happens during a netsplit), the server would not allow any user to use that nickname or join that channel, respectively, until a certain period of time (the *delay*) had passed. The idea behind this was that even if a netsplit occurred, it was useless to an abuser because they could not take the nickname or gain operator status on a channel, and thus no collision of a nickname or 'merging' of a channel could occur. To some extent, this inconvenienced legitimate users, who might be forced to briefly use a different name (appending an underscore was popular) after rejoining.

Timestamping

The alternative, the timestamp or *TS* protocol, took a different approach. Every nickname and channel on the network was assigned a timestamp – the date and time when it was created. When a netsplit occurred, two users on each side were free to use the same nickname or channel, but when the two sides were joined, only one could survive. In the case of nicknames, the newer user, according to their TS, was killed; when a channel collided, the members (users on the channel) were merged, but the channel operators on the "losing" side of the split lost their channel operator status.

TS is a much more complicated protocol than ND/CD, both in design and implementation, and despite having gone through several revisions, some implementations still have problems with "desyncs" (where two servers on the same network disagree about the current state of the network), and allowing too much leniency in what was allowed by the 'losing' side. Under the original TS protocols, for example, there was no protection against users setting bans or other modes in the losing channel which would then be merged when the split rejoined, even though the users who had set those modes lost their channel operator status. Some modern TS-based

IRC servers have also incorporated some form of ND and/or CD in addition to timestamping in an attempt to further curb abuse.

Most networks today use the timestamping approach. The timestamp versus ND/CD disagreements caused several servers to split away from EFnet and form the newer IRCnet. After the split, EFnet moved to a TS protocol, while IRCnet used ND/CD.

Networks

There are thousands of running IRC networks in the world. They run various implementations of IRC servers, and are administered by various groups of IRC operators, but the protocol exposed to IRC users is very similar, and all IRC networks can be accessed by the same client software.

One can join servers by clicking on an "irc://irc.network.example:port/channel" hyperlink.

The largest IRC networks have traditionally been grouped in *The Big Four* — a designation for networks that top the statistics. The Big Four networks change periodically, but due to the community nature of IRC there are a large number of other networks for users to choose from.

The Big Four[*citation needed*]:

- EFnet
- IRCnet
- QuakeNet
- Undernet

For network statistics, rankings, and a list of smaller networks, see netsplit.de, Search IRC and Gogloom.

Usage Share

As of March 2009, the top 100 IRC networks served more than half a million users at a time, with hundreds of thousands of channels (the vast majority of which stand mostly vacant), operating on a total of roughly 1,500 servers worldwide.

According to statistics by netsplit.de, the top 10 populated networks accounted for 66 per cent of usage in the top 100 populated networks. That is, more than 370,000 users at a time. These networks had an average of just less than 1,500 users per server. The top 20 populated networks, accounted for 77 per cent of usage (again, in the top 100 networks). That is, more than 430,000 users at a time. These networks had an average of a 1,000 users per server. According to this statistics, the top 100 networks served more than 560,000 users at a time, on 1,450 serves, with an average load of 390 users per server.

Statistics from gogloom shows similar results, with more than 570,000 users served at a time. According to this statistics, 78 per cent of users were concentrated on the top 10 networks. That is, more than 450,000 users at a time. Further on, the top 20 networks house 86 per cent of users, with almost half a million users at a time.

According to statistics by Search IRC, as of March 2009, it monitored more than 760,000 users on 650 different networks spread over 7,600 servers. Giving an overall server load of a 100 users per server. Here too 90 per cent of the users were concentrated in 250 (a third) of the monitored networks, with the vast majority of networks being small/local with less than 200 users per network.

CLIENTS

Client software

For more details on this topic, see Comparison of Internet Relay Chat clients.

Scheme of an IRC-Network with normal clients (green), bots (blue) and bouncers (orange)

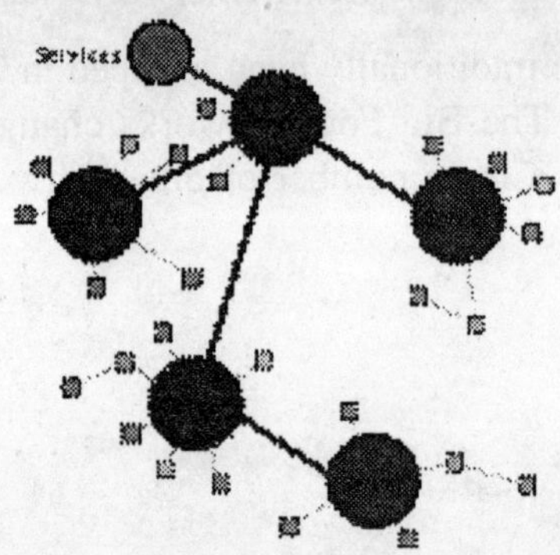

People most commonly will connect to an IRC network via an IRC client. The client takes the raw IRC traffic and turns it into an easy-to-use interface.

There are many IRC clients available, and are mostly separated by operating system. On Windows-based systems, one of the most popular IRC clients is mIRC.[55] However, with the recent introduction of new clients such as Miranda IM, Bersirc, KVIrc, Trillian, Pidgin, Visual IRC, ChatIRC and XChat, mIRC is beginning to see much more competition, especially with clients that are not commercial. Many people still use mIRC most likely due to the fact that it has been around for quite some time and has a wide variety of scripts available.[who?] One of said scripts is NoName Script (NNS) which is a common one to use due to its wide set of features.[56]

ircII is the canonical Unix and Linux IRC client, but its userbase has declined with the appearance of competing clients such as ircII-EPIC, BitchX, irssi, XChat, Konversation, etc. For Mac OS X, the most widely used clients are Snak, Ircle and Colloquy. OS X can also run most Unix-like command line and X11 IRC clients. Recently, X-Chat Aqua, a special build of XChat, has been gaining ground on OS X systems. Amiga IRC clients are AmIRC, WookieChat, BenderIRC. Amongst AmigaOS clones there is MomosIRC for MorphOS.

There are a number of web browsers with IRC clients. Opera has a built in IRC client. Mozilla Firefox does not have a built-in IRC client, though ChatZilla, a Firefox add-on, can be installed to provide access to IRC in the browser. Chatzilla is part of the SeaMonkey internet suite.

Built-in IRC is utilized by many computer games, such as *War§ow*, *Unreal Tournament*, *Uplink*, *World of Warcraft*, *Zdaemon* and *EVE Online*. The SoulSeek file sharing network is based on IRC.

For novice users, mIRC and other large-window clients can seem unnecessarily large and complex. New users may prefer instant messaging clients like Miranda IM, Pidgin or Trillian that support IRC and provide a familiar interface to the application. Alternatively web based clients such as Mibbit and webirc provide an easy way for people to access IRC.

Few clients exist for DOS, examples of which are LeetIRC, Trumpet and IRCjr.

A client called ERC, written entirely in Emacs Lisp is included in v.22.3 of Emacs. Therefore, any platform that can run Emacs can run ERC.

Bots

Automated clients are called bots. As bots evolved, they began to serve as permanent points of contact for information exchange and protection agents for the channels they served, because of their superior speed when compared to humans. Presently, although many of these functions are often delegated to network-provided services which allow for registration and management of both nicknames and channels, bots remain popular and continue to be adapted to new and unexpected tasks.

Bots have been written in a variety of languages, and a wide array of implementations exist. Most modern IRC services typically implement bot-like interfaces, through which users can communicate with and control the functionality. Bots have also been created for malevolent uses, such as flooding or taking over channels, ousting their rightful owners.

Bouncer

A program that runs as a daemon on a server and functions as a persistent proxy is known as a bouncer. A bouncer's purpose is to maintain a connection to an IRC server, acting as a relay between the server and client. Should the client lose network connectivity, the bouncer will archive all traffic for later delivery, allowing the user to resume his IRC session without disrupting their connection to the server.

Furthermore, as a way of obtaining a bouncer-like effect, the old UNIX user's way of doing this is to run a (typically text-based) client on a remote server, inside a piece of screen-detaching software (e.g. GNU Screen), and using a secure shell to connect to this server, letting it relay all information, and thus letting the client archive all traffic should the connectivity be lost.

Search engines

There are numerous search engines available to aid the user in finding what they are looking for on IRC. Generally the search engine consists of two parts, a "back-end" (or "spider/crawler") and a front-end "search engine".

The back-end (spider/crawler) is the work horse of the search engine. It is responsible for crawling IRC servers to index the information being sent across them. The information that is indexed usually consists solely of channel text (text that is publicly displayed in public channels). The storage method is usually some sort of relational database, like MySQL or Oracle.

The front-end "search engine" is the user interface to the database. It supplies users with a way to search the database of indexed information to retrieve the data they are looking for. These front-end search engines can also be coded in numerous programming languages. The more popular languages for such search engines and indexing spiders are Perl, PHP and C.

Most search engines have their own spider that is a single application responsible for crawling IRC and indexing data itself. However, others are "user based" indexers. The latter rely on users to install their "add-on" to their IRC client (like mIRC); the add-on is what sends the database the channel information of whatever channel[s] the user happens to be on. IRC search engines have completely automated the process of finding information on IRC and have thus contributed greatly to the popularity of IRC in recent years.

Modern IRC

IRC has changed much over its life on the Internet. New server software has added a multitude of new features.

- Services: Network-operated bots to facilitate registration of nicknames and channels, sending messages for offline users and network operator functions.
- Extra modes: While the original IRC system used a set of standard user and channel modes, new servers add many new modes for such features as removing color codes from text, or obscuring a user's hostmask ("cloaking") to protect from denial of service attacks.
- Proxy detection: Most modern servers support detection of users attempting to connect through an insecure (misconfigured or exploited) proxy server, which can then be denied a connection. An example is the Blitzed Open Proxy Monitor or BOPM. This proxy detection software used by several networks, although that real time list of proxies is defunct since early 2006.
- Additional commands: New commands can be such things as shorthand commands to issue commands to Services, to network operator only commands to manipulate a user's hostmask.
- Encryption: For the client-to-server leg of the connection SSL might be used (messages cease to be secure once they are relayed to other users on standard connections, but it makes eavesdropping on or wiretapping an individual's IRC sessions difficult). For client-to-client communication, SDCC (Secure DCC) can be used.
- Ident: Provides identification to the IRC server, but in modern Internet that RFC 1413 identification is almost useless.
- Connection protocol: IRC can be connected to via IPv4, the current standard version of the Internet Protocol, or by IPv6, the next-generation version of the Protocol.

Character encoding

IRC still lacks a single globally accepted standard convention for how to transmit characters outside the 7-bit ASCII repertoire. IRC servers normally transfer messages from a client to another client transparently, just as byte sequences, without any interpretation or recoding of characters. The IRC protocol (unlike e.g. MIME or HTTP) lacks mechanisms for announcing and negotiation character encoding options. This has put the responsibility for choosing the appropriate character codec on the client. In practice, IRC channels have largely used the same character encodings that were also used operating systems (in particular Unix derivatives) in the respective language communities:

- **7-bit era:** In the early days of IRC, especially among Scandinavian and Finnish language users, national variants of ISO 646 were the dominant character encodings. These encode non-ASCII characters like Ä Ö Å ä ö å at code positions 0x5B 0x5C 0x5D 0x7B 0x7C 0x7D (US-ASCII: [\ ] { | }). That is why these codes are always allowed in nicknames. According to RFC 1459, { | } in nicknames should be treated as lowercase equivalents of [\ ] respectively.[57] By the late 1990s, the use of 7-bit encodings had disappeared in favour of ISO 8859-1, and such equivalence mappings were dropped from some IRC daemons.

- **8-bit era:** Since the early 1990s, 8-bit encodings such as ISO 8859-1 have become commonly used for European languages. Russian users had a choice of KOI8-R, ISO 8859-5[*citation needed*] and CP1251, and since about 2000, modern Russian IRC networks convert between these different commonly used encodings of the Cyrillic alphabet.

- **Multi-byte era:** East Asian IRC channels with ideographic scripts in China, Japan, and Korea have used for a long time multi-byte encodings such as EUC or ISO-2022-JP. With the common migration from ISO 8859 to UTF-8 on Linux and Unix platforms since about 2002, UTF-8 has become an increasingly popular substitute for many of the previously used 8-bit encodings in European channels. Some IRC clients are now capable of reading messages both in ISO 8859-1 or UTF-8 in the same channel, heuristically autodetecting which encoding is used. The shift to UTF-8 began in particular on Finnish-speaking IRC (fi:IRC#Merkistö (Finnish)).

Today, the UTF-8 encoding of Unicode/ISO 10646 would be the most likely contender for a single future standard character encoding for all IRC communication, if such standard ever relaxed the 510 bytes message size restriction. UTF-8 is ASCII compatible and covers the superset of all other commonly used coded character set standards.

File sharing

Using scripts like Sysreset, UPP, Sooplex, Polaris, users can create file servers that allow them to share files with others.

Due to the large number of people who use IRC for file sharing[*citation needed*], some think of IRC as a form of P2P file sharing. Conversely, many users try to defeat this view by persistently discouraging it or refusing to help with it. Technically, IRC provides no file transfer mechanisms itself; file sharing is implemented by IRC *clients*, typically using the Direct Client-to-Client (DCC) protocol, in which file transfers are negotiated through the exchange of private messages between clients. The vast majority of IRC clients feature support for DCC file transfers, hence the view that file sharing is an integral feature of IRC.

Questions

(1) Expain how E-mails are important? How they are sent?

(2) Explain the various requires that are available on internet?

(3) What are E-Mails? and how they are sent?

(4) What is World Wide Web?

(5) Explain the various components of your web browser?

(6) What do mean by URL? How will you visit a specific site?

(7) What are attachment files? How are the attachments downloaded?

(8) What do you mean by Internet? Give a brief account of growth of Internet?

❑ ❑ ❑

Unit IV

CHAPTER 6

Electronic Commerce - Overview

E-commerce is a technology-mediated exchange between parties (individuals or organizations) as well as the electronically based intraor inter-organizational activities that facilitate such exchanges.

E-commerce consists primarily of distributing, buying, selling, marketing and servicing of products or services over electronic systems such as the Internet and other computer networks. The information technology industry might see it as an electronic business application aimed at commercial transactions. It can involve electronic funds transfer, supply chain management, e-marketing, online marketing, online transaction processing, electronic data interchange, automated inventory management systems and automated data-collection systems. It typically uses electronic communications technology such as the Internet, extranets, e-mail, Ebooks, databases and mobile phones.

E-commerce brings the universal access of the Internet to the core business processes of buying and selling goods and services. It helps generate demand for products and services and improves order management, payment and other support functions. The overall goal is to cut expenses by reducing transaction costs and streamlining all kinds of processes

According to Forrester Research (as cited in Kessler, 2003), electronic commerce generated sales worth US $12.2 billion in 2003.

Definition of E-Commerce

According to Dictionary.com, the definition of E-Commerce is "The conducting of business communication and transactions over networks and through computers. As most restrictively defined, electronic commerce is the buying and selling of goods and services and the transfer of funds, through digital communications. However EC also includes all inter-company and intra-company functions (such as marketing, finance, manufacturing, selling and negotiation) that enable commerce and use electronic mail, EDI, file transfer, fax, video conferencing, workflow or interaction with a remote computer."

Electronic commerce also includes buying and selling over the WorldWide Web and the Internet, electronic funds transfer, smart cards, digital cash (e.g. Mondex) and all other ways of doing business over digital networks.

E-commerce describes the process of buying, selling, transferring or exchanging products, services and/or information via computer networks, including the Internet. E-commerce can be defined from the following perspectives:

Communication – From a communication perspective, e-commerce is the delivery of goods, services, information or payments over computer networks by any other electronic means.

Commercial (trading) – From a commercial perspective, e-commerce provides the capability of buying and selling products, services and information on the Internet via other online services.

Business process – From a business process perspective, e-commerce is, doing business electronically by completing business processes over electronic networks.

Service – From a service perspective, e-commerce is a tool that addresses the desire of governments, firms, consumers and management to cut service costs while improving the quality of customer service and increasing the speed of service delivery.

Learning – From a learning perspective, e-commerce is an enabler of online training and education in schools, universities and other organizations.

Collaborative – From a collaborative perspective, e-commerce is the framework of inter and intra-organizational collaboration.

Community – From a community perspective, e-commerce provides a gathering place for community members to learn, transact and collaborate.

Electronic Commerce, commonly known as (electronic marketing) **e-commerce** or **ECommerce**, consists of the buying and selling of products or services over electronic systems such as the Internet and other computer networks. The amount of trade conducted electronically has grown extraordinarily with widespread Internet usage. The use of commerce is conducted in this way, spurring and drawing on innovations in electronic funds transfer, supply chain management, Internet marketing, online transaction processing, electronic data interchange (EDI), inventory management systems and automated data collection systems. Modern electronic commerce typically uses the World Wide Web at least at some point in the transaction's lifecycle, although it can encompass a wider range of technologies such as e-mail as well.

A large percentage of electronic commerce is conducted entirely electronically for virtual items such as access to premium content on a website. But most electronic commerce involves the transportation of physical items in some way. Online retailers are sometimes known as e-tailers and online retail is sometimes known as **e-tail**. Almost all big retailers have electronic commerce presence on the World Wide Web.

Electronic commerce that is conducted between businesses is referred to as business-to-business or B2B. B2B can be open to all interested parties (e.g. commodity exchange) or limited to specific, pre-qualified participants (private electronic market). Electronic commerce that is conducted between businesses and consumers, on the other hand, is referred to as business-to-consumer or B2C. This is the type of electronic commerce conducted by companies such as Amazon.com.

Electronic commerce is generally considered to be the sales aspect of e-business. It also consists of the exchange of data to facilitate the financing and payment aspects of the business transactions.

Often referred to as simply e-commerce, business that is conducted over the Internet using any of the applications that rely on the Internet, such as e-mail, instant messaging, shopping carts, Web services, UDDI, FTP, and EDI among others. Electronic commerce can be between two businesses transmitting funds, goods, services and/or data or between a business and a customer.

See Understanding "Web Services" in the "Did You Know...?" section of Webopedia.

Also See "How Affiliate Marketing Works" in the "Did You Know..." section of Webopedia.

Also see Refer-It.com, a directory of referral & affiliate programs for e-commerce, featuring information on over 6,500 affiliate programs.

2. History of E-Commerce

The origin of commerce by exchanging goods occurred before recorded history, now commerce is a basic activity of goods trading and buying in everyday life. Entering into the electronic era, the way individuals and organizations do business and undertake commercial transactions have been changed. This indicates the movement towards electronic commerce. This means there is no paper work and physical interaction is limited, if at all. The emergence of electronic commerce started in the early 1970s with the earliest example electronic funds transfer (EFT), which allows organizations to transfer funds between one another electronically. Then another technology electronic interchange (EDI) was introduced. It helps to extend interbusiness transactions from financial institutions to other types of business and also provides transactions and information exchanges from suppliers to the end customers. However, the early system development was limited to special networks such as large corporations and financial institutions, which are costly and complex to administer for small business. So EDI was not widely accepted as expected.

With the progress of Internet technology and a highly developed global Internet community, a strong foundation of prosperous electronic commerce continues to be built. During the 1990s, the Internet was opened for commercial use; it was also the period that users started to participate in World Wide Web (WWW), and the phenomenon of rapid personal computer (PCs) usage growth. Due to the rapid expansion of the WWW network; e-commerce software; and the peer business competitions, large number of *dot-coms* and Internet *start-ups* appeared. Integrated with the commercialization of the Internet, Web invention and PC networks these three important factors made electronic commerce possible and successful.

Early development

The meaning of electronic commerce has changed over the last 30 years. Originally, electronic commerce meant the facilitation of commercial transactions electronically, using technology such as Electronic Data Interchange (EDI) and Electronic Funds Transfer (EFT). These were both introduced in the late 1970s, allowing businesses to send commercial documents like purchase orders or invoices electronically. The growth and acceptance of credit cards, automated teller machines (ATM) and telephone banking in the 1980s were also forms of electronic commerce. Another form of e-commerce was the airline reservation system typified by Sabre in the USA and Travicom in the UK. Online shopping was invented in the UK in 1979 by Michael Aldrich and during the 1980s it was used extensively particularly by auto manufacturers such as Ford, Peugeot-Talbot, General Motors and Nissan. From the 1990s onwards, electronic commerce would additionally include enterprise resource planning systems (ERP), data mining and data warehousing.

The earliest example of many-to-many electronic commerce in physical goods was the Boston Computer Exchange, a market place for used computers launched in 1982. The first online information market place, including online consulting, was likely the American Information Exchange, another pre-Internet online system introduced in 1991.

Until 1991, commercial enterprise on the Internet was strictly prohibited.[1] Although the Internet became popular worldwide around 1994, it took about five years to introduce security protocols and DSL allowing continual connection to the Internet. And by the end of 2000, a lot of European and American business companies offered their services through the World Wide Web. Since then people began to associate a word "ecommerce" with the ability of purchasing various goods through the Internet using secure protocols and electronic payment services.

Timeline

- **1990:** Tim Berners-Lee writes the first web browser, WorldWideWeb, using a NeXT computer.
- **1992:** J.H. Snider and Terra Ziporyn publish Future Shop: How New Technologies Will Change the Way We Shop and What We Buy. St. Martin's Press. ISBN 0312063598.
- **1994:** Netscape releases the Navigator browser in October under the code name Mozilla. Pizza Hut offers pizza ordering on its Web page. The first online bank opens. Attempts to offer flower delivery and magazine subscriptions online. Adult materials also becomes commercially available, as do cars and bikes. Netscape 1.0 is introduced in late 1994 SSL encryption that made transactions secure.
- **1995:** Jeff Bezos launches Amazon.com and the first commercial-free 24 hour, internet-only radio stations, Radio HK and NetRadio start broadcasting. Dell and Cisco begin to aggressively use Internet for commercial transactions. eBay is founded by computer programmer Pierre Omidyar as AuctionWeb.
- **1998:** Electronic postal stamps can be purchased and downloaded for printing from the Web.

- **1999:** Business.com sold for US $7.5 million to eCompanies, which was purchased in 1997 for US $149,000. The peer-to-peer filesharing software Napster launches. ATG Stores launches to sell decorative items for the home online.
- **2000:** The dot-com bust.
- **2002:** eBay acquires PayPal for $1.5 billion. Niche retail companies CSN Stores and NetShops are founded with the concept of selling products through several targeted domains, rather than a central portal.
- **2003:** Amazon.com posts first yearly profit.
- **2007:** Business.com acquired by R.H. Donnelley for $345 million.
- **2008:** US eCommerce and Online Retail sales projected to reach $204 billion, an increase of 17 percent over 2007.

3. Business applications

Some common applications related to electronic commerce are the following:

- Email
- Enterprise content management
- Instant messaging
- Newsgroups
- Online shopping and order tracking
- Online banking
- Online office suites
- Domestic and international payment systems
- Shopping cart software
- Teleconferencing
- Electronic tickets

4. Government regulations

In the United States, some electronic commerce activities are regulated by the Federal Trade Commission (FTC). These activities include the use of commercial e-mails, online advertising and consumer privacy. The CAN-SPAM Act of 2003 establishes national standards for direct marketing over e-mail. The Federal Trade Commission Act regulates all forms of advertising, including online advertising and states that advertising must be truthful and non-deceptive. Using its authority under Section 5 of the FTC Act, which prohibits unfair or deceptive practices, the FTC has brought a number of cases to enforce the promises in corporate privacy statements, including promises about the security of consumer's personal information. As a result, any corporate privacy policy related to e-commerce activity may be subjected to enforcement by the FTC.

The Ryan Haight Online Pharmacy Consumer Protection Act of 2008, which came into law in 2008, amends the Controlled Substances Act to address online pharmacies.

5. Forms

Contemporary electronic commerce involves everything from ordering "digital" content for immediate online consumption, to ordering conventional goods and services, to "meta" services to facilitate other types of electronic commerce.

On the consumer level, electronic commerce is mostly conducted on the World Wide Web. An individual can go online to purchase anything from books or groceries to expensive items like real estate. Another example would be online banking i.e. online bill payments, buying stocks, transferring funds from one account to another and initiating wire payment to another country. All of these activities can be done with a few strokes of the keyboard.

On the institutional level, big corporations and financial institutions use the internet to exchange financial data to facilitate domestic and international business. Data integrity and security are very hot and pressing issues for electronic commerce today.

6. Overview of E-commerce technology

Electronic commerce

Any web site that offers products and/or services for sale is a commercial web site. There are thousands of commercial web sites on the Internet. Some of them have been successful and some weren't so lucky. What elements make up a good commercial web site? Of course, web pages should look attractive to a customer. However, even the most attractive web pages will not make a person come back to a web site where it takes too long to find the right product or where order forms don't work. In this lecture we will discuss what functionality is needed for a successful commercial web site and what technology implements various web site elements.

Examples of commercial web sites

Let's browse the following two web sites which are fairly typical web sites for online shopping:

- Online bakery. A web site for a small business.
- Trains.com Online sore of model trains and related products. An example of a larger commercial web site.

Components of a well-functioning commercial web site

A well-organized web site should be easy for a customer to use and easy for the owner to maintain. It takes a lot to build a well-organized web site. Below is a list of the most important elements that a good web site should have:

1. **A well-organized collection of products and/or services.** Smaller web sites can just list all their products on one or several web pages. Larger sites provide indices of

products and search engines so that customers can find what they need. There should be a way for customers to get all necessary information about products, compare several products, get an advice on related products that they might want to get etc.

To maintain a web site, the owner should be able to change product information easily. A web site where a price change of a single product requires changing 3 web pages is just bound to have inconsistencies. The owner should be able to add or remove products based on everyday's availability, change prices, add product cross-references, etc. without making the web site inconsistent even for a minute.

2. **A convenient way for a customer to select products.** Usually implemented as a shopping cart or a shopping basket. The customer should be able to select and delete products while browsing the web site.

3. **Convenient order forms.** The form should be flexible enough to allow to specify a different address for the product delivery, a gift message etc. It should have as few required fields as possible. A returning customer should be provided default information so that not to type it every time. For both the customer and the owner it is essential that the form catches simple typos (s.a. 4 digits in a zip code).

4. **Convenient ways of payment.** There should be options of paying by a credit card, by a cheque (not everyone has credit cards!) and by a credit card over the phone if the customer is not comfortable sending his/her credit card number. The options may include some electronic payment systems.

   For the owner, there should be a quick way to verify the credit card information or in some other way to check that the payment is valid.

5. **Secure communication system.** Not only to protect transmission of a credit card number, but also to guarantee privacy of the customer (including details of the purchase). A web site might have a user registration system with a password, in which case all transactions by the user should be private. It is also important to prevent unauthorized access to the web site (by a hacker or accidental).

6. **Some way of storing information about customers.** This is convenient for customers so that they don't need to re-enter their information every time they access the site. It also allows to "customize" the web site for someone's interests. This can be done via customer registration or by means of "cookies", which we will discuss later.

   The owner can benefit a lot from storing information about a customer. He/she can customize ads based on the customer's profile or send an e-mail advertising a new product (but keep in mind that many people don't like this!) However, the greatest benefit is the owner's ability to monitor customer's behaviour: which pages have the customer visited and which purchases (if any) he/she have made afterwards.

7. **A way of keeping information about orders.** This allows customers to track their orders, and for owners to get all kinds of financial and statistical information. It is also important to keep order information in case of later disputes.

8. **The last, but not the least, customer support and feedback.** There should be online documentation for all products ever sold on the web site, various FAQs, and ideally, a way for customers to post their opinion about the product. Easy access to this information may make a difference between a frequently visited web site and a lonely online looser.

This aspect of a web site cannot be completely mechanized; a human being has to answer e-mail, judge the relevance of customer's comments (otherwise the web site may be flooded with nonsense), organize comments by topics and so on. However, there is a lot that can be computer-aided in this process, for instance sorting incoming messages by their title and/or return address to forward them to an appropriate customer support person.

Note that we are only considering business-to-customer interactions here (so-called **B2C**), leaving out all the features related to business-to-business (**B2B**) interactions. While such interactions are basically similar to B2C, they can be optimized if a company has stable business partners which have more powerful computers than an average customer does. Even a customer oriented web site has a B2B part when dealing with vendors of products. We are not considering B2B connections in designing a web site.

Some technologies used to implement all this

1. **Convenient storage and retrieval of information about products and customers require a database.**

Some terminology: *A database is a collection of data organized in such a way that it can be easily accessed, managed, and updated. A query is a request to a database written in a form that's supported by the database. Every brand of databases has its own language of queries (a query language).*

A well-organized database allows you to store each piece of information only once. So if you need to change it, you change it in one place. Databases allow you to store information about orders, needed both for you and for customers. For instance customers can track their orders by requesting information from the database, which will automatically reply whether the order has been shipped. You can use customer information to fill in forms for returning customers with their recorded information. You can store statistics about customers (how many times they have visited the web sites, which pages, what did they buy and so on). Customer's feedback about products can be organized and displayed later when someone else is interested in the same product. It's hard to imagine an interesting web site that does not have a database behind it.

There are various kinds of databases, from a simple one, which is a collection of "flat" files storing data, to very sophisticated commercial products, s.a. ORACLE. The most common kind is a relational database.

A relational database is a database organized as a collection of tables.

In this course we will use a simple relational database called *McKoi database*.

2. A convenient interface to the database from the web site. A customer does not need to know anything even about the existence of the database, not to mention details of its organization. He/she should be able to get all necessary information by typing in keywords and filling in electronic forms.

Various programming languages (for instance Java, JavaScript) provide libraries to implement a remote connection to a database server.

A server is a computer that provides a remote access to some service, for instance a web page server "serves" web pages i.e., sends HTML files, graphics files, etc. in response to http requests, a database server provides responses to database queries and so on. One machine can provide several different services at the same time.

A client is a computer that makes a request for a service.

We will use a Java **JDBC (Java Database Connectivity)** package to facilitate a connection to a relational database. It does not depend on a particular kind of the database, as long as the database supports **SQL (Structured Query Language).**

SQL is a standard for a query language of a relational database.

An interface has to provide way for customers to fill in forms, press buttons etc. We will use javax.swing package to build an interactive graphical interface.

3. We need to be able to process user's forms, for instance order forms, and produce various web pages, depending on the request. Ways of processing electronic forms include various server-side scripts, s.a. CGI, PERL, asp (Active Server Pages– an extension of JavaScript) and others. We will use **Java Servlets** for this purpose.

4. A web site responds to requests for web pages. It doesn't "know" where the requests have come from, so it can't tell if two requests for web pages have been made by the same user. To keep track of a user during a session (and sometimes between sessions), a web server uses **cookies.**

A cookie is a small text file placed by a web server on the client machine. The file gets sent back every time the client requests a web page from the server. A cookie has an expiration time, which may be just for the session or longer.

Java Servlet package also implements cookies.

5. Encryption and security. A common way to secure communications are implemented, is via SSL (Secure Sockets Layer), which allows various forms of encryption, depending on the maximum level of encryption provided by the server and the client and on geographic location of the machines (a different level of encryption is allowed in the US for connections to domestic and foreign computers). We will study and compare several encryption algorithms. On the practical side, we will use Java packages which implement encryption and secure communications.

6. Electronic payment systems are based on customer's accounts with one of trusted vendors. A customer obtains certificates "signed" by the vendor which are analogous to cheques ("personal money") and cash ("anonymous money"). The implementation should be such that mere copying of any piece of information transmitted in the transaction does not allow the thief to use the "money". We will study protocols for verifying validity of "cheques" and "cash" in electronic transactions. We will also study ways of implementing "coins" on the Internet, i.e. certificates for small amounts of money (this allows some shortcuts in implementation, since the process of breaking even a simpler protocol may not be worth the money stolen).

7. Electronic Commerce (Internet Marketing)

Uses of the Internet In Marketing

Online marketing can serve several purposes:

- **Actual sales of products:** e.g. Amazon.com.
- **Promotion/Advertising:** Customers can be quite effectively targeted in many situations because of the context that they, themselves, have sought out. For example, when a consumer searches for a specific term in a search engine, a "banner" or link to a firm selling products in that area can be displayed. Print and television advertisements can also feature the firm's web address, thus inexpensively drawing in those who would like additional information.
- **Customer service:** The site may contain information for those who no longer have their manuals handy and, for electronic products, provide updated drivers and software patches.
- **Market research:** Data can be collected relatively inexpensively on the Net. However, the response rates are likely to be very unrepresentative and recent research shows that it is very difficult to get consumers to read instructions. This is one of the reasons why the quality of data collected online is often suspected.

Economics of electronic commerce: Selling Online Is Usually More Expensive

Some people have suggested that the Internet may be a less expensive way to distribute products than traditional "brick-and-mortar" stores. However, in most cases, selling online will probably be *more* costly than selling in traditional stores due to the high costs of processing orders and direct shipping to the customer. Some products may, however, be economically marketed online. Some factors that are relevant in assessing the potential for e-commerce to be an effective way to sell specific products are:

- "*Value-to-bulk" ratio*. Products that have a lot of value squeezed into a small volume (e.g., high end jewellery and certain electronic products) are often more cost-effective to ship to end-customers than are bulkier products with less value (e.g., low end furniture).
- *Absolute margins*. Some products may have a rather high *percentage* margin — e.g., a scarf bought at wholesale for $10 and marked up 100% to be sold at $20. However, the *absolute* margin is only $20-$10=$10. In contrast, a laptop computer may be bought at $1,000 and be marked up by only 15%, or $150, for a total price of $1,150. Here however, the absolute margin will be larger—$150. This allows the merchant to spend

money on processing, packaging, and shipping the order. Ten dollars, in contrast, can only cover a small amount of employee time and very limited packaging and shipping. Some online merchants do charge for shipping, but doing so will ultimately make the online merchant less competitive.

- *Extent of customization needed.* Some products need to be customized — e.g., checks have to be personalized and airline tickets have to be issued for a specific departure site, destination time, and travel time. Here, online processing may be useful because the customer can do much of the work.

- *Willingness of customers to pay for convenience.* Some consumers may be willing to pay for the convenience of having products delivered to their door. For example, delivering high bulk, generally low value groceries is generally not efficient. However, for some customers, it may be worthwhile to pay to avoid an inconvenient trip to the grocery store.

- *Geographic dispersal of customers.* Electronic commerce, when value-to-bulk ratios and absolute margins are not favorable, is often not viable when customers are located conveniently close to a retail outlet. However, for some products — e.g., bee keeping equipment — customers are widely geographically dispersed and thus, a centralized distribution center may be more economically viable. Speciality books — e.g., for collectors of vintage automobiles — may not be worthwhile for bookstores to stock, and these may thus be economically sold online.

- *Vulnerability of inventory to loss of value.* Some products — especially high tech products — have a very high effective carrying costs. It has been estimated that because of the rapid technological progress made in the computer field, computer parts may lose as much as 1.5% of their value per week. If shipping directly to the customer can reduce the channel time by five weeks, this potentially "rescues" as much as 7.5% of the product value. In such a situation, then, trying to reach the customer directly may make sense, even if the direct costs of distribution are higher, because of the inventory value issue.

There are a number of economic realities of online competition:

- As discussed, costs of handling online orders is often higher than that of distributing through traditional stores.

- Even if online selling is more cost effective in some situations, a firm selling online will in the long run, be competing with other online merchants—not just against traditional "brick-and-mortar" stores. By the forces of supply and demand, online prices will then be driven down so that the profit from selling online will be no greater than that from traditional retailing. Any reduced costs would then be expected to go to customers.

- Competition will be greater for products that have large markets than for those where markets are smaller and more specialized. Amazon.com, for example, has found it necessary to discount best selling books deeply. Higher prices — closer to the list price

— can be charged for speciality books, but for a large part of the market, competition will be intense.

- A new online merchant will face competition from established traditional merchants. These will often have the cash reserves to stay in business for a long time even with temporary competition. The online merchant, if it has no cash reserves other than stockholders investment, may run out of cash before it can become profitable.

Issues in Web Site Design

Web site design: The web designer must take various issues into consideration:

- **Speed vs. aesthetics:** As we saw, some of the fancier sites have serious problems functioning practically. Consumers may be impressed by a fancy site, or may lack confidence in a firm that offers a simple one. Yet, fancier sites with extensive graphics take time to download — particularly for users dialing in with a modem as opposed to being "hard" wired — and may result in site crashes.

- **Keeping users on the site:** A large number of "baskets" are abandoned online as consumers fail to complete the "check-out" process for the products they have selected. One problem here is that many consumers are drawn away from a site and then are unlikely to come back. A large number of links may be desirable to consumers, but they tend to draw people away. Taking banner advertisers on your site from other sites may be profitable, but it may result in customers lost.

- **Information collection:** An increasing number of consumers resist collection of information about them, and a number of consumers have set up their browsers to disallow "cookies," files that contain information about their computers and shopping habits.

Cyber-consumer behavior. In principle, it is fairly easy to search and compare online, and it was feared that this might wipe out all margins online. More recent research suggests that consumers in fact do not tend to search very intently and that large price differences between sites persist. We saw above the problem of keeping consumers from prematurely departing from one's site.

Site content. The content of a site should generally be based on the purposes of operating a site. For most sites, however, having a clear purpose to be evident is essential. The site should generally provide some evidence for this position. For example, if the site claims a large selection, the vast choices offered should be evident. Sites that claim convenience should make this evident. A main purpose of the Internet is to make information readily available, and the site should be designed so that finding the needed information among all the content of the site is as easy as possible. Since it is easy for consumers to move to other sites, the site should be made interesting. To provide the information and options desired by customers, two-way interaction capabilities are essential.

Web Site Traffic Generation

The web is now so large that getting traffic to any one site can be difficult. One method is search engine optimization, a topic that will be covered below. Other methods include "viral" campaigns wherein current users are used to spread the word about a site, firm, or service. For example, Hotmail attaches a message to every e-mail sent from its service alerting the recipient that a free e-mail account can be had there. Google offers a free e-mail account with a full gigabyte of storage. This is available only by invitation from others who have such e-mail accounts. Amazon.com at one point invited people, when they had completed a purchase, to automatically e-mail friends whose e-mail addresses they provided with a message about what they had just bought. If the friend bought any of the same items, both the original customer and the friend would get a discount!

Another method of gaining traffic is through online advertising. Sites like Yahoo! are mainly sponsored by advertisers, as are many sites for newspapers and magazines. Individuals who see an ad on these sites can usually click to go to the sponsor's web site. Occasionally, a firm may advertise their sites in traditional media. Geico, Dell Computer, and Progressive Insurance do this. Overstock.com has also advertised a lot on traditional TV programs. Conventional advertising may also contain a web site address as part of a larger advertising message.

Viral marketing is more suitable for some products than for others. To get others involved in spreading the word, the product usually must be interesting and unique. It must also be simple enough so that it can be explained briefly. It is most useful when switching or trial costs are low. It is more difficult, for example, getting people to sign up for a satellite system or cellular phone service where equipment has to be bought up front and/or a long term contract is required makes viral marketing more difficult. Viral marketing does raise some problems about control of the campaign. For example, if a service is aimed at higher income countries and residents there spread the word to consumers in lower income countries, people attracted may be unprofitable. For Google's one gigabyte e-mail account, for example, there are large costs that may be covered by advertising revenues from ads aimed at people who can afford to buy products and services. Advertisers, however, may not be willing to pay for targets who cannot afford their products. It is also difficult to control "word of mouth" (or "word of keyboard"). Measuring the effectiveness of a campaign may be difficult. When a viral campaign relies on e-mail, messages received may be considered spam by some recipients, leading to potential brand damage and loss of goodwill.

Online promotions. One way to generate traffic is promotions. Many sites often offer new customers, discounts or free gifts. This can be expensive, but sometimes, the gifts can be ones that have a low marginal cost. For example, once the firms pays for the development of a game, the cost of letting new users download it is modest. The U.S. army uses this approach in making a game available. To be allowed to use some of the "cooler" features, the user has to go through various stages of "basic training."

Search Engine Optimization

Many Internet users find desired information and sites through search engines such as Google. Research shows that a large proportion of the traffic goes to the first three sites listed, and few people go to sites that appear beyond the first "page" or screen. On Google, the default screen size is ten sites, so being in the top ten is essential.

Because of the importance of search engines, getting a good ranking or coming up early on the list for important keywords is vitally important. Many consultants offer, for large fees, to help improve a site's ranking.

There are several types of sites that are similar to search engines. Directories involve sites that index information based on human analysis. Yahoo! started out that way, but now most of the information is accessed through search engine features. The Open Directory Project at http:\\www.dmoz.org indexes sites by volunteer human analysts. Some sites contain link collections as part of their sites — e.g., business magazines may have links to business information sites.

Several issues in search engines and directories are important. Some search engines, such as Google, base rankings strictly on merit (although sites are allowed to get preferred paid listings on the right side of the screen). Other search engines allow sites to "bid" to get listed first. Some sites may end up paying as much as a dollar for each surfer who clicks through. If a potential customer is valuable enough, it may be worth paying for enhanced listings. Often, however, it is better to be listed as number two or three since only more serious searchers are likely to go beyond the first site. The first listed site may attract a number of people who click through without much serious inspection of the site.

Some search engines are more specific than others. The goal of Google, Yahoo! and MSN is to contain as many sites as possible. Others may specialize in sites of a specific type to reduce the amount of irrelevant information that may come up.

Search engines often have different types of strategies. Google is very much technology oriented while Yahoo! appears to be more market oriented. Another major goal of Google is speed. Some sites may contain more content of one type than another. For example, AltaVista appears to have more images, as opposed to text pages, indexed.

Search engine rankings. The order in which different sites are listed for a given term is determined by a secret **algorithm** developed by the search engine. An algorithm is a collection of rules put together to identify the most relevant sites. The specific algorithms are highly guarded trade secrets, but most tend to heavily weigh the number of links from other sites to a site and the keywords involved. More credit is given for a link from a highly rated site — thus, having a link from CNN.com would count much more than one from the site of the *Imperial Valley Press.* On any given page, the weight given from a link will depend on the total number of links on that page. Having one of one hundred links will count less than being the only one. One source reports that the weight appears to be proportional so that one out of one hundred links would carry one percent of the weight of being the sole link, but that may change and/or vary among search engines.

For Google, some of the main ranking factors appear to be:

- Number and quality of links to the site, as discussed above.
- Relevant keywords. Note that the ranking algorithm tests for "spam." Reckless repeating keywords may actually count *against* the rating of the site.

- The "click-through" share of the site. Since late 2006 or early 2007, Google reportedly fine-tunes rankings by observing the percentage of the time that a particular site is chosen for a given set of search terms. Sites that are selected more frequently may improve in rank and those less frequently selected – despite their merits presumed from the other factors — may move down.

Types of search engines. Some engines, such as Google, are general purpose search engines. Some are specialized. Some are hybrids, containing some directory structure in addition to search engine capabilities. Some "reward" sites such as iwon.com attract people by allowing them to enter a lottery when doing a search. Some sites are aggregator sites — they do not have their own databases but instead combine the results from simultaneous searches on other search engines.

Text optimization. It is important to repeat important words as much as possible subject to credibility. Search engines today are increasingly sophisticated in identifying "spamming" through frivolous repetition of the same words or early use of words that are not relevant to the main content of the site. Words that appear early in the text and on the index page will tend to be weighed more heavily. For some search engines, it may be useful to include common misspellings of a word so that the site will come up when that spelling is used. For aesthetic reasons, many firms may object to having much text on the front page, but text may be put below the graphic elements — e.g., see http://www.LarsPerner.com. Some web site owners have attempted to include hidden text so that a search engine would find the desired words while the visitor would see something else. Some web designers, for example, would hide text behind a graphic, make the text in a very small font, and/or make the font color the same, or nearly the same, as the background. Other web site designers have made a "legitimate" site, only to have a command to move the visitor to another site when they go to the searched site. Search engines today are increasingly able to detect this type of abuse, and sites may be penalized as a result.

Early search engines relied heavily on "meta tags" where the web site creator specified what he or she believed to be appropriate keywords, content descriptions and titles. Because these tags are subject to a lot of abuse, these no longer appear to be significant.

Link optimization. Many web sites engage in "link exchanges" — that is, complementary sites will agree to feature links to each other. It may be useful for a webmaster to ask firms whose content does not compete for a link. Sites should register with the Open Directory Project at http://www.dmoz.org since, if a site is classified favorably, this may help rankings.

The bottom line on Google. Today, the most significant factor in search engine rankings appears to be the "value" of the links that reach a site. Links from "low value" sites (those that are not rated highly, and especially those considered to the "spam") count for very little. Links from highly rated sites on the relevant keywords count for literally thousands — sometimes tens and hundreds of thousands — times as much as less important sites. In the past, the presence of important key terms on a site was the main driver of rankings, subject to some rudimentary safeguards against obvious "spamming" sites which used the words as a way to gain rankings without providing relevant information. Now, the effect of keywords is secondary except for searches that involve a very unique key term. Within the last year, it appears that Google has incorporated the frequency of "click-through" for a site when it is listed in search ("organic") results. That is, if a relatively high proportion of searchers go to the site, its ranking is likely to decrease. However, if relatively few searchers actually end up going to a highly ranked site when it shows up in search listings, that site is likely to lose rank. Search engines cannot usually measure the amount of traffic that goes to a site. Traditionally, then, the traffic of a site was not directly incorporated into the ranking system. Today, however, Google is reported to weigh the percentage that a site is chosen for click-through when the site comes up in a search. That is, if a site is initially highly ranked, if a small proportion of searchers actually choose to go to that site, this site is likely to have its rank reduced.

Google now offers a set of "Analytics" tools, including a set of web traffic statistics. Webmasters can sign up voluntarily to participate in this by placing certain "meta tag" code in their web pages. (This code is invisible to people viewing the respective web page in its regular display mode). Therefore, for such sites, Google does, in principle, have access to traffic information from all sources, including other search engines or links from other sites. However, it is not clear whether Google actually uses this information.

8. Advantages/Disadvantages of E-Commerce

There are many advantages and disadvantages for customers, business and non-profit organisations to apply electronic commerce. Through the Internet, different levels of product information can be accessed online globally, which makes it easy for customers to compare and evaluate. Business can provide wide range of choices to extend markets and opportunities. With contribution to digital goods and services, customers could save delivery time, business could reduce operating cost and increase profit. The drawback of E-commerce is the different expectations of goods such as clothes sales online when customers are purchasing. Another disadvantage is the privacy and security issues of customer's credit card detail.

9. Impact of E-Commerce

The introduction of E-Commerce has impacted on the traditional means of online exchanges. It is creating a new market place and opportunity for the reorganization of economic processes, in a more efficient way. The open structure of the Internet and the low cost of using it, permits the interconnection of new and existing information and communication technologies. It offers businesses and consumers an innovative and powerful information system and another form of communication. This changes the way they search and consume products, with these products increasingly customized, distributed and exchanged differently (Anonymous, 2000:193).

In 1991, the Internet had less than three million users and the concept of e-commerce was non existent. By 1999 an estimated two hudred and fifty million users accessed the Internet and and approximately one quarter made purchases online from e-commerce sites (Anonymous, 2000:193).

The advent of e-commerce has seen a dramatic impact on the traditional ways of doing business. It has brought producers and consumers closer together and eradicated many of the costs previously encountered (Wyckoff, 1997:5).

It is evident that the supply industry will benefit from e-commerce which includes those producing computers, networking equipment and the software necessary (Wyckoff, 1997:6).

It is also evident that a negative impact will be targted at direct substitutes, such as retail travel agencies, retailers of software and "bricks and mortar" music stores. However, these impacts will be small comapared to the developments imaginable (Wyckoff, 1997:5).

10. Management of E-Commerce

Referring back to E-Commerce overview, E-Commerce consists of distributing, buying, selling, marketing and servicing of products or services over electronic systems such as the Internet and other computer networks. The information technology industry might see it as an electronic business application aimed at commercial transactions. Moreover, it can involve electronic funds transfer, supply chain management, e-marketing, online marketing, online transaction processing, electronic data interchange, automated inventory management systems, and automated data-collection systems. In order to implement the above mentioned functions (such as electronic funds transfer and automated inventory management systems) required by running E-Commerce and to systemically deal with the data involves in performing E-Commerce, an Enterprise Information System is necessary for managing E-Commerce and provides an overall control structure to organize and manage all the transaction data within the organization or across all other organizations such as suppliers and customers.

Enterprise System

According to Wikipedia 2005, Enterprise System is "more or less any kind of computing system that is of "enterprise classýÿ?. This means typically offering high quality of service, dealing with large volumes of data – capable of supporting some large organization ("an enterpriseýÿ?). An Enterprise Information System would typically be operated by professional system administrators and be deployed on dedicated servers .It would typically offer network connectivity and provide services that supported the operations carried out by the enterprise.

"Enterprise Systems can be defined as customizable, standard application software, which includes integrated business solutions for the core processes and the main administrative functions of an enterprise.ýÿ?

An enterprise wide system is an off-the-shelf package that provides an integrated suit of applications which provide transaction processing and management information systems for the common core of business processes found in accounting, human resource management, manufacturing and sales and distribution. (Hernandez 1999)

Originally, Enterprise System was known as Enterprise Resource Planning (ERP), which supports broad set of activities by multi-module application software that helps a manufacturer manage the important parts of its business. These include product planning, parts purchasing, maintaining inventories, interacting with suppliers, providing customer service, and tracking orders. ERP is now known as Enterprise System, which extends beyond resource planning, with extensive complex of databases and support multi-online transactions. There are numbers of suppliers that provide Enterprise Systems for business and the examples of major well-known suppliers are SAP, Oracle, PeopleSoft and Baan.

E-commerce — Advantages

The advantages of E-commerce are basically increased sales and decreased costs through the use of electronical media, especially the Web. The advantages of E-commerce will be divided into the benefits it provides to organizations, consumers, and society.

Advantages to Organizations

Due to the global reach of the Internet, business organizations are able to send messages worldwide, exploring new markets and opportunities. This breaks down geographic limitations and reaches narrow markets that traditional businesses have difficulty accessing. Through the Internet, business now offer a wide range of choices and higher levels of customer information and details for individuals to search and compare. Some build-to-order companies such as Dell Computer Corp can even provide a competitive advantage by inexpensive customization of products and services.

In terms of cost reduction, E-commerce helps organizations decrease costs in creating, processing, distributing, storing and retrieving information. For example the communication and advertising costs could be lower by sending e-mails and using online advertising channels, than by using television commercials or the print media. In terms of online ordering and online auction organizations, the costs could be lower than running an actual shop with the associated manpower.

Extended trading hours is another benefit, the 24 hours a day, 7 days a week in 365 days allows business free to open on the Internet without overtime and extra cost. Other advantages includes the up-to-date company material, current inventories, improved customer service, better customer communication, increased operating and trading flexibility

Advantages to Consumers

For customers, the advantages occur in the buying process, product research, evaluation and execution. E-commerce provides customers with a platform to search product information through global markets with a wider range of choices, which makes comparison and evaluation easier and more efficient. With the ubiquity in accessing the Internet, consumers are able to search for shops or perform other transactions anytime in almost any location. Cheaper goods and services is one of the benefits for consumers who purchase online. Furthermore, delivery time and costs can be saved by buyers when they purchase digital goods and services. Examples are e-books, music, audio clips, software, games, and distance education delivered via the Internet.

Advantages to Society

By telecommuting, individuals can nowadays work and do their purchasing at home rather than by traveling around. This will result in less traffic and air pollution. For people in Third World countries, many service and products are now available which were unavailable in the past; opportunities and higher education services are more achievable for students. Non-profit organizations, including government services, also benefit from E-commerce by the online payment system which supports the payment of tax refunds and pensions quickly and securely. Public services such as health care, education and public social service also benefit from E-commerce.

For example, rural doctors and nurses can access professional information and the latest health care technologies. Overall, e-commerce makes products and services more easily available without geographic limitations.

11. The Guidelines for Consumer Protection in the Context of Electronic Commerce

The Guidelines are established to encourage a global approach to consumer protection in the e-marketplace, a sector that is international and borderless .These guidelines are able to facilitate online commerce consumer protection mechanisms without causing barriers to trade and by increasing consumer confidence in e-commerce and assist in worldwide economy.

The Six Concepts Outline for Consumer Protection

Transparent and Effective Protection

Consumers are to be protected regardless when shopping through the e-marketplace or through local stores. This will ensure consistency and gives assurance to the consumers while shopping (Australian Competition and Consumer Commission, 2005).

Fair Business, Advertising and Marketing Practices

Fairness and equality are important during business transactions. For example, advertising should be clear and understandable for people of all ages. Consumers are to be respected and businesses should take special consideration (language, information) when targeting different target markets (Australian Competition and Consumer Commission, 2005).

On-line Disclosures About the Business, the Goods and Services and the Transaction*

When purchasing goods online, disclosure should include complete and accurate information about the business, about the goods and services for sale and about how the transaction is made. This will keep the consumer well-informed and aware of the transaction going on (Schneider, 2002:119).

Confirmation Process

The confirmation process for a sale should give the consumer a chance to see what he has agreed to buy and to change his mind if he wants, before the purchase is completed (Australian Competition and Consumer Commission, 2005).

Secure Payment Systems

Payment systems need to be secure and consumers should be taken through a step by step procedure to assist them (Australian Competition and Consumer Commission, 2005).

Education

These guidelines also encourage governments, business and consumers to work together to educate consumers about electronic commerce, to foster informed decision making by consumers participating in electronic commerce, and to increase business and consumer awareness of the consumer protection framework that applies to their on-line activities (Australian Competition and Consumer Commission, 2005).

12. Digital Wallet

Definition

Electronic wallet (E-wallet) is a software component in which a user stores credit card numbers and other personal information. When shopping online, the user simply clicks the e-wallet to automatically fill in the information needed to make a purchase.

E-wallet is basically another online payment scheme that functions as a carrier of e-cash, in the same way that a wallet is used to carry real cash for doing a physical transaction in an actual shop. The purpose is to offer a secure and easy means of online payment.

Four steps of using E-wallet:

Decide on an online shop website.

Download the wallet form from the website and fill out the personal information such as credit card number, phone number, and address. By filling out the details once, personal information will be completed automatically when customers click the E-wallet, when purchasing in the future.

Fill out the personal information as to where customers want the merchandise to be shipped.

When customers are ready to buy, one way is to click the E-wallet button to execute the process or drag information out of the wallet and drop it into the online form.

Cooperating companies

The Electronic Commerce Modeling Language (ECML) is an organizational attempt to set standards for e-wallet vendors in the industry. It provides guidelines for Web merchandise in exchanging data for shipping, billing, and payment between users and merchants. Supporting companies include: American Express, America Online, Brodia, Compaq Computer, CyberCash, Discover, IBM, MasterCard International, Microsoft, Novell, Sun Microsystems and Visa International (Casselman, 2000).

Other on-line merchants who use e-wallet mode and support ECML include 1800-Batteries, Beyond.com, Dell Computer, Fashion.com, Healthshop.com, Nordstrom, Omaha Steaks and Reel.com (Casselman, 2000).

Advantages and disadvantages

Jupiter Communications report that 27% of online buyers abandon orders before checking out because of the hassle of filling out forms (Graphic Arts Monthly, 1999). E-wallet shortens and simplifies the process of repeatedly filling out detailed information, in a safe environment. Customers not only save time but also have control of personal data by being able to drag the proper card from the E-wallet pop-up screen (Quinton, 1999:32).

However, the drawback is that users must download the wallet form and software, after the download is complete, the wallet is installed as a plug-in or ActiveX control which is within a browser that must also be installed. (Kerstetter, 1998:10).

E-wallet in the future

Due to the popularity of the mobile phone, mobile phone bill payments will predictably increase in the future. In Scandinavian countries such as Finland and Sweden, it is estimate that over 60% of the population has mobile phones and already has wireless mobile devices to pay for everyday purchases (Rayport and Jaworski, 2002:567).

13. Disadvantages of E-commerce

The advantages and limitations of e-commerce can be classified as technological and nontechnological.

Overall

According to the research done by CommerceNet in 2000 of the top 10 barriers to E-commerce, the main disadvantage of E-commerce is the lack of a business model, lack of trust and key public infrastructure, slow navigation on the Internet, the high risk of buying unsatisfactory products, and most of all lack of security.

Technological

For the E-commerce system itself, there is no universally accepted standard for quality, security and reliability. The software of e-commerce development tools are always evolving, and have difficulties in integrating the Internet and E-commerce software with parts of the existing applications and databases.

For general users of e-commerce, the accessibility to Internet, such as Digital Divide, is unstable, expensive and insufficient in particular areas. This will generate limitations for business in accessing wider markets. Another problem is that if a business system's scalability is not sufficient and upgradeable, it will result in degradation, slowdown and eventually loss of customers. (Turban, 2004:19, Awad, 2003:18).

Nontechnologies

The lack of trust is one main reason why customers are unwilling to accept E-commerce due to privacy and security concerns. According to a 2000 *Economist* article, 95 per cent of Americans showed reluctance to release their credit card number via the Internet. Some C2C action organizations are under an unencrypted payment environment, in which a customer's number number might be stolen in the payment process. However, recent payment systems such as PayPal can solve this kind of problem (Turban, 2004:52). The danger of hackers accessing customer files and corrupting accounts is also related to privacy and legal issues (Awad, 2003:18).

For some customers, it is hard to change their habit of viewing merchandise online; those customers resist traditional ways of purchasing physical goods in actual shops and have difficulties in changing from a real to a virtual store.

Another drawback is that there are some products that people will not buy online. For some high-cost and unique item, businesses such as those involved with jewellery or antiques have difficulties in offering the items in the e-commerce mode in the same way as online books and CD sales. Another example is furniture companies: many of them have websites that allow customers to browse, but most customers still want to feel and touch the item before they make a decision. Different expectations of goods and services from customers are typical of the online purchasing environment. An example is in the perception of colour. Due to different monitor settings, inaccurate information about colour makes it difficult for customers to make an accurate decision when purchasing online. Because customers are unable to triy or access the actual goods before purchasing and delivery, many customers will not take the risk of purchasing via the Internet.

14. Benefits of E-Commerce

1. Reduce Production Cost

   Replacing paper-based business operations
2. Better Information System

   Faster data retrieval rate
3. Better Management System within organization

   Central database for different departments of the company
4. Better Management System across different organizations

   Data exchanges and transactions between different organizations from suppliers to customers
5. Better Business Strategy

   Extending the business to cover more customers
6. Globalization

   E-Commerce is the essential pathway to implement globalization

15. Five E-commerce Drivers

There are five drivers that promote e-commerce.

1. Digital convergence: The digital revolution has made it possible for almost all digital devices to communicate with one another. The Internet's massive growth during the past 10 years, which is completely a creation of market forces, will continue (Awad, 2004:6).

2. Ubiquity: Today's e-commerce is available to anyone, anywhere, in the world, 24 hours a day, 7 days a week. E-commerce ties together the industrial sector, merchants, the service sector, and the content provider using text, multimedia, video, and other technologies (Awad, 2004:6).

3. Changes in organizations: More and more today's business empower front-line workers to do the kind of work once performed by junior management. A trend also is developing towards partnering owners and managers across departments to develop a chain of relationships that adds value to the enterprise (Awad, 2004:6).

4. Information Density: Global competitions and the proliferation of products and services worldwide have added unusual pressure to keep a close watch on operating costs and maximize profit margins. E-commerce addresses their concerns quickly, efficiently, and at a low cost (Awad, 2004:6).

5. Personalization/Customization: Today's customers are collectively demanding higher quality and better performance, including a customized way of producing delivering and paying for goods and services. Mass customization puts pressure on firms to handle customized request on a mass-market scale.

16. Six key components of E-commerce

1. Placement: This component is vital to any E-commerce business. It focuses on the business being highly visible and easy to access.

2. Merchandise and audience size: This component focuses on ensuring that product lines are kept in stock and that delivery is on time. The audience size of the e-business marketplace, spans across all geographical boundaries. It is important to create capabilities that facilitate global commerce.

3. Presentation: This focuses on two key context dimensions: function and aesthetics. Businesses can employ presentation that is predominantly focused on one or the other in its presentation. At times, the two contexts are combined (McGraw-Hill, 2002:132).

4. Payment: The marketplace capability integrates with other applications for financial and payment processing. Applications include the ability to purchase using a credit card and require integration to provide supplier invoice information to the buyer and to indicate invoice payment status.

5. Security: This component must be given particular attention by e-businesses as it is an ongoing concern for consumers. E-businesses must instill trust in its users by ensuring the security of all transactions and this can be achieved through many methods such as encryption and authentication.

6. Fulfillment: Once the online purchase order has been generated, the marketplace can allow buyers and sellers to manage the fulfillment process. The fulfillment process must be enabled to ensure delivery.

17. Four Major Categories of E-Commerce

Electronic commerce has been divided into four distinct categories:

1. Business-to-Consumer(B2C): Business to Consumer commerce, according to Patton "applies to any business or organization that sells its products or services to consumers over the Internet for their own useÿÿ?. In other words, it provides a direct sale between the supplier and in the individual consumer.

B2C commerce created much hype when it first took off. The first noticeable success arrived around 1995, where companies like eBay.com and Amazon.com were launched. When the success of these companies took off, many other imitations were born. However, the market turned sour and many of the B2C companies crashed, including Australian company dstore.com.au.

2. Business-to-Business (B2B): Business-to-Business involves online transactions between businesses. Examples of B2B include online companies that specialise in marketing strategies, advertising, email companies, internet consultants, website development etc. Also, as an offshoot of these companies, there are various internet resources such as online magazines, including the E-Commerce Times and BtoBOnline.com.

3. Consumer-to-Consumer or Peer-to-Peer (C2C/P2P): Consumer-to-Consumer or Peer-to-Peer is defined as exchanges between/among consumers (McGrawHill, 2002, p.xiv). These exchanges can involve a third-party involvement, which can facilitate and provide the infrastructure, place and governance for the transactions/exchanges. Perhaps the most well known example of this is the online market place, eBay.com. Here consumers can bid for and sell items of any description, for any price. An example of P2P exchanges are file swapping sites/programs, such as Kazaa and eDonkey.

4. Consumer-to-Business (C2B): Consumer-to-Business is when consumers present themselves as a buyer group. Examples of this include CTB and SpeakOut.com. These sites provide consumers with market strategies and businesses also use them to gain insight into consumer wants. These groups may be economically motivated, as with demand aggregators, or socially orientated.

18. Ethical issues

It is contended that we are all living in a transitional economy and given the implications of globalisation and information technologies for business and commerce, no economic system displays stability. The Internet poses fundamental challenges to issues central to society, namely free speech, privacy and national sovereignty. With the advent of e-commerce, it brings with it a host of ethical issues surrounding customer privacy. The topic of protecting individual and corporate privacy as a major ethical issue, has triggered a wave of governmental legislation and has created an entire segment of Internet industry firms whose mission is to help consumers protect sensitive and personal data on the web. Privacy violations, pornography, transaction security breaches, unsolicited e-mail and other questionable or illegal activities being conducted on-line have become serious issues. Some see regulation as the only answer to protection from unwelcome intrusion. However, due to the universal nature of the Internet, regulation will be extremely difficult, if not impossible. It is believed that ethical issues involving Internet marketing are basically the same as in other forms of marketing. If a firm has been able to gain the confidence of the consumer through demonstrated fair practices, the same level of confidence should be imputed to the e-transaction. The real challenge is for the true "virtual business" that lacks the traditional brick and mortar image of stability and consumer access.

As more "bricks and mortar" firms use e-commerce as a channel of distribution in their industries, personalization and customer information is becoming increasingly important in a firm's marketing strategies, with privacy protection becoming an important factor. As more firms rely increasingly on individualized customer information to achieve marketing success, they will seek flexibility and speed of response in using such data. Under these circumstances, firms might implement self-regulation as a means of preserving their edge in fast-changing environments, rather than concur with government-set privacy regulations.

Many individuals have perceived a lack of regulation as an opportunity to engage in conduct that raises serious ethical questions. It is this concept of self-regulation that affords the greatest opportunity for ethical growth. It forces Internet companies to think about their attitudes regarding consumer privacy, to decide whether or not they will disclose their policies, and to determine what sort of protections they put into place. More and more web sites have risen to the challenge and have been posting privacy policies (Maury, 2002:21).

Generally accepted guides to ethical behavior are being developed and adopted by professional organizations. These guidelines often have common themes such as customer consent to the dissemination of their private information. Since social responsibility has become expected by the general public, firms are being forced to subscribe to at least the minimum standards or run the risk of going out of business (Peeples, 2002:32).

19. The Future of E-Commerce

E-commerce introduces incredible benefits, such as the diffusion of information, the development of new technologies, the promotion and sales of products and services, and the collaboration between those in a supply chain(Aljifri,2003:130). It has been suggested that ultimately a single chain of e-commerce will emerge and this chain will be a superset of B2B, C2B, B2C abd C2C. E-commerce still represents a minor percentage of total commerce but is likely to become a major force in the future. The factors driving this push are convenience, reduced cost of operations, lower risk, more timely information and control over processes and the ability to deliver customisation and control on a mass scale. More recently attention has been focused on standards for secure communication, encryption and authentication of both sender and receiver of information on the Internet. This will continue into the future, as a broad range of new value added services built around trust and security will be found on the Internet. Initiatives for the future must be developed within a common framework or risk introducing isolated, non-interoperable implementations that will inhibit progress towards truly free, open and spontaneous e-commerce.

Most of the current solutions being prototyped over the Internet differ in some way in its approach to security and privacy and the ability to handle micropayments and the applicability to various types of transactions. They also differ in their business models. For example, in the pricing strategies and in assumptions as to who bears the risk in case of insufficient funds or disputes. Some of these variations are the inevitable result of competitors offering different solutions and are a part of the open mareketplace that characterise the Internet. Other differences reflect a more serious lack of standardisation that could threaten the acceptance and deployment of secure commerce solutions. It is important for e-commerce to devlop the next generation of network based products and services and that primary goals and standards must be agreed upon. It is especially important to build an infrastructure around the following characteristics (Cronin, 1998:178):

inter-operability

flexibility for innovations

increased accessibility

adequate security

adequate search capabilities

e-payment options

20. E-Commerce: Legal Issues

Electronic Commerce: Legal Issues.

Electronic commerce is one of the newest and fastest developing business environments. One of the advantages of online business, as outlined by Reinsch (p167, 2005) is the ability for businesses to access larger markets. One location can serve the world with fast customer relations, less transaction and manpower costs, smaller start up costs, ease of reinvention and upgrade, greater consumer access and low barriers to entry.

While these advantages attract businesses and consumers alike, there are a number of disadvantages. One of these disadvantages includes the legal environment surrounding e-commerce.

Legal Issues

Reinsch argues that the cyber legal environment is unknown, and can only be known once a law suit develops (p167, 2005). This is due to the fact that businesses on the internet are subject not only to the laws from their country of origin, but also potentially subject to many international laws.

The kinds of legal barriers cyberspace has delivered exist primarily in areas of intellectual property, security (including consumer protection), copyright, free speech, gambling, privacy and taxation (McGraw Hill, 2003).

Perhaps the most relevant legal landmine on the Internet are the rights to intellectual property. Mykytyn and Mykytyn in the importance of the law in e-commerce strategies (2005) include copyright, trademark, defamation and patents as part of the intellectual property subgroups.

Mykytyn notes that one of the biggest shifts towards protecting intellectual property has been the ability to place patent protection on software (2005). One of the landmark cases on this is in the U.S, where Amazon.com sued Barnesandnoble.com. Barnesandnoble.com was accused of infringing on Amazon.com's "1-click ordering system" patent awarded in 1999, and Amazon.com now has the right to allow other companies use the system if they receive royalties.

Copyright is also another major issue for e-commerce. Software, articles and even advertising on websites for instance can be construed as a copyright infringement, if the appropriate permission and authority is not granted. One of the biggest issues in internet copyright laws at the moment is the downloading of web content, such as music files and movies.

Legal Landmines

The internet has no physical borders and is always changing. Furthermore, a clear advantage has risen from the lack of regulation, that being the boom in economy, particularly in the U.S (McGraw-Hill, p 260, 2003). There are fears if strict regulation was placed on the internet and was successful there would be significant economic losses.

From these barriers and possible legal landmines, another area has developed. There is a sense of uncertainty and hesitation to create an internet start-up because of the many possible legal nightmares. In his article Potential of custom in overcoming legal uncertainty in global electronic commerce, Polanski (2002, p1) addresses these issues.

Polanski argues that the current model for addressing e-commerce restricts rather than encourages electronic commerce. The current attitude towards e-commerce legal issues provides too many possible outcomes, including possible negative outcomes. This is because the laws are uncertain, untested and hard to apply.

21. Definition of online Banking

Online banking is a growing part of E-Commerce which provides interactive services such as accessing account summary information, paying bills and accessing other banking products and services.

22. History of Online Banking

October 18 1995 Security First Network Bank opened to the public as world's first Internet bank (Cronin, 1998:75). Banking executives needed to find more cost effective delivery channels to overcome limitations of labour intensive, high cost branch banking models. The world wide web with its ubiquitous browser based access offered a completely different delivery model for banking, one in which customers could tap into their accounts to conduct transactions at any hour.

23. Online Banking Advantages

Online banking provides the opportunity for bank customers to find out information or make a payment when a visit to a branch is not convenient .

For the bank, it reduces the cost of processing each transaction and has the potential to enable the bank to reduce the overhead of the branch network.

24. Online Banking Disadvantages

While online banking can provide considerable convenience for users who require out of branch banking facilities, the user is also vulnerable to potential risks of virus attacks, unauthorised access, fraudulent transactions and identity theft.

The use of the Internet, young prosperous customers may require and can certainly cope with. For the old and the poor, these developments are less likely to be welcome. There is a problem of exclusion from financial services and the retrenchment of the branch network (i.e.

country towns closing branches) will do nothing to help the situation. Social exclusion is a growing problem both in and for society.

25. Online Banking-the target market

Companies that take advantage of targeting the appropriate customers with the products and services customised for them, will have a lasting competitive advantage. Electronic delivery of these products and services will be one of the means of achieving this edge because it provides convenience and ability to customise products and services on a mass scale.

26. Online banking-the increased momentum

1. New distribution channel: The reach and delivery capabilities of computer networks such as the Internet, far exceeds any proprietary bank network ever built and makes it continually easier for customers to manage their money anytime, anywhere (Cronin, 1998:20).

2. No barriers to entry: Through increased technology, a trend can be seen in the area of bill paymens where recent innovations have provided an opportunity for non-banks to break into the banking business, threatening one of the most profitable services provided by banks.

In the borderless "marketspace" of the Web economy, any business can go global with unprecedented ease and low costs. E-Commerce will reduce the barriers that distribution channels traditionally offered the market leaders. The barriers represented by channels, particularly to smaller manufacturers that lack volume and economies of scale to create end-user demand and by limited shelf space, mind share or financial resources, are eliminated. With E-Commerce, the shelf space is virtually unlimited and the networks will probably compete on the basis of the number of manufacturers and products represented (Savoie, 1999:247).

3. Changing customer expectations: Customers want to bank at their convenience and want banks to provide more interesting financial products. This change is evident in the increased purchase of investment products and has been one of the fastest growing industries (Cronin, 1998:24).

New technology has not only enabled an ever increasing range of products, it has also had far reaching effects on consumer expectations. Fincancial institutions understand that to meet these expectations, they need to be flexible by separating the content (financial product) from the distribution channel (the branch). The traditional model of one stop integrated financial shopping has outlived its usefulness and is keeping banks from being agile enough to meet new consumer demands (Cronin, 1998:20).

4. Digital convergence of financial management: Technology has enabled a convergence of a broad range of financial management activities that previously were consuidered disparate. Only recently has software been written that makes it possible to perform diverse transactions through one common interface (Cronin, 1998:20).

27. The future of online banking

Few managers have a clear vision of tomorrow's banking environment. Few institutions have strategic plans in place today that anticipate the future of online banking. The challenge for the banking industry lies in creating the right incentives for customers to use PCs regularly for banking.

Financial instutions today have reason to worry that if they do not offer online banking services, affluent customers will look to competitors. In addition to wanting to protect their existing franchise, financial institutions can look to online and related services to expand their product offerings and win new business.

28. Online shopping

Definition: Online shopping, also known as internet shopping, online purchasing or internet buying which also includes activities such as online auction. It is same as customers purchase goods or service by exchanging values in actual shops. Internet enables transactions occur through electronic ways by computers. Due to the growing population of internet users, online shopping now is popular and as an accepted way in which to purchase various types of goods and services. Statistics show that in 2001, online sales were $48.3bn, representing an annual growth of 45.9%, and was expected to grow more dramatically in the future. Therefore online shopping will be a promising and prosperous business in the following generation .

Types of online shopping shops

There are several different types of online shops with advantages and disadvantages.

Online autions

Online auctions are popular places for trading goods. Individuals registered as users can buy and sell almost anything online. Online auction companies are, for instances, eBay and Yahoo. The price is normally cheaper than market price; with "past history" functions, users can evaluate a sale's honesty and trustworthy before buying; more information is also provided online, or could be answered in QnA section. However some vendors refuse to ship overseas and risks are that vendors are registered but arc not official business. Hence the credibility is unknown.

Classifieds

It is similar to newspaper classifieds. There are many hard to get or used items with sometimes good discount. On the other hand the traders history is hard to evaluate, the risks is relatively higher.

Portals

It is like a shopping center gathering a number of shopping destinations together in one location, but online however. The benefit is the variety of shops and the navigation between shops is simplified. The drawback will be the move of site without being told.

Manufacturers/retailers

They are online outlets for small or large stores and manufacturers to sell products, such as Super E-store. The advantage will be the sufficient information provided by retailers or producers, and the credibility due to the direct purchase. The drawback might be the price is average without any discount and promotion.

Steps

1. Decide on a online shop and browse items.
2. Put interested items in a virtual shopping cart (goods can be added and deleted as wanted).
3. Log in with user name and password and fill out personal information (this could contain shipping address, billing address, phone number etc).
4. Choose a way of payment and delivery method.
5. Confirm order.
6. Log out

Types of payment

Common payments are Credit Card, Cash on delivery (C.O.D.), cheque (personal cheques, cashier's cheque) money order money transfer/delivery on payment.

Or with online shopping website payment systems such as PayPal. (eBay, 2005)

Online purchase industries

In October 2001, several main industries had large shares of online sales, which included:

Airline tickets

Apparel

Computer hardware

Hotel reservations

Consumer electronics

Online shopping demographics

Gender

The United States female Internet population grew at a triple rate of male's growing rate in 2002.

In many Asian countries such as China, Hong Kong and Singapore, the average online shopper is male.

Age

There are up to 50% of online shoppers whose age various from 18 to 49, and they account for 71% of sales in the United States [www.baltimoresun.com].

In China, Hong Kong and Singapore the average online shoppers are under 36 as well.

Culture

Scandinavian countries have the highest level of Internet usage, however Sweden is least likely to shop online. (Pastore, 2001)

British Internet users are highly keen online shoppers. It is suggested almost half of United Kingdom internet users who visit an e-tailing shop actually make a purchase.

Chinese Internet users on the other hand are more interested in internet games than online shopping, with statistics show that 43% of Chinese Internet users doing online gaming activities while only 16% made online purchases.

29. Introduction to Government regulation

Government regulation has encountered new challenges with the emergence of the Internet. The Internet presents many challenges to government regulation. Throughout the world, countries must decide not only how to regulate, but how much to regulate.

Challenges the Internet brought to Regulation

The two major challenges the Internet has brought to regulation are new technology and lack of physical borders. New technology affects issues like privacy and intellectual property, the lack of borders affects taxation and gambling. Free speech is affected by both issues (Rayport & Jaworski, 2002:596).

Main Regulation Issues on the Internet

The five main issues are:

Privacy

Privacy is an issue because Internet companies have new technology that can track a user's every movement.

Intellectual property

Intellectual property has become an issue because new technology makes it easy to copy high-quality music such as Napster and trade them over the Internet.

Taxation

Taxation is an issue because e-commerce companies do not have to collect sales tax on their customer's purchases. While this is an advantage to customers, it costs the states billions of dollars a year.

Gambling

Gambling is an issue because the Internet makes it difficult to decide where the transaction take place, and therefore, which region's law should regulate that transaction.

Free Speech

Free speech has become an issue because the internet now allows millions of people to speak their mind annoymously, something that has never happened before.

30. United States and Europe

The United States and Europe have been working together on both privacy and cybercrime issues. While Europe has stricter laws regulating privacy than the United States, U.S e-commerce companies are reluctant to adopt them since the regulations would limit their ability to do personalised advertising. Europe wants to ban American companies from doing business with its citizens until European privacy standards are implemented (Queensland University of Technology, School of International Business, 2004) . The European Union and the United States are also working together to create laws prohibiting cybercrime. These laws have come under attack from privacy advocates wno are concerned with giving governments the right to monitor online behaviour.

31. Security

One of the critical success factors of e-commerce is its security. Without a great degree of confidence by the customers that credit card numbers and other extremely sensitive personal information will be kept secure, e-commerce will simply not work. However, the successful functioning of e-commerce security depends on a complex inter-relationship between several components, including the applications development platforms, database management systems, systems software and network infrastructure. The following, outline the needs and threats of e-commerce.

Access control

If access control is properly implemented many other security problems like lack of privacy, will either be eliminated or mitigated. Access control ensures only those that legitimately require access to resources are given access and those without valid access cannot have access. This includes both physical access as well as logical access to resources. Various types of threats exist for access control. For example, being able physically to enter a building or having access to network equipment is one example of a threat.

Privacy

Privacy ensures that only authorized parties can access information in any system. The information should also not be distributed to parties that should not receive it. Issues related to privacy can be considered as a subset of issues related to access control.

Protection of privacy requires access control. However access control deals with the larger picture. Due to this, the threats to privacy are similar to that of access control. Integrity ensures that only authorized parties make changes to the documents transmitted over the network. Lack of integrity of the system can be devastating for e-commerce. While the threats to integrity are similar to the threats to access, being a threat to integrity is possible only when one has access at a level consistent with someone having the rights to alter a document. For example, if a customer places an order, and someone can access the system as the customer, they may be able to alter the contents of the order placed.

Authentication

Authentication ensures that the origin of an electronic message is correctly identified. This means having the capability to determine who sent the message and from where or which machine. Without proper authentication, it will be impossible to know who actually placed an order and whether the order placed is genuine or not.

Non-repudiation

Non-repudiation is closely related to authentication and this ensures the sender cannot deny sending a particular message and the receiver cannot deny receiving a message. If this happens infrequently, it may not significantly harm e-commerce, however, on a large scale this can be devastating. For example, if many customers receive goods and then deny placing an order, the shipping, handling and associated costs with the order can be significant for the company processing the orders.

Availability

Availability ensures that the required systems are available when needed. For an e-commerce site this means that the customer order systems are available all the time. Two major threats to availability problems are virus attacks and denial of service.

One complicating factor for any e-commerce venture is security for customer information, such as credit card numbers and personal data, that most customers do not wish to have shared. Hardly a month goes by without media reports of security breaches over the Internet. Internal security problems, as well as hackers, can plague firms. Guarantees, seals of approval, testimonials, etc., can help ease consumer worries since most sites lack track records.

Transaction security has kept many customers from purchasing products on the Internet. Much resistance has come from privacy issues such as giving credit card number and personal information. There are continual reminders of how unsafe these practices can be, even though "secure" software programs have been developed and continue to become more protective. Foolproof systems may never be developed and therefore the customer is left to weigh the potential cost of privacy with the benefits of conducting business over the Internet.

Internet Startups

Internet startups are viewed by many with a very cautious lens. Companies and individuals begin new businesses and services on the Internet every day. Reuters reported in 2002 that one in five dot-com companies became "dot-bombs? .During the 1990s, there was a massive Internet boom, where thousands of startups began yet never took off and failed with massive losses. The survivors however became very successful, with companies such as Google Inc, eBay and

Amazon.com leading examples of very successful startups. The craze has since slowed significantly and more strategic and planned approaches are being developed.

Risk and Failure

The biggest issue for Internet startups is the high level of risk and failure. Professor Sea Jin Chang in his article Venture Capital Financing, Strategic Alliances, And The Initial Public Offerings Of Internet Startups identifies some key factors that affect Internet startups. These are:

The liability of newness and establishing legitimacy

An initial public offering (first sale of stock to the public) is a measure of success, yet many startups never reach this goal. This is due to the fact that there is a great amount of promise and risk involved with startups that have no "bricks and mortar? type backing. Startups have a higher rate of failure than established firms because of the added uncertainty that already surrounds internet startups, doubled with the lack of legitimacy or an established reputation.

Initial Public Offering

Strategic alliances and the reputations of the venture-capital firm had a significant impact on the success of the initial public offering (Chang, 2004, p721). Companies that were backed by venture-capital firms with a higher IPO success rate enjoyed returns far higher than those with a lower success rate, suggesting investors look for venture-capital firms previous success rate before buying stock (Chang, 2004, p721).

There are also many legal risks. Elliot (2005, p67) identifies some being liabilities of web site hosts, internet service providers, manufacturers, privacy and a host of other potential traps. All of these are suggested to form part of the scepticism of many internet startups.

Success

After all of the failures and loss of investments, there have been many insights into what makes a startup successful. Finkelstein (2001, p16) argues there are four main strategic elements a startup needs to be successful. These are customers, capabilities, internal consistency and competitive advantage.

For all businesses, customers are the heart-beat. Particularly for business-to-consumer businesses, it is essential for startups to develop and retain customers (Finkelstein, 2001, p16). Startups fall into the traps when they overspend and over estimate their profits, become too niche orientated (for example Kneehighsocks.com instead of Clothing.com) or underestimating customer acquisition costs (Finkelstein, 2001, p16). The buyer needs to be assured of two things before they purchase online: trust and experience (Finkelstien, 2001, p16). For this too happen, many organisational elements need to be put into place. Simple activities that sort the organisation of the Startup often do not happen, and therefore there are no buyers. Internal operations that will make the company run smoothly and cost efficiently need to fall into place before a customer will place trust into the system (Finkelstein, 2001, p17). Once these systems are in place, these systems must be consistent.

Competitors include not just other internet companies, but also bricks and mortar companies. Developing strong internal capabilities is essential. However if all other companies have similar strategies, then there is not much of a competitive advantage (Finkelstein, 2001, p17).

32. E-commerce and Australia

A global entity

E-Commerce involves the application of Web-based information technologies towards automating business processes, transactions, and work flows, and buying and selling information, products, and services using computer networks? (MacGregor and Vrazalic, 2005, p1). The biggest advantage (and sometimes disadvantage) is that electronic commerce provides an immediate global marketplace. Business transactions can occur seamlessly and very quickly from opposite sides of the world. As a global marketplace, movement is increasing. Electronic commerce within one specific area however is interesting to watch.

E-commerce within Australia

Jing Gao (2005, p20) describes e-commerce within Australia as growing. Specifically within the Australian manufacturing industry, the use of the Internet as a business tool is increasing, yet there are still some significant problems that need to be overcome. One of the main problems according to Gao is the lack of media attention given to e-commerce businesses.

MacGregor and Vrazalic (2005) suggest that e-commerce is disruptive in Australian small businesses. This is because they now have more similar businesses to compete with, not only on a local scale, but globally.

However Dunt and Harper (2002) argue that given Australia's physical distance with the major commerce centres in Europe, America and Asia, e-commerce helps close those gaps. In times before e-commerce, the physical distance has been considered a disadvantage, dubbed the "tyranny of distance?.

Within Australia, there are two main sources of B2B e-commerce: migration of existing buyer and supplier transactions to e-commerce; and new B2B products made possible by the advent of e-commerce (Dunt and Harper, 2002, p330).

Some of the factors that are improving and increasing e-commerce in Australia are outline by Dunt and Harper (2002). They include ease and greater access to the internet, low internet costs, increase in demand, placement in the global e-commerce network and some long-term advantages including increase of knowledge. However they warn that e-commerce could do more harm than good, and it's success depends on Australia's ability to generate and sustain increases in productivity (2002, p18).

Australian exports

The major types of e-commerce businesses within Australia are predominantly service and manufacturing industries (Gao, 2004). Madden and Coble-Neal (2002, p343) write, "Australian Internet involvement began in the early 1970s with small and isolated networks of agency connections to ARPANET via an international dial-up service offered by the Australian Overseas Telecommunications Commission?. Since then, many existing and new businesses have taken advantage of the opportunities made available by e-commerce. Companies include the failed then 'born again' online store dstore.com.au and many food, clothing and other service industries. One of Australia's biggest export markets is Asia, with AusTrade making noticeable developments and trades with Asian Industries.

33. E-commerce and Europe

A global entity

"E-commerce involves the application of Web-based information technologies towards automating business processes, transactions, and work flows, and buying and selling information, products and services using computer networks? (MacGregor and Vrazalic, 2005, p1). The biggest advantage (and sometimes disadvantage) is that electronic commerce provides an immediate global marketplace. Business transactions can occur seamlessly and very quickly from opposite sides of the world. As a global marketplace, movement is increasing. Electronic commerce within one specific area however is interesting to watch.

E-commerce within Europe

Europe as a whole consists of a highly developed network of countries. The European Union is the closest concept of a centralized government across twenty-five independent states. E-commerce is also a highly developed business institution within Europe. Although there may be physical boundaries between the nations of Europe, e-commerce is not restricted by physical borders, perhaps one of the most attractive elements of this developing business environment. E-commerce is now embedded within most European corporations (Ellis, 2002).

E-Commerce Barriers

E-commerce in Europe is not however, without barriers. Ellis (2002) writes there are two major barriers facing the advance of e-commerce in Europe. They are currency differences, and language and cultural differences.

The introduction of the euro currency in 2002 was a step towards improving this barrier, with 12 countries adopting this currency (Ellis, 2002). Money exchange costs are one of the primary deterrents when buying between different currencies.

Language and culture also provide significant barriers. Eastern Europe for example, has the lowest amount of e-commerce usage (ECD, 2003). The link between language and cultural attitudes and percentage of e-commerce retail sales are linked.

Another important barrier restricting the development of e-commerce in Europe are the legal barriers and jurisdiction. The inability to place boundaries on the Internet makes it virtually impossible to regulate the Internet (Eang, 2005). Eang writes "From the second a consumer places an online order until the payment is complete, consumers already have moved in and out of numerous regulatory realms. The transaction could be national or international, and consumers do not know when they are leaving a regulated zone and entering an unregulated area? (2005, p75). The current debate at the forefront of this legal issue is how and where disputes and regulations should be governed.

European E-commerce Developments

With the development of the euro, it is now argued that the euro is providing more advantages for the progress of e-commerce. Ellis writes "combined impact of the single currency and e-commerce can be expected to forge powerful synergies across the euro zone, strengthening and deepening the single market? (2002). In other words, e-commerce is not only encouraged, but it is developing because one of the barriers has been lowered.

Market integration in Europe is still significantly high and rivals the US, which promotes usage of e-commerce (Ellis, 2002). Countries that generally understand English benefit the most from the advantages and profits of e-commerce, including countries like Finland, Germany, Denmark, Sweden, The Netherlands and of course the UK (ECD, 2003).

34. Major E-Commerce Issues and Impediments

Protection of Privacy: The Korea Information Security Agency states that it received 12,329 complaints on privacy infringement through November 2001, which is roughly a 530% increase over the previous year. Based on that figure, 18,000 to 20,000 complaints on privacy infringement are expected in 2002 (Bae, 2005).

Damage, infringement, and misusage of private information by other persons were the primary types of privacy infringement reported in 2000, followed by reception of unwanted information, non-compliance with requests for private information queries, requests for changes or deletion, and collection of private information without consent from users. Resolution of complaints was the most frequent response to complaints followed by self-correction and reconciliation between related parties (Bae, 2005).

Consumer Protection: Consumer protection entails establishment of fair competition/trade practices, protection of consumer rights, and resolution of e-commerce related disputes. In the area of fair competition and trading practices, major issues include dissemination of false and/or exaggerated advertisements and information via the Internet, disputes related to domain name usage, network fraud, and unfair competition arising from other unfair collective actions. In consumer rights protection, major concerns are protecting consumer rights in online purchasing, eradication of unfair trade practices, preventing harm to consumers, and protection of privacy. Lastly, in the area of dispute resolution, major concerns include conflicts between jurisdictions and overlapping applicable laws and identifying alternatives to legal action for effective dispute resolution (Bae, 2005).

Security & Certification: The Basic Act on e-Commerce and the Electronic Signature Act are the two laws related to security and certification in Korea. The Basic Act on e-Commerce gives e-documents the same legal force as written documents. The law was formulated to improve the viability of e-commerce, protect consumers, and to help implement government policies for promoting electronic commerce. The Electronic Signature Act was passed in February 1999 as a means to ensure the identity of the other party in remote communications in non face-to-face situations and to guarantee the integrity and authenticity of electronically signed documents. Both the Basic Act on e-Commerce and the Electronic Signature Act came into effect on July 1, 1999 (Bae, 2005).

Impediments: The growth of e-commerce is also giving rise to related problems. Korea possesses the basic requisite conditions to foster a thriving e-commerce such as an advanced IT infrastructure, rising investments in e-commerce led by large companies and robust growth of the e-commerce market. However, despite the fact that external indices are showing rapid growth, e-business implementation by the business sector as the new engine for growth in the digital age is still lagging behind advanced countries. The reasons the government cites for the delay in the proliferation of e-commerce include lack of collaboration among businesses; uncertainties about the outcome; insufficient investment resources among small and medium-sized companies; lack of corporate innovation and sincere pursuit of non-transparent business practices; lack of standardization; shortage of trained manpower and the absence of a standardized payment system (Bae, 2005).

Questions

(1) What do you mean by E-commerce?

(2) What are the prospects of E-commerce in India?

(3) Explain the E-commerce Buzzwords?

(4) How is electronic commerce useful in online selling?

(5) Define Electronic commerce at the view of market?

❐ ❐ ❐

CHAPTER 7

Information Technology

Information technology (IT) is "the study, design, development, implementation, support or management of computer-based information systems, particularly software applications and computer hardware", according to the Information Technology Association of America (ITAA). IT deals with the use of electronic computers and computer software to convert, store, protect, process, transmit, and securely retrieve information.

Today, the term *information* has ballooned to encompass many aspects of computing and technology, and the term has become very recognizable. IT professionals perform a variety of duties that range from installing applications to designing complex computer networks and information databases. A few of the duties that IT professionals perform may include data management, networking, engineering computer hardware, database and software design, as well as the management and administration of entire systems. Information technology is starting to spread farther than the conventional personal computer and network technology, and more into integrations of other technologies such as the use of cell phones, televisions, automobiles, and more, which is increasing the demand for such jobs.

When computer and communications technologies are combined, the result is information technology or "infotech". *Information technology* is a general term that describes any technology that helps to produce, manipulate, store, communicate and/or disseminate information.

In recent days ABET and the ACM have collaborated to form accreditation and curriculum standards for degrees in Information Technology as a distinct field of study separate from both Computer Science and Information Systems. SIGITE is the ACM working group for defining these standards.

Marketing is the process by which companies determine what products or services may be of interest to customers, and the strategy to use in sales, communications and business development. It is an integrated process through which companies create value for customers and build strong customer relationships in order to capture value from customers in return.

Marketing is used to identify the customer, to keep the customer and to satisfy the customer. With the customer as the focus of its activities, it can be concluded that ***marketing management*** is one of the major components of business management. The evolution of marketing was caused due to mature markets and overcapacities in the last 2-3 centuries. Companies then shifted the focus from production to the customer in order to stay profitable.

The term *marketing concept* holds that achieving organizational goals depends on knowing the needs and wants of target markets and delivering the desired satisfactions. It proposes that in order to satisfy its organizational objectives, an organization should anticipate the needs and wants of consumers and satisfy these more effectively than competitors.

Evolution of marketing

An orientation, in the marketing context, relates to a perception or attitude a firm holds towards its product or service, essentially concerning consumers and end-users. Throughout history marketing has changed considerably as consumer tastes are changing faster.

Earlier approaches

The marketing orientation evolved from earlier orientations namely the production orientation, the product orientation and the selling orientation.

Orientation	Profit driver	Western European timeframe	Description
Production	Production methods	until the 1950s	A firm focusing on a production orientation specializes in producing as much as possible of a given product or service. Thus, this signifies a firm exploiting economies of scale, until the minimum efficient scale is reached. A production orientation may be deployed when a high demand for a product or service exists, coupled with a good certainty that consumer tastes do not rapidly alter (similar to the sales orientation).
Product	Quality of the product	until the 1960s	A firm employing a product orientation is chiefly concerned with the quality of its own product. A firm would also assume that as long as its product was of a high standard, people would buy and consume the product.
Selling	Selling methods	1950s and 1960s	A firm using a sales orientation focuses primarily on the selling/promotion of a particular product and not determining new consumer desires as such. Consequently, this entails simply selling

			an already existing product, and using promotion techniques to attain the highest sales possible. Such an orientation may suit scenarios in which a firm holds dead stock, or otherwise sells a product that is in high demand, with little likelihood of changes in consumer tastes diminishing demand.
Marketing[8]	Needs and wants of customers	1970 to present day	The *marketing orientation* is perhaps the most common orientation used in contemporary marketing. It involves a firm essentially basing its marketing plans around the marketing concept, and thus supplying products to suit new consumer tastes. As an example, a firm would employ market research to gauge consumer desires, use R&D to develop a product attuned to the revealed information, and then utilize promotion techniques to ensure persons know the product exists.

Contemporary approaches

Recent approaches in marketing is the *relationship marketing* with focus on the customer, the *business marketing* or *industrial marketing* with focus on an organization or institution and the *social marketing* with focus on benefits to the society. New forms of marketing also use the internet and are therefore called *internet marketing* or more generally *e-marketing*, *online marketing*, search engine marketing, *desktop advertising* or *affiliate marketing*. It tries to perfect the segmentation strategy used in traditional marketing. It targets its audience more precisely, and is sometimes called personalized marketing or one-to-one marketing.

Orientation	Profit driver	Western European timeframe	Description
Relationship marketing / Relationship management[9]	Building and keeping good customer relations	1960s to present day	Emphasis is placed on the whole relationship between suppliers and customers. The aim is to give the best possible attention, customer services and therefore build customer loyalty.
Business marketing / Industrial marketing	Building and keeping relationships between organizations	1980s to present day	In this context marketing takes place between businesses or organizations. The product focus lies on industrial goods or capital goods than consumer products or end products. A different form of marketing activities like promotion, advertising and communication to the customer is used.

Social marketing	Benefit to society	1990s to present day	Similar characteristics as marketing orientation but with the added provision that there will be a curtailment on any harmful activities to society, in either product, production or selling methods.

Customer orientation

A firm in the market economy survives by producing goods that persons are willing and able to buy. Consequently, ascertaining consumer demand is vital for a firm's future viability and even existence as a going concern. Many companies today have a customer focus (or market orientation). This implies that the company focuses its activities and products on consumer demands. Generally there are three ways of doing this: the customer-driven approach, the sense of identifying market changes and the product innovation approach.

In the consumer-driven approach, consumer wants are the drivers of all strategic marketing decisions. No strategy is pursued until it passes the test of consumer research. Every aspect of a market offering, including the nature of the product itself, is driven by the needs of potential consumers. The starting point is always the consumer. The rationale for this approach is that there is no point spending R&D funds developing products that people will not buy. History attests to many products that were commercial failures in spite of being technological breakthroughs.

A formal approach to this customer-focused marketing is known as ***SIVA*** (Solution, Information, Value, Access). This system is basically the four Ps renamed and rewarded to provide a customer focus. The SIVA Model provides a demand/customer centric version alternative to the well-known 4Ps supply side model (product, price, placement, promotion) of marketing management.

Product	→	Solution
Promotion	→	Information
Price	→	Value
Placement	→	Access

If any of the 4Ps had a problem or were not there in the marketing factor of the business, the business could be in trouble and so other companies may appear in the surroundings of the company, so the consumer demand on it's products will become less.

Organizational orientation

In this sense, a firm's marketing department is often seen as of prime importance within the functional level of an organization. Information from an organization's marketing department would be used to guide the actions of other departments within the firm. As an example, a marketing department could ascertain (via marketing research) that consumers desired a new type of product, or a new usage for an existing product. With this in mind, the marketing department would inform the R&D department to create a prototype of a product/service based on consumer's new desires.

The production department would then start to manufacture the product, while the marketing department would focus on the promotion, distribution, pricing, etc. of the product. Additionally, a firm's finance department would be consulted, with respect to securing appropriate funding for the development, production and promotion of the product. Inter-departmental conflicts may occur, should a firm adhere to the marketing orientation. Production may oppose the installation, support and servicing of new capital stock, which may be needed to manufacture a new product. Finance may oppose the required capital expenditure, since it could undermine a healthy cash flow for the organization.

Herd behaviour

Herd behavior in marketing is used to explain the dependencies of customer's mutual behaviour. *The Economist* reported a recent conference in Rome on the subject of the simulation of adaptive human behaviour.[12] It shared mechanisms to increase impulse buying and get people "to buy more by playing on the herd instinct." The basic idea is that people will buy more of products that are seen to be popular and several feedback mechanisms to get product popularity information to consumers are mentioned, including smart card technology and the use of Radio Frequency Identification Tag technology. A "swarm-moves" model was introduced by a Florida Institute of Technology researcher, which is appealing to supermarkets because it can "increase sales without the need to give people discounts."

Other recent studies on the "power of social influence" include an "artificial music market in which some 14,000 people downloaded previously unknown songs" (Columbia University, New York); a Japanese chain of convenience stores which orders its products based on "sales data from department stores and research companies;" a Massachusetts company exploiting knowledge of social networking to improve sales and online retailers who are increasingly informing consumers about "which products are popular with like-minded consumers" (e.g.: Amazon, eBay).

Further orientations

- An emerging area of study and practice concerns *internal marketing* or how employees are trained and managed to deliver the brand in a way that positively impacts the acquisition and retention of customers, also see *employer branding.*
- *Diffusion of innovations* research explores how and why people adopt new products, services and ideas.
- With consumer's eroding attention span and willingness to give time to advertising messages, marketers are turning to forms of *permission marketing* such as *branded content, custom media* and *reality marketing.*

MARKETING RESEARCH

Marketing research involves conducting research to support marketing activities and the statistical interpretation of data into information. This information is then used by managers to plan marketing activities, gauge the nature of a firm's marketing environment and attain information from suppliers. Marketing researchers use statistical methods such as quantitative research, qualitative research, hypothesis tests, Chi-squared tests, linear regression, correlations, frequency distributions, poisson distributions, binomial distributions, etc. to interpret their findings and convert data into information. The marketing research process spans a number of stages including the definition of a problem, development of a research plan, collecting and interpretation of data and disseminating information formally in the form of a report. The task of marketing research is to provide management with relevant, accurate, reliable, valid, and current information.

A distinction should be made between ***marketing research*** and ***market research***. Market research pertains to research in a given market. As an example, a firm may conduct research in a target market, after selecting a suitable market segment. In contrast, marketing research relates to all research conducted within marketing. Thus, market research is a subset of marketing research.

Marketing environment

Market segmentation

Market segmentation pertains to the division of a market of consumers into persons with similar needs and wants. As an example, if using Kellogg's cereals in this instance, Frosties are marketed to children. Crunchy Nut Cornflakes are marketed to adults. Both goods aforementioned denote two products which are marketed to two distinct groups of persons, both with like needs, traits and wants.

The purpose for market segmentation is conducted for two main issues. First, a segmentation allows a better allocation of a firm's finite resources. A firm only possesses a certain amount of resources. Accordingly, it must make choices (and appreciate the related costs) in servicing specific groups of consumers. Furthermore the diversified tastes of the contemporary Western consumers can be served better. With more diversity in the tastes of modern consumers, firms are noting the benefit of servicing a multiplicity of new markets.

Market segmentation can be defined in terms of the ***STP*** acronym, meaning ***Segment***, ***Target*** and ***Position***.

Types of marketing research

Marketing research, as a subset aspect of marketing activities, can be divided into the following parts:

- Primary research (also known as field research), which involves the conduction and compilation of research for the purpose it was intended.
- Secondary research (also referred to as desk research), is initially conducted for one purpose, but often used to support another purpose or end goal.

By these definitions, an example of primary research would be market research conducted into health foods, which is used *solely* to ascertain the needs/wants of the target market for health foods. Secondary research, again according to the above definition, would be research pertaining to health foods, but used by a firm wishing to develop an unrelated product.

Primary research is often expensive to prepare, collect and interpret from data to information. Nonetheless, while secondary research is relatively inexpensive, it often can become outdated and outmoded, given it is used for a purpose other than for which is was intended. Primary research can also be broken down into quantitative research and qualitative research, which as the labels suggest, pertain to numerical and non-riumerical research methods, techniques. The appropriateness of each mode of research depends on whether data can be quantified (quantitative research), or whether subjective, non-numeric or abstract concepts are required to be studied (qualitative research).

There also exists additional modes of marketing research, which are:

- Exploratory research, pertaining to research that investigates an assumption.
- Descriptive research, which as the label suggests, describes "what is".
- Predictive research, meaning research conducted to predict a future occurrence.
- Conclusive research, for the purpose of deriving a conclusion via a research process.

MARKETING PLANNING

The area of **marketing planning** involves forging a plan for a firm's marketing activities. A marketing plan can also pertain to a specific product, as well as to an organization's overall marketing strategy. Generally speaking, an organisation's marketing planning process is derived from its overall business strategy. Thus, when top management are devising the firm's strategic direction or mission, the intended marketing activities are incorporated into this plan. There are several levels of marketing objectives within an organization. The senior management of a firm would formulate a general business strategy for a firm. However, this general business strategy would be interpreted and implemented in different contexts throughout the firm.

Marketing strategy

The field of marketing strategy encompasses the strategy involved in the management of a given product.

A given firm may hold numerous products in the marketplace, spanning numerous and sometimes wholly unrelated industries. Accordingly, a plan is required in order to manage effectively such products. Evidently, a company needs to weigh up and ascertain how to utilise effectively its finite resources. As an example, a start-up car manufacturing firm would face little success, should it attempt to rival immediately Toyota, Ford, Nissan or any other large global car maker. Moreover, a product may be reaching the end of its life-cycle. Thus, the issue of divest, or a ceasing of production may be made. With regard to the aforesaid questions, each scenario requires a unique marketing strategy to be employed. Below are listed some prominent marketing strategy models, which seek to propose means to answer the preceding questions.

Marketing specializations

With the rapidly emerging force of globalization, the distinction between marketing within a firm's home country and marketing within external markets is disappearing very quickly. With this occurrence in mind, firms need to reorient their marketing strategies to meet the challenges of the global marketplace, in addition to sustaining their competitiveness within home markets. [13]

Buying behaviour

A marketing firm must ascertain the nature of the customers buying behaviour, if it is to market its product properly. In order to entice and persuade a consumer to buy a product, marketers try to determine the behavioural process of how a given product is purchased. Buying behaviour is usually split in two prime strands, whether selling to the consumer, known as business-to-consumer (B2C) or another business, similarly known as business-to-business (B2B).

B2C buying behaviour

This mode of behaviour concerns consumers, in the purchase of a given product. As an example, if one pictures a pair of sneakers, the desire for a pair of sneakers would be followed by an information search on available types/brands. This may include perusing media outlets, but most commonly consists of information gathered from family and friends.If the information search is insufficient, the consumer may search for alternative means to satisfy the need/want. In this case, this may be buying leather shoes, sandals, etc. The purchase decision is then made, in which the consumer actually buys the product. Following this stage, a post-purchase evaluation is often conducted, comprising an appraisal of the value/utility brought by the purchase of the sneakers. If the value/utility is high, then a repeat purchase may be bought. This could then develop into consumer loyalty, for the firm producing the pair of sneakers.

B2B buying behaviour

Relates to organizational/industrial buying behaviour. B2C and B2B behaviour are not exact, as similarities and differences exist. Some of the key differences are listed below:

In a straight re-buy, the fourth, fifth and sixth stages are omitted. In a modified re-buy scenario, the fifth and sixth stages are precluded. In a new buy, all aforementioned stages are conducted.

Use of technologies

Marketing management can also note the importance of technology, within the scope of its marketing efforts. Computer-based information systems can be employed, aiding in a better processing and storage of data. Marketing researchers can use such systems to devise better methods of converting data into information, and for the creation of enhanced data gathering methods. Information technology can aid in improving an MKIS' software and hardware components, to improve a company's marketing decision-making process.

In recent years, the netbook personal computer has gained significant market share among laptops, largely due to its more user-friendly size and portability. Information technology typically progress at a fast rate, leading to marketing managers being cognizant of the latest technological developments. Moreover, the launch of smartphones into the cellphone market is commonly derived from a demand among consumers for more technologically advanced products. A firm can lose out to competitors, should it refrain from noting the latest technological occurrences in its industry.

Technological advancements can facilitate lesser barriers between countries and regions. Via using the World Wide Web, firms can quickly dispatch information from one country to another, without much restriction. Prior to the mass usage of the Internet, such transfers of information would have taken longer to send, especially if via snail mail, telex, etc.

Services marketing

Services marketing, as the label suggests, relates to the marketing of services, as opposed to tangible products (in standard economic terminology, a tangible product is called a good).

A typical definition of a service (as opposed to a good) is thus:

- The use of it is inseparable from its purchase (i.e. a service is used and consumed simultaneously)
- It does not possess material form, and thus cannot be smelt, heard, tasted, or felt.
- The use of a service is inherently subjective, in that due to the human condition, all persons experiencing a service would experience it uniquely.

As examples of the above points, a train ride can be deemed as a service. If one buys a train ticket, the use of the train is typically experienced concurrently with the purchase of the ticket. Moreover, a train ride cannot be smelt, heard, tasted or felt as such. Granted, a seat can be felt, and the train can be evidently heard, nonetheless one is not paying for the permanent ownership of the tangible components of the train.

Services (by comparison with goods) can also be viewed as a spectrum. Not all products are pure goods nor are all pure services. The aforementioned example of a train ride can be deemed a pure service, whilst a packet of potato chips can be deemed a pure good. An intermediary example may be a restaurant (as the waiter service is intangible and the food evidently is tangible in form.

Questions

(1) What is Information Technology?

(2) Differentiate between Information System vs.Information Technology.

(3) What is the role of Information Technology in Indian market?

(4) What is the role of information Technology in finances?

(5) What is the role of information Technology in production?

EXAMINATION 2004-2005

Time: 3 Hours **Total Marks: 100**

Note: (i) Attempt ALL the questions.

(ii) All questions carry equal marks.

(iii) In case of numerical problems assume data wherever not provided.

(iv) Be precise in your answer.

Q.1 Attempt any two of the following:

(a) Distinguish between Primary storage devices and Secondary Storage devices.

(b) What is the importance of memory buffers and input/output buffers?

(c) How is the information processing techniques evaluated?

Q.2 Attempt any two of the following:

(a) How does and MS-PowerPoint help a manager?

(b) Write a lucid Note on OOPS.

(c) Discuss the Significance of JAVA.

Q.3 Attempt any four of the following:

(a) Distinguish Between a Multiprogramming and a Time-Sharing operating system.

(b) What are the basic features of the Window Operating System? why has it become so popular?

(c) Discuss the Menus, Tools and Commands of WINDOWS 98 Operating System.

(d) Name and briefly describe any two types of networks.

(e) As a manager how will you make the maximum use of Internet?

(f) Discuss the different applications of single and a multi-user operating systems.

Q.4 Attempt any four of the following:

(a) Discuss the various functions supported by Internet.

(b) What are the precautions one should take while developing a website?

(c) What is the significance of World Wide Web?

(d) "Internet Service Provider is and integral part of Internet." comment.

(e) How does searching an down-loading from Internet helps a manager?

(f) Why and how websites are updated ?

Q.5 Write notes on any two of the following:

(a) MS-Office's usage in Documentation

(b) Advancements in SQL

(c) Information Technology and Materials Management

(d) On-line Management system.

EXAMINATION 2005-2006

Time: 3 Hours **Total Marks: 100**

Note: (i) Attempt ALL the questions.

(ii) All questions carry equal marks.

(iii) Be precise in your answer.

Q.1 Attempt to any two parts of the following:

(a) What do you understand by information? What are the benefits of accurate information? Discuss the various information techniques.

(b) Differentiate between the following:

(i) Primary and Secondary memory

(ii) CPU and Control unit

(iii) RAM and ROM

(iv) Sequential access storage devices and Direct access storage devices.

(c) Answer the following questions:

(i) What is buffer?

(ii) What is the role of memory buffer and input/output buffer in computer?

(iii) Explain the advantages of working with graphics interface.

Q.2 Attempt any four of the following:

(a) Explain any four points to differentiate between a compiler and an interpreter.

(b) What is SQL? What do you understand by DML and DDL commands in SQL? Give two examples for each.

(c) Why Java is said to be a platform indepedent language? Differentiate between a class and an object with suitable example.

(d) Write down the purpose of the following in references to the MS word:

(i) Recycle Bin

(ii) My Briefcase

(iii) Network Neighborhood

(iv) Control Panel

(v) Desktop

(e) What is a spreadsheet? Write down the advantages of using Excel for accounting purposes?

(f) What is the purpose of Power Point? Describe the steps involved in creating a new presentation using AutoContent Wizard.

Q.3 Attempt any four part of the following:

(a) What is Internet? How is it different and similar to a computer network in your institute?

(b) How do you send an e-mail to your friend? Also explain the purpose of the following in e-mail, I) CC, II) BCC, III) Forward mail

(c) What is an operating system? What are its important functions?

(d) Write down the advantages of using a computer network over a cluster of stand alone computers.

(e) Differentiate between LAN and WAN.

(f) Discuss the different types of operating system by giving one example for each.

Q.4 Attempt any two parts of the following:

(a) Answer the following question:

(i) What is an ISP? How do you select this ISP as per your need?

(ii) Define WWW and Hyper text.

(b) Write down the various steps needed to develop a corporate Web site.

(c) What is the need of updating a Web site? How do you update a Web site?

Q.5 Write short notes on any two of the following:

(a) Maketing information system.

(b) Creating a database using MS Access

(c) Function and expression in MS Excel

EXAMINATION 2006-2007

Time: 3 Hours **Total Marks: 100**

Note:(i) Attempt ALL the questions.

(ii) All questions carry equal marks.

(iii) In case of numerical problems assume data wherever not provided.

(iv) Be precise in your answer.

Q.1 Attempt any four parts of the following: (5 x 4 = 20)

(a) What do you understand by the quality of information? The quality of information could be called good or bad depending upon some characteristics. Discuss those characteristics.

(b) Differentiate between the following:

(i) CPU and control unit

(ii) Primary and secondary storing devices

(c) What do you mean by the generation of computers? Discuss the key features of the current generation of computers?

(d) What type of interface is provided by windows operating system? How it differs with the previously used interface (Command line Interface) for computer?

(e) What is the role of memory buffer and input/out put buffers in a computer?

(f) What is an I/O processor? Also differentiate between the single user and multi-user environments.

Q.2 Attempt any four parts of the following: (5×4=20)

(a) What do you understand by the compiler for a high level language? How it differs with the interpreter used for high level language?

(b) Discuss the important features of $OOP_{s7.}$

(c) Write a small Java program and explain all steps to compile and run it in Windows environment.

(d) What is MS-Word? Explain the following in reference to the MS Word:

(i) Alignment

(ii) Font selection

(iii) Table Auto Format

(iv) Header and Footer

(e) What is the purpose of Power Point? Describe the steps involved in creating a new presentation using AutoContent Wizrd.

(f) How do you perform the followings in MS-Excel?

(i) Rename a worksheet

(ii) Add the values of two cells

(iii) Arrange the values of column in ascending order

(iv) Print a document

(v) Save the current workbook as other workbook.

Q.3 Attempt any four parts of the following:

(a) Discuss the role of an operating system as a resource manager and coordinator of devices.

(b) How do you perform the following in Windows?

(i) Copy a file from one directory into another directory

(ii) Rename a file

(iii) Delete a file permanently

(iv) Search a file

(v) Change the background of your desktop

(c) Write down the advantages of using a computer network over a cluster of standalone computers.

(d) Answer the following question:

(i) What is Web browser? Name any two Web browsers.

(ii) What is URL? Give one example.

(iii) What is the purpose of Favorites option on Internet Explorer?

(iv) What is Multi-task computer system?

(v) What is a Gopher?

(e) What is the structure of an e-mail address? Write down the advantages of the following in e-mail:

(i) Address book

(ii) Signature

(iii) Attachment

(f) Differentiate between LAN and WAN.

Q.4 Attempt any two parts of the following: **(10 x 2 = 20)**

(a) Answer the following questions: (5 + 5 = 10)

(i) Discuss the architecture of Internet.

(ii) Write down the reasons for the popularity of Internet.

(b) Write down various steps needed to develop a corporate Web site.

(c) Answer the following questions:

(i) How do you search a Website on Internet? Explain with the help of an example

(ii) How can you download a text file and save a picture from Internet?

(iii) What do you mean by uploading?

(iv) What is the role of ISP? Name any two ISPs.

Q.5 Write short notes on any two of the following: (10 x 2 = 20)

(a) Use of information technology in Marketing.

(b) Use of information technology in Productions.

(c) Function and expression in MS Excel.

Examination, 2007-2008

Time: 3 Hours **Total Marks: 100**

Note:(i) Attempt ALL the questions.

(iii) The figures in the right hand margin indicate marks.

Q.1 Attempt any two of the following: **(10×2=20)**

(a) Differentiate between RAM and ROM. Discuss various types of RAM and ROM in detail

(b) Draw a block diagram to illustrate the basic organization of a computer system and explain the function of the various units

(c) Write short notes on:

(i) Digital Computers

(ii) Hybrid Computer

(iii) Analog computer

(iv) Graphic interfacing

(v) Language Translators.

Q.2 Attempt any two of the following: **(10 x 2 = 20)**

(a) Discuss the following in context to object oriented programming:

(i) Polymorphism

(ii) Object/class

(iii) Information hiding

(iv) Inheritance

(b) What are fourth generation languages? Discuss DDL and DML features of SQL.

(c) Discuss the salient features and utilities of following packages:

(i) MS-Word

(ii) MS-Excel

(iii) MS-PowerPoint

Q.3 Answer any four of the following: **(5 x 4 = 20)**

(a) What is operating system? Give various services provided by the OS. Distinguish between single user and multi-user operating systems

(b) What is the role of task bar in Windows? List the steps to perform the following actions in windows:

(i) Start a program

(ii) Open a recently used document

(iii) Search a file

(iv) Delete a file or folder permanently.

(c) What is computer network? Compare and Contrast LAN and WAN

(d) Write the role of following:

(i) My computer

(ii) Network neighborhood

(iii) My document

(iv) Recycle bin

(v) My briefcase

(e) Write steps to create a folder in "D" drive and to put a shortcut of this folder on Desktop in Windows based system.

Q.4 Attempt any four of the following: (5 x 4 = 20)

(a) Discuss the architecture and functioning of Internet.

(b) Write steps to send an E-mail message on a dial-up terminal. Distinguish between "Cc" and "Bcc" fields of address part of your E-mail.

(c) What is an ISP? Can you get connected to internet without an ISP?

(d) What is WWW? How are the addresses defined on the internet?

(e) What do you mean by downloading from and uploading to the internet?

(f) Discuss, why owning a website is felt a must for any organization now a days.

Q.5 Write notes on any two of the following: (10 x 2 = 20)

(a) Information processing techniques

(b) Use of computers in management.

(c) Generations of computer languages

(d) Database management system

EXAMINATION 2008-2009

Time: 3 Hours **Total Marks: 100**

Note: The question paper contains three parts. All parts are compulsory

Q.1 Attempt all parts: **1 x 8**

State True or False

(i) Cache memory is used in Pen Drives

(ii) Windows XP is a network operating system.

(iii) Open source software does not have to be purchased.

(iv) MS Excel can be used for creating a database.

(v) Switches are used for switching a network on or off.

(vi) World Wide Web is another name for Internet.

(vii) An intranet is a corporate network that works like the Internet.

(viii) Cookies are a type of virus.

Choose Correct Answers from the Following:

(ix) MICR is a technology used in

(a) Input (b) Output

(c) Communication. (d) E-banking.

(x) If a disk has a bad spot on its recording surface it is called

(a) Disk scratch. (b) Disk crash.

(c) Disk error. (d) Disk sector.

(xi) Common keyboard layouts are called

(a) QWERTY (b) QRWTY

(c) QYRWET (d) QERTWY

(xii) In a word processor, you ______ text for formatting or editing it.

(a) Copy (b) Move

(c) Block (d) Select

(xiii) A field which can hold only one of the two possible values is of the type.

(a) Binary (b) Logical

(c) Boolean (d) Assembly code

(xiv) The process of converting digital data into analogue by a modem is called

(a) Modularization (b) Modulation

(c) Modification (d) Moduliation

(xv) For providing services such as www, the Internet acts as a

(a) Server (b) Provider
(c) Host (d) Carrier

(xvi) When you register at a shopping site, it may place on your computer

(a) Cooking (b) Catalogue
(c) Shopping cart (d) Digital signature

Fill in the Blanks

(xvii) Softwares that control system software are called _____ software.

(xviii) In a spreadsheet, a set of worksheets in the same file are called _____.

(xix) The process of copying a file from a remote computer into your computer is called _____.

(xx) A web page is a document designed in hypertext _____ language.

Ans.

(i) F	(ii) F	(iii) T	(iv) F
(v) F	(vi) F	(vii) T	(viii) F
(ix) a	(x) a	(xi) a	(xii) d
(xiii) c	(xiv) b	(xv) c	(xvi) b
(xvii)	(xviii) workbook		
(xix) Downloading	(xx) Markup		

Q.2 Attempt all questions given at the end of the case study.

(a) Why are many companies not planning to switch to Windows Vista?

(b) Make a business case for switching to Windows Vista.

(c) What are several improvements you would like to see Microsoft make in to next version of Windows?

Q.3 Describe the characteristics of Fourth generation languages. How is programming code reused to simplify a programmer job?

Or

3 Describe the role of Network Operating Systems.

Q. 4 Explain the process of generating a bar graph in Excel and including it in a report being typed in Word.

Or

4 What is a filter? How do we apply a filter in MS Access?

Q.5 Discuss benefits that networks provide to business users.

Or

5 What are the common uses of e-mail? Why e-mail is not considered a real time communication system?

Q.6 Explain common payment methods used online.

Or

6 Choose any production/operations activity and describe how efficiency can be increased by the use describe how efficiency can be increased by the use of computers.

IMPORTANT QUESTION FOR FORTHCOMING EXAMINATION COMPUTER APPLICATION IN MANAGEMENT 2009-2010

UNIT I

Q.1 What do you understand by the quality of information? The quality of information could be called good or bad depending upon some characteristics. Discuss those characteristics.

Q.2 Answer the following question:

(i) What is buffer?

(ii) What is the role of memory buffer and input/output buffer in computer?

(iii) Explain the advantages of working with graphics interface

Q.3 What type or interface is provided by Windows operating system? How it differs with the previously used interface (Command Line Interface) for computers?

Q.4 Write short notes on:

(i) Digital Computers (ii) Hybrid Computer (iii) Analog Computer.

(iv) Graphic interfacing (v) Language Translator.

Q.5 Discuss the different applications of single and a multi-user operating systems.

UNIT II

Q.1 how do you perform the followings in MS-Excel?

(i) Rename a worksheet

(ii) Add the values of two cells

(iii) Arrange the values of column in ascending order

(iv) Print a document

(v) Save the current workbook as other workbook

Q.2 What is MS-Word? Explain the following in reference to the MS Word:

(i) Alignment (ii) Font selection

(iii) Table Auto Format (iv) Header and Footer

Q.3 What is the purpose of PowerPoint? Describe the steps involved in creating a new presentation using AutoContent Wizard

Q.4 What is a filter? How do we apply a filter in MS Access?

Q.5 Discuss the salient features and utilities of following packages:

(i) MS-WORD

(ii) MS-EXCEL

(iii) MS-POWERPOINT.

UNIT III

Q.1 Discuss benefits that networks provide to business users.

Q.2 Discuss the architecture and functioning of Internet.

Q.3 What do you mean by downloading from and uploading to the Internet

Q.4 What is WWW? How are the addresses defined on the Internet

Q.5 Answer the following questions:

(i) What is Web browser? Name any two Web browsers.

(ii) What is URL? Give one example.

(iii) What is the purpose of Favorites option in Internet Explorer.

(iv) What is a Gopher?

UNIT IV

Q.1 Use of information technology in marketing.

Q.2 Choose any production/operations activity and describe how efficiency can be increased by the use of computers.

Q.3 Use of information tcchnology in Productions.

Q.4 Information Technology and Materials Management

Q.5 Explain common payment methods used online